Doors, Entrances and Beyond...

Doors, Entrances and Beyond...

Various aspects of entrances and doors of the tombs in the Memphite necropoleis during the Old Kingdom

Leo Roeten

Archaeopress Egyptology 33

ARCHAEOPRESS PUBLISHING LTD
Summertown Pavilion
18-24 Middle Way
Summertown
Oxford OX2 7LG

www.archaeopress.com

ISBN 978-1-78969-871-8
ISBN 978-1-78969-872-5 (e-Pdf)

Photo cover: Entrance into the tomb of Inty at Abusir.
(From: M. Bárta and V. Dulíková, “The Afterlife Existence Captured in Stone”, in P. Jánosi and H. Vymazalová (eds), *The Art of Describing. Studies in Honour of Yvonne Harpur* (Prague, 2018)).
(With the kind permission of Prof. Dr. M. Bárta; Czech Institute of Egyptology, Charles University, Prague)

This book is available direct from Archaeopress or from our website www.archaeopress.com

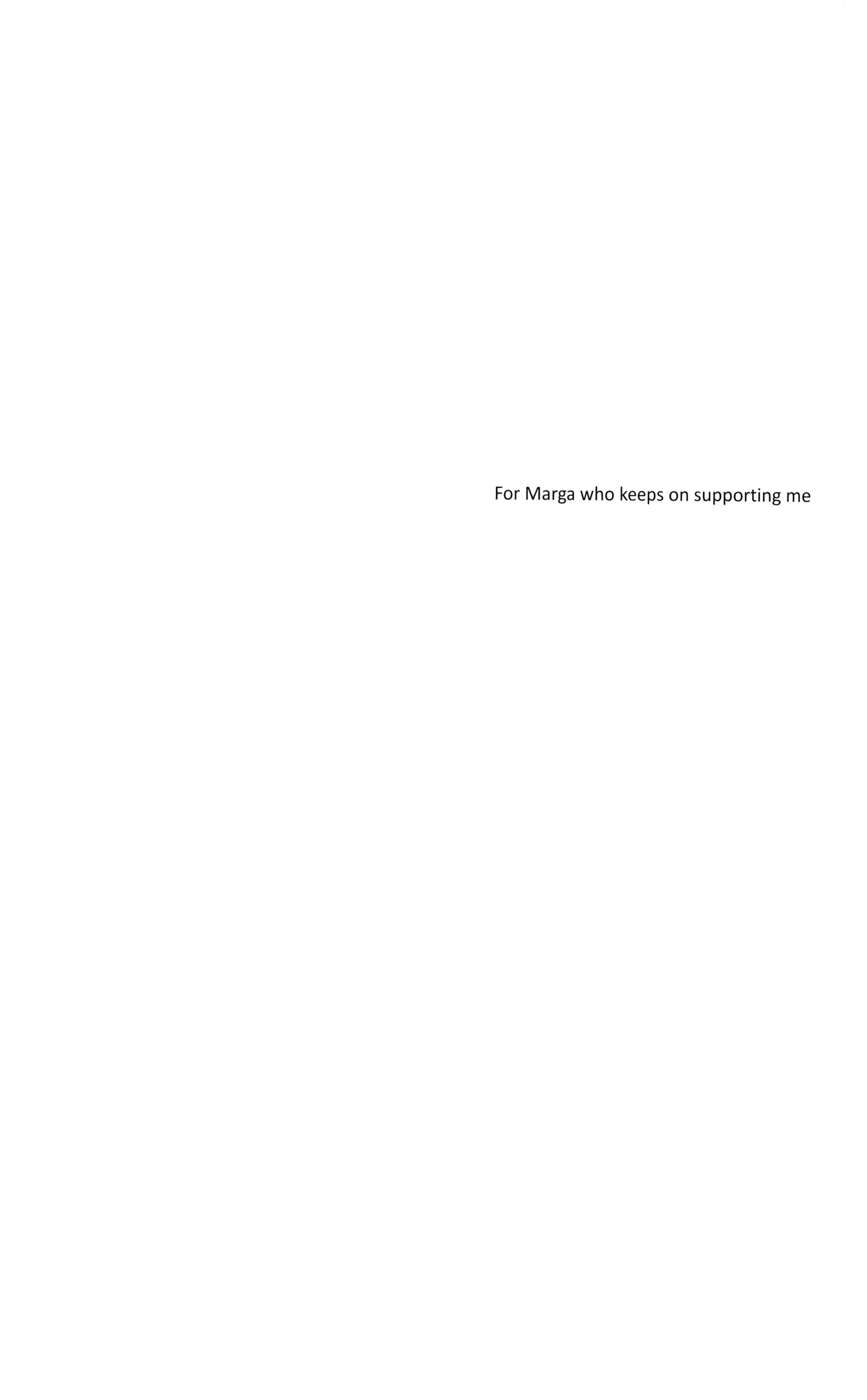

For Marga who keeps on supporting me

Contents

Entrances and Decoration

Offering Places

List of Figures

Chapter Eight

Chapter Nine

Chapter Ten

Chapter Eleven

Chapter Twelve

Chapter Thirteen

Chapter Fourteen

List of Tables

Chapter One*

About this Study

I. Introduction

Throughout pharaonic times a tomb, particularly an elite tomb, was a monument that was erected for, and usually exclusively paid by the tomb owner, and it had multiple functions. The most obvious of them were:

1. The purely prosaic purpose of serving as a burial place for the mortal remains of a deceased person.
2. To be a monument that marked the place where the deceased had been buried, thus enabling the relatives to pay respect to the deceased and to bring offerings for the sustenance of his/her *k3*.
3. To ensure that the personality of the deceased was retained within the context of the society whence he/she came.
4. To show the social status not only of the tomb owner but also of his or her family.[1] This status was shown not only in the titles the deceased had held, in the dimensions and the decoration of the tomb, but also in texts that stated the relation the deceased had had with royalty. These texts could also make reference to presents given or decrees made by the king.[2]

The tomb owner dead and the monument had been finished or nearly so, the first of its functions was to be the stage for the final phases of the burial ceremony and the funerary rituals pertaining to it.[3] For this short-term but important part of its functions some provisions were made. These were usually removed after the funeral, but nevertheless they left enough marks to be noticed and interpreted during excavation.[4] After the funeral, the monument became the focus of its second, and in fact its most important, function: acting as the daily stage for the 'eternal' mortuary rituals, a recurrent offering ritual, necessary for the sustenance of the *k3* of the deceased.[5]

The construction of the tomb had to permit the necessary architectural facilities for both its funerary and the mortuary aspect, although more was required for the total ritual functioning of the monument than just the building itself, including movable items as ritual furniture, equipment and model offerings. The architectural necessities for the funerary and mortuary rituals were not identical; if part of the funerary rituals were performed on the roof of the tomb,[6] the construction of a ramp would have been necessary,[7] of which remnants have indeed been found near some mastabas.

In some tombs most of the stages of the funeral were depicted on various walls of the chapel,[8] but a relatively small number of chapels have decoration themes depicting the funeral ritual in the vicinity of the tomb itself. The observation that this part of the overall funerary activities was not frequently depicted could be a consequence of the scene being considered not important enough to be indispensable. In view of a hypothesis concerning this specific part of the funeral that will be put forward in the present study, this explanation is not probable. A more valid argument is based on the same proposal which interprets the statue during the opening of the mouth ritual as a facsimile of the dead body of the tomb owner, and this, in combination with the reluctance to depict dead bodies that was still strong during the Old Kingdom, would explain the low frequency of depiction.

The mortuary monument consists of a set of architectural elements that are completely inter-independent. Yet they have to form two separate sets in order to make it possible both for the funerary and the mortuary rituals to take place in the traditional manner

* I would like to thank Mr. David Sexton (former literary editor 'Evening Standard', London) for going over my English; of course mistakes of any kind are entirely of my hand.

1 Alexanian, *Tomb and social status.*

2 Kloth, *Biographische Inschriften,* 185.

3 For the definition of the terms 'mortuary' and 'funerary', see 'Bibliography, abbreviations and technical terms'.

4 Friedman, *Hierakonpolis,* Figure 4.13.

5 For sustenance the deceased was not solely dependent on the daily mortuary offering ritual in the chapel; during the funeral food had been left behind in the burial chamber or in the shaft leading to it (Ikram, *Food,* 361). In the course of the Old Kingdom the importance of the magical part of the sustenance showed a continuous increase (Roeten, *Decoration*).

6 LD, *II*, 35. On the false door of *ṯp-m-ꜥnḫ* (PM, III/2, 483) is written '*causing to stand on the roof, an invocation-offering is made to you....*' (Mariette, *Mastaba,* 195). Forshaw, *Lector*, 91 suggests that this liturgy was performed in the chapel, although in view of the dimensions of the average chapel, this statement might be valid for the tombs of the members of the highest social stratum, but certainly not for the smaller tombs.

7 This ramp might at first have been used for the construction of the higher layers of the mastaba. Alexanian, *Netjeraperef,* 38, note 110, Plates 4, 7b, Figure 15; Abu-Bakr, *Giza,* Figure 3; Junker, *Giza IX*, Figures 2, 3; Plate IIc/d; Reisner, *Estate stewards,* Figure 3, for further examples see: Arnold, *Building,* 84 – 5, notes 94, 95 (page 105).

8 OEE, scene-detail database, item 15 (funerary rites and funeral scenes); Forshaw, *Lector,* 83 – 94.

that is necessary for the deceased to obtain afterlife. The decision that both sets can and should be studied separately is based on an interpretation of a definition given by Hoffmann concerning the evidential value of the conclusions drawn from various parts of an architectural whole:

> *'Architectural elements are portions of structures which can be dissociated from their original context but which still provide evidence of the architectural competence of the period under consideration'* [9]

Elements that played an important role in the tomb-bound part of the funerary rituals are the shaft and the burial chamber, while the chapel and its entrance, although they had a role in the funerary functioning of the monument, played a major role in the ensuing mortuary activity. An example of the inter-relation between the two sets is that, although the shaft and the burial chamber were prominent in the funerary rituals, the chapel must have been the centre of some of these rituals too. It is certain that, due to their inaccessibility, the latter two architectural elements cannot have been implicated in the mortuary rituals. This leads to the realization that the offerings that had been placed in the burial chamber were not considered sufficient sustenance in the longer term and a mortuary cult had to be installed to continue sustaining the *k3* of the deceased.

In the literature it is usual to consider the offering place in the chapel as the most important area of the total monument. Seen from a ritual point of view, this is correct, but it takes more than an offering place to get people to enter the chapel of a person with whom they are not directly affiliated. The primary task of the entrance is to introduce, to invite and to warn. This makes the entrance in its totality an area of interest in its own right, but not just because it is a way to get into the chapel. The importance of the entrance lies in the realization that it represents a non-physical aspect of the monument in that it is where the worlds of the living and the dead meet. In the richer tombs this threshold between the two worlds was marked by a door; in this way marking the transition and giving it a special significance. This underlying meaning makes a door not only a physical object; it makes it also an integral part of the totality of an entrance, granting access not only to ordinary rooms, but also to rooms with a liminal function. Based on this assumption the various types of entrances and their inter-connectivity will be further studied, which gives rise to a hypothesis concerning their ritual function and meaning.

Part of the study will investigate whether the decoration themes of the various architectural elements of the entrance of the mortuary monuments are chronologically interconnected, possibly indicating a chronological development of the ritual meaning of the entrance.

The various parts of the chapel, whether exterior of interior, are the most obvious ritual elements of the tomb. Yet, there are parts, either subterranean or above ground, that, although hidden, nevertheless can be interpreted as part of the total ritual combination. The most obvious example of this hidden, ritually important, element is the serdab, and where necessary this part of the mortuary ensemble will be included in this study.

II. Preliminary considerations

- The names of kings are written according to Verner, *Chronology.* Private names are written in transliteration font and are spelled according to Harpur, *DETOK,* 265 – 84. The place of the king within the dynasty is determined in the table given in Stadelmann, *Pyramiden,* 310 – 2.
- Within the context of this study the type of tomb, whether mastaba, rock-cut or a combination of both, is irrelevant.
- The tombs that are subject of this study and that are accepted in eventual catalogues are those situated in the necropoleis of Giza, Saqqara and Abusir.
- If in the course of this study it becomes necessary to investigate a possible connection between the signalling and inviting function of the entrance decoration and the themes placed on this architectural element, solely those placed on the real (outside) entrance of the mortuary installation are taken into account.[10] Entrances that are suitable for inclusion in the catalogues can be either those of interior or exterior chapels.
- Due to the chronological limits set for this study, only tombs that can be dated from the 4th up to and including the 6th dynasty are usually accepted in the catalogues. In case of necessity for the study at hand, it is possible that tombs that can be dated to the 1st, 2nd and 3rd dynasty can be included in the catalogues also, and thus incorporated in curves describing various chronological developments.
- The northern and southern walls of the corridor of a cruciform chapel are considered as entrance thicknesses; if these walls are decorated, the tomb is included in the relevant catalogue.

[9] Hoffmann, *Amratian house,* 135.

[10] This condition has been added because in the multi-chambered mastabas (e.g. *Mrrw-k3.j* (PM, III/2, 525 – 34)) the room with the offering place is deep in the substructure of the monument (room A-11 in the aforementioned tomb).

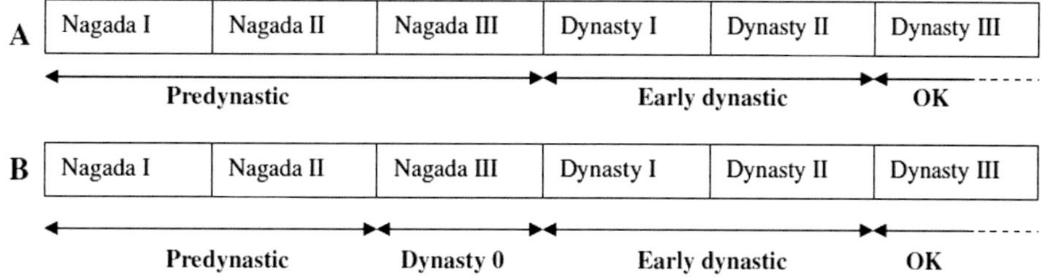

Figure 1.1 The two main naming systems for the periods prior to the Old Kingdom.

- If a tomb has two chapels (e.g. in tomb M6 at Maidum the separate chapels of *Rꜥ-ḥtp* and his wife), the decoration of both chapels is taken into consideration.[11]
- A tomb with an offering place in the form of a niche can be included in the relevant catalogue if decoration is present on its jambs. This type of offering place has no corridor and consequently has no entrance thicknesses in the usual sense of the word.
- If the entrance of the tomb is what is called 'a portico', only the decoration at both sides of the real entrance or the false door that functions as such is interpreted as door jamb decoration, while the decoration on the northern and southern walls of the portico is not included in the catalogue (certain aspects of the portico will be discussed in later chapters).
- Because there is the possibility of a difference between the architectural and mortuary background of the tombs in the Memphite area and the provinces, only the tombs in necropoleis of Giza, Saqqara and Abusir are included in the catalogues.[12]
- In view of the relatively careless use of the terms funerary, mortuary, funerary offerings and mortuary offerings, the definitions of the terms as they will be employed in this study are those given in the table 'Bibliography, abbreviations and technical terms'.
- In some parts of this study material aspects of periods before the Old Kingdom are discussed. In the literature the nomenclature of these periods is somewhat confused due to the intermingling of two systems, while other terms have been added too. In Figure 1.1 the two main naming systems are shown, and in this study system A will be employed.[13]
- If the gender of the tomb owner has to be given in the form of a possessive pronoun the male form 'his' is used, unless the context demands the use of a female pronoun.

Dynasty	Number	Name	Kings per period	Period
IV	IV.1	Sneferu	IV.1 – IV.3	IV.E
	IV.2	Khufu		
	IV.3	Radjedef		
	IV.4	Rakhaef	IV.4 – IV.6	IV.L
		(Baka)		
	IV.5	Menkaure		
	IV.6	Shepseskaf		
		(Thampthis)		
V	V.1	Userkaf	V.1 – V.3	V.E
	V.2	Sahure		
	V.3	Neferirkare		
	V.4	Shepseskare	V.4 – V.6	V.M
	V.5	Raneferef		
	V.6	Niuserre		
	V.7	Menkauhor	V.7 – V.9	V.L
	V.8	Djedkare		
	V.9	Unas		
VI	VI.1	Teti	VI.1 – VI.2	VI.E
	VI.2	Pepy I		
	VI.3	Merenre	VI.3 – VI.4E	VI.M
	VI.4	Pepy II	VI.4M – VI.4L	VI.L

Figure 1.2 Table of the kings of the Old Kingdom and the division in periods (after Harpur, *DETOK*, 43).

III. The chronology employed

The following considerations are taken into account for the chronology employed in this study, which is the same as the one used in the author's two prior studies of the author related to this subject (Figure 1.2).[14]

1. This study is based on the order of kings in a dynasty as given in Figure 1.2.[15]

[11] An example of this is the tomb of *Sꜣbw* and *Ptḥ-špss*; PM, III/2, 460-1.

[12] Because the cemetery of Abû Rawâsh can be interpreted as one of the Memphite necropoleis, tombs from this cemetery can be included in the catalogues. The excavation reports of this necropolis as given by the Institut Français d'Archéologie Orientale in Cairo (BIFAO) give two tombs with entrance decoration (tomb F 19, Baud, *F 19*, 29 and Figure 4; tomb F 48, Baud, *F 48*, Figure 14), both of them dated to the earlier part of the 4th dynasty. These tombs are included in the catalogue of the necropolis of Giza.

[13] In system B the period 'predynastic' is sometimes called 'dynasty 00'.

[14] Roeten, *Decoration*, Figure II.9 (page 48) and Roeten, *Economic decline*, Figure 18 (page 18).

[15] Harpur, *DETOK*, 34.

		Verner, *Chronology*	Harpur, *DETOK*
IV.E	Sneferu	24	24
	Khufu	23	23
	Djedefre	8	8
		55	55
IV.L	Rakhaef	20 + x	25
	Menkaure	18/28	18/28
	Shepseskaef	4	7
		Min. 43, max. 53 + x	Min. 50, max. 60
V.E	Userkaf	7	7
	Sahure	12	12
	Neferirkare	?	≤ 20
		19 ?	Min. < 39, max. 39
V.M	Shepseskare	7	7
	Raneferef	1	≤ 10
	Niuserre	11 (+ x)	> 11
		Min. 19, max. 19 + x	Min. 20, max. 18 + x
V.L	Menkauhor	8	8
	Raneferef	28	28
	Niuserre	30	30
		66	66
VI.E	Teti	lost	15?
	Pepy I	20	≤ 30 (25?)
	Merenre	6	7
		26 + x	Min. 47?, max. 52
VI.L	Pepy II	90 + x	85
		90 + x	85

In total Verner = 98 – 108+x and Harpur = 105-115

In total Verner = 85 + x and Harpur = (< 125) – (123 + x)

In total Verner = 116+x and Harpur = 132?

Figure 1.3 Comparison of the reign lengths given by Harpur, *DETOK* and Verner, *Chronology*.

2. The dating given to the tombs that are accepted in the various catalogues is based on the literature and databases available (e.g. PM, the Giza Mastabas Series of the Boston Museum of Fine Arts, the Abusir series published by the Faculty of Arts of the Charles University in Prague, the databases 'Mastabase' of the University of Leiden (Walsem, van, *Mastabase*) and OEE (Oxford Expedition to Egypt: Scene-details Database (Linacre College, Oxford)).
3. Because of the small number of tombs that can be dated to one particular reign, they are only assigned to the various Old Kingdom periods as given in Figure 1.2.
4. If additional information is available concerning the dimensions of the tombs, the methodology developed and employed in Roeten, *Economic decline* can be used to check the reliability of the given date.
5. This methodology can be applied when in the literature a dating like IV.L/V.E or V.L-VI is given. If the additional data about the dimensions do not lead to a decision; then the date in the catalogue is given as a 'flowing' date between the two periods; for 'IV.L/V.E' this becomes 'IV.L - V.E'. The date 'V.L or VI' is interpreted as V.L - VI.E.
6. A date 'V – VI' is not included unless the dimensions of the tomb enable the determination of a more precise date (e.g. *Ḥwtj*, PM, III/2, 482).[16]

The abbreviations used in the chronology of Figure 1.2 are the following:

IV.E and IV.L mean resp. 4th dynasty early and late.

V.E, V.M and V.L resp. 5th dynasty early, middle and late.

VI.E, VI.M and VI.L resp. 6th dynasty early, middle and late.[17]

Although there is still a lot of debate about the length of the reign of some of the kings of the Old Kingdom,[18] the approximate length in years of the three dynasties of the Old Kingdom as given in Harpur, *DETOK,* 34 – 5 is IV = 110, V = 140 and VI = 140[19]

16 Mariette, *Mastaba*, 99 gives a plan that omits the width of the mastaba.

17 In this dynasty the division in periods is hampered by the long reign of Pepy II (VI.4). This problem is treated in accordance with Harpur, *DETOK*, 43.

18 Harpur, *DETOK*, 33 – 5; Verner, *Chronology;* see Figure 3.

19 The shortened length of the reign of Teti according to Harpur, *DETOK*, 35.

The division of the dynasties as given in Figure 1.2 provides a distribution of sub-periods that have, according to Figure 1.3 some equilibrium in length. Because for the period-divisions the number of tombs and not the equilibrium in length of time is statistically important, in this study two kinds of time-line are used:

System I: IV – V.E – V.M – V.L – VI

System II: IV.E –IV.L –V.E – V.M – V.L –VI.E – VI.L

The choice of dating system depends largely on the number of tombs in the population.

Chapter Two

The Rituals and Tomb Elements

I. About the funerary rituals

After a person died those left behind had to take care of the mortal remains. For the poorest that care consisted of wrapping the body in a reed mat or a skin,[1] digging a hole in the desert sand and leaving the body in it, usually in a contracted position, and sometimes accompanied by gifts.[2] In some graves a kind of protection in the form of a lining of twigs placed directly on the body or spanning the hole was added.[3] The placing of grave gifts points to ideas about an after-life, and it is also possible that a form of funerary ritual was performed, but the latter is difficult to trace in the poorer graves.

Funerary activities were sometimes depicted on the walls of the chapel, thus making it possible to form a relatively well founded idea about its course. Basically the funeral proceeded along a line of fixed sub-ceremonies and rituals,[4] which could be extended at will in length and number depending on need and financial resources. This series of different stages of the ceremony was determined by the practicalities inherent to escorting a deceased person to its tomb; a series of actions that consists of the transport from the residence to the western bank of the river, and, depending on the period and the financial status of the deceased, taking the body to the embalming place, the embalming itself, transport of the mummy and the funerary offerings to the tomb and finally the burial.[5]

For the richer part of the population more elaborate ceremonies were possible, together with a small mortuary monument, some care taken to preserve the mortal remains from total decay, some funerary rituals and a burial in an underground chamber.

Although for the elite the ceremonies and rituals were the same as those for the lesser social stratum, their overall execution would be in keeping with the wealth of the family; the entire funeral would be led by a large group of priests who were assisted by mourners and dancers, the voyage to the west bank of the river was made with a fleet of ships,[6] the mummification was the best that could be obtained, and the ceremonies at the tomb were extensive, lengthy and expensive.[7]

These steps are also mentioned in the Pyramid Texts:

> *Nephthys has collected all your members for you in this her name of 'Seshat, lady of Builders'.*
> *(She) has made them hale for you, you having been given to your mother Nut in her name of 'Sarcophages',*
> *She has embraced you in her name of 'Coffin',*
> *and you have been brought to her in her name of 'Tomb'*
> (PT, § 616).

The main purpose of these funerary rituals was to enable the deceased to achieve an eternal afterlife. In order to live this afterlife the deceased needed sustenance and because the deceased needed hands, sight, smell, hearing, and a mouth; un addition to other rituals, this necessitated one of the main funerary rituals, 'The opening of the mouth', after which the first offering ritual took place. At first the opening of the mouth ritual was performed on a statue;[8] later, when the representation of a mummy had become more common, depictions show that the ritual was performed on the mummy itself

After the more or less comprehensive funerary ceremonies and rituals had taken place and the body of the deceased had been lowered into the burial chamber, the main purpose of the monument that marked the

---

1 Petrie, *Tarkhan I,* Plate XXV.

2 Petrie, *Tarkhan I,* PlateXXII(1035).

3 Brunton, *Badarian,* 18, Plate IX; Clark, *Tomb security,* 15 – 6.

4 LÄ, I, 745 – 65, s.w. 'Bestattungsritual', there 745.

5 Forshaw, *Lector,* 83 – 95; Hayes, *Funerary rituals,* 1. The details of the various steps of the funerary ritual were highly dependent on the financial capacity of the deceased's family.

6 In some cases the group of ships clearly is not part of a funeral procession (LD, *II,* 76(e)), and distinctly shows that it is the tomb owner travelling to estates or destinations connected with his functions (LD, *II,* 15).

7 Forshaw, *Lector,* 83 ff..

8 Roth, *Opening of the mouth,* 117; Chapel of *Rḫ-mj-Rʿ* (PM, I, 206 14; TT100) (www.osirisnet.net); LÄ, IV, 223 – 4, s.v. 'Mundöffnung(sritual)'; *Dbḥnj* (PM, III/1, 235 – 6); LD, *II,* 35. It is doubtful whether the representation of the ceremony on top of the ramp, as represented in the chapel of *Dbḥnj,* has any connection with reality because of the fact that the entrances to the burial chamber of this tomb were inside the rock-cut chapel and not on top of the escarpment (Hassan, *Giza IV,* Figure 120) or the doubtful mastaba on top of it (Reisner, *Mycerinus,* 258). Bolshakov , *Tomb-cult,* 206 states that the opening of the mouth ritual took place in the workshop after the statue was finished and not in the vicinity of the tomb after it had been transported to the cemetery (Duell, *Mereruka I,* (Plate 29 – 30). The scene in the chapel of *Dbḥnj* (LD, *II,* 35) might be interpreted as the bringing of offerings, a ritual which only took place after the mouth of the statue had been opened, which could indicate that this particular ritual had already taken place before the statue arrived at the tomb.

place of the burial changed from funerary to mortuary.[9] One of the consequences is that for this new aspect of the function of the monument a new set of rituals had to come into play, a new set which required its own architectural peculiarities and its own decoration themes.

In the course of time enough written texts and tomb decoration have come down to us to give a reasonably reliable picture not only of the components of the various acts that constituted the funerary ceremony and rituals but also of the order in which they were performed.

The conviction that the deceased needed sustenance in the afterlife goes as far back as the predynastic period, because in the cemetery of Tarkhan (Nagada III) tombs have been found that are divided in a part intended for the burial, and another at first used for funerary and after that for mortuary rituals, thus continuing the bipartite character of the Nagada II tombs at Hieraconpolis.[10] Against the low wall surrounding the burial pit of grave Tarkhan 1845 (the only not plundered grave in the cemetery) a small building had been erected that could be entered from the north and had one (Tarkhan 1889) or two slot-like openings (Figure 2.1) in the eastern wall of the mastaba.[11] In view of the fact that it was not possible for a living person to really look inside the grave pit, these were probably intended for the deceased to magically participate in the rituals that took place in the chapel and to benefit from the offerings that were placed in front of those slots.[12] The fact that an open connection existed between the two parts of the tombs shows that the *k3* was not yet considered to be able to traverse a solid wall (the same is also the case in tomb U-j at Abydos).

These offerings were brought to the chapel by priests and/or members of the family and therefore were undeniably physically present, but it is only by means of magic that the deceased could benefit from the sustenance thus offered.[13] It remains a problem to know whether or not after the burial and the funerary rituals a mortuary cult was maintained, it is a question that might be answered by solving the question as to whether or not the pottery found lying inside and in the vicinity of the chapel is the result of an accumulation of offerings brought over the course of time or a one-time result of ritual activities during the funeral.

The photos in the excavation report show that in the chapel itself it was mainly cups and dishes that were used for the ritual activity and that jars were not present there. Outside the chapel pottery was laid out in a certain degree of order. A scene on one of the walls in the chapel of *Dbḥnj* (PM, III/1, 235 – 6; IV.L) shows a semblance of this situation.[14] The scene shows a phase of the funeral of the tomb owner where pottery and food offerings are placed in orderly rows in the vicinity of the ramp leading to the roof of the tomb and next to the entrance of the chapel. That this depiction has a core of truth is shown by the excavation results of mastaba II/1 in the Lepsius Mastaba Field of Dahshur (datable to IV.F).[15] Around the southern offering place, beer jars were found in large quantities, while cups and plates are also present but in significantly smaller numbers. In the area around the south-eastern corner of the mastaba, beer jars were present in quantities comparable with those around the southern niche, but cups and plates were *not* present. From the additional observation that hardly any pottery of later periods was present it can be concluded that the mortuary cult for the deceased did not last long. The conclusion from these data could be that the situation excavated around mastaba II/1must have a strong similarity to that in which it was left after the funeral. The short period of active mortuary cult could have resulted in a few more cups and plates in the chapel, and some more beer jugs for the transport of water for the rituals being left

[9] The conclusion is that the main function of the monument is mortuary and not funerary (Roeten, *Decoration,* 27).

[10] A well known bipartite tomb from this area is tomb 100. Snape, *Egyptian tombs,* states that each of the two components of the Tarkhan bipartite tombs had a function that was distinctively different from the other, but that the two of them acted together as a unit.

[11] In Petrie, *Tarkhan II,* Plate XII, in the photos upper- and middle right the two openings are visible and it is evident that they are vertically elongated.

[12] Petrie, *Tarkhan II,* 2 proposes that the slots were meant for the offerings to reach the deceased. The total plan of the tomb in Figure 2.1 has a remarkable resemblance with the primitive mastaba GW 76 that has been uncovered in the 'Wadi cemetery' north of the Plateau of Giza (Giza Archives photo C 10392; Der Manuelian, *Wadi cemetery,* Figure 27 and in ibidem Figure 11 a longer opening has been constructed in the wall of the tomb). Mawdsley, *Tarkhan,* 27 states that the two slots might have been meant to provide the deceased with the means to reach the world of the living and the afterlife.

[13] Often the supply of sustenance for the deceased was not entirely dependent on the kindness of the family; instances are known in which the deceased, while still alive, had already arranged for the later provision of his mortuary cult. An example of this can be found in the tomb of *Ḏf3(.j)-Ḥꜥpj,* nomarch of the 13th nome of Upper-Egypt during the reign of Sesostris I (XII.2) (LÄ, V, 890 – 9, s.v. 'Sesostris I'), who (tried) to secure the perpetuity of his (mortuary) cult by having chiselled in the walls of his chapel the ten contracts he had concluded with the various persons who were directly or indirectly involved in taking care of this cult. Bolshakov, *Man and double,* 194 objects against the use of the term 'mortuary cult' because he claims that the cult started already during the life-time of the tomb owner from the moment that the decoration of the monument had been finished, because the cult is considered to be for the *k3* of the tomb owner, and not for the perishable part of his person. Bolshakov concludes, in support of his hypothesis, that two of the contracts (no. II and VIII) lead to the conclusion that the cult started the moment the contract had been concluded. An earlier example of this type of contract can be found in the mastaba of *Nb-k3w-Ḥr* (PM, III/2, 627 – 9) (Abdou, *Nebkauhor,* 126 – 36, Plate IVA, IVB.

[14] LD, *II,* 35.

[15] Alexanian, *Netjeraperef,* 163 and Figure 70.

behind in the vicinity of the chapel, but this would not appreciably change the original situation.

Due to the relatively small 'distance' in time and place it is tempting to extend this conclusion to the situation around the older tomb Tarkhan 1845 that is dated to the early dynastic period (Figure 2.1). Here too the mortuary cult lasted only one generation, implying that the kind, the number, and the position of the artefacts that have been excavated approximately reflect the situation after the burial.[16]

The scenario after the burial of the deceased could have been that the funerary ritual(s) took place in the chapel and its vicinity, after which the sustenance necessary for the after-life of the deceased was deposited in front of the entrance into the chapel.

The way the jars were placed in front of the entrance of the chapel indicates that further entry was apparently deemed unnecessary, leading to the conclusion that the intention of the offerings was identical to that of the masses of jars that were placed in the sub-terranean magazines of the elite tombs of the first and second dynasty in Saqqara.[17] The difference in social status and the concomitant economic power meant that, for the elite, these items of sustenance were placed inside the tomb, but for the less rich just in the open, and possibly only protected by the respect one would have for the deceased in his mortuary environment.

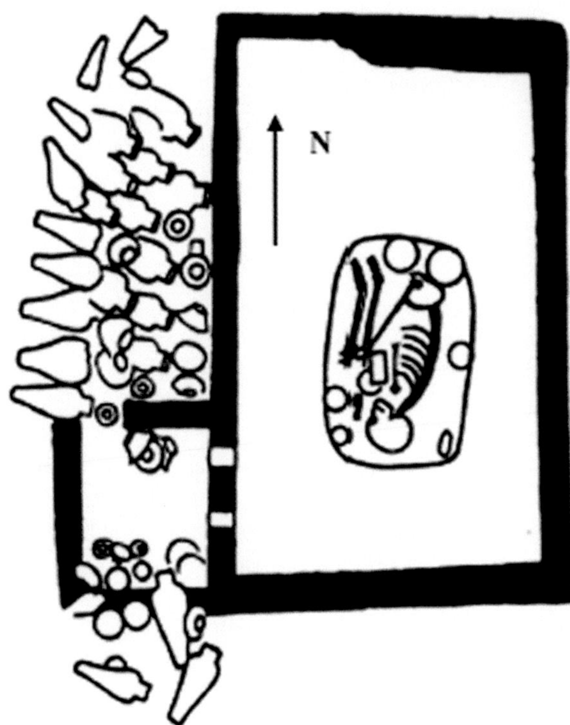

Figure 2.1 Tarkhan tomb 1845 (from Petrie, *Tarkhan II*, Plate XIV).

II. About the mortuary ritual

From the moment the ritual of the opening of the mouth had taken place, the monument started to serve as a focus for daily offerings for the *k3* of the deceased and as a place for ritual contact between the deceased and the living. The observation that for this purely magical contact the facsimile of a door was a necessity indicates that special meaning was attached to this object that is basically no more than a piece of architectural equipment. Because the mortuary ritual was primarily focused on the sustenance of the *k3* of the deceased and not on his or her veneration, the main component of the ritual must have been depositing the offerings at the place intended for this purpose.[18]

Compared with the information available about the funeral ceremony, far less is known about the daily offering ritual. There is much indirect evidence of its existence in the form of a part of the offering formula,[19] but its various components, their order of performance and the way they were executed during the Old Kingdom, has never been as clearly and completely described as any of the other rituals.[20] Furthermore, the way in which this daily ritual is represented in the decoration of some chapels gives the impression of an extensiveness in the actions and the number of persons involved that can be expected to be present during an elite funeral, but that for a daily mortuary ritual can be dismissed as unlikely.

If for some reason the daily offering ritual was not performed by the son or another member of the family, it is probable that that duty had been taken on by a priest. The contracts of *Ḏf3(.j)-Ḥ*ʿ*pj* clearly state that

[16] Grajetzki, *Tarkhan*, 111.

[17] Emery, *Archaic Egypt*, Plates 13, 20. The orientation of the first dynasty tombs at Tarkhan as given in Reisner, *Tomb development*, Figure 126 shows that that feature does not play the major role that it would do in later periods.

[18] The first phase of providing sustenance for the *k3* of the deceased was the placing of food in the burial chamber (Emery, *Archaic Egypt*, Plate 29) or the magazines around it (Emery, *Archaic Egypt*, Plate 13). The latter was gradually replaced by the stele with the offering table scene which was placed in a specially marked offering place in the chapel, and in this way magically provided the needs of the deceased (O'Neill, *Setting the scene*, 16). Originally the provision of real offerings was the main way of providing the sustenance of the *k3* of the deceased, and it was only later that this aspect was pushed into the background (Roeten, *Osiris*, Figure 108).

[19] An important component of this collection of evidence is the offering formula of which Junker states that its first known appearance is in the inner recess of the southern false door in the tomb of *R*ʿ*-ḥtp* at Maidum (Junker, *Giza II*, 41 – 2; Harpur, *Maidum*, 112, Figures 98 and 171). In the decoration of many chapels the daily ritual is represented in a stereotyped form that does not give much information about the actual ritual.

[20] The aforementioned contracts of *Ḏf3(.j)-Ḥ*ʿ*pj* just give an inkling of the content of the ritual.

Figure 2.2 False door area in the chapel of *3ḫtj-mrw-nswt* (PM, III/1, 80 – 1; G 2184; ASAE 13-14(1914), Plate 11B).

for his services the priest received payment in the form of his share of the offerings. Undoubtedly, the priest in attendance had such contracts on a daily basis, and as a result the ritual could not have been lengthy; it may have consisted of burning some incense on the offering standard(s),[21] placing some bread on the offering stone and pouring out some water (or beer) into the libation basin,[22] and because that was an extremely important part of the magical content of the ritual, spells must have been pronounced. This means that two of the three components of the magical part of the procedure, the spells and the ritual, were present. The third component, one or more ritual instruments wielded by the officiant,[23] cannot always be determined with certainty, due to the limited and certainly stereotyped information that is available.

III. Ritually important tomb elements outside the chapel

In the tomb five ritually charged areas can be designated, of which one, the entrance, had partly lost its direct ritual meaning:[24]

1. The entrance into the chapel is the first ritually important element to be met on the way to the interior of the chapel. This entrance element had once been the offering place and only later became a real entrance. This indicates that the interpretation of the offering place had always that of a door. The result of the change from an offering place into a real entrance was that a new offering place with the underlying idea of a door had to be created in the chapel. This means that being the focal point of offering activities is the main function of the door. The statement by Scharff that the offering function of the false door is only of secondary importance is contradicted by the consideration that it is unlikely that the *k3* of the deceased, who could go anywhere in the tomb, needed a door-like construction to pass through, if it had been attracted there by the presence of offerings placed at the other side. The observation that in that case the *k3* needed the facsimile of a door might indicate that the chapel was not part of the tomb interior, a space that was neither the world of the living nor the world of the dead.
2. In the superstructure the area of the offering place against the western wall of the chapel or the eastern wall of the tomb contained an offering stone or basin often flanked by offering stands,[25] sometimes a statue, and the false door itself (Figure 2.2). It was the place where the deceased was invited to leave his house and partake in the offerings. This made it the area where a direct contact was made between the living and the spirit of the deceased.
3. The serdab is one of the tomb elements that was important for the afterlife of the deceased. In the course of the Old Kingdom its placement in the mortuary monument had been subject to change, indicating a gradual alteration in the ritual meaning of the element. Its role in the monument is somewhat dualistic; in some tombs they are completely closed off from the world

[21] Giza Archives, Photos B11816_OS and B11817_OS.

[22] Junker, *Giza VII,* 121 observes that in some chapels small canals were constructed from the offering basin out of the chapel; this might indicate that during the ritual a considerable quantity of water was poured out. Because the number of basins with a drain that have been found is not large, this copiously pouring of water cannot have been a binding part of the ritual. The abundant pouring of water can also be seen as a token of reverence for the deceased because water for the rituals had to be carried over a long distance, and on the edge of the desert water was equivalent to an item of luxury.

[23] Forshaw, *Lector,* 27 ff..

[24] Scharff, *Wohnhaus,* 40.

[25] Giza Archives, photo A675-NS gives the impression that on the platform next to the offering stone a standard had been placed; in tomb G 1452 + 1453 two offering stands have been excavated *in situ* (Giza Archives, photos B11816_OS and B11817_OS).

outside; in others they have a small opening, theoretically giving the visitor an opportunity to see the statue of the deceased (e.g. the mastaba of *Ṯjj* at Saqqara), although in most cases the statues remained invisible due to their small length or the lack of light. This dualism has led to several opposing opinions about the function of the serdab, making it the subject of ongoing scholarly discussion.[26]

4. The burial chamber in the subterranean part of the mortuary monument is a room that was cut out of the underlying rock and consequently lay below the level of the chapel. However, when considered from a three-dimensional point of view, it was, if possible, oriented in such a way that it was close to the false door in the chapel. The burial chamber itself not only was the place where the mortal remains of the deceased were deposited, it was also seen as part of the world where the deceased 'lived'. The closure, 'the door', between the entrance of the burial chamber and the shaft was the place where, temporarily, the world of the living and of the dead were in direct open contact.[27]
5. The shaft to the burial chamber forms the connection between the world of the living and the burial chamber. Excavation results have made it likely that after the burial chamber had been closed the shaft remained part of the world of the living, while the burial chamber became part of the world of the dead. The number of shafts is not identical with the number of burials in all tombs, in some an extra shaft is present that has no burial chamber connected to it.[28]

III.1. The burial chamber and the shaft

Some remarks have to be made about the last two items, because these parts of the monument as a whole are the most complex, due to the existence of the real and direct connection between them, forming a link between the world where the deceased will live for eternity and the world of the living.

In some tombs, the burial chamber opened directly into the shaft, in others the connection was made by means of a small corridor. Once the connection closed, the space behind the closure not only became part of the world of the dead, but also the residence of the deceased.

The connection was frightening not only because it was a connection between these two worlds, but also due to the complicating factor that the demise of the tomb owner had released two forces, the *k3* and the *b3,* two forces that were inherent to his being the person that he was. These two forces were considered to be potentially dangerous for living persons.

Although the funerary ritual united the *k3* with the body, in which vicinity it stayed thereafter, the survival of the *k3* by way of the offering of food and drink in the offering place was of the utmost importance for the continuation of the after-life of the tomb-owner, thus necessitating the perpetual maintenance of the mortuary cult, and in order to be able to partake in the offerings, the *k3* had some mobility in the tomb and could move through its interior to the false door and through it into the chapel.[29]

The *b3* can be interpreted as the personification of the vital forces of the deceased that come into being at the moment of death. It is mobile in that it can move in the realms of after-life and in the physical world outside the tomb,[30] using the burial shaft as the way out of the tomb. In the literature there is no indication that the *b3* must be provided with offerings. If the fact that the *k3,* in contrast to the *b3,* needed sustenance is combined with offerings that have been found placed in the shaft to the burial chamber, the conclusion is that the mobility of the *k3* in reality extended beyond the burial chamber and the chapel.

Once the body of the deceased had been placed in the burial chamber, care was taken to physically *and* magically close the opening between these two worlds.[31] Normally this opening was closed with stones or mud-bricks (and white-washed at the shaft side, thus making it a sacred place), but in tomb M16 of *Nfr-m3ʿt* in Maidum the opening was closed with a stone wall *and* a wooden door.[32] In view of the sometimes indifferent way in which these connections were closed,[33] it has the

[26] Bolshakov, *Man and double;* Warden, *Serdab.*

[27] Rzeuska, *Funerary customs,* 361. The closure could be a wall of mud-brick, smaller stones, custom cut stones or a monolithic portcullis. A wall made of mud-brick or smaller stones was the most common way of closing the entrance; only for the upper social stratum was a portcullis sometimes used (Alexanian, *Netjeraperef,* Plate 3), while in the entrance of the burial chamber of *Nfr-m3ʿt* at Maidum a wooden door was placed (Harpur, *Maidum,* Figures 54 and 55).

[28] Rzeuska, *Funerary customs,* 371 ff..

[29] Bárta, *Funerary rites,* 21 – 2 discusses a tomb in which, according to the excavators' opinion, this idea has been worked out in the lay-out of the super- and substructure.

[30] LÄ, I, 588 – 90, s.w. 'Ba'; Junker, *Giza XI,* 106 – 7; Žabkar, *Ba concept,* 162 only mentions its mobility in the realm of the dead. Kanawati, *The tomb,* 24 brings forward that the *b3* of the deceased has a greater freedom of movement than the *k3* and was able to traverse both the realm of the living and the dead, but at night had to reunite with the corpse of the deceased.

[31] For a discussion of the rituals see Rzeuska, *Funerary customs,* 362 ff..

[32] Harpur, *Maidum,* Figures 54, 55; Clark, *Tomb security,* Figures 281 and 282.

[33] Petrie, *Meydum and Memphis,* Plate 1. Clark, *Tomb security,* Figures 276 – 81. This way of closing the connection was not done in all tombs, because during the early 4th dynasty the portcullis was also used

appearance that the belief was that the real 'security' came from rituals performed in front of the burial chamber once it was closed, rituals that must have been partly for the sustenance of the *k3* and partly apothropaic.[34]

In the necropolis of Abusir in the (disturbed) shaft leading to the burial chamber of tomb AC 31 at the height of the entrance into the burial chamber, items have been found that are partly apothropaic (the head and lower legs of a bovine) and partly non-apothropaic (offering stands, *bḏ3* bread forms), it is probable that tomb-robber disturbance caused the latter to mix with the apothropaic items.[35] The deposits of a variety of goods that were sometimes placed at a certain height in the shaft can only be interpreted as food offerings, due to the presence of *bḏ3* and *ʿpr.t* bread forms. The excavation of the burial shaft in the mastaba of *Ἰntj* at Abusir showed layers of offerings at various levels.[36] Garstang reports that in tomb K1 at Bêt Khallâf vessels had been placed on the descending staircase.[37]

In the burial shaft of some tombs excavation showed that further apothropaic measures were taken in the form of objects placed in a niche higher up in the shaft.

The prevalent opinion is that measures like closing the door physically and magically were meant to keep robbers out of the burial chamber. Excavation has taught that tomb robbers could not be stopped, either by physical, or by magical means; after all the physical blocking could easily be pushed aside while the magical protection could be bypassed by a corridor directly into the burial chamber, and apparently fear of the world of the dead could be overcome by greed.[38] That this fear was not entirely overcome can be deduced from the observation that whenever statues are found, they are nearly always broken, probably by the robbers to 'break' their magic in this way.[39]

Both facts had undoubtedly also been observed by the Egyptians themselves, and yet they continued to take these protective measures. That means that the continuation cannot just be 'protection against.... '; but this expression works in two ways. While the physical measures in most cases do not effectively protect the deceased against living intruders, the apothropaic measures protect

- the deceased against evil spirits from the world outside the tomb that might be dangerous for the continuation of the afterlife of the deceased.
- the living against intrusion by evil spirits that can find their way out of the world of the dead by way of the burial chamber and the shaft into the world outside the tomb.
- the living against the deceased, who was not always considered as a benevolent force.

The offerings in the shaft might indicate that they were meant to support and facilitate the passage of the *k3* that apparently developed a greater degree of freedom of movement and in that case appeared not to be influenced by the apothropaic measures.

III.2. The shaft niches

In the shaft of the tomb of *Ḥm-jwnw* (PM, II/1, 122 – 3; IV.E) a(n) (unfinished) niche has been found that might have served as a place where offerings were left behind.[40] The same type of niche has been found in the shaft to the burial chamber of queen *Ḥtp-ḥr.s,* (IV.E), but in this niche items had been placed that cannot be interpreted as only food offerings;[41] possibly the content of the niche was meant to be partly apothropaic (the skull), partly food offering (the legs), although the latter can be apothropaic too. In the tomb of *Ἰtj* (IV.E) the same type of niche, but this time empty, has been found in the southern shaft.[42] If the relative depth of the three niches in the shaft is gathered, it is evident that the tomb of *Ḥtp-ḥr.s,* which is completely different from other tombs, also deviates strongly in the depth of the niche in the shaft from the two mentioned in the table (Figure 2.3).

in private tombs (Alexanian, *Netjeraperef*, Figure 4, Photo 2a; some mastabas in cemetery G 2100 (Jánosi, *Giza*, 151, Plan 2). In tomb G 2100-A the opening between the shaft and the burial chamber has been closed with cut stones (Der Manuelian, *Gmast 8*, Figure 1.12).

34 The apothropaic elements in these rituals were connected with animal skulls (Rzeuska, *Funerary customs*, 361), this is also evident in elements of the rituals around the laying of the foundation of a large construction like the temple of a royal mortuary complex, these incorporated apothropaic elements like a bovine skull placed upside down (Krejči, *Abusir XVIII*, Figure 6.2). Also see Junker, *Giza I*, 204. This ritual apparently still existed in the 12th dynasty, since in the burial shaft of the tomb of *Ḏḥtj-nḫt* at Deir el-Barsha the feet of calves have been found, placed in front of the wall of the burial chamber from the shaft (Willems, *Djehutinakht*, 36).

35 Krejči, *AC 31*, 15; Bárta, *Abusir V*, 90. In the disturbed shaft 4 of the tomb of *Ḥtpj* 0.50m over the entrance of the burial chamber a layer containing bread moulds, stands and animal bones has been found. On the bottom of the shaft to the burial chamber of *Nṯr-ʿpr.f* (tomb II/1 at Dahshur) offerings next to model vessels parts of a calf have been found that can be interpreted as apothropaic (Alexanian, *Netjeraperef*, 100).

36 Bárta, *Inty*, 2; Bárta, *Funerary rites*, Figure 2.

37 Garstang, *Bêt Khallâf*, 10.

38 See the by-passing robbers tunnel in Alexanian, *Netjeraperef*, Plate 3c/d.

39 Another terrifying aspect of robbing a tomb was the severe punishment upon being caught.

40 Junker, *Giza I*, Figure 21.

41 In the niche the horned skull and three legs of a bull packed in a reed matting have been found (Lehner, *Hetep-heres*, 33).

42 Bárta, *Abusir V*, 90 – 10; Junker, *Giza V*, 190 (mastaba 4498) ; A discussion of the burial shaft niche in Junker, *Giza V*, 180 – 2. The double recessed niche that has been found in the shaft of the mastaba of *Ἰnty* at Abusir, and that can be dated to the 6th dynasty, is different in design and meaning.

name		% depth niche (from top)
Ḥtp-ḥr.s	PM, III/1,179 - 82	27
Ḥm-jwnw	PM, III/1,122 - 3	62.5
Ꜣty	Bárta, *Abusir V*, 9-10	60 - 75

Figure 2.3 The depth of shaft niches.

With regard to this type of niche another aspect has to be taken into account: observations about the placing of the serdab lead Junker to propose a development of the placement of the statues that leads from a serdab in the mass of the mastaba, [43] to a serdab in the vicinity of the entrance of the burial shaft,[44] followed by a place in a niche in the shaft itself,[45] first higher up in the shaft,[46] later at the bottom in front of the entrance of the burial chamber,[47] finally ending up in the burial chamber itself.[48] Junker based his hypothesis on a growing lack of space in the superstructure caused by the decline of the dimensions of the tombs which took place in the course of the Old Kingdom, a development in accordance with the observations in an earlier study by the author.[49]

This gradual displacement of the statues stresses the magical connection between the chapel, the shaft and the burial chamber, a connection that was visible even in the mastaba of *Ꜣty* at Abusir South.

Another conclusion is that the development indicates a decreasing connection between serdab statues and the need for offerings brought to them by visitors, a development that can be connected with the change in the mode of sustenance of the *k3* of the deceased.[50] The latter conclusion is strengthened by the observation that the earlier statues were placed closer to the outside of the tomb, in some cases even in an exterior chapel.

The possibility that these niches were not solely intended to place goods in them can be deduced from the niche that has been found in the mastaba of *K3.j-m-nfrt* (PM, III/1, 218). In the shaft a niche opposite the entrance of the burial chamber had been cut out, that turned out to be empty. Reisner proposed that the niche was meant to enable the sarcophagus to be placed in the burial chamber, but according to Junker this is not the case.[51] The niche at the bottom of the shaft is not necessarily there for protective and ritualistic purposes, while a niche higher-up in the shaft is clearly intended for that purpose.

[43] Junker, *Vorbericht 1914*, 12 – 4; Junker, *Giza VII*, 85 – 6.

[44] Junker, *Giza VII*, 25.

[45] In a niche in the shaft of the tomb of *Ṯn3* (PM, III/1, 149) a limestone statue and two wooden ones of the tomb owner have been found (Junker, *Giza VII*, 85 – 8, Figure 28, Plate XVII) ; in a niche in the shaft of the tomb of *Ꜣṯtj* (PM, III/2, 609) several wooden statues of the tomb owner and servants had been placed (Drioton, *Ishethi*, 214 – 5).

[46] Bárta, *Abusir V*, Figure 3.3 (tomb of *Ḥtpj*).

[47] Junker, *Giza VII*, 86.

[48] The excavation of Abusir tomb AC 33 of *K3-jr.s* (press release Czech Institute of Egyptology, Prague 02.10.2018) revealed a statue of the tomb owner standing behind a low wall in front of the sarcophagus.

[49] Roeten, *Economic decline*.

[50] Roeten, *Decoration*.

[51] Junker, *Giza X*, 31 - 3.

Chapter Three

Introduction

I. The tomb, its facade and chapel

Earlier elite tombs had outer walls that were frequently constructed in a stylized imitation of what many scholars have interpreted as the facade of the royal palace (Figure 3.1).[1] In order to enhance the similarity with a door, the inner recess of all the niches of the palace façade panelled outer walls of mastaba XVII at Abusir were painted brown.[2] The panelling can be constructed with different degrees of complexity, in Figure 3.1 the panelling is simple (two double niches separated by three single niches), but more complicated constructions are possible.[3]

Figure 3.1 Palace façade panelling (Shunet el-zebib, Abydos).

Because in the early period of the Old Kingdom the *k3* of the deceased was supposed to 'live' in the tomb itself, the door in front of which the offerings were placed, and which was often marked with a wooden or stone floor plate,[4] served as a chapel and was seen as a door

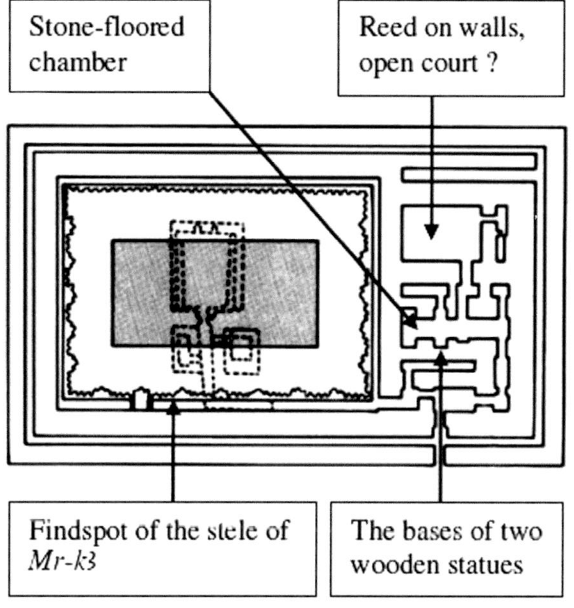

Figure 3.2 Plan of the mastaba of *Mr-k3* (PM, III/2, 446; S 3505; date: reign of Qa'a (I.8)). Findspot according to Snape, *Egyptian tombs,* Figure 1.4.

through which the *k3* of the deceased could pass in order to benefit from the offerings placed in front of it.[5] At first it was just one of the many 'doors' in these walls that could serve as a point of contact between the worlds of the living and the dead,[6] but a preference developed to consider one of the doors in the southern part of the eastern wall as the main place of contact.

An example of this preference is the offering place with a (displaced) stele that has been found in the southern part of the eastern wall of the tomb that probably belonged to the official *Mr-k3* (PM, III/2, 446; S 3505; date: reign of Qa'a (I.8)) (Figure 3.2).[7]

---

[1] According to Wilkinson this type of decoration was even used in places where it could not been seen, like in the burial chamber of tomb 2275 at Minshat Abu Omar where three of the interior walls had niches (Wilkinson, *Early dynastic,* 192 - 7, Figure 6.8(4), although the figure gives the impression that only the northern wall has niches. However, there is a distinct possibility that these protruding parts were not part of niches but supports for a wooden inner-room like the ones in the burial chamber in the tombs of Djer (I.3), Djet (I.4) and Merneith (I.4?) in the first dynasty necropolis of Abydos.

[2] Radwan, *Mastaba XVII,* 512. This tomb is dated to the first dynasty. The conclusion that this is done in order to imitate a door is not unequivocal because it is also possible that the palace was constructed of wood reinforced with stone or mud-brick pilasters. This construction has an equivalent in that of the construction of the burial chamber in the tombs of some of the first dynasty kings at Abydos; here the wooden inner chamber (the residence of the deceased) is supported at first by thin wooden (?) uprights, later by larger mud-brick pilasters (Kaiser, *Königsfriedhof,* 217 – 8, Figure 12).

[3] Alexanian, *Chasechemui,* Plate 5. Reisner, *Tomb development,* Figures 129 – 134.

[4] Petrie, *Tarkhan I,* Plates XV(2) and XVIII.

[5] Tomb U-j at Abydos, a tomb that is dated to the period just before the first dynasty (pre- or protodynastic period, Nagada IIIa2), had no palace façade panelling and no discernible offering place. The somewhat older tomb 100 at Hieraconpolis (Nagada II) consists of one room that is partly divided into two separate spaces: the northern is a magazine for supplies, the southern (probably) is the actual burial chamber (Quibell, *Hierakonpolis II,* 21 – 2, Plate LXVII). It is not possible to determine whether tomb 100 had a chapel, but at the southern side of tomb U-j evidence of a cult has been found in the form of model vessels, offering tables and a alabaster basin (Dreyer, *Royal burial,* 129).

[6] Reisner, *History mastabas,* 580. The larger mastabas were enclosed by a wall at a certain distance from the mastaba itself . This created an open air area in front of the doors, and an open air chapel in front of the special door.

[7] Emery, *Archaic Egypt,* Figure 53 (page 89). Morris, *Saqqara mastabas,*

This mastaba has another feature that makes it exceptional; at its northern side is an extension that can be interpreted as a chapel. One of the several rooms in the chapel had a stone covered floor and in a niche in that room the bases of two wooden statues with the feet of a striding figure were found (Figure 13.1). The design of the extension resembles the plan of mastaba S 3121 (dated to Qa'a (I.8)) which has an entrance at the northern side of the eastern wall which splits up into one corridor with an offering place and another leading to a chapel with painted walls.[8]

Over the course of time the palace façade panelling disappeared and all that remained were two offering places on the eastern wall of the tomb of which the one at the southern end of that wall was usually the most important.[9] At first this place, which was outside the body of the tomb, offered little protection against climatic conditions.[10] As early as the 1st dynasty a wall was constructed in front of some of the offering places,[11] which not only created a space hiding it from direct view, but also created something new: a real entrance.[12] The next step in the development was the construction of a roof over the chapel,[13] while from the start of the 4th dynasty on the exterior chapels of the richer tombs were constructed of stone.

At a somewhat later stage the chapel was constructed inside the body of the tomb, thus introducing a type of chapel which offered the maximum in privacy and protection. The consequence was that the exterior chapel slowly got into disuse,[14] although, possibly for reasons of financial capacity, it was never completely abandoned, while sometimes both types of chapels were installed in the same mortuary monument (Figure 13.4).

II. The constituent parts of a structure for ritual purposes

The tomb acts as the focal-point of two different sets of rituals, the funerary rituals, a set that is enacted only once, and the mortuary rituals, that are, theoretically, performed not only every day ('for eternity'), but certainly during every festival or on every festive day.

> *'An offering which the king and Osiris give, may an invocation offering come forth for him at the opening of the year feast, the Thoth feast, the first of the year feast, the Wag feast, the Sokar feast, the great feast, the fire-lighting feast, the first of the year feast, the coming forth of Min (feast), the Sag-feast, at the monthly feast, the half-monthly feast, at the course of every day from the bread, beer, from meat, birds, from the lit incense, perfumes, from all the sweet things (to) the inspector of the royal domain, Themi'*
>
> (Soleiman, *Ptahshepses*, 108 – 9).

For each of these sets the monument contains several elements; some of these are only meant to serve one set of rituals, others can serve both of them. However, for each of the sets it is necessary that the sum of the elements relevant to them acts as a unit.

In a monument with an interior chapel the following elements can be distinguished:

For the above-ground part:[15]

- The entrance which can be sub-divided into:
  - The door jambs.
  - The drum over the entrance into the corridor.
  - The architrave over the entrance.
  - The entrance thicknesses.
- The chapel and its walls, the number of which depends on the ground-plan of the chapel.
- The false door(s).
- The serdab(s).

171, 183 – 4. In this tomb there is no northern niche, but the chapel-like construction north of the tomb can be seen as the northern offering place.

[8] La Loggia, *Engineering*, 136, and note 379.

[9] Mastaba S 3505 (Figure 3.2) departs from this in that what seems to be the chapel has been placed at the northern side of the tomb, while the stele, although not found *in situ*, could have been the marker of the southern offering place. The person who was buried here must have been of high social status (possibly royalty closely linked to the king by blood line, which would explain the dimensions of the mastaba and the northern 'chapel').

[10] Often the offering place had an appreciable depth and in this way could provide some protection to the decoration eventually placed on and in it.

[11] Later in the Old Kingdom, if the entrance of a chapel led directly to a public space, possibly for the sake of privacy, a wall was sometimes placed in front of it ('curtain wall' (Hassan, *Giza I*, General plan)).

[12] The tomb of king Den (I.5; PM, V, 83-5) at Abydos incorporates a building constructed against the south-eastern wall of the tomb. This building can be interpreted as a chapel with a stair-case that descends through a right angle into a chapel with a niche, in which possibly a statue of the king had been placed (Emery, *Archaic Egypt*, Figure 40; O'Connor, *Abydos*, 154). O'Connor remarks that this set-up is anomalous for the royal tombs of the 1st dynasty. It is possible that all the royal tombs had a chapel against the super-structure, but they have disappeared over time. For unknown reasons the chapel of the tomb of this king is subterranean and thus less exposed (O'Connor, *Abydos*, 154). In the early-dynastic cemetery of Abusir a non-royal tomb (tomb V; date: 1st dynasty) has the same type of ground-plan with a chapel at the top of a staircase descending to the burial chamber (Bárta, *Serdab*, Figure 2, Radwan, *Abusir*, Figure 2).
This set-up made the subterranean room invisible from the outside world and possibly stelae with the tomb owner's name had been placed at the top of the staircase. An example of a first-dynasty non-royal tomb with an above-ground chapel connected to it is mastaba XVII at Abusir (Radwan, *Mastaba XVII*).

[13] The corridor chapel in the mastaba of *Ḥsjj-Rʿ* (early dynasty III; PM, III/2, 437–9) had been roofed with wood (Quibell, *Hesy*, 5).

[14] Examples of tombs with both an interior and exterior chapel are *K3.j-w3b* (PM, III/1, 187 – 8) and *ʿnḫ-ḥ3.f* (PM, III/1, 196), both dated to IV.E.

[15] Not every tomb design gives rise to all elements mentioned in the list.

For the subterranean part:

- The shaft to the burial chamber.
- The burial chamber.
- In tombs that are intended for the burial of one person, sometimes a second shaft has been constructed that is less deep and has no burial chamber connected to it: this is called the 'subsidiary' or 'ritual' shaft.[16]

II.1. The chapel entrance

Whatever the construction of the offering place or the entrance of the interior or exterior chapel, it remained of the utmost importance that visitors and passers-by were informed about the person that was buried in the monument. This was not only necessary for the continuation of life in the world of the dead, but also for the deceased to keep his place in the community of the living. In addition, the monument was also important to demonstrate the social status not only of the deceased but of the family too. For this reason at first in or around the offering place architectonic elements were installed that carried information stating the name and titles of the deceased (this can be called 'person signalling information').[17] As long as the offering place was visible from the path leading to or passing by the tomb, the indispensable information could be restricted to the offering place itself.

Figure 3.3 The entrance of the exterior chapel of *K3(.j)-m-nfrt* (PM, III/1, 263-4; date: V.L); after Hassan, *Giza II*, Figure 112, Plate XXXIII.

However, after the introduction of the exterior chapel, and later the interior chapel, the information carrying architectonic elements of the offering place were no longer directly visible to the passer-by. This invisibility made it necessary to place the signalling information on the architectural elements of the entrance of the exterior or interior chapel (Figure 3.3 is an example of an exterior chapel with door jambs that carry the information (the architrave is lost)).[18] Early examples of entrances with information carrying architectural elements around the entrance of an interior chapel are those of *Nfr-m3ʿt* (PM, IV, 92 – 3; IV.E) at Maidum, where the architrave, door jambs and entrance thicknesses have been used to depict the tomb owner, his wife and his titles,[19] and the entrance of the cruciform chapel of *Mṯn* (PM, III/2, 493 – 4; IV.E) where his name and titles are given on the architrave, on the drum over the entrance, while on the first vertical line of the entrance thicknesses only his name is written; the other lines on

[16] Garstang, *Bêt Khallâf*, Plate VII calls these shallow shafts 'offering wells'.

[17] Although they have been found but never *in situ*, it is probable that steles had been placed near the royal burial place in order to indicate the name of the person that had been buried there; that it was a king was shown by the *serekh* with the name and the falcon depiction of the god *Ḥr* on top of it (Aldred, *Egyptian art*, Figure 11 (page 41)). Near the tombs of the first dynasty kings at Abydos, rows of lower class graves have been found that surrounded the royal tombs. The name of the deceased was given by way of a simple stele just stating the name, although some stelae that were placed in graves around the tomb of later kings give the impression that sometimes additional information like a profession, or other data had been added (Petrie, *Royal tombs II*, Plates XXVI and XXVII; O'Connor, *Abydos*, Figure 83). In all probability we are dealing here with *sati* burials, which makes it questionable whether an offering place was present (the victims had given up their after-life to serve that of another, thus being dependant on the other (Morris, *Sacrifice*,17)). An example of a stele placed as a marker and giving the name, titles and a depiction of the deceased is the one of *Mr-k3* (PM, III/2, 446; date: dynasty I.L). The stele, on which the deceased was represented sitting without an offering table, was placed in a niche in the eastern side of mastaba S 3505 at Saqqara (Stevenson Smith, *Art and architecture*, Figure 21 (page 40)). In the cemetery of Tarkhan mastaba 2038 (datable from king Den (I.5) to the end of the 1st dynasty) has two subsidiary burials between the mastaba itself and the temenos and two stelae were placed on the topside of the tombs (Petrie, *Tarkhan II*, Plate XV). If the offering place was a niche, not only the name and some titles of the tomb owner were mentioned, but further themes could be added, like depictions of the tomb owner, offering bearers, offerings, an offering table with loaves, an ideographic offering list (Alexanian, *Netjeraperef*, Plates 14-8). During a short period in the 4th dynasty the offering place was indicated with a slab stele showing a depiction of the tomb owner, the name, some titles and an offering list (Der Manuelian, *Giza slab stelae*).

[18] On the entrance thicknesses of the chapel of *K3(.j)-m-nfrt* (PM, III/1, 263 – 4) the tomb owner is depicted in company of priests and family (Hassan, *Giza II*, Figures 114A and B). For a reconstruction of the exterior chapel of *K3.(j) - w'b* (PM, III/1, 187 – 8), see Simpson, *Gmast 3*, Figures 4 and 5.

[19] Harpur, *Maidum*, Figure 176. On the architrave of the chapel of his wife *Jtt* (PM, IV, 93 – 4) the deceased has been depicted in a marsh environment, stating her name and showing her husband and sons (Harpur, *Maidum*, Figure 82).

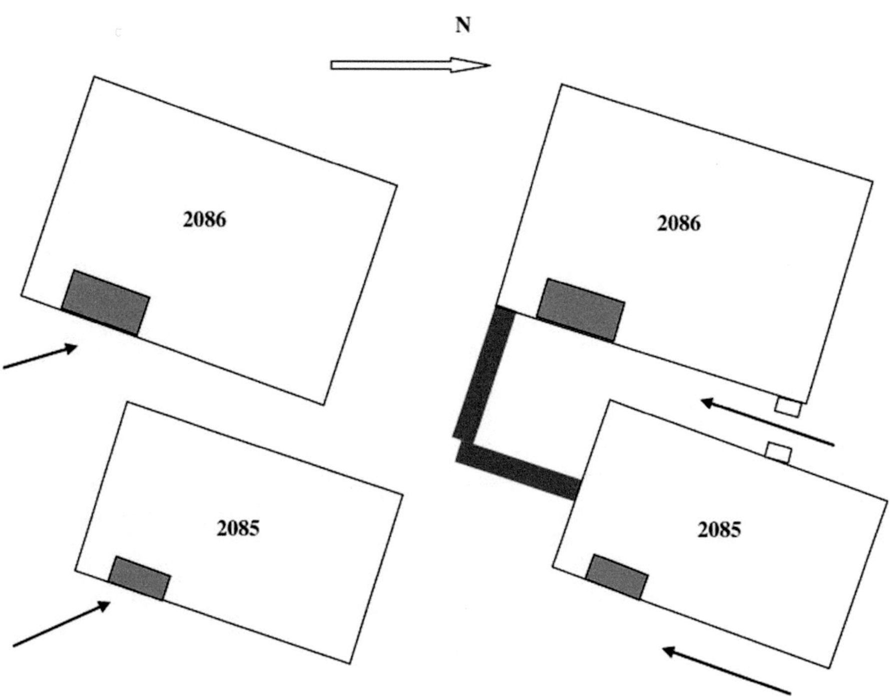

Figure 3.4 The adjustment of the lay-out of the mastaba to a shift in a change of the direction of approach.

this element contain the autobiography of the tomb owner.[20]

During the Old Kingdom elite tombs were often gathered in clusters;[21] that were organised in such a way that the offering place or the entrance of the chapel faced an already existing path through the cemetery or faced a new path that connected the valley and the cluster (Roth, *Gmast 6*, 23, 25). These paths could be the result of restrictions imposed by the landscape, as was the case in the necropolis of Abusir where the location of the lake of Abusir meant that the cemetery had to be approached from the north (Bárta, *Hetepi*, 34). It could also be the shortest way between the valley and the cluster. Sometimes over the course of time the trajectory of these paths altered (for reasons not always clear), often necessitating architectural adjustments at the tombs. The latter is clear from the development as shown in Roth, *Gmast 6*; in Figure 3.4 the mastabas G 2085 and G 2086 are placed next to each other with their offering places exposed to the path that runs at their south side (Figure 3.4 left). On the architectural elements forming the access to the offering chapel of mastaba G 2086 the necessary information had been placed with that direction in mind.[22]

In the next phase of development of the cluster the path had shifted to the northern side of the cluster which reduced the visibility of the offering place of mastaba G 2086 markedly. In order to enhance the visibility the courtyard in front of the chapel was closed and a new entrance with door jambs carrying signalling information was constructed (Figure 3.4 right).[23]

An apparent departure from the idea of the necessity of visibility is the situation in the mastaba of *N-sḏr-k3.j* (PM, III/1, 72 – 4; G 2101 or G 2100-II.ann.); in front of the portico-entrance is a courtyard that is surrounded by a high wall (2.50m). This courtyard can be entered through a gateway with an anepigraphic architrave, and a (no longer present) door. This suggests that, were the entrance into the courtyard to be blocked, the identity of the tomb owner would remain unknown. However, the height of the pillars of the portico-hall in front of the entrance of the chapel itself enabled the passer-by to see the text on the architrave supported by them at the other side of the courtyard.[24]

II.2. The corridor into the chapel

A direct result of the introduction of the interior chapel was that a corridor to the chapel itself had to be constructed with the consequence that more

20 LD, *II*, 7a.

21 Often these clusters were determined by social status and/or profession.

22 Roth, *Gmast 6*, Plates 14c, 15 and 139.

23 Rothe , *Gmast 6*, 71 – 2, Plates 110/b/c and 138.

24 Junker, *Giza II*, 104 – 5, Plate IIa.

Figure 3.5 Northern entrance thickness of the tomb of *Kȝw-njswt* (PM, III/1, 274); after Hassan, *Giza II,* Plate XXIV.

Figure 3.6 Southern entrance thickness of the chapel of *Kȝ-pw-nswt* [I] (PM, III/1, 135); after Junker, *Giza III,* Plate VIIIb.

wall space became available in the vicinity of the entrance, and as well as from the name and titles, other decoration themes could now be placed on the entrance thicknesses that were introduced by this development. The dimensions of these entrance thicknesses also made it possible to place more voluminous themes that, due to the glare of the sun light reflected on the sand outside, would be visible without entering the corridor into the chapel.

Examples of this type of voluminous decoration themes are the tomb owner and his wife either standing (the female adult could be depicted at the same size as the male or much smaller, though bigger than children used to be depicted (for the same male/female size version see Figure 3.5) or sitting (Figure 3.6); another example is the depiction of the tomb owner sitting at the offering table which was placed for a short period in the chapel entrances of the tombs in the necropolis of Giza (Figure 3.7).[25]

Very often rooms in interior or exterior chapels, including the chapel itself, could be closed with a door,[26] thus making it impossible for passers-by to enter the chapel and to place offerings in front of the false door.

This made the entrance and the corridor to the chapel likely to become a place where the offering formula could be cited and possibly offerings could be placed, although Figure 13.17 shows that a more spacious place was preferred.

The most direct indication of this function of the entrance thicknesses is the depiction of the tomb owner sitting at the offerings table (Figure 3.7), a depiction that can be interpreted as purpose signalling. In a later stage of this study the feasibility of the corridor as an

[25] Roeten, *Decoration,* Table XII.1.Ann. (page 384 ff.). In Table II of the present study it is obvious that this decoration theme in any of its three forms (themes 4, 5 and 6 in Figure 11.1) is present on the entrance thicknesses of the chapels in the necropolis of Saqqara (Harpur, *DETOK,* 53).

[26] Reisner, *Giza I,* 187. Bárta, *Abusir XIX,* Plate 2.6. In this photo it can be seen that the false door could be closed off with a door. It is probable that not every tomb owner was financially able to close the entrance of his chapel in this way because wood was an expensive commodity. In the tomb of *Rʿ-wr* (PM, III/1, 265 – 9, Plan XXXIII) the pivot holes of several doors closing interior rooms have been found (Hassan, *Giza I,* 4 – 32, Plates VIII and XXVII). The various doors in the total complex give the impression that they were meant to close small rooms that were intended as chapels.

Figure 3.7 Northern entrance thickness of the chapel of *K3.j-nj-nswt* (PM, III/1, 78-9); Junker, *Giza, II,* Plate Va; Der Manuelian, *Gmast 8,* Figures 13.28 and 13.29.

alternative offering place will be discussed (Annex Chapter XIV).

The functions of the themes of the entrance decoration, combined with the functions that these themes have within the total cultual functioning of the chapel, have already been touched upon by the author in two preliminary studies which, however, remained limited to the tombs in the necropolis of Giza.[27]

27 Roeten, *Decoration,* 342-5; Roeten, *Functions.*

Doors

(photo author)

There are always two sides to each door
and in the end, who is inside and who is out

(Free after Dr. H.G.S. Snijder,
'Een beetje gek' in 'Spiegelingen"
(Literaire Tafelstonden, Brugge, 1963).

Chapter Four

Doors, Closing the Monument

I. Introduction

Earlier in this study it has been remarked that in many tombs the possibility of closing parts of the interior rooms had been included in their architecture. This conclusion follows from various archaeological finds that indicate that doors were frequently used in funerary monuments. The finds lead to the conclusion that the primary function of doors was to make the passage 'impassable', but their construction did not allow them to keep out sand or wind.

It is possible, and even probable, that our approach to the purpose of the doors that obviously have been present in many of the passages is etic.[1] From our point of view we interpret doors as a means to make entering into a place difficult if not impossible, while here the doors were placed in the passage without being locked in our sense of the word.[2] Because a device to lock the door was unknown, a door could only indicate that it was considered to be within good taste that this space be respected in case of a closed door. The large number of different representations of doors, either two-dimensional or three-dimensional, that have come to us indicates a wide range of employment, and in the following sections these applications will be further studied.

II. The door: an entrance, a passage, and an object

The definition of the noun 'door' is *'a hinged, sliding, or revolving barrier at the entrance to a building, room, or vehicle, or in the framework of a cupboard'*, and refers solely to the physical object. Closely connected to this object is the noun 'doorway', that is defined as *'an entrance into a building or a room'*, a definition that has the non-substantial meaning of passage in it. However, one of the synonyms for 'doorway' is 'door' which thus also has the meaning of an entrance. This means that the word 'door' can be interpreted in two different ways, first as the material object that closes an opening, second as the opening itself.

Until now excavations have not completely solved the problem of when the Egyptians developed the technical ability to lock a door instead of merely closing it. Perhaps the basic idea was that an entrance, possibly even that of a private dwelling, had a special meaning that was embedded within the sphere of decorum. This consideration is supported by the observation that in a chapel a low wall could already indicate the separation between public and ritual environment.[3] An argument against this is that entering and robbing a burial chamber, a place that was supposed to be really protected by decorum and even magic, evidently did not raise any problems.

As a passage it can act in two ways; the first one is as a real passage where a human being can go through in order to enter into another room or to reach the other side of an obstacle. A famous example of the latter is 'The Wall of the Crow' that forms a physical division between the workers village and the royal necropolis on the Plateau of Giza (Figure 4.1).

An early precursor of the passage between rooms is found in tomb U-j at Abydos. In the interior of the tomb every room was connected with at least one other room by way of a slot-like opening. The slots making a north-south connection resembled low and narrow doors,[4] while those connecting east-west were taller, had a lintel and could be closed with a mat.[5] These features give the impression that the tomb was intended as an early facsimile of a house that was in accordance with the social status of the deceased. This would make these slots doors and windows in order to give the deceased a house that resembled his earthly home and it is apparently for that reason that Dreyer calls these slots 'Scheintür-Mauerdurchlässen',[6] where the word 'Scheintür' is not used in its magical meaning.

---

[1] Tavares, *House*, 11, the reconstruction of a residence in the pyramid town of Queen *Ḫnt-k3w.s.* shows that not only could the entrance be closed with a door, but also that several interior spaces were separated by doors.

[2] The explanation of the locking of doors in the pyramid temple of Menkaure (IV.6) is not convincing because it postulates holes in the door leaves where strings can pass through to pull the bolt, which would leave the door closed but still unlocked (Reisner, *Mycerinus*, 95). Another argument against this solution is that in the doors that have been excavated such holes were not present. Reisner introduces the use of a type of lock and key based on tumbling pegs, which was indeed known to Egyptian technology, but only from a much later period on. Koeningsberger, *Tür* does not mention a construction with which a door could really be locked, except than in the Late Period.

[3] Chauvet, *Tomb environment*, 48.

[4] Dreyer, *Royal burial*, Figure 14.5 (page 130).

[5] Dreyer, *Royal burial*, 129 states that the construction of the passage was such that an actual, but not preserved, curtain could be lowered in front of it.

[6] Dreyer, *U-j*, 35.

Figure 4.1 Heit el-Ghurab (The Wall of the Crow) at Giza.

In Dreyer, *Royal burial,* 130 the phrase 'These openings were intended to give the owner of the tomb symbolic access to the grave goods' suggests that these slots were present to give the *k3* of the deceased the possibility to move from one room to the other, and this in its turn would lead to the conclusion that in that period the *k3* could not pass through a wall. This would be contrary to the statement that the *k3* of the deceased could move around freely in the interior of the tomb.

A photo of the excavated 2nd dynasty tomb of Peribsen (II.5) gives the impression that passage ways of this type in the walls between the various rooms in the substructure were still in use,[7] although Petrie claims that they have been made by grave robbers.[8]

In the tombs of Djer (I.3) and Djet (I.4) the wooden walls of the inner burial chamber were supported by retaining walls standing perpendicular against the outer walls of the tomb.[9] On some of these retaining walls rectangular recesses are visible that have been painted red which, in view of the colour, might have served as doors for the *k3* of the deceased.[10]

The other type of passage, of which the false door is the most important representative, plays a major role in the interaction between the world of the living and the world of the dead. These were meant as passages for the *k3* of the deceased to enter into the chapel. This second type of passage will be discussed further in this study.

Excavation experience has revealed that in the majority of archaeological contexts only the non-wooden parts of door installations like the stones with the holes for the pivots that serve as part of the 'hinge-system' of the door (Figures 4.10, 4.11 and 4.12), or the holes in the jambs of the door opening that were intended for the bolt with which the door could be closed, are likely to be found (this type of bolt is only valid for single doors; double doors are locked in another way)).[11]

However, even with the scarcity of archaeological proof, the multiple uses that were made of doors can be deduced from the various forms in which the door is shown in two or three dimensional material culture. Examples of three-dimensional depictions are:

1. The dummy doors in the pyramid complex of Djoser (III-2) (Figure 4.10).
2. The dummy doors in the serdab of the mastaba of *Sšm-nfr* [II] (PM, III/1,146 – 8) (Figures 4.3 and 6.10).

Examples of two-dimensional depictions

1. Possibly in the decoration of Nagada II pottery (Figure 5.2).
2. Decoration on one of the walls of the chapel of the tomb of *Idw*.[12]
3. The decoration of the walls of the rock-cut tombs of El-Amarna,[13] for an example from Thebe see Figure 5.22.

According to Arnold Egyptian architecture had rules about the direction in which the door had to open, a rule stating that the door opened following the direction of the main movement through it. This supposition is not valid for the entrance of chapels, because in chapels of private tombs there is only one entrance. The rule is valid for the interior rooms of multi-chambered private or royal chapels.[14]

III. The door as a physical object

Apart from the various aspect of the material, the door as a total installation consists of several parts:

1. The door
    a. The door itself
    b. The bolt(s)
    c. The pivots
    d. The battens

7 Clark, *Tomb security,* Figure 46. Petrie, *Royal tombs II,* Plate LVII/2.

8 Petrie, *Royal tombs II,* 12.

9 Petrie, *Royal tombs I,* 10, Plates LXIII and LXIV(1). Adams, *Djet,* Plate XXXII. In passage systems leading to the burial chamber in later pyramid tombs doors were placed too (Petrie, *Kahun,* 15).

10 In Petrie, *Royal tombs II,* 8 it is mentioned that these recesses might be 'spirit-entrances to the cells of offerings'. Adams, *Djet,* 186 proposes that the recesses are the precursors of false doors.

11 Apart from the door of *K3.j-m-ḥst,* McFarlane, *Kaiemheset,* 43, note 117 mentions two other doors dating to the Old Kingdom that have been preserved.

12 Simpson, *Gmast2,* Figure 35

13 Davies, *Amarna II,* Plates XVIII, XIX.

14 Arnold, *Pyramidentempel,* 3.

2. The frame of the opening
   a. The upper beam
   b. The door jambs and rebates

III.1. The material

Only a small number of doors that can be dated to the earlier dynasties of the Pharaonic period have been found in excavation situations.[15] The reason for this is the small resistance of most types of wood against the devastations of time in the form of climate and insects,[16] but another and even more radical reason is that in a country poor in good quality wood the first things that will disappear in a tomb where the care for the cult of the deceased has ended, are the plainly visible wooden utility items like doors, their wooden pivot coatings and cultic objects like statues placed in the chapel in such a way that they were visible.[17]

The number of wooden statues that 'survived' the latter type of attack is greater, possibly due to the fact that most of them were placed in a serdab, a space in the mortuary monument that was nearly always closed to the outside world, and therefore hidden somewhere in the body of the mastaba.[18] Although tomb robbers must have been well aware of the existence of serdabs, apparently their content was less interesting, and thus worth less the trouble than that of the burial chamber. The robbers were not specifically searching for the serdab, but when it was found, the statues were broken, due to the danger of their magical power.

Even if the serdab had not been robbed or violated, in most cases the state of conservation of wooden statues was deplorable.[19] Regarding the difference in conservation of the statues found in the serdab of the mastaba of *Ḫkrt-nbty* and *Ḥdt-nbw* in the cemetery of Djedkare at Abusir,[20] the conclusion is that this difference cannot be the result of a distinction in microclimate, because the mastabas are built against each other. The difference might be due to the use of different types of wood;[21] because scientific research has pointed out that termites have a preference for certain wood species and avoid other types.[22]

The effect that time has on wood can also be concluded from the remains of the wooden statues that have been placed in the northern temple of mastaba S 3505 at Saqqara (PM, III/2, 446) of which only the bases and part of the feet are still extant (Figures 3.2 and 13.1).[23]

The state of conservation of an archaeological artefact is not solely dependent on the wood used, or on the micro-environment of the artefact; there is a certain degree of the arbitrariness in it too. An example is the, in spite of its age, relatively well preserved wooden mask (or the face part of a hollow statue) that has been found in the early dynastic cemetery of Abydos. The exact location where it was found, it is lost in the haze of incomplete reporting, but it might be one of the royal tombs of the 1st dynasty. In the same cemetery a fragment of a wooden statue has been found in a far worse state of conservation than the wooden mask.[24] This arbitrariness is even clearer in the chapel of the tomb of *Ḥsjj-Rᶜ* (PM, III/2, 437 -9), where the difference in the state of conservation of the wooden tablets is remarkable even within one chapel (Figure 4.2), and in this situation the use of different timber is not likely.

The definition of a door as given by Oxford Dictionaries and already earlier mentioned in the text does not specify the material that the object has to be made of, but, due to weight and cost, certainly for the less rich, the material had to be local wood.[25] The doors of the *main entrance* of buildings that are constructed for and maintained by the state system, like temples and palaces, could be made of imported wood (e.g. cedar of Lebanon (*Cedrus libani*)).[26] Possibly the use of

15 Due to the fragility of most types of wood this statement is also valid for wooden objects in general.

16 Regarding insects, the worst is the white ant or termite, which has a preference for soft, moist wood. Ebony and other types of hard wood are hard enough to resist climate and insect attack to a certain degree. The resistance of resinous wood (Cedar, Cypress, Redwood) against insect attack is based on the resin keeping the wood dry and being poisonous for termites. Wood is also easily destroyed by environmental influences like humidity and salt. Organic materials like wood can survive in very dry (Sahara desert) or very wet circumstances.

17 Wooden coffins were subject to theft too because of the re-use that could be made of them, either as coffin or as a source of wood. The costliness of wood can be deduced from the anonymous coffin in Borchardt, *Denkmäler II*, 1791 A -D, a coffin that is doweled together from little bits and pieces of wood. Petrie, *Arts & crafts*, 137 claims that in the early period of the Old Kingdom wood was less scarce than in later periods, basing the statement on the extensive use of wood in the tombs of the kings of the first dynasty at Abydos, although this wood was undoubtedly imported from the Lebanon.

18 Harvey, *Wooden statues*, 2 states that the statues were not placed in the tomb in order to receive offerings.

19 It is interesting to observe that in many tombs the statues were deliberately destroyed; due to the large number of cases this cannot always be the result of damnation memoriae, and it is rather the result of the conviction that the image of a person (or of even any living entity) has magical power and can be harmful to people entering the tomb with bad intentions.

20 Verner, *Abusir VI*, Plates XI and XXIII.

21 For a discussion of the usability of various types of Egyptian indigenous wood, see Deglin, *Wood*, 86.

22 Forschler, *Wood preference.* The various types of wood used in ancient Egypt, either indigenous or imported are listed in www.ucl.ac.uk/museums-static/digitalegypt/wood/types.html .

23 Emery, *Archaic Egypt*, Plate 27; Dreyer, *Dewen.*

24 Stevenson Smith, *Archaic sculptures.*

25 Wood, *Archaic tombs Helwan*, 62, states that during the archaic period probably only local wood was used for construction. The increasing importance of building in stone after the first dynasty might by caused by the progressing aridification, which resulted in a decreasing availability of wood, and a concomitant rise in its economic value.

26 Kemp, *Ancient Egypt*, Figure 90 shows an Aten temple with the

imported wood for the doors in the constructions made for the members of the highest social stratum was less widespread, and might have been limited to the use of local wood of higher quality.[27] Doors were such luxury items that their production was important enough to place a depiction thereof on the walls of the chapel.[28] The dimensions of the great mastabas in the cemetery around the pyramid of Teti (VI.1) show that the tomb owners were not only wealthy and must have had a high office in the state system,[29] but also that they maintained a special status that enabled them to build these mastabas. The plans of these mastabas show that the number of doors in the various rooms and chapels was large, thus corroborating their wealth and special status

Figure 4.2 The difference in state of conservation. Two tablets from the chapel of *Ḥsjj-Rꜥ* (Quibell, *Hesy*, Plate XXIX).

A closer study of the plans of tombs of persons belonging to the lower social strata shows a scarcity of rebates which might indicate that for them the use of doors in chapel entrances was exceptional.

It was in the later periods, when major temple precincts like in Thebe and Luxor were (and remained) under construction that doors of metal, probably bronze, came into use.[30]

Only constructions meant for 'eternal' use, like temples and tombs, could be built of stone. Even the king's palace was made of mud-brick, which, like every construction of this material, necessitated the installation of stronger supporting constructions for the doors in the entrance and the passages.[31] This need of a stronger construction was caused by the horizontal pulling force of the weight of the door, which was also disadvantageous for the upper pivot hole which, strangely enough, was often made of wood.[32]

III.2. The door, the pivots, the battens, and the bolt(s)

The standard door was constructed of vertical boards which were held together and stabilized by a number of horizontal battens fixed to the boards by means of wooden pegs. It is mentioned that the boards could be held together by means of dowels;[33] the fact that sometimes one relied nearly completely on dowels alone can be deduced from the 19th dynasty door held in the British Museum (EA 705; PM, I/2, 613),[34] a door that originally had one batten in the middle of its back side.[35]

This horizontal batten construction can be discerned

1. In the door that is depicted on the Narmer palette (Figure 5.20), although in that context it is not meant as an utensil to close an entrance, and is just a depiction of such used in a linguistic context.
2. In some false doors, were they are depicted in order to strengthen afterlife ideas connected with this ritual object.[36]

---

double door closed, while in Figure 93 the door is open with the two leaves depicted.

[27] In the pyramid town of Queen *Ḫntj-k3w.s* (PM, III/1, 288 – 9; LG 100), what appears to be a single door was installed to close the eastern entrance of the causeway leading to the pyramid temple, a door that had to bridge a distance of about 1.00m (Lehner, *Khentkaues*, 152 – 3, Figure 9).

[28] Petrie, *Deshasheh*, Plate XXI. Drenkhahn, *Handwerker*, 107 – 11.

[29] Roeten, *Economic decline*, Figure 104 (page 93).

[30] LÄ, VI, 778 – 87, s.w. ' Tür und Tor ', there 779. The casting of such a door can be seen in the chapel of *Rḫ-mj-Rꜥ* (www.osirisnet.net, Rekhmire, TT 100, Photo bs-38556).

[31] Reisner, *Mycerinus*, 94.

[32] Hayes, *Scepter I*, 257 mentions that door frames were made of wood.

[33] LÄ, VI, 778 – 87, there 779.

[34] Quirke, *Religion*, 53.

[35] At both ends and in the middle of the door, planks have been fastened that can be interpreted as later attempts to hold the door together (personal communication of Mr. A. Almásy, acting curator of the Department of Ancient Egypt and Sudan of the British Museum, London). The front side has a small decoration on it of the owner standing in front of Osiris and Hathor.

[36] In the mastaba of *Mrrw-k3.j* (PM, 525 – 34) in room A-XI (www.osirisnet.net) and *Wꜥtt-ḫt-ḥr*, (PM, III/2, 534 -5) in room B-V (Lauer, *Saqqara*, Plate 42). These depict double doors that are closed with a bolt on one side. The false door of Queen *T3tjt* (Borchardt, *Denkmäler I*, CG 1425; Callender, *Queen Tatjet*, 172). On many false doors with this representation of a door the battens were not indicated, and the indication that it was a double door was limited to a vertical incised line, the bolt and sometimes the pivots (Jéquier, *Pyramides reines*, Figure 5). In the mastaba of *K3r* (Bárta, *Abusir XIII*, Figure 5.3.9.) one of the false doors has battens depicted on the door in its central niche.

3. In the substructure of the south tomb in the funerary complex of Djoser (III.2). As under the pyramid itself, here too three niches have been constructed in a subterranean corridor that are evidently meant as doors through which the king enters, while in a parallel corridor the back sides of these doors are shown complete with the battens (Figure 5.1).[37]

'You have ascended to the portal, having appeared as king......' (PT, § 1638).

4. On the dummy doors of limestone that have been found in the statue cult room in the tomb of *Sšm-nfr* [II] (PM, III/1, 146 – 8; G 5080) (Figure 4.3).[38] The observation that the door has two pivots at the underside indicates that a double door is represented. The battens are visible from the cult room and this indicates that, as in the cabinets for the transport of statues, these doors were used to close a space in which a statue was waiting to step into the room behind the doors, once they were opened.
5. In the fragment of a door from the 11th dynasty that is constructed of seven vertical planks with battens (Metropolitan Museum of Arts, New York).[39]

About the door mentioned in item 5, Hayes writes: 'The battens are half round in section except at the ends over the pivot, where they are flattened to permit the door to swing fully back against its jamb'.[40] This remark itself does not permit a conclusion about the battens being on the outside or inside of the door when closed.[41] However, wear marks left by battens in the wall behind the door prove that both the doors of chapels and houses open inwards,[42] this means that, when completely opened, the battens of the door were invisible. The doors that have been excavated all have battens which are flattened at the side of the pivot, while the other side sometimes does not reach right to the end of the door, or is, as is the case with the doors of the boat of Khufu, only roughly finished. The observation that the battens were flattened only at the side of the pivots indicates that the other side of the opening had been constructed in such a way that the door could close flat against it, or that the door was one of the leaves of a double door. Because the dummy door of Figure 4.3 is a double door the battens are flattened on both sides.

The door could turn by placing it with 'pins' (pivots) in holes made in the lintel and the door sill. In order to prevent the sagging of the door the pivots were not installed in the form of dowels or pieces of copper fixed to the door, but both of them were made in one piece out of the terminal vertical board.[43] Reisner states that the both pivots were made longer than necessary in order to compensate for wear.[44]

Often the pivot hole was made in a harder type of stone than that used for the construction of the door frame itself or for the tomb; in the chapel of the mastaba of *K3-wʿb* (PM, III/1, 187 – 8; G 7110 + 7120) diorite is used for the stone in which the holes for the pivots are made.[45] If the frame of the door was made of wood, the pivots holes were dug out in the floor and the bottom covered with a flat stone.[46]

The basic intention of a door was that it could be closed, and in the entrance of the tomb of *Jnw-Mnw* in the cemetery around the pyramid of Teti (VI.1) not only door sockets have been found but also the holes for the fixation of the bolt necessary to close the door, which, in view of the description, must have been a single door. Strangely enough in this entrance the holes for the bolt were made in blocks of stone inserted into the (stone) door jambs, which could be the result of a repair, while the upper pivot of the door (probably) was held in a block of wood.[47]

From the description of the construction of this door bolt it could be concluded that it was placed on the inside of the door.[48] The consequence is that in that case a special provision should have been foreseen to be able to lock and unlock the door from the outside.[49] That the bolt is not always on the inside of the door is apparent

37 Lauer, *Saqqara,* Plate 101.

38 Martin, *CAA 3,* 1540. This design was also used to depict the door in a *serekh* false door (Ćwiek, *Relief decoration,* Figure 39, here the pivots are not represented).

39 Hayes, *Scepter I,* Figure 163.

40 Hayes, *Scepter I,* 257. Donadoni, *Sarcofagi,* 85, Plate X.2 states that de battens are slanted to allow opening of the door.

41 LÄ, VI, 778 – 87, s.w. 'Tür und Tor' does not make a statement about the physical in- and outside of a door, just that it exists for those coming in. Kemp, *Ancient Egypt,* Figure 54 places the battens outside, but this conclusion is not right.

42 Reisner, *Mycerinus,* 95.

43 Clarke, *Construction,* 163; Fischer, *Varia nova;* LÄ, VI, 778 – 87, s.w. 'Tür und Tor', there 779 – 80. The false door of *Ḥnw* (Borchardt, *Denkmäler I,* 1401) shows the pivot construction (the door does not represent battens, it only gives an indication of the two leaves and two bolts).

44 Reisner, *Mycerinus*

45 Simpson, *Gmast 3,* 2 (left column); Junker, Giza II, 104; Hassan, Giza III, 33 ff.

46 Der Manuelian, *Gmast 8,* Figures 6.6 and 6.7.

47 Kanawati, *Teti cemetery VIII,* 19. Regarding the block of wood for the upper pivot; the choice of a harder type of wood would make this possible, while the same choice for the lower pivot would be unpractical due to the heavy wear caused by the weight of the door. In the chapel of *Idwt* (PM, III/2, 617 -9) the lintel in one of the passages has a round hole with a wooden block in it for the upper pivot (Lauer, *Saqqara,* Plate IX).

48 Kanawati, *Teti cemetery VIII,* 19; the same is the case in the mastaba of *Ptḥ-ḥtp* [I] (Mourad, *Ptahhotep I,* 18).

49 LÄ, V, 658 – 61, s.w. 'Schloss', corroborates this conclusion.

in the closing mechanism of the main entrance door of the pyramid complex of Queen *Jpwt* (PM, III/2, 432) which clearly shows that the combination of vertical and horizontal bolt(s) is on the outside of the door.[50] If a door bolt had been placed on the outside of the door, one way of closing it was with a bolt with a hook and a 'closing' mechanism based on a clay sealing.[51]

Vertical bolts were also used for the double doors with which the ramps leading to the valley temple of Rakhaef (IV.4) were closed.[52] The mechanism used to close the doors of the valley temple itself is also on the outside.[53]

However, when a passage has been closed with a double door, the design of the bolt is different. An example of this design has been found in one of the rooms in the mastaba of *Sšm-nfr* [II] (PM, III/1, 146 – 8), of which the architecture and archaeology lead to the interpretation that it was meant for the cult of statues (Figure 4.3).[54]

In the southern wall of the room dummy double doors with bolts have been found.[55] These bolts slide over the joint of the two leaves of the door, and a pillar in the middle of the door is neither mentioned nor shown.

In the subterranean chapel of *Mrs-ꜥnḫ* [III] the entrance of the main room (room A in Dunham, *Gmast 1*, plan D) could be closed with a single door that opened inward to the left and had a square hole in the jamb on the opposite side (here too the information is not sufficient to determine on which side of the door the bolt has been placed).[56] All the openings between the pillars in the chapel could be closed with double doors. Although the door between the main and north room had no rebates, their existence could be deduced from grooves in the floor.[57] This indicates that not only the passage connecting the chapel with the outside world could be closed, but also passages between interior rooms, which might have been done in order to obtain a multi-chambered residence impression.

Figure 4.3 Limestone dummy door in the serdab of *Sšm-nfr* [II] (PM, III/1,146 – 8) (Pelizaeus Museum, Hildesheim, M 1540).

Another use of doors was to close the cabinets in which statues were placed for transportation. Because the transport of statues is often depicted without cabinets protecting them, the cabinet appears not to be of the utmost importance, but not depicting the doors could also be the result of the wish to show the statues.

Due to the location of the residence, transport of the deceased and the goods that had to be placed in the mortuary monument that was situated on the limits of the western desert, had to be done partly over land and partly over water. Normally statues were placed on sledges and were dragged over land and shipped over water.

The doors of the cabinets used for the transport were depicted either opened or closed. The doors of a cabinet that is transported by water are normally closed.[58] The cabinets that are transported by sledge can either be standing still with one or more priests in front of its

50 Jéquier, *Pyramides reines*, Figure 23. This also led to one of the drawbacks of this installation: the bolt would have to be drilled so close to the side of the stone that it would easily break off (see Jéquier, *Pyramides reines*, 42, note 1).

51 Bussmann, *Door bolt sealing*. For a depiction of such a bolt see Petrie, *Kahun*, Plate IX, there Figure 21.

52 Lehner, *Giza*, 212; Hawass, *Khafre*.

53 Hölscher, *Chephren*, 41 – 2; Plate XI.

54 Junker, *Giza III*, 188. The description gives the impression that the excavator has seen the bolts, but no further depiction is given (the dummy door in the Pelizaeus Museum in Hildesheim (M 1540 (Martin, *CAA 3*, 1540)) has been excavated by E. Von Sieglin in 1910).

55 Junker, *Giza III*, Figure 34, on page 188 is stated 'In der Mitte zwischen diesen vier in Relief gearbeiteten Türen ist eine weitere einfach durch einen Strich angedeutet, der den Spalt zwischen den beiden Flügeln andeuten soll.'.

56 Dunham, *Gmast I*, 9.

57 For an example of these grooves see: Ptahshepses, *Preliminary report*, Figure 11.

58 The eastern wall of the portico of the tomb of *Nj-ꜥnḫ-H̱nmw* and *H̱nmw-ḥtp* (PM, III/2, 641 – 4) is decorated with a funeral procession in which several cabinets with statues are transported.

open doors; in that case the doors, of which the battens are not visible, are directed toward the spectator. If the statues are actively under transport, the cabinet is directed in accordance with the movement and normally the doors are invisible, although some exceptions exist where the statue, while being transported on land, is standing looking in the direction of the movement with the doors open toward the beholder.[59] In the tomb of *Ptḥ-šsps* (PM, III/2, 340 – 2) at Abusir a cabinet with two statues in it is dragged with the side open and the doors are invisible;[60] during the transport over land rituals could be performed.[61]

The observation that the battens are visible when the doors are closed and invisible if opened leads to the conclusion that the face of the statue is turned toward the smooth side of the door, the side which is normally turned to the world outside the residence. The consequence is that the statue, although it is standing inside the cabinet, is in fact outside, waiting for the doors to be opened.

To my knowledge there are no depictions of cabinets with opened doors while they were transported on a ship, although there was no special taboo of the statue being without protection while on the river as is visible in the transport by ship of statues of *Tjj* (PM, III/2, 468 – 78). In view of the aforementioned observation the following statue transport sequence can be proposed for the funeral ceremony:

- After the preliminary rituals in front of the statues, their transportation to the tomb started in the direction of the river.
- During transport over land the doors can be opened at will; possibly only during transport over water do they remain closed.[62]
- Once arrived at the tomb, the doors are opened, and when the necessary rituals are performed the deceased can now enter his or her eternal residence.

III.3. The frame of the opening, the lintel, door jambs and rebates

From an architectural point of view, the entrance of a mortuary monument was a relatively simple construction consisting of a lintel resting on two door jambs that sometimes were standing on a threshold. The sole purpose of this construction was to furnish a solid frame where the door could be hung. Smaller tombs sometimes had the false door(s) in the eastern wall of the tomb, and had a chapel of which the wall with the entrance was made of mud-brick or small stones put together with mortar. In that case no re-enforcing construction for the entrance was present and no door-frame could be installed, thus leaving the chapel open to the outer-world.

Normally, if a door had to be installed, rebates were foreseen in the posts, however, in some of the walls that were not strong enough to support a door, rebates had nevertheless been constructed.[63]

The opposite is also possible, the mastaba of *Nfrn* (PM, III/2, 120 – 1) is built of smaller stones, and the entrance into the vaulted chapel had a supporting stone construction (stone door posts, a drum over the entrance and an architrave), yet no rebates are present in the wall at either side of the entrance.[64] This means that deducing the presence of a door from the presence or absence of rebates is not completely reliable.

The style of the lintel of the door opening depended strongly on the financial situation of the tomb owner and his family. For the poorer tombs this often was a piece of limestone without any inscriptions, but there are also tombs in which the lintel tells an extensive story with the request for offerings given every day and also on festival days by the king and several gods, with titles and with a biographical text.[65]

The frame of the opening, together with the rebates therein, are constructed to support a door and to enable it to be opened and closed. In many chapels the width of the passage was such that an open door would form an obstruction.[66] In order to avert this or to reduce it to a minimum adapted door placements were designed. The first step is depicted in Figure 4.4; its disadvantage is that the door cannot be opened completely, and would form an obstacle in a chapel if this passage is placed near the middle of the wall.[67] This factor led to two customized designs:

[59] On the eastern wall of corridor II in the tomb of *Tjj* (PM, III/2, 468 – 78) a standing statue is transported in a cabinet with the doors open, while there is no sign of a ritual because the priest is walking behind the cabinet. On the northern wall of the pillared courtyard a ship is transporting statues of the tomb owner that are not placed in a cabinet.

[60] Verner, *Abusir I*, Plate 60.

[61] Verner, *Abusir I*, Plate 56.

[62] Steindorff, *Ti II*, Plate 13.

[63] Junker, *Giza V*, 168 (mastaba 4470); Junker, *Giza V*, 136 and note 1 (door jambs made of mud-brick, while pivot holes have not been found). The question here is whether this is done in imitation of richer tombs; another possibility is that visitors provided part of the sustenance of the deceased, and for that reason it was important to attract them by showing an entrance a bit more luxurious than was inherent to the status of the tomb owner.

[64] Junker, *Giza VI*, 198 and Figure 73.

[65] Soleiman, *Ptahshepses*, Figures 6 – 12.

[66] An example is the chapel of *Mrsw-ʿnḫ* (PM, III/1, 269 – 70) which has a width of 0.68m (Hassan, *Giza I*, 105).

[67] Apparently special configurations of door rebates are visible in the chapel of mastaba G 7152 (PM, III/1, Plan XXIX) and in the tomb of *Jj-nfrt* (PM, III/2, Plan LXIII (between 11 and 12)). Undoubtedly these are rebates that were not intended to accommodate a door; they were

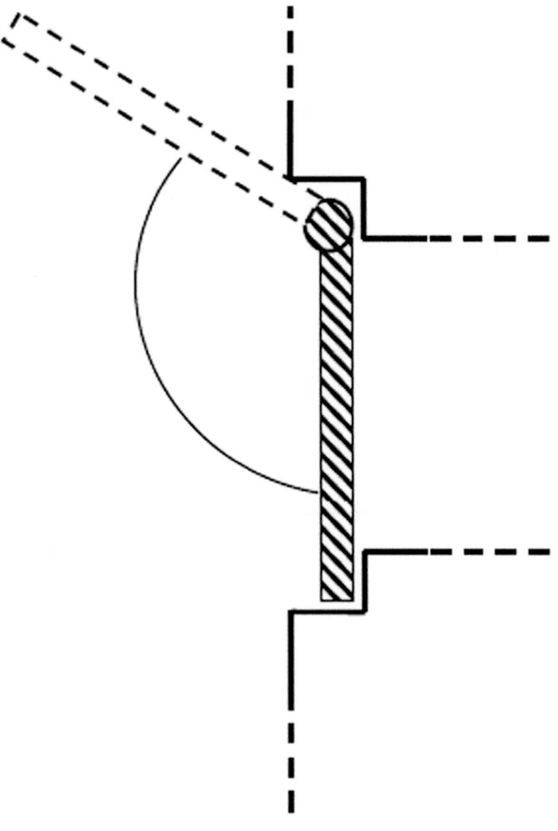

Figure 4.4 The door opening in a straight wall.

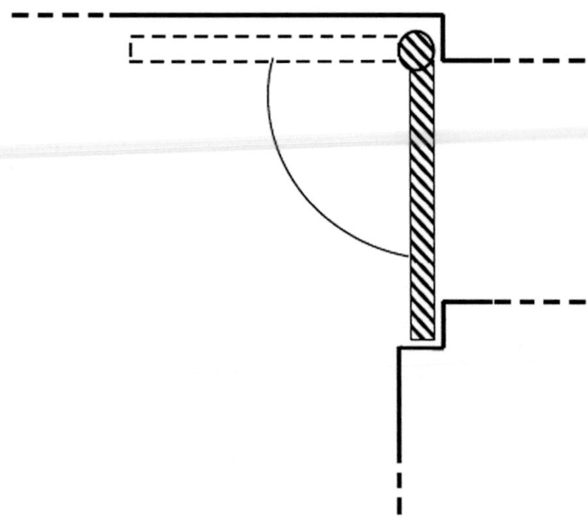

Figure 4.5 The door opening in the tomb of *Nswt-nfr* (Kanawati, *Giza II,* Plate 49).

1. One or both of the walls next to the passage were placed in line with the corridor.

The type of design shown in Figure 4.6 of a passage that becomes wider before opening into the main room is common in chapels with corridors that come out near the centre of the wall, like the rock-cut tomb of *Dbḥnj* (PM, III/1, 27 – 6),[68] or long and narrow chapels,[69] but the design is sometimes used at the end of the eastern wall of L-shaped chapels too.[70] Although these entrances could be closed with double doors,[71] because many of the passages to the chapel were of the design given in Figure 4.5 and not of the design in Figure 4.6, they were practically always closed with a single door.[72] It is for that reason that the door installation in Figure 4.5 and its opposite form with the door opening to the left are common in L-shaped chapels with the entrance at the northern or southern end of the eastern wall.[73]

constructed because the rebate had become an object of decoration..

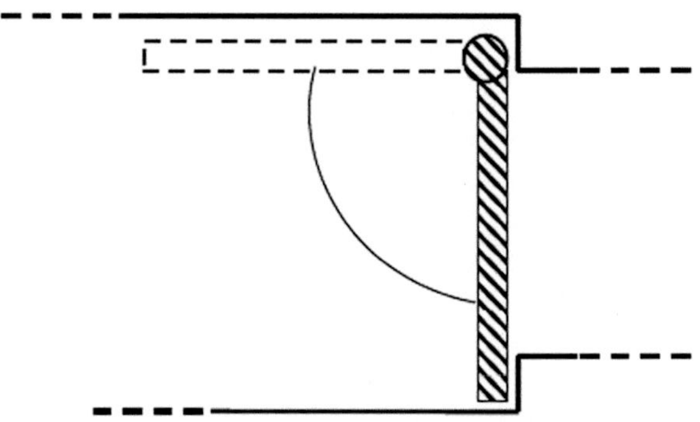

Figure 4.6 The door opening in the tomb the *Hsj* (Kanawati, *Teti cemetery V,* Plate 47).

2. The door, when opened, falls into a recess in the wall; this is a situation that is in fact identical with that in Figure 4.4, the difference being that the door now can be opened completely without placing the door as an obstacle in the passage. This design can be divided in two sub-groups; the first one is given in Figure 4.7, of which a possible example can be found in the entrance of the chapel of *Wsr* (PM, III/1, 285).[74]

68 Hassan, *Giza IV,* 161, 167.

69 Hassan, *Giza IV,* 106, 109.

70 The rock-cut tombs in the Central Field of Giza are equipped with this type of door installation (Jánosi, *Giza,* 308 ff.). An example of an entrance corridor with a wider end-part is found in the chapel of *Kꜣ.j-nj-nswt* [I] (PM, III/1, 78 – 9). Junker, *Giza II,* 139 remarks that the part of the northern wall of the corridor that was covered when the door was open, was not decorated.

71 *Sḫm-kꜣ-Rꜥ* (PM, III/1, 233 – 4), Hassan, *Giza IV,* 109;

72 The rock-cut tomb of *Nj-wsr-Rꜥ* (PM, III/1, 272) (Jánosi, *Giza,* 382).

73 The pivot hole has been found in the ceiling (Kanawati, *Teti cemetery* V, 18). In the entrance of the interior chapel of *N-sḏr-kꜣ.j* (PM; III/1, 72) bottom pivot holes have been found at both sides, indicating a double door (Giza archives, photo PDM_1993.084.25).

74 Hassan, *Giza I,* Figure 161, Plate LVIII, Hassan does not mention the existence of door sockets. This placement of the doors is less likely due to the fact that in that case they would be on the exterior side of the entrance corridor.

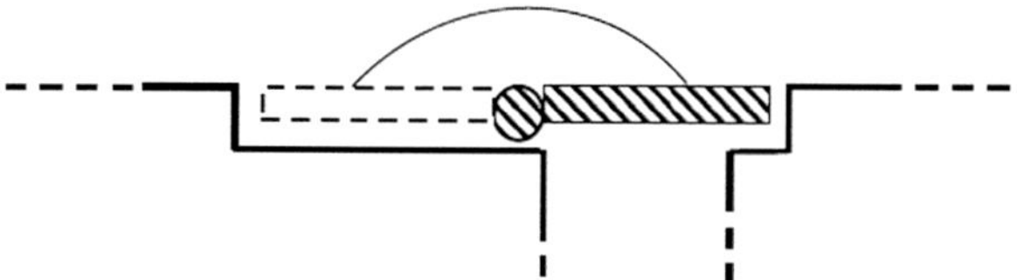

Figure 4.7 The door opening in a recess.

The second possibility is given in Figure 4.8; this design can be found in the building in front of the chapel entrance of the mastaba of *Ḥm-jwnw* (PM, II/1, 122 – 3; G 4000). Opening the door from the ante-room to the main room can have the door axis in the rebate at the western side, in which case the door cannot be opened completely (Figure 4.4). The other possibility is to have the door axis at the eastern side, but this would place the open door in the entrance without being hidden from sight by a rebate.[75]

A possible but not likely reason why a niche and not a rebate has been constructed could be because the width of the entrance is, within the reliability of the plan given in Reisner, *Giza I,* Figure 121, about 0.8m and the thickness of the open door (ca. 7 – 8cm) would have diminished the opening, but would not have made it impassable (Figure 4.8).[76] The design of Figure 4.8 is rare, and apart from the chapel of *Ḥm-jwnw* another example only exists in the chapel of *Ḫwtꜣ* (PM, III/1, 279).[77]

If the rebate construction for a door was present at the entrance of the chapel, either for mechanical reasons of suspension and/or closing, or in order to enlarge the space available for introductory decoration, the door suspension was situated at the chapel-end of the entrance thicknesses.

If the ground-plan of the rooms in the superstructure of a tomb is available, the conclusion whether rooms can be closed could initially, within certain limits, be drawn from the representation of the door rebates. However, in a land where wood is a valuable building material, it is possible that not every passage with rebates automatically had a door installed. It is quite possible that rebates between certain types of rooms in the course of time changed from an architectonic necessity to a decorative object without any further

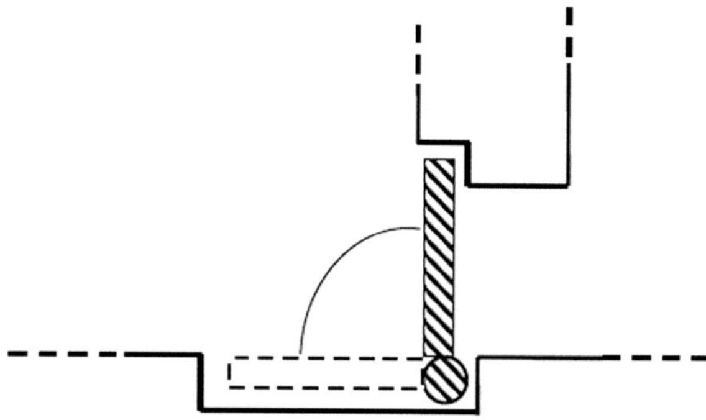

Figure 4.8 Internal passage in the chapel of tomb G 4000. (Schematically after Reisner, *Giza I,* Figure 121).

purpose.[78] Furthermore, what looks like a short bulge against a long wall, suggestive of a rebate, can also be a construction meant to make an opening smaller in order to create some privacy.

In the tomb of *Ḥtpj* (Bárta, *Abusir XIX,,* tomb AS 20), the presence of a pivot hole in the entrance of the southern chapel indicates that it could be closed with a door; rebates are present too, unlike in the entrance of the northern chapel of this tomb.

In front of the western wall of the chapel two pivot holes indicate that a double door had been placed there, of which is claimed that they acted as a facsimile of the expected false door.[79] These doors made it possible to cover up a no longer present false door or the western wall itself (Figure 4.9).[80] In view of the small dimensions of the chapel compared to those of the three doors, opening them in order to perform the cult for the deceased could not have been easy. Bárta, *Abusir XIX,* 8 states that the western wall of this chapel was completely missing; the consequence is that the distance between the doors and the western wall cannot be determined.

The following questions emerge:[81]

- What arguments are there to state that a false door was *not* placed against the western wall of the chapel?

[75] Junker, *Giza I,* 140 remarks that the purpose of the niche is not clear.

[76] Junker, *Giza I,* Figure 18. The result of a further study of the width of chapel entrances in a population of 50 tombs in the necropolis of Giza (Table VI) shows that their mean value is 72cm which indicates that in Figure 4.8 the remaining width of the entrance of 80 – 8cm = 72cm is within the range of normal values. The thickness of the door is estimated at 7 – 8cm in accordance with the door found in the chapel of *Kꜣ.j-m-ḥst* (PM, III/2, 542 – 3; McFarlane, *Kaiemheset,* 42).

[77] Hassan, *Giza III,* 45.

[78] In the mastaba of *Mhw* (PM, III/2, 619 – 22), Altenmüller, *Mehu,* 25 -6, Plan A, evidence for the presence of doors in the form of rebates has be found in all the passages.

[79] Bárta, *Abusir XIX,* 8.

[80] Bárta, *Abusir XIX,* Figure 2.6 (page 8).

[81] Bárta, *Inty,* 55 gives the 132 x 78 x 38cm (H x W x D) as dimensions of the false door that has been found in the burial chamber of *Jntj* in Abusir-south. The thickness of the door must have been given with the cavetto cornice included. Because in the period of the construction of the chapel of *Ḥtpj* this decorative element of the false door was not yet in use, the thickness of the false door in the chapel must have been much less than 38cm.

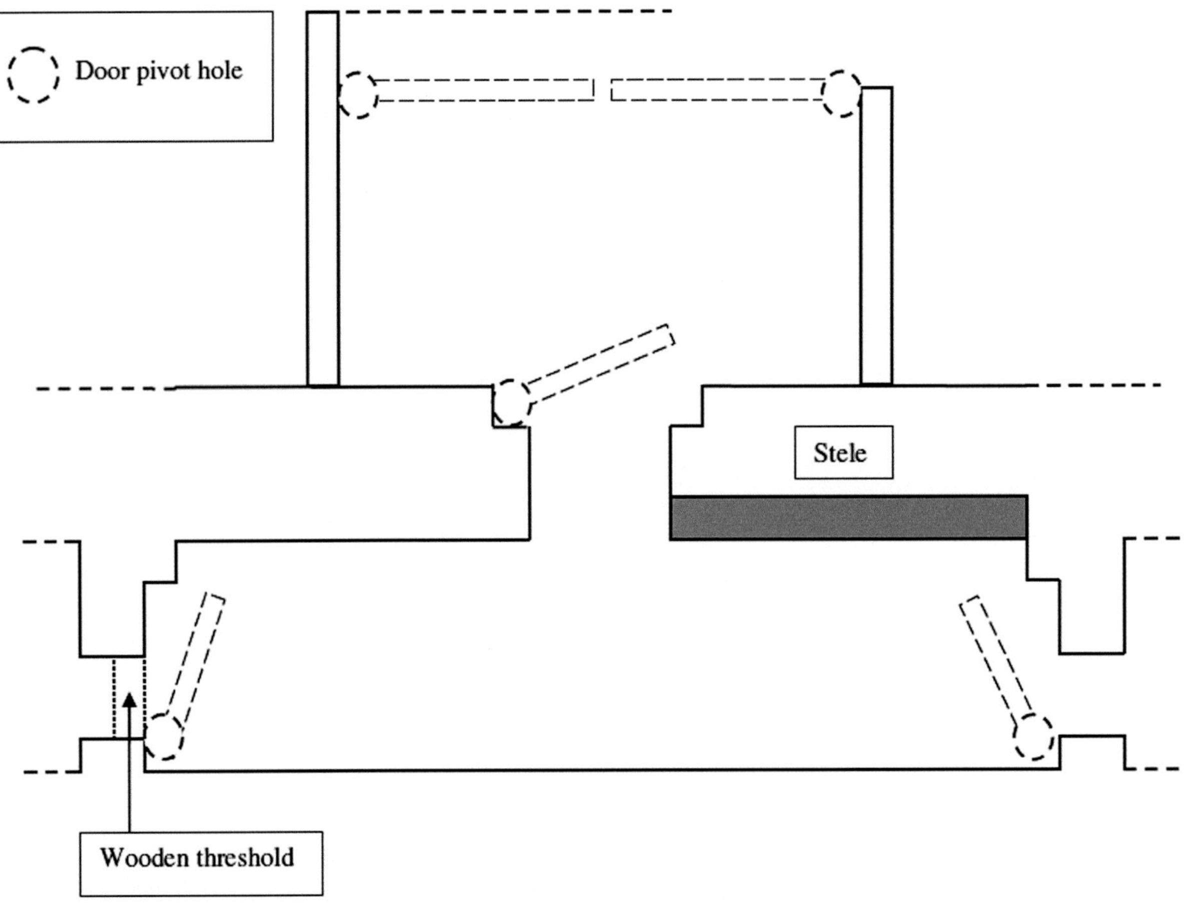

Figure 4.9 The chapel in the mastaba of *Ḥtpj* (Abusir, tomb AS 20). (schematically after Bárta, *Abusir XIX*, Figures 2.1 and 2.9).

- If a false door had been placed against that wall, why was it considered necessary to cover it up with a door or a facsimile of it?
- If the two doors were placed in front of the wall, could it be opened, or was it a dummy door, like the one in Figure 4.3?
- If a false door was not placed against the wall, what was behind the double door, or was it just the plain wall, because the two real doors had taken over the role of the magical (false) door.

The doors in the corridor in front of the chapel were possibly placed there in order to form an ante-room with the intention of performing the cult in front of the stele, an activity that is permissible within the dimensions of this room which are 3.12 x 1.50m. In that case this would be an early example of the presence of closed doors compelling visitors to come up with an alternative solution.

An apparently similar situation for both niches is found in the tomb of *K3-mn* (PM, V, 175; date: IV) at El-Kab where the southern niche appears to have rebates, indicating that probably the niche could be closed.[82] Fragments of decoration have been found in the vicinity of the niches.

IV. The various uses of the door as a utilitarian object

1. In the dummy buildings that have been erected in the mortuary complex of Djoser (III.2) at Saqqara some doors are shown in a non-functional form. If these dummy-doors are not present doors are indicated by the hollowed out stones for their lower-pivots and by the rebates into which they fall (Figures 4.10 and 4.11).

In many tombs one or more rooms could be closed with a door (as was also the case in the houses of members of the higher social strata), because in passages between the various rooms in the super-structure pivot-stones were often still present, while rebates can be seen as an indication that a door might have been present. The latter is not always reliable, because in the tomb of Peribsen (II.5) at Abydos rebated dividing walls are present that form rooms that could, in view of the width of the corridor in front of them, only be closed

[82] Quibell, *El Kab*, Plate XXIII. The date IV given in PM, V is not in accordance with the remark that on one of the pieces of niche decoration an indication has been found that could point to a Nagada date.

Figure 4.10 (Dummy) pivot hole in the funerary complex of Djoser (III.2) at Saqqara. (Photo author).

Figure 4.11 Dummy stone for upper pivot hole in mortuary complex of Djoser (III.2).

with a double door.[83] However, the width of the corridor is such that even then it would have been difficult to open the doors completely, although this conclusion depends on the accuracy of the plan.[84]

In view of the distance between the door rebates and the pivot holes (Figure 4.10), it is clear that the 'closing efficiency' of the doors is doubtful.[85]

Figure 4.12 shows the 'modern' edition of a door hinge system, and it is plain that the essence of the old form has been preserved.

2. Apparently the construction which enabled the turning of a door is of a remote date because in the temple precinct of Nekhen (Hieraconpolis) a block of basalt has been found that was sculpted in the form of a bound enemy with the pivot hole for a door in its back and a door jamb next to it still in place. This pivot has been dated to the late-predynastic period.[86]

Figure 4.12 Stone with upper-pivot. (Detail photo Wikipedia, "Hinge").

3. In the tomb of Den (I.5) at Abydos halfway down the stairs descending from the east and leading to the burial chamber two pilasters were constructed that marked the beginning of the underground part of the staircase. This part could be closed with a door of which the lower pivot support was still in place, while another door was placed at the end of the staircase.[87]

4. In the main constructions in the 4th dynasty settlement south-east of the Giza Plateau are galleries that served as barracks for the crews working at

[83] The use of doors in the subterranean part of a tomb has already been seen in the tomb of Den (I.5) at Abydos (see below).

[84] Clark, *Tomb security,* Figure 47.

[85] Reisner, *Mycerinus,* 94 describes a pivot hole that is designed in such a way that the door slides automatically toward the post in order to obtain a less pronounced opening between post and door.

[86] Quibell, *Hierakonpolis I,* 6, Plate III (University of Pennsylvania Museum of Archaeology and Anthropology, Philadelphia, registration number E 3959).

[87] Dreyer, *Abydos, Den,* 73; Clark, *Tomb security,* Figure 32.

the pyramids on the Plateau; every gallery of both complexes opened to the north into their own main street and each of them had a door that could be closed, because the sockets for the pivots have been excavated.[88] In other parts of that settlement houses were constructed that had several interior doors of which the sill and pivot socket were still present.[89]

5. From the same period examples of door emplacements have been found in the tomb of *N-sḏr-kȝ.j* (PM, III/1, 72; G 2101) where the entrance to the courtyard had a single door,[90] and where the upper and lower sockets for a double door in the passage between the courtyard and the chapel are still in place.[91] In the entrance of the chapel of *Nfr* (PM, III/1, 72 – 4; G 2110) the pivots for a double door are present.[92]

6. One of the oldest doors that has been found *in situ* is the wooden door closing the burial chamber in the mastaba of *Nfr-mȝʿt* at Maidum (in the same passage a stone wall had been constructed too),[93] nevertheless tomb robbers reached the burial chamber, but possibly this door survived because its dimensions made transport through the narrow robbers tunnel too complicated compared to the intrinsic value of the object.[94]

7. Sometimes wooden cabinets that were equipped with doors and that were apparently intended to house a statue were depicted in the decoration of the chapels of Old Kingdom tombs.[95] These doors were placed in such a way that they opened to the outside.[96] In the course of the burial and the accompanying rites funerary offerings, including statues, were transported to the tomb. These statues were standing on sledges, even while crossing the river. Examples of depictions of the transport by ship of such cabinets are placed in the chapels of *Snfrw-jn-štf* (PM, III/2, 891),[97] *Ḥtp-ḥr-ȝḫtj* (PM, III/2, 593 – 5, date: V.6),[98] and *Nj-ʿnḫ-Ḫnmw* & *Ḫnmw-ḥtp* (PM, III/2, 641 – 4),[99] in all three examples the doors of the cabinets are closed while their battens are visible.

Figure 4.13 Transport of a cabinet with a statue of *Ḥtp-Ḥr-ȝḫtj* (Mohr, *Hetep-her-akhty*, Figure 2).

In a scene in the latter chapel the dragging of a statue of the deceased is shown; the statue is standing in a cabinet on a sledge with the double door opened, on which no battens are visible.[100] This confirms that, once the cabinet is closed, the battens are on the outside and thus visible, and apparently important enough to depict the cabinet rotated in order to show the double door and its battens and bolt.

A possible explanation for these observations is the following course of events when the statue is transported standing in a cabinet of which the battens of the doors are on the outside if the doors are closed:

- The statue of the deceased in its cabinet with closed doors is placed on a sledge and dragged to the bank of the Nile and from there it is shipped to the other bank.
- The statue is dragged to the tomb, and once arrived there the doors are opened, rituals are performed and offerings are brought.[101]

The visibility of the battens in the various situations indicates that the deceased is standing in a cabinet 'facing' the smooth side of the doors. That means that the deceased is 'looking' at the outside of a residence's door and waits for the moment the doors will be opened and he/she can enter. After the arrival of the statue at the tomb, and after the opening of the mouth ritual,

[88] Aeragram, 6.1.2002, figure on page 5.

[89] Aeragram, 7.2.2004, page 7 Figure 3.

[90] Der Manuelian, *Gmast 8*, Figure 5.13.

[91] Der Manuelian, *Gmast 8*, Figures 5.41 and 5.42. Giza Archives, photos PDM_1993.063.14 and PDM_1993.084.02.

[92] Der Manuelian, *Gmast 8*, Figure 6.6. The width of the chapel entrance is 0.70m, which is rather narrow for a double door.

[93] Harpur, *Maidum*, Figure 54; Petrie, *Labyrinth*, 25.

[94] Harpur, *Maidum*, 37. Also in later periods the closing of a burial chamber with a wooden door was still in use (*Snnḏm*, PM, I, 1 – 5, JE 27303).

[95] Fischer, *Varia nova*, Plate 11a.

[96] Spencer, *Naos Nekhthorheb*, 1 states that, based on the position of the rebates, in this naos of the 30th dynasty the double door opened to the inside. The naos found by Naville in Deir el-Bahari was closed by a double door and the leaves show battens on the outside and decoration on the inside (Naville, *Deir el Bahari II*, Plates XXXVI, XXIX).

[97] Forshaw, *Lector*, Figures 25, 94.

[98] Fischer, *Varia nova*, Plate 12; Oxford Expedition to Egypt: Scene-details Database (Linacre College, Oxford (2006) *Oxford Expedition to Egypt: Scene-details Database* [data-set]., gives for article 15, sub-article 15.2.1. only one example, and that concerns several statues on sledges on the eastern wall of corridor II in the tomb of *Ṯjj* at Saqqara.

[99] Osirisnet, Niankhkhnoum Khnoumhotep, Photo 7b (www.osirisnet.net).

[100] Mohr, *Hetep-her-akhty*, Figure 3, the sledge is dragged by two bulls, but more often this is done by a row of men (Fischer, *Varia nova*, page 97, Figure 6); Cherpion, *Mastabas*, Plate 37.

[101] LD, *II*, 35.

the deceased can come out of the cabinet into his or her eternal residence.

While on a closed door the visible battens define the inside of the dwelling, it does *not* define whether a person is going in or out of the house. This ultimately led to a dualism in the way the false door was depicted on the sides of the coffins. On the outside of some coffins, the door is shown without battens and on some with them.[102] At the end of the Old Kingdom the inside of coffins started to be decorated too, and part of the decoration was a false door. Here that dualism occurred too because the door could be depicted with two leaves as usual but without battens.[103]

Although the *k3* of the deceased has a degree of freedom of movement within the tomb, it remains primarily within the vicinity of the sarcophagus and 'lives' within it, especially during the night. This means that the battens should be inside once the doors were closed.[104] It is possible that the original meaning of the visibility of the battens had become obsolete and their presence or absence was just a result of the custom of the producing workshop.

8. In burial chambers too, doors were depicted, either in the form of false doors (in the case of the tomb of *Ỉntj* in Abusir in the burial chamber an actual false door has been placed against the sarcophagus and opposite the entrance of the chamber), or in the form of doors of silos, warehouses or workshops.

On the western wall of the burial chamber of *K3.j-m-ʿnḫ* (PM, III/1, 131 – 3) storerooms are painted that are closed with doors with visible battens.[105]

9. Pavilions with a receiving function could be closed with doors; an example of this has been excavated on the terrace in front of the valley temple of Rakhaef (IV.4) at Giza and also on the ramps leading to the temple. These are constructions supported by four pillars and one or two double doors.[106]

10. Of a later date is the model of a house that has been found in the tomb of *Mʿkt-Rʿ* (PM, I/1, 359 – 64, 11th dynasty) which shows the rear façade of a residence with eight pillars supporting a portico.[107] Two doors and a window with a blind have been installed in the façade, the doors being a large double and a small single one.[108] Both doors have battens on the inside.

The double door is of special design, consisting of two separate single doors which do not overlap or touch in the middle but close on a middle frame,[109] a design resembling the doors of heaven of Figure 5.22.[110] Above the door is a half-round fanlight with a decoration composed of djed-pillars and lotus flowers.[111] The other side of the rear wall shows the front façade of the house. The care that has been taken to depict both sides of the residence, the fanlight and the portico indicates the importance of the model in a funerary context; this is corroborated by the fact that in the hidden chamber of the tomb two models of the residence of the tomb owner were present.

11. In the tomb of *K3.j-m-ḥst* (PM, III/2, 542 – 3) a decorated door (Cairo JE 47749) with a width of 0.68m has been found with the depictions of the tomb owner and a smaller male figure both facing left.[112]

In the part of the mastaba complex that was meant for *K3.j-m-ḥst* there are three passages with rebates:[113]

- The passage from outside to room I.E has a corridor width of 0.70m and a recess width of 1.10m. The door of 0.68m could be used for this entrance because the door (just) covers the opening of the passage. However, if the door is opened with the decoration visible while entering (Figure 4.14) it nearly closes off the passage (width = 0.94m) at the right side of the column, leaving 0.25m to 0.3m as an opening.

---

102 Compare the coffin of *Ḫnmw-nḫt* (13th dynasty) (Adams, *Mummies*, Figure 13), and that of *Spj* (11th – 12th dynasty) (Taylor, *Coffins*, Figure 13). The latter coffins (inner and outer) have the bolts of the doors visible at the outside.

103 Donadoni, *Sarcofagi*, Plate XXXIX(1), Junker, *Giza VIII*, Figure 45.

104 The coffin of *Nfrj* (PM, IV, 184) has a false door with the battens visible, but not the pivots (Deir el-Bersha, 12th dynasty; CG 28088); www.sl.wikipedia.org/wiki/slika:Coffin_Nefri.

105 Kanawati, *Giza I*, Plate 36.

106 Hölscher, *Chephren*, 38; Hawass, *Khafre*.

107 Metropolitan Museum Arts, New York, no. 20.3.13; Hayes, *Scepter I*, Figure 169.

108 Winlock, *Models*, 18; Kemp, *Ancient Egypt*, Figure 54.

109 Drenkhahn, *Handwerker*, Figures 36 - 8. Winlock, *Models*, Plate 57. Winlock, *Models*, 18 describes the double door as 'There is no groove marking the place where the two leaves of the closed door meet......' and does not mention the frame in the middle visible in the drawing of Plate 57. Koeningsberger, *Tür*, 43 – 4 explains this strange construction as the result of the Egyptian way of depiction. This way of depicting can also be found on a false door in the 19th dynasty temple of Sethi I at Abydos. The explanation given in Kemp, *Ancient Egypt*, Figure 54 that states that the back side of the doors and window are a representation of the façade adjacent to the street is erroneous.

110 Davies, *Townhouse*, Figure IA shows this type of door in a wall painting in tomb TT104 (PM, I, 217 – 8).

111 This form strongly resembles the panels in the subterranean corridors of the pyramid complex of Djoser (Lauer, *Saqqara*, Figure 102). The design of the door, the middle post and the half-round top is still in use during the later part of the 18th dynasty (Kemp, *Ancient Egypt*, Figure 99).

112 McFarlane, *Kaiemheset*, 42 – 4, Plates 15 and 50; in PM, III/1, 542 the door is named a 'door wing', but it is highly improbable that in the complex a door entrance can be found that is wide enough to accommodate two of these doors. The width of 0.68m is not exact because due to the influence of time the dimensions must have changed somewhat.

113 McFarlane, *Kaiemheset*, Plate 40. The dimensions of the entrances are from this excavation report.

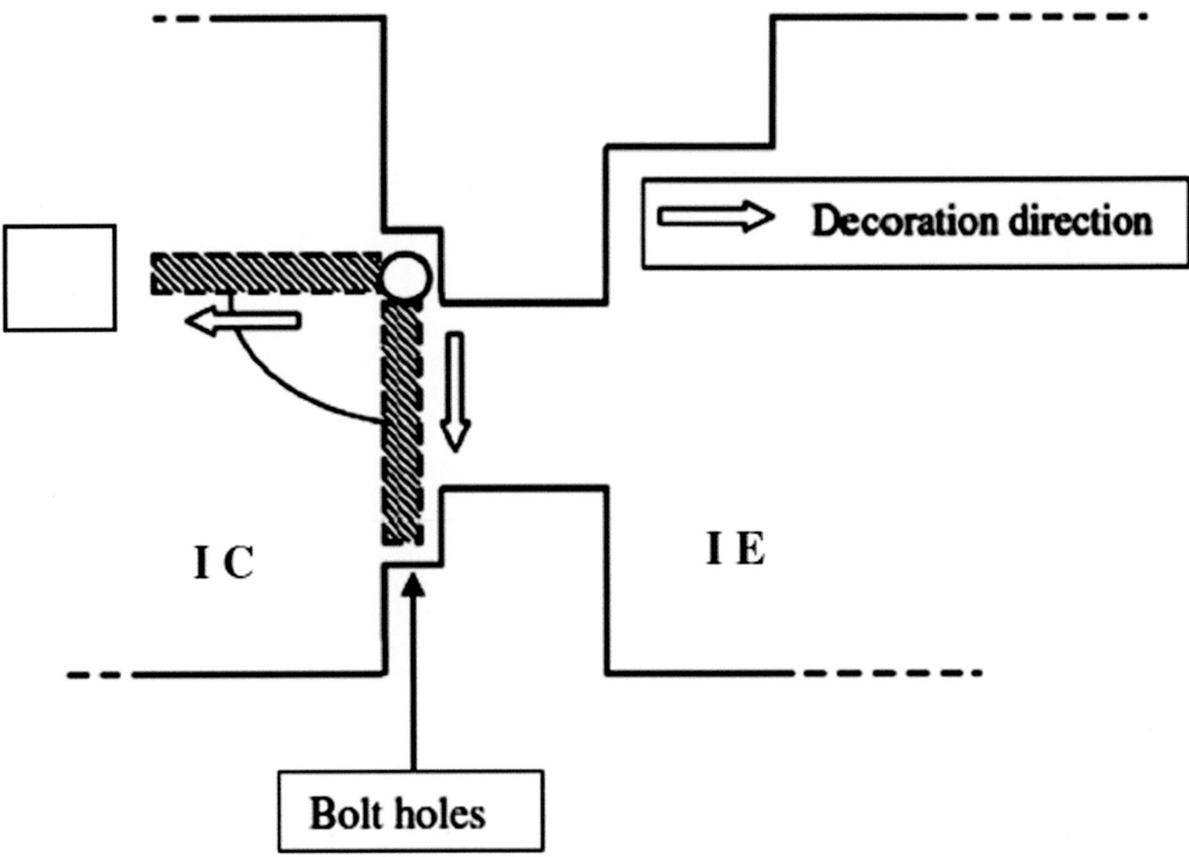

Figure 4.14 The possible position of door JE 47749 in the chapel entrance of the mastaba of *K3.j-m-ḥst* (after McFarlane, *Kaiemheset*, Plate 40).

- The passage from room IC to IA has a minimum width of 0.70m and a maximum width of 1.20m. If the door had been placed in this passage, the presence of the offering basin standing there would have hindered the movement of the door, while, due to the width of the chapel (0.70m) and the location of the door in the middle of the eastern wall, the door would close off the chapel.
- The passage from room I.E to I.C has a width of 0.70 m and a recess of 1.10m, and has two bolt holes on the inside. According to Figure 4.14 the door would nearly close the opening between the northern pillar and the wall (width = 0.94m), but if thus opened, would lead the visitor in the direction of the entrance of the chapel (1A). Apparently the door has not been placed at the other side of the opening because the bolt holes are in the eastern rebate of the opening.

The above perceptible discrepancy between door and entrance dimensions could be reason for some doubt whether this door actually was placed in the tomb of *K3.j-m-ḥst.*[114] All the more because the door was not found in the tomb itself. However, the text on the door might be seen as proof that it was indeed placed in one of the passages of this complex, and in that case the most probable place would be the passage from 1E to 1C.

It has to be remarked that a door is used not only to close a space; it can also be used to identify by means of text (Figure 4.3), and to guide in a desired direction by means of the depiction of a human figure (Figure 4.14).

The depiction of the tomb owner shows a reversal of the hands normally holding the staff and the sceptre. Possibly this has been done because the door could not be placed on the other side of the opening, although in that way it would show the paraphernalia in the proper hands. The depiction of a standing person is preferentially directed to the right because, while following the convention that the sceptre is held in the right hand, this direction gives the least distortion of the hands and arms. In this presentation of the tomb owner the convention (staff in the left hand and the sceptre in the right hand) has been

[114] A doubt that was already expressed by Quibell (McFarlane, *Kaiemheset*, 42).

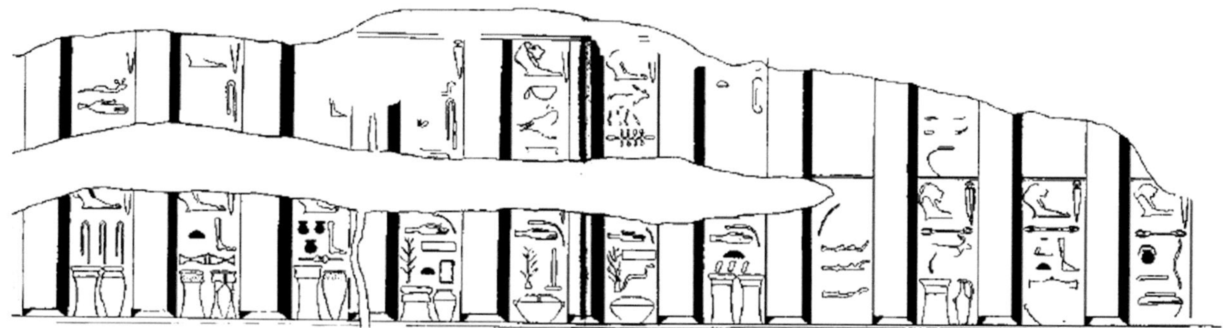

Figure 4.15 Cupboards with doors (Quibell, *Hesy,* Plate XXI).

12. Between the parts of the ship in the boat pit alongside the pyramid of Khufu five doors have been found that were constructed of boards fixed with dowels and strengthened by battens that were perpendicularly placed over the boards.[115] Some of the doors had a copper bolt sliding in two rings of the same metal.[116] The battens were tapered at the end nearest the pivots, but the other ends of the battens were rather carelessly finished off and not equal in length,[117] and this could indicate that the ship had not been used as such and that that had never been the intention.

13. On the eastern wall of the corridor chapel of *Ḥsj-Rˁ* (PM, III/2, 437 – 9) the precursor of an offering list had been painted. One of the items depicted is a row of cupboards that can be closed with what looks like a double door, and which contains vases and pots with various oils and ointments (Figure 4.15).[118] The cupboards have one shelf like the cupboards in the decoration of the chapel of *Rˁ-ḥtp* at Maidum.[119] Battens are not depicted on the doors; the reason for this could be that the doors are made of one piece of wood, or that the battens are at the other side of the door (in which case the battens would become visible on closing the door, and give the same picture as the store room doors depicted on one of the walls in the burial chamber of *K3.j-m-ˁnḫ* (PM, III/1, 131 – 3).[120]

The way the doors of these cupboards are depicted can be interpreted in two ways:

- The door is drawn at one side of the cupboard, but in order to show that it is a double door the two pivots are depicted. This is done because the artist has decided that, apart from the cupboard and its content, the fact that the door is double is important information too.[121] Thus what looks like a single door consists in reality of two half doors each of a different cupboard, although a dividing line is not present. This would mean that the cupboards are placed at a certain distance from each other, which might be the case in reality, but it can also be a consequence of the aspective way of rendering a three-dimensional object (Figure 4.16).
- The door post of the cupboard that has been drawn in bold is the sole post and the door is a single door. In that case the second pivot might be a contraption to close the door by lifting it and letting the lower pivot slide in a hole, while the upper pivot is not present at that side of the door (Figure 4.17).

In order to make the up- and downward movement possible in Figure 4.17 the upper pivot has been changed into a longer and round pole. This proposed change in pivot design from triangular to round is based on the observation that as early as the first dynasty (Figure 5.21) as well as in later periods this pivot design occurred in decoration themes (Figure 5.22).[122]

Bárta endorses the proposition of Balcz that this is the depiction of a rack with cupboards placed in them.[123]

14. In the chapel of *Nfr-sšm-Ptḥ* (PM, III/2, 645) a bedroom scene has been depicted with a bed that is probably placed in a separate room. The door seems to close the entrance into the antechamber, but it is probable that here the artist also considered the presence of the door between the antechamber and the bedroom itself important enough to depict it in an aspective way.[124] The door is constructed of

115 Nour, *Cheops boats*, 9. Plate XIV.

116 Fischer, *Varia nova,* Plate 11b (page 99).

117 Nour, *Cheops boats*, Plates XLVII, XLVIII and LII.

118 Reisner, *Grave stelae,* 326 calls this the 'cupboard list', and considers it the precursor of the compartment list.

119 Harpur, *Maidum,* Figures 98, 172. No indication of a door is present.

120 Kanawati, *Giza I,* Plate 36.

121 LÄ, I, 474 – 88, s.w. 'Aspektive', there 476.

122 Hornung, *Book of the dead,* 142 – 3.

123 Bárta, *Opferliste,* 29.

124 Moussa, *Craftsmen,* Figure 1; Altenmüller, *Geburtsschrein,* Figure 2.

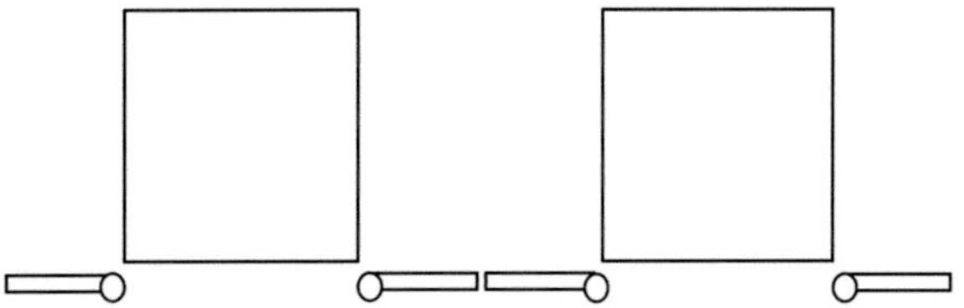

Figure 4.16 A possible interpretation of the cupboards in Figure 4.15.

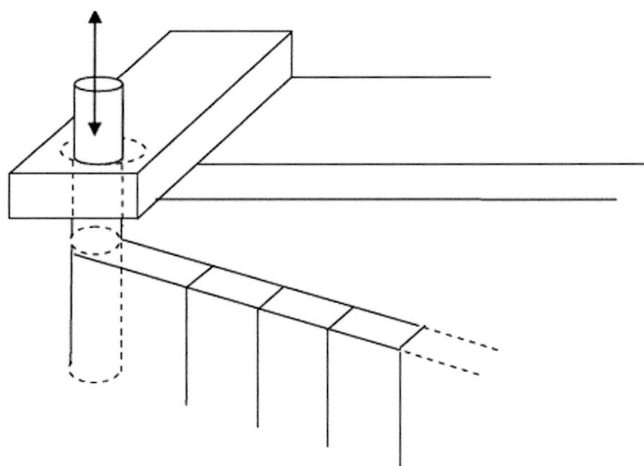

Figure 4.17 Closing the single door by lifting it.

vertical boards with two bolts and the battens are not visible (Figure 4.18). If in reality the door had been placed between the bedroom and the antechamber, and presuming that the bolts would have been in the bedroom, the battens would have been on the antechamber side of the door. This would make the bedroom part of the outside world, corroborating the use of the word 'Geburtsschrein' for the bedroom in the sense that the tomb owner after being reborn comes back in the outside world by opening the door.[125]

Figure 4.18 The bedroom scene (after Moussa, *Craftsmen*, Plate I).

[125] Altenmüller, *Geburtsschrein*.

Chapter Five

Doors, Other uses

I. The south tomb of Djoser's pyramid complex

The substructure of the southern tomb of the mortuary complex of Djoser (III.2) at Saqqara consists of a system of corridors some of which form an inter-connected sub-system that is based on physical representation of contact between the world of the living and the world of the dead.

In Figure 5.1 three niches are placed in the western wall of corridor A depicting the king in a running or walking position. West of and parallel to corridor A is a corridor C with the depictions of the back side of doors displayed by their battens on the eastern wall. The existence of this corridor C indicates that the niches were intended as doors. In the literature corridor A is interpreted as the residence of the king,[1] but in view of the hypothesis presented in this study regarding the meaning of doors and battens, this is incorrect.

The hypothesis previously mentioned in this study proposes that the niches in corridor A are the view of the doors from the 'street' side, and the battens in corridor C show the 'residence' side of the doors, meaning that in corridor C not only the western side of the door is shown but also the inside of the house, and this statement is strengthened by the fact that this is also the direction in which the burial chamber, the centre of the residence of the deceased king, lies.

The western walls of corridors A and B represent the eastern outside wall of the royal residence,[2] a statement that is not contradicted by the richness of the faience tiling of these walls, because, if this represents the royal residence in the world of the living, it would make it visible from all sides and from far away.

> *I built myself a house decked with gold, its ceiling of lapis lazuli,*
> *walls of silver, floors of acacia wood, doors of copper, bolts of bronze.......*
>
> Instruction of Amenemhet,
> (Lichtheim, *Literature I*, 137)

In this design corridor A shows some of the doors into the residence, while corridor B gives an example of the decorated wall of the palace.[3]

Nearly the same situation is found in the galleries under the pyramid itself. In the equivalent corridor A are three panels with the king running or walking placed against the western wall; corridor C is also (partly?) present but the cutting out of the back side of the doors has never been started. Some galleries have the same blue faience tiles covering the walls as well as the galleries of the south tomb.

II. The naos

The naos or shrine is a construction, that is, depending on its purpose, made either of wood or of stone. It is intended to house and/or transport the statue of a deceased person or a god.[4] In this definition the words naos and shrine have more of the sense of being the place where the statue of a god or a deceased person remains permanently.[5] If in the context of this part of the study, the construction is intended to transport statues to the tomb, the word 'cabinet' will be used for it. Normally these constructions, be it naos or cabinet, could be closed with doors that were in most cases made of wood. An example of wooden doors that were meant for the (ebony) naos of the statue of the god *Jmn* has been found in the temple of Deir el-Bahari (Cairo, CG 70001). One side of one of the doors is decorated with the king worshipping the statue of the god in the naos and the other side bears battens.[6] The doors, which were intended to open to the outside,[7] are made in such a way that the battens are outside when the door is closed, thus showing that the god lives in the naos, and offering the god the possibility to enter into the world of the living and have contact with them. This situation

---

1 Friedman, *Djoser.*

2 Friedman, *Cosmos*, 343 states that the faience tiles have a connection with the 'Field of Reeds' and thus with the afterlife. The bluish colour and the shiny surface of the tiles would refer to the glistening of the primeval waters. This supports the above mentioned proposition that the tiles are placed against the outside façade of the royal palace, to call forth a mental link between royalty and the world of creation and the gods.

3 For an example of such a wall see Lauer, *Saqqara*, Plate 102.

4 A wooden naos for a statue of *Jnpw* is on exhibit in the MMA under catalogue number 14.3.18 (Fischer, *Varia nova*, Plate 11a (page 99)); this naos is constructed of wooden boards and beams. Most naos that are made of stone are monolithic.

5 An example of a space that was intended as a naos and that could be closed by a double-door of which the pivot-holes are still present is the 'brick chamber' in the tomb of *Rʿ-wr* (PM, II/1, 265 – 9), Hassan, *Giza I*, 24 – 6, Plate XXVII.

6 Naville, *Deir el Bahari II*, Plates XXVI and XXIX ; on page 2 it is stated that the door itself was made of smaller pieces of wood while the battens were made out of one piece of the same wood.

7 Spencer, *Naos Nekhthorheb*, 1 concludes that, based on the position of the rebates, the conclusion is that in this naos of the 30th dynasty the double door opened to the inside.

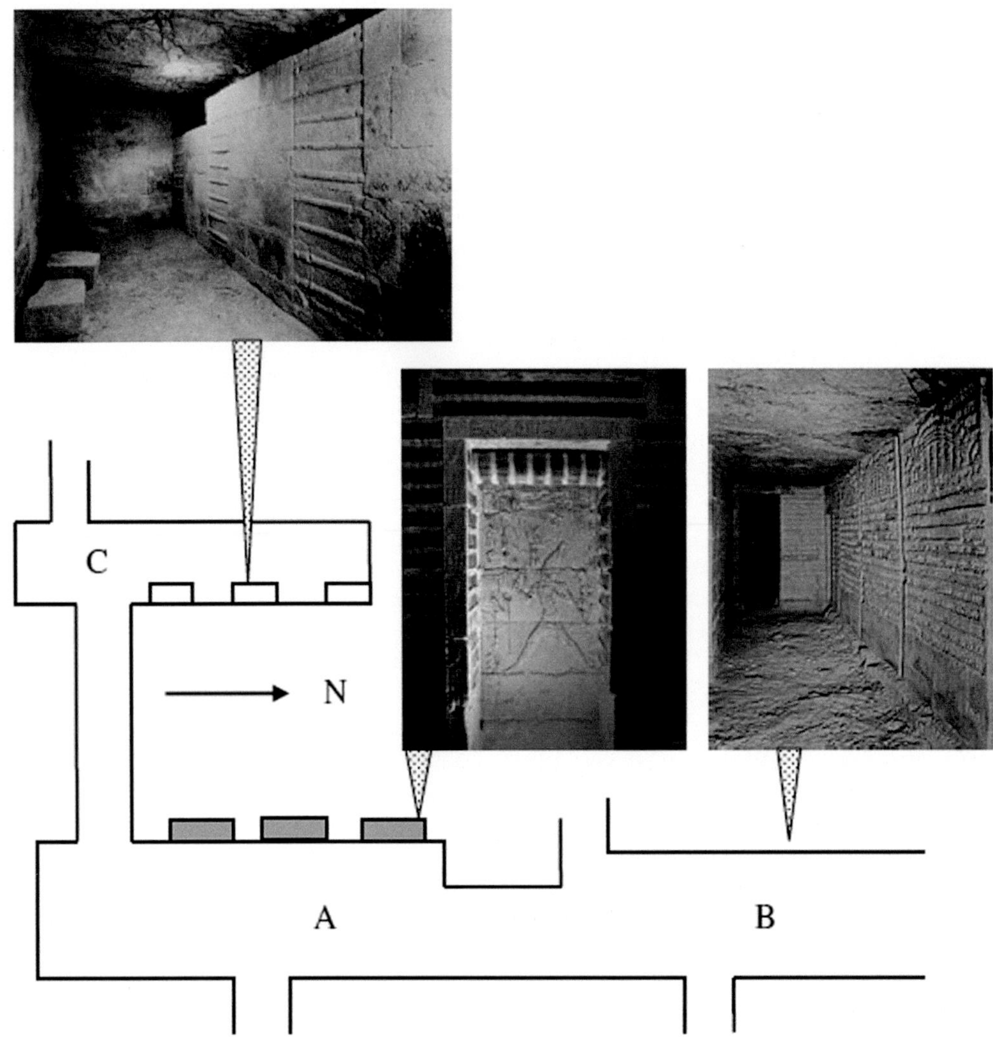

Figure 5.1 Plan of part of the substructure of the south tomb in the mortuary complex of Djoser (III.2).

Figure 5.2 Ceramic vase, predynastic period. (Nagada II.L – III.E). MMA 20.2.10

is identical with the wooden cabinets in which statues of deceased private persons were transported to the necropolis (Figure 4.13).

Depictions of shrines with human figures around them can be dated back to predynastic times.[8] On the vase in Figure 5.2 two shrines standing on what is usually called a boat can be seen and the image gives the impression that a *sḥ - nṯr* shrine with the statue of a god in it is depicted.[9] Several interpretations of the scene are possible:

[8] Hendrickx, *Decorated pottery.* This motif has also been used on the Gebel el-Arak knife (Dreyer, *Messergriffe,* Figure 4 (page 218).

[9] Monnet Saleh, *Tomb 100,* note7 states that similar images have been found in which the oars were provided with peddle-shaped ends and were displayed sticking out above the ship's deck (Gebelein cloth, Museo Egiro, Torino, 17138). From these observations it can be concluded that these were representations of real boats; in contrast, on the images on the vases the 'oars' probably were poles of a platform on which the shrines were standing.

1. The small construction at the lower part of the shrine can be interpreted as a door. The large number of horizontal lines in it makes it unlikely that they are meant as battens,[10] which would make it the depiction of a door with horizontally placed narrow boards, thin branches or reeds, the latter two possibilities being the more plausible. The construction above the shrine could be the aspective rendering of its interior, with the small construction against the right side of the shrine indicating its depth. The little construction to the left might be a shrine without the aspective depiction of the interior. The boat-like construction on which the shrines are standing could be a platform, having this form because shrines used to be depicted while being transported on a boat (Gebelein cloth,[11] date: Nagada I; Hierakonpolis, Tomb 100, date: probably Nagada II)), and apparently the original connection between shrines and boats was so strong that even when they were no longer standing on a real boat, the depiction of the platform they were standing on retained this form.
2. In order to give an interpretation of the 'oars' Kemp links them to a row of vertical lines in a construction depicted on a tablet that can be dated to the reign of Den (I.5)).[12] Kemp interprets these lines, visible under what looks like a platform, as a panelled brick enclosure. In that case in Figure 5.2 the 'oars' could be seen as an enclosure with two shrines constructed out of wicker standing inside it on a boat-like platform, or a flat platform that has been depicted in the form of a boat, thus honouring the old tradition.[13] On some labels the boat-like shrine is standing on a platform that in length exceeds that of the boat;[14] the fact that the poles are outside the boat indicates that this type of pole has no connection with oars.

In none of the shrines gathered in the catalogue of predynastic (Nagada) decorated pottery is the door divided into two halves and this might lead to the conclusion that either the shrines were closed with a single door or the object depicted was not a door.[15]

The argument that the two shrines could be pylons of a temple because on some vases a connection that might be a lintel is visible between them is not strong because in only 6.5% of the depictions is this lintel present.

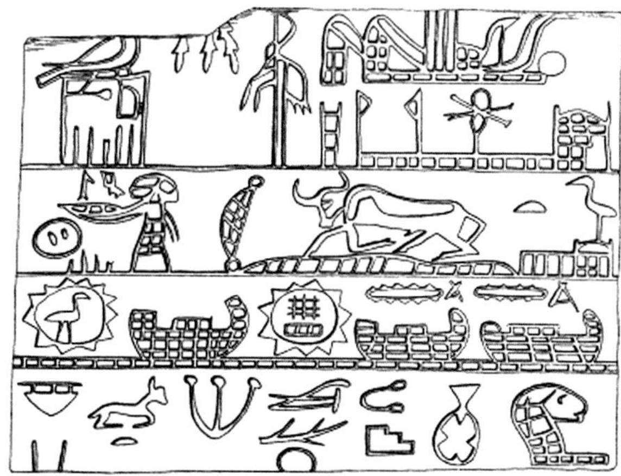

Figure 5.3 Ebony tablet of Hor-Aha (I.1). From Petrie, *Royal tombs II,* Plate X(2).

Another type of entrance into what looks more like a sacred precinct than a shrine was visible in a now lost rock inscription in the vicinity of Aswan.[16] One of the themes can be interpreted as a ship with the deck as a platform. The row of vertical lines is probably an enclosure with an entrance flanked by masts, or perhaps this is an aspective depiction of two shrines standing within an enclosure and with a sign on each of the shrines.

This way of indicating a shrine or a ritually important building is visible on a tablet of Hor-Aha (I.1) where a fenced area next to a *Pr-nw* shrine shows the standard of the goddess Neith and two poles carrying a triangle (Figure 5.3),[17] possibly a sign indicating the city of Sais, still in use during the Old Kingdom to mark places that were connected with the (magical) journey that the funeral procession had to make to the city of Sais.[18]

On seals that have been found in the tombs of the first dynasty at Saqqara a construction is depicted that gives the impression of a temple, with a (small) door in what looks like the side of the building. The front has the appearance of a high façade with two narrow door-like openings in it that give the impression of being high monumental gates (Figure 5.4).[19]

10 The ivory label of Djer (I.3) (Berlin Äg. Museum no. 18026) shows two shrines with horizontal lines that can be interpreted as doors with one resp. two battens.

11 The stick like objects on the Gebelein cloth are clearly oars; on the vase in Figure 5.2 these sticks end under the platform and cannot be interpreted as oars.

12 Kemp, *Ancient Egypt,* 93 (Figure 33(1)).

13 In view of the shrine-like entrance in the left-lower corner of the tablet, in all probability the shrine and its enclosure are standing in one of the 'royal enclosures' of Umm el-Qa'ab.

14 Endesfelder, *Entstehung staates,* Figures 2 and 30.

15 Hendrickx, *Decorated pottery.*

16 Hendrickx, *Royal scene,* Figure 3.

17 On the 'hunters palette' (Louvre E 11254 and British Museum BM 20792) a *pr-nw* shrine has been depicted.

18 Moussa, *Nianchchnum,* Plate 9 (Pfeilerportiko, Ostwand, Bestattungsritual des Chnumhotep, 'Saisfahrt').

19 Badawy, *Stèle funéraire,* 222 interprets the building as a chapel with

Figure 5.4 Seal impression from a first dynasty tomb at Saqqara (from Emery, *Hor-Aha,* Figure 21).

III. The *serekh*

Already by late predynastic times the name of a king was written in a space above the depiction of what, in early dynastic *serekh* of higher quality, looked like a row of towers with entrances in between while a Horus falcon stood over the name of the king (Figure 5.5).[20] This way of stating the royal name could also be used on statues,[21] and in jewellery.[22]

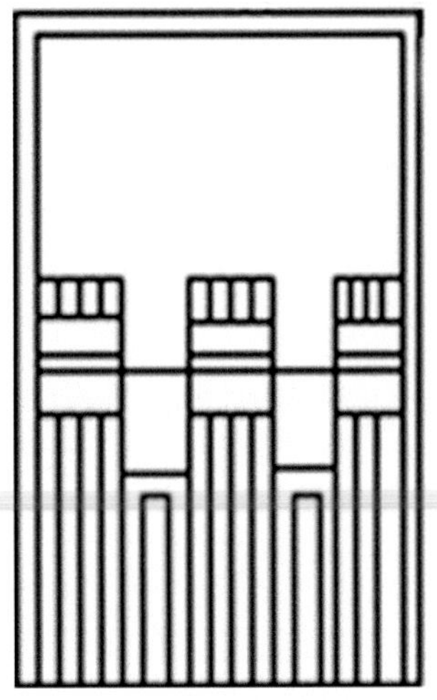

Figure 5.5 Schematic rendition of a *serekh* (after Hor-Djet (I.4)).

The rendering of the palace façade in the *serekh* is probably an aspective depiction of the panelling of the wall (Figure 5.6(A)), which in reality has no towers or battlements (Figure 5.6(B)). The serekh is an iconographical element that represents the wall of a building, undoubtedly with one of the niches being the entrance of the building; it is also possible that it represents a false door (for the connection between these three elements see Figure 6.21).[23]

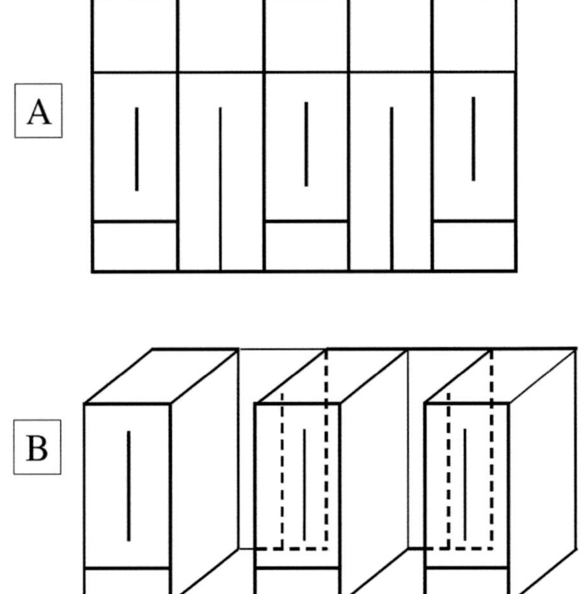

Figure 5.6 The aspective rendition of the panelled wall (schematically after *serekh* in Petrie, *Royal tombs I,* Plate VI(2)).

III.1. The entrances

In work of higher quality like the steles of Djet (I.4) and Qa'a (I.8) the entrance has been worked out more extensively than the one in Figure 5.6, and this group leads to the observation that there are several types of entrances.

The *serekh* of Djet (I.4) (Figure 5.7) has a very elaborate representation of the entrances between the 'towers' and they have the appearance of a plain single niche with sets of uprights to support beams holding up the ceiling of the entrance, as it has been done in the entrance of the pyramid complex of Djoser (III.2). But this would make it a perspective view, which is not habitual in the Egyptian way of displaying objects.[24]

The conclusion is that the entrance must be seen as a three-step plain compound niche (Figure 5.12), possibly with an increasingly low ceiling (perhaps meant as psychological pressure on those who came in?). Further

the figure of Anubis laying on it.

[20] The British Museum Dictionary of Ancient Egypt defines the serekh thus: 'The serekh is usually employed to refer to a rectangular frame surmounted by the Horus falcon, within which the king's 'Horus name' was written'.

[21] Romano, *Royal sculpture,* Figures 10 and 19. Emery, *Hor-Aha,* Figure 2.

[22] One of the bracelets on the mummified arm that has been found in the tomb of Djer (I.3) consists of small platelets in the form of a *serekh* (Petrie, *Royal tombs II,* Plate I).

[23] O'Brian, *Serekh,* 123.

[24] Stele of Djet, Louvre, E 11007, Stele of Qa'a, University of Pennsylvania Museum of Archaeology and Anthropology, E6878.

study showed that this number of steps in a *serekh* is rare and that the one and two stepped entrances must be seen as the standard (Figures 5.8 and 5.9).

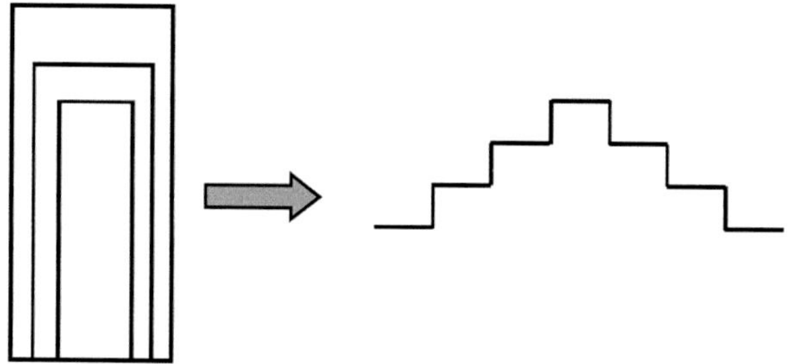

Figure 5.7 The entrance in the *serekh* of Djet (I.4) (see Figure 5.5).

The *serekh* of Qa'a (I.8) that is also a plain compound niche, but this entrance is executed with one step less than the entrance in the *serekh* of Djet (Figure 5.8).[25]

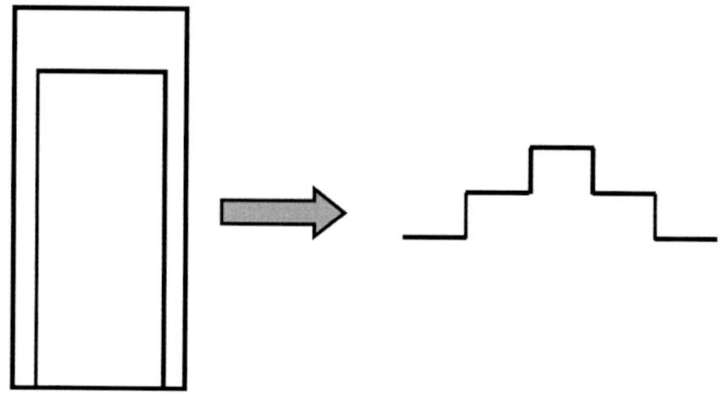

Figure 5.8 The entrance in the *serekh* of Qa'a (I.8).

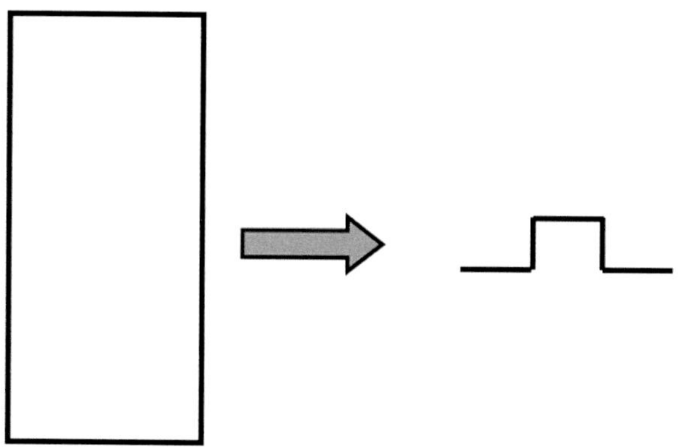

Figure 5.9 The entrance in the *serekh* of Raneb (II.2).

The entrance as shown in Figure 5.7 is also visible on the older incense burner from Qustul (Lower Nubia, OIM E24069, A-group, Nagada III-early(?)), which was found in the largest tomb in the cemetery. The number of steps in this niche is not three but five.[26] Although it is not part of a *serekh*,[27] it is probably a compound entrance (Figure 5.10).

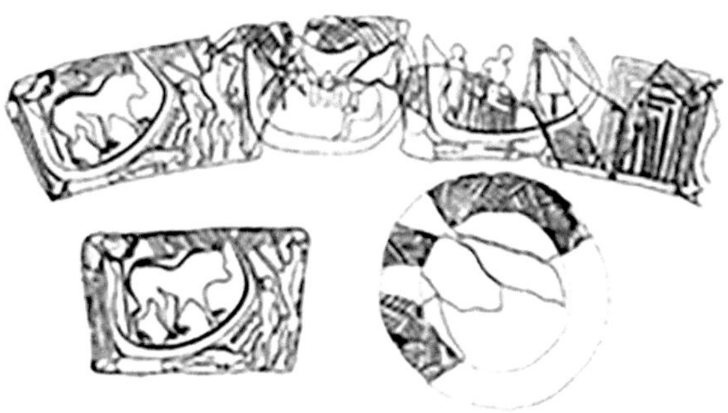

Figure 5.10 The decoration of the incense burner of Qustul (Williams, *A-group*, Plate 34).

It can be observed that in the predynastic period the number of niches in a *serekh* was random and that only later was the strong penchant for units of three items that is observed in this study developed. This leads to the conclusion that the depiction of a niche on the incense burner can have a connection with the Nagada culture, but has no subsequent link with the later *serekh* designs of the first and second dynasty.

III.2. The palace façade panelling and the serekh *false door*

Because both palace façade panelling and the *serekh* false door are decorative themes that are derived from doors and frequently used on sarcophagi, coffins, as well as on architectonic elements of the tomb, it is necessary to further define their resemblances and differences.

Figure 5.11 Palace façade panelling on the eastern wall of mastaba G 5080 (photo author).

In her study of false doors Wiebach discusses the various hypotheses that have existed and still exist about the origin of the palace façade panelling and the

[25] The Metropolitan Museum, New York, 60.144.

[26] Teeter, *Origins*, 162 – 3.

[27] Williams, *A-group*, 138 interprets the niche as a *serekh*.

Figure 5.12 The different types of niches according to Reisner.

serekh type false door that is closely connected to it.[28] In the context of the present study the origin of the decorative theme is not important; more significant is the apparent difference between the two themes and whether it is possible to make an irrefutable distinction between them.

The literature makes it clear that in this field some of the definitions in use are not sufficiently substantiated to be unambiguous.

Reisner describes the true false door (Reisner's 'false-door stele'), and the *serekh* false door (Reisner's 'great *k3*-door of the palace façade panelling), [29] and defines the true false door as a long and small doorway set in the wall of the tomb (his *k3*-door), while the *serekh* false door developed from the palace façade panelling (Figure 5.11) through the cruciform palace façade chapel to the *serekh* false door (Borchardt's 'Prunkscheintür').

These definitions by Reisner lead to the conclusion that the basic feature that makes up the palace façade panelling is the small *k3*- door,[30] although variations are possible (on the long side of the sarcophagus of *Ỉry-n-wr* (PM, III/1, 205) at both sides the row of small *k3*-doors is closed by a larger door of the same design).[31] According to Reisner in the necropolis of Giza this type of panelling is not found on the exposed outside of mastabas; the only (unfinished) example, consisting of a row of small *k3*-doors (plain compound niches) (Figure 5.12),[32] is on the eastern wall (which in reality is the western wall of the exterior chapel) of mastaba G 5080 of *Sšm-nfr* [II] (PM, III/1, 14 – 7).

This type of decoration has not only been placed on stone sarcophagi,[33] but also on wooden ones (Figure 5.15).[34]

The Reisner *k3*-door can be divided in two types of niche, the plain single niche and the plain compound niche (Figure 5.12), with the great door niche as a third type derived from these two (Figure 5.13). The two basic niches can also be combined into a group consisting of three plain single niches, one plain compound niche and again three plain single niches as in the Shunet el-zebib at Abydos (Figure 3.1). This type of decoration appears to have been used on the southern wall of the tomb of *Ḫnt-k3w.s* (PM, III/1, 288 – 9; LG 100) too.[35]

Each of the two kinds of niches can form a palace façade panelling. The total (compound) *serekh* false door design is made up of three units of three plain compound niches of which the middle niche of the middle unit develops a somewhat different form (Figure 5.13). This indicates a degree of preference for three related elements in a group.[36]

In the central niche of both a true and a *serekh* false door the depiction of a door could be displayed.[37]

In the temple of the queen's pyramid III-c next to the pyramid of Menkaure (IV.5) the panelling combination

[28] Wiebach, *Scheintür*, 29 – 34.

[29] Reisner, *Giza I*, 372.

[30] Donadoni, *Sarcofagi*, Plate XXXII(2).

[31] Donadoni, *sarcophagi*, Plate XXIX(1).

[32] Giza archives, Photos A644_NS, A645P_NS.

[33] Donadoni, *Sarcofagi*, B 35 (Plate XXVIII).

[34] Donadoni, *Sarcofagi*, Sarcophagus of *Sš3t-ḥtp*, C 10, Plate XI.

[35] https://www.researchgate.net/publication/327043367_Khentkawes_Tomb_Giza_A_layman's_guide
Photos on pages 28 and 29.

[36] Examples of this tendency are:
- The western wall of the chapel of *Ḥʿ-b3w-skr*, (PM, III/2, 449 – 50), (Figure 8.1).
- The western wall of the chapel of *Ḥsjj-Rʿ* (PM, III/2, 437–9), (Figure 7.3).
- The eastern wall of the Shunet el-zebib at Abydos is composed of three plain single niches with at each side a plain compound niche (Adams, *Shunet el-Zebib*, Figure 3).
- The standard panelling of the *serekh* false door consists of a tripartite central niche at both sides flanked by a unit of three small entrances each topped by a papyrus dolde.
- Often sarcophagi had a *serekh* panelling on the exterior sides which was based on a tripartite *serekh* false door flanked by a combination of three plain compound niches (Figure 5.15).
- The false doors in tombs of members of the higher social strata relatively often have three jambs, and some of them also have three columns of text on every jamb (*SAbw*, PM, III/2, 461) (Borchardt, *Denkmäler II*, no. 1565).

[37] In the chapel of *Sṯw* [II] (PM, III/2, 490 – 1) two *serekh* false doors are placed against the western wall of the chapel with doors in the central niche that swing in opposite directions (Borchardt, *Denkmäler I*, Plates 1377 – 8). In the chapel of *Q3r* at Abusir the false door in chapel 2 has a double door with battens in the central niche (Bárta, *Abusir XIII*, Figure 5.3.9).

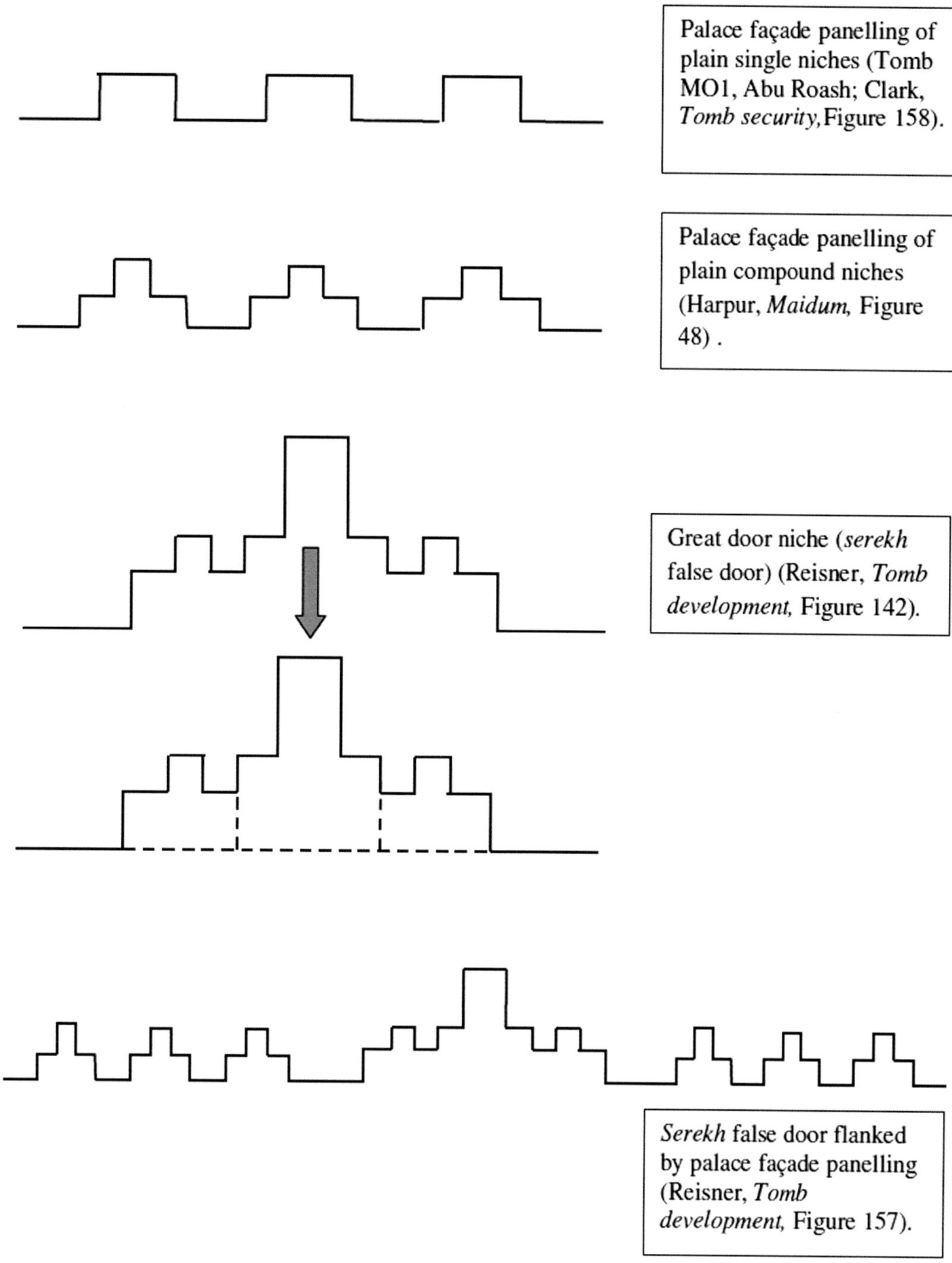

Palace façade panelling of plain single niches (Tomb MO1, Abu Roash; Clark, *Tomb security,* Figure 158).

Palace façade panelling of plain compound niches (Harpur, *Maidum,* Figure 48) .

Great door niche (*serekh* false door) (Reisner, *Tomb development,* Figure 142).

Serekh false door flanked by palace façade panelling (Reisner, *Tomb development,* Figure 157).

Figure 5.13 The different types of panelling and the resulting compound *serekh* false door.

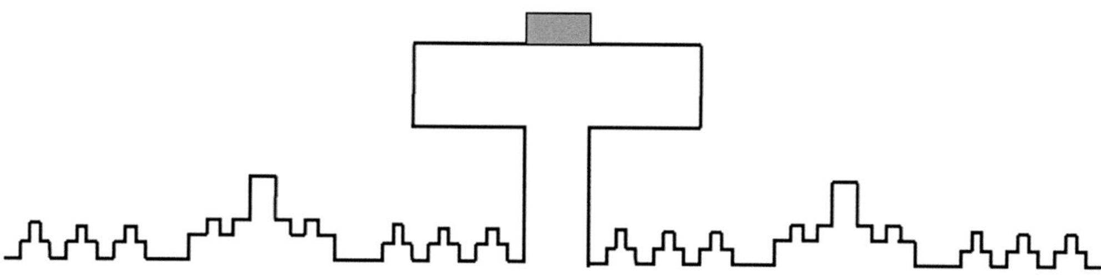

Figure 5.14 The panelling decoration of the entrance into the chapel of queen's pyramid III-c at Giza.

of Figure 5.13 has been used on both sides of the entrance into a T-form chapel (Figure 5.14).

Reisner proposes a total development that can be described as follows:

- During the first dynasty larger mastabas had palace façade panelling (composed of plain or compound niches) on all four sides.
- At the end of the dynasty this design was abandoned and only two of the niches remained in use as an offering place on the eastern wall of the mastaba, of which the southern one eventually ended up as a plain single or compound niche with an identifying tablet over it, thus turning into a 'true false door'.
- This design remained in use until the end of the second dynasty, when the offering place was withdrawn into the body of the mastaba and a 'great door niche ' (= the door of a *serekh* type false door) was placed on the western wall of the interior chapel. This false door, which was a combination of three plain compound niches, was flanked on both sides by three small plain single or compound niches, thus making up the (compound) *serekh* type false door. The deeper *serekh* false door turned this originally T-shaped chapel into a cruciform one. The re-appearance of the multiple plain niches panelling on the western wall of this chapel indicates a partial return to the original panelling as was used during the first dynasty.

Figure 5.15 Anonymous sarcophagus (Cairo Museum 54934; Donadoni, *Sarcofagi*, Plate XXIV).

Apart from on chapel walls the compound *serekh* false door could also be placed

1. On sarcophagi. The *serekh* false doors in Figure 5.15 show that they are divided in two leaves each with its own pivots and are thus fully intended as depictions of real doors.
2. On wooden coffins.[38]
3. On the slots flanking the panel of the true false doors.[39] In view of the context of the false door acting as a passage between the world of the living and the dead, the depiction of the *serekh* false door can only have been placed there as a decorative theme.
4. On walls of interior spaces, as in the pyramid temple of the queen's pyramid III-c belonging to the pyramid complex of Menkaure (IV.5).[40]
5. At the end of the 5th dynasty this type of false door was painted on the walls of the burial chamber of Unas (V.9).
6. During the 6th dynasty the false door could be painted on the walls of burial chambers of private tombs.[41]

That other combinations of these decoration elements exist can be seen in the remnants of the walls of the courtyard of the pyramid temple of Menkaure which has a design consisting of the repetition of a plain compound niche flanked by a panelling of three plain single niches.[42] In the same complex an identical design has been used in the temples of the queen's pyramids III-a and III-c. In the subterranean structure of the pyramid of Menkaure, the four walls of one of the rooms are decorated with shallow and narrow plain compound niches.

Some false doors can be interpreted as a mixed form of both types, an example being the false door of *Pḥn-wj-kȝ.j* (PM, III/2, 491 – 2) which has a normal true false door design, but also shows several characteristic features of the *serekh* false door.[43] The compound *serekh* false door flanking the panel of the true false door (see item 3 above) is another example of the mixed form. This observation leads to the conclusion that the purpose of the two types of false doors is basically identical.

III.3. The door as part of the sarcophagus or coffin [44]

The earliest graves, other than a hole in the desert sand, had their sides strengthened (Figure 2.1), and

38 LD, *II*, 98(d).

39 Cherpion, *Mastabas*, Plates 21, 32.

40 Reisner, *Mycerinus*, Plans IV and V.

41 Duell, *Mereruka II*, Plates 204 and 209.

42 Reisner, *Mycerinus*, Plan I. The same design is used in the outer walls of the Shunet- el-Zebib at Abydos

43 LD, *II*, 48.

44 Although sarcophagus, coffin or mummy case can all three be defined as containers meant to hold and protect the remains of a deceased person, the definitions of the three are not quite equal. A

then the body of the deceased was placed in the pit without further substantial envelopes, but often with grave goods directly next to the body.[45] Not only the *k3* of the deceased had direct access to the goods in the pit itself, but also to offerings that had been laid down just outside by way of traversing the slits in the walls around the pit.[46]

When the tombs of members of the richer social classes were progressively provided with a burial in a subterranean space, a container for the protection of the mortal remains became necessary.

The result was that in the tombs of members of the higher social strata a chest was placed in the burial chamber during the funeral which was meant to be the container that would hold and protect the mortal remains of the deceased 'for eternity'. Although the body was no longer lying in a small pit with grave goods placed close by it, the custom of these goods being near the body of the deceased continued and a small quantity of goods was placed inside the container, and some outside of it.[47]

A funerary container could either be a coffin which was made of terracotta or wood (in the latter case depending on the wealth of the family, local or imported), or a sarcophagus which was normally made of stone (here the type of stone depended on the social status of the deceased).[48]

Because the *k3* of the deceased had to be able to enter and leave the coffin, some kind of (magical) passage was necessary.[49] Often, but not always, this passage was indicated by means of a palace façade panelling, thus emphasizing the underlying idea of a dwelling,[50] or with a *serekh* false door decoration which could be of variable complexity.[51] Coffins of the First Intermediate Period and the Middle Kingdom were regularly decorated with a (painted) false door of the *serekh* design. In the following periods the theme became less frequent, although even in the Late Period a coffin was still sometimes decorated with it.[52]

In Figure 5.16 a 4th dynasty wooden coffin for a contracted burial is shown. The literature interprets the type of decoration on the eastern wall of the coffin as a 'palace façade',[53] but it is possible to interpret this façade in another way:

Starting from the premise that the coffin is the facsimile of a house, and in order to be able to support the vaulted roof, the walls had to have a certain thickness. However, it was possible to reduce the wall to one or more pillars by taking away thickness in the parts A, which as a consequence became thinner but remained closed and were decorated,[54] while the parts B were transformed into two doors with a pillar in between. This proposal would lead to the conclusion that, in that case, the battens of the door are on the outside of the coffin, but because both sides of the door are in the world of the dead, the world where the *k3* lives, the hypothesis about the proper place for the battens is not valid here. This conclusion is supported by the observation that the battens were not always present;[55] meaning that, based on the position of the battens, a definitive conclusion about the location of the world of the dead is not fully reliable. In later periods there is a tendency to use a simplified version of the door more as a decorative element than as a magical passage.[56]

Petrie describes a nearly identical coffin found in Tarkhan (tomb 532),[57] and states that the parts equivalent to part A in Figure 5.16 are doors and the parts B are barred windows to let wind in when the shutters are opened, which is in contradiction with that which is previously proposed.

However, an argument against this is the realization that Egypt is a country with a prevailing northern

sarcophagus is defined as typically a stone coffin (!), while a coffin is made of wood (but the word 'sarcophagus' is given as a synonym). It is clear that the definitions are inaccurate, and the ones that will be used in this study are given in the table of technical terms.

45 Emery, *Archaic Egypt*, Pate 22.

46 These slits cannot only be interpreted as openings through which the *k3* of the deceased could leave the burial place to get to the offerings; they can also be seen as the pair of eyes that in later periods would be painted on the coffin so that the deceased could look at the world outside and at the rising sun.

47 Bárta, *Abusir XXIII*, Plate 3.1a; Emery, *Archaic Egypt*, Plate 29.

48 During the Old Kingdom the king and the highest echelon were often buried in sarcophagi of hard stone (for the cemetery of Abusir, see Nováková, *Sarcophagi*, Chart 2 (page 146)).

49 PT § 2009.

50 Donadoni, *Sarcofagi*, Plate XXIX(1). The palace façade panelling could be cut out in the stone (sarcophagus of *Mrs-ʿnḫ* [III] (Dunham, *Gmast 1*, Plate XV), painted on wood (Marochetti, *Gebelein*, Figure 13), or directly made out of wood (Marochetti, *Gebelein*, Figure 8). The stone sarcophagus with palace façade panelling was still in use during at least the 18th dynasty as is shown in the tomb of *Rḫ-mj-Rʿ* (PM, I/1, 206 – 14) Davies, *Rekh-mi-Re'*, Plate 24.

51 Donadoni, *Sarcofagi*, Plates XXIV and XXV; Fischer, *Varia nova*, Plate 14a/b (page 102).

52 The coffin of Asru (25th – 26th dynasty, Manchester Museum no. TN R4567/1937).The depiction of the door in the compound *serekh* false door resembles the door of Figure 5.22 which is interpreted as the double doors of heaven. This type of decoration was rare in later periods, because here the doors were painted on the lid of a wooden coffin.

53 Marochetti, *Coffin Gebelein*, 237.

54 Marochetti, *Coffin Gebelein*, Figure 5.

55 Emery, *Archaic Egypt*, Plate 24a.

56 The coffin of *Ḥpj-ʿnḫ-tḫfj* (The Metropolitan Museum number: 12.183.11b, 12th dynasty); The coffin of *Ḥr* (The Metropolitan Museum, O.C.800; Late Period).

57 Petrie, *Tarkhan I*, 27, Plate XXVIII.

wind,[58] and a window intended to cool the house would be placed at its northern side. Coffins were placed in the pit or the burial chamber with a predominant north-south orientation, and the conclusion is that it is doubtful that the decoration on the eastern side of the coffin had been placed there as the facsimile of a window of the residence of the deceased.

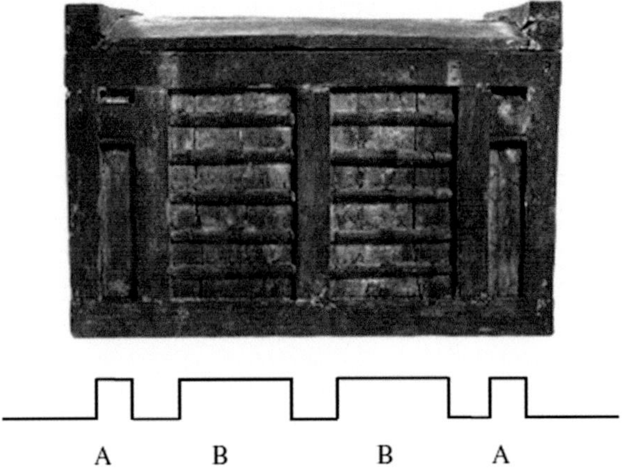

Figure 5.16 Wooden coffin (4th dynasty) (Museo Egizio Torino, Suppl. 14061).

The cedar wooden coffin of *Sšt-ḥtp* (PM, III/1, 149 – 50; V.E) shows six plain single niches on the long side, while the horizontal interior boards give the impression of battens thus emphasizing that it is a door which is depicted.[59]

Decorated stone sarcophagi of the Old Kingdom with a *serekh type* false door have been gathered in Figure 5.17. From the figure it appears that as early as the Old Kingdom a development took place in which the double door was abandoned and only single doors were used, while the number of items defining a door decreased. Apparently the most common way of displaying doors was in their most simple, nearly symbolic, way.

Within the context of this study the invisibility of the battens would imply that the inside of the sarcophagus is the house of the deceased and that the *k3*, upon opening the doors, could enter into another world, a world that was still the world of the dead, but that had a place of contact with the world of the living. However, if this consideration is combined with the conclusion about the sarcophagus in Figure 5.16 it seems obvious that, although the door plays an important role, the place of the battens does not matter.

This can be based on the consideration that when the *k3* goes from the coffin to the burial chamber, it remained within the residence; it only went to a part of the residence with another function. The whole inner world of the tomb could be seen as the residence; this would make the false door in the chapel its entrance, the dividing line between the outside and inside world; the burial chamber is the private part of the house, and the coffin the sleeping quarters of the deceased (Figure 14.2). In order to cross all these dividing lines, indications of passageways were required, indications that could be quite obvious, as in the slits in Tarkhan tomb 1845 (Figure 2.1), but that could also be purely symbolic and thus magical as in the doors on the sarcophagus in Figure 5.15.

III.4. The door in the burial chamber

From the start of the 6th dynasty in an increasing number of tombs the walls of the burial chamber were decorated, and later in the 6th dynasty in an increasing percentage of these tombs one or more doors were included, doors that could be either ritual (a false door) or utilitarian (the door of a granary or a store room).

An example of the latter is found in the burial chamber of the tombs of *K3.j-m-ʿnḫ* (PM, III/1, 131 – 3 (V.L)) and of the former in the burial chamber of *Ppy-ʿnḫ S̱tw* (PM, III/2, 672).[60] In the burial chamber of *K3.j-m-ʿnḫ* , on the wall opposite the entrance three registers showing granaries and storerooms are painted (Figure 5.18).[61] The top register depicts three storerooms with doors of which two doors have battens. One door without visible battens and a strange construction that looks like a double pivot at the top leads into a work shop, while the other two doors are of store rooms.[62] The register under this shows four vaulted rooms that are closed with doors with battens.[63]

In this burial chamber no other doors are displayed on the walls, and these doors were not intended to serve as passages for the *k3* of the deceased; they were just

[58] Information concerning the prevailing direction of the wind over the year is obtained from websites giving the current predominant wind of the various locations. Delta and northern Nile valley: north-west; Sinai: north; Siwa: north to north-east; Farafra: north-west; Dakhla: north-east; Kharga: north-west; Baharia: north to north-west.

[59] Although the coffin has the form of a *ḳrsw* sarcophagus, according to the given definition the container is a coffin.

[60] Dated VI according to PM, III/1; Kanawati, *Giza I*, 18 gives V.L. For the burial chamber of *Ppy-ʿnḫ S̱tw* see Jánosi, *Burial chamber.*

[61] Kanawati, *Giza I*, Plate 36.

[62] Junker, *Giza V*, Plates IX, X.

[63] PM, III/1, 132(18) states that these are granaries although a granary with this type of door (they all show pivots, thus indicating that the doors turn around a vertical axis) would not be able to hold grain. The same vaulted structure is visible in the burial chamber of *Ppy-ʿnḫ S̱tw* (PM, III/2, 672) but with another type of door (Brovarski, *South Saqqara*, Figures 5E and 8A). This leads to the question of whether the artist somehow interpreted the idea of a door according to his own knowledge and not in accord with reality.

Name	Reference	Date	Battens	Pivot(s)	Bolt	door	
						Single	Double [1]
Mrs-ꜥnḫ [II] [2]	PM, 194	IV.M	x	x	?	---	x
Ḫwfw-ḏd.f	PM, 219	IV.M	---	---	---	x	---
Ḥr-ḏd.f	PM, 191	IV.M	---	---	---	x	---
Anonymous	PM, 192	IV.M/L	---	x	---	---	x
Mnw-ḫꜣ.f	PM, 195	IV.M/L	---	---	---	x	---
Mrs-ꜥnḫ [III]	PM, 197	IV.L	---	---	---	x	---
Anonymous	PM, 201	IV	---	---	---	x	---
Ḫwfw-ꜥnḫ [3]	PM, 216	IV	---	---	---	x	---
Anonymous	PM, 10	IV	---	---	---	x	---
Bꜣ-bꜣ.f	PM, 155-7	IV.L-V.E	---	---	---	x	---
Ptḥ-sḏf	PM, 285	V.M/L	---	x [4]	---	x	---
Wr-jrnj	PM, 205	V(?)	---	---	---	x	---
Rꜥ-wr [III]	PM, 242	V.L-VI.E [5]	---	---	---	x	---

1. If a door is not divided in two leaves by means of a line, the door is included in the table as a single door. Sarcophagi without decoration are not included.
2. MFA 27.441a/b, the decoration is on both long sides of the sarcophagus. The presence of a bolt is not clear in the photos.
3. Cairo Museum CG 1790, in PM dated to IV-V, in Borchardt, *Denkmäler II,* Plate 112; 209 – 12, dated to IV.
4. This is a real single door because there are only pivots at one side. Hassan, *Giza I,* Plate LXII; Donadoni, *Sarcofagi,* Plate XXV.

Figure 5.17 Door representations on stone sarcophagi with *serekh* type false doors.

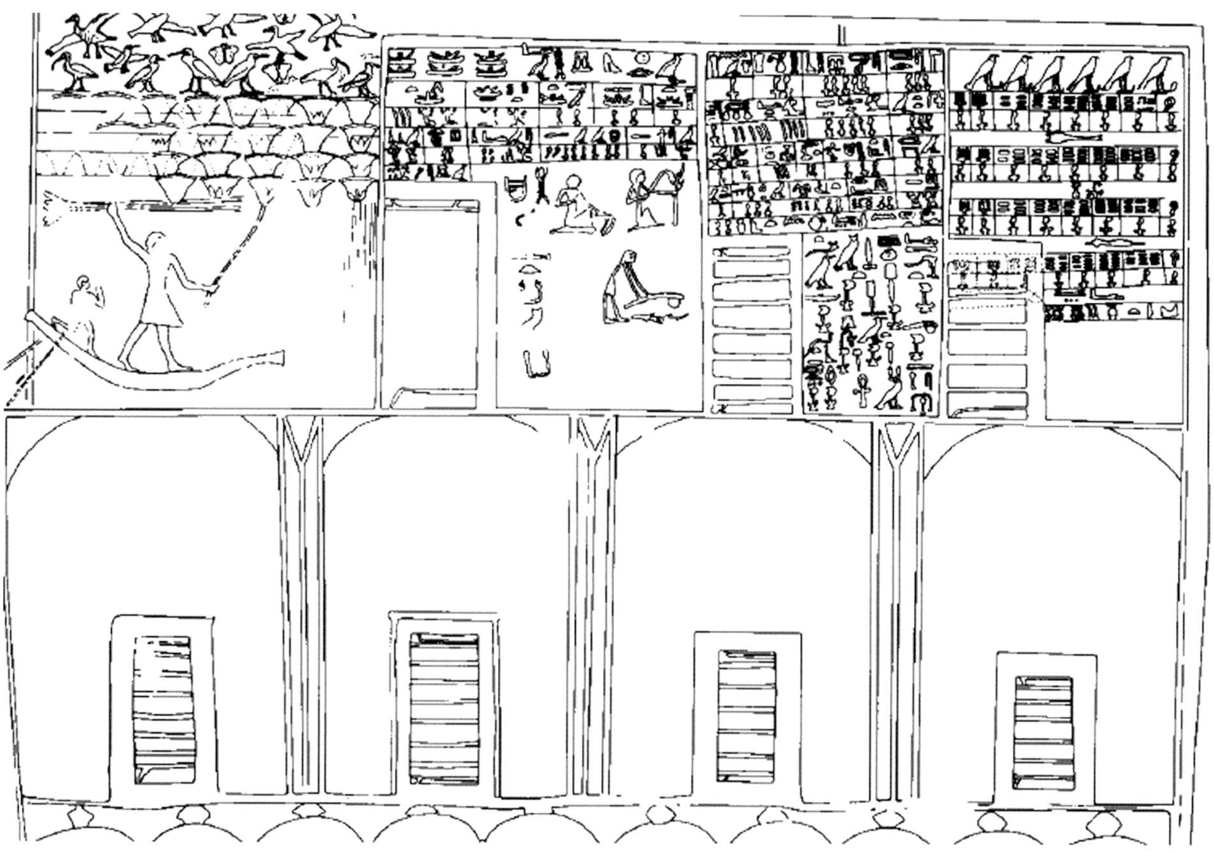

Figure 5.18 Detail of the western wall in the burial chamber of *Kꜣ.j-m-ꜥnḫ* (PM, III/1, 131 – 3).

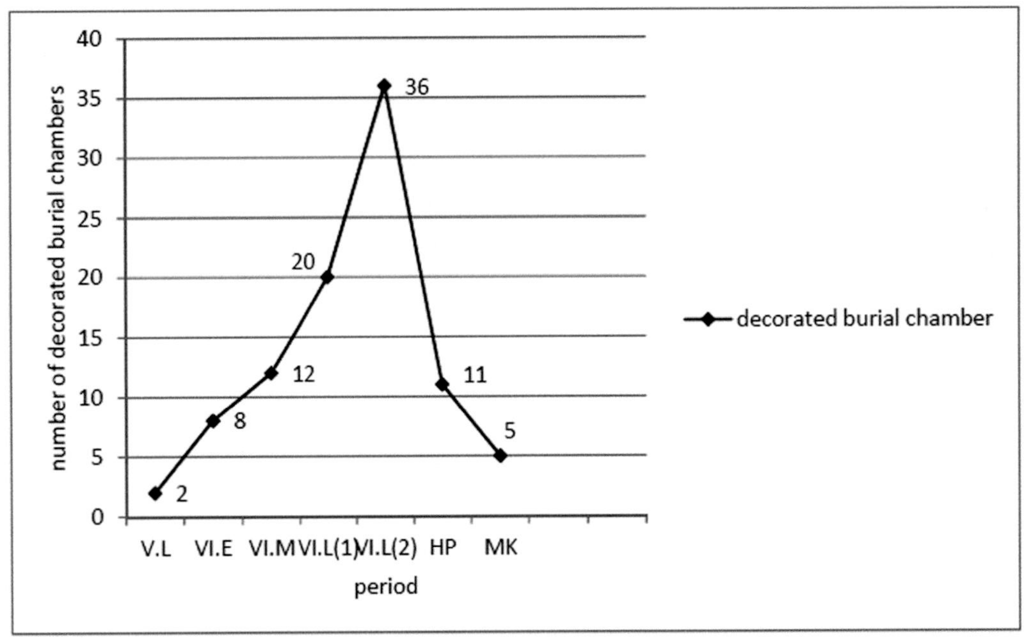

Figure 5.19 The number of decorated burial chambers in the Memphite necropolis (from the catalogue in Dawood, *Burial chamber decoration*).

depictions of objects that had played a role in the daily life of the tomb owner, and were strictly utilitarian.

In the burial chamber of *Ppy-ʿnḫ Sṯw* (PM, III/2, 672) two *serekh* false doors are painted on the eastern and western walls. Of both false doors the door part shows a double door with pivots.

Another situation is found in the burial chamber of the tomb of *Mrrw-k3.j* (PM, III/2, 525 – 34 (VI.E)), where the sarcophagus is standing with a ramp going up to the rim. On both sides of the ramp, a *serekh* false door has been painted on the sarcophagus.[64] The painting at the left side of the ramp is in a state of conservation which enables one to see the pivots of the double door. On the other walls of the burial chamber a less door-like *serekh* design has been painted.[65]

An even more realistic situation exists in the burial chamber of the tomb of *Ỉnty* (date: VI.M) at Abusir, where a monolithic false door was placed against the sarcophagus.

There is a difference between the '*serekh type*' false doors on the walls of the burial chambers and the *serekh* type false doors in the chapel, because the false door in the burial chamber is not a false door in the sense of the one in the chapel; it is not a place where offerings can be placed; in reality it is a highly decorated passage.[66]

A possible reason for the dominant presence of *serekh* type false doors in burial chambers might be that the period in which decorating the walls of the burial chamber started was V.L (see Figure 5.19), and this development increased markedly until the end of the 6th dynasty. But this period was also the one in which the cult of Osiris rose above the threshold of consciousness and began to expand strongly.

One of the main ideas of this new cult was that the *k3* of the deceased was no longer confined to the tomb but could be reborn and move to the Field of Offerings. Although the *k3* could move freely through the tomb, it mainly stayed in the vicinity of the mortal remains of the deceased. When the cult of Osiris became more popular, the *k3* of the deceased that descended together with the coffin to the burial chamber could now leave through the 'false' door in the burial chamber and go on its way to the Field of Offerings. Against this explanation is the fact that the burial chamber was not decorated in every tomb.[67]

IV. The door in script

IV.1. The door in writing

On the palette of Narmer (Cairo, CG 14706, JE 32169) an object is depicted that can be interpreted as a door

64 Duell, *Mereruka II*, Plate 209A/B.

65 Duell, *Mereruka II*, Plate 204A

66 Jánosi, *Burial chamber*, 224 – 5.

67 Dawood, *Burial chamber decoration*, 117 – 20; due to the long reign of Pepy II (VI.4) the period VI.L has been divided into two sub-periods VI.L(1) and VI.L(2); HP = Heracleopolitan Period, MK = Middle Kingdom).

wing (Figure 5.20),[68] and which possibly has a narrative function as part of a series of signs.

The door is part of the written language with the phonetic value of ꜥꜣ (= door) and can serve as an ideogram and a determinative (Gardiner O31). An uncertain translation of the word is 'false door'.[69]

On a sealing of Djet (I.4) a double door (Figure 5.21) with pivots and battens is depicted over the hieroglyphic sign of the human mouth (Gardiner D21). The translation of these signs is uncertain due the fact that it is not possible to determine whether the signs should be read or interpreted. If the doors are used as determinatives it might be translated as 'a double door entrance', the doors possibly being those of the palace in which Djet resided, because both the *serekh* of Djet and a building with palace façade panelling with the name of the king and the Horus falcon in it are visible in the sealing.[70]

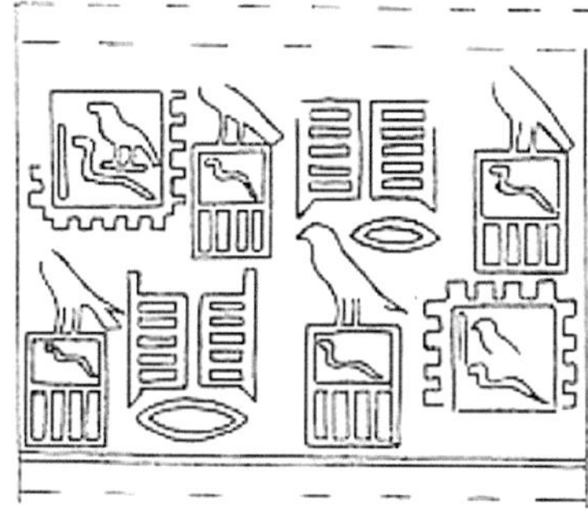

Figure 5.21 Sealing of Djet (I.4) (Petrie, *Royal tombs I*, Plate XVIII(4)).

Figure 5.20 Detail of the obverse side of the Narmer Palette (JE 32169).[71]

On some ebony tablets of king Den (I.5), in what is probably the royal palace, a text has been placed that contains the door wing O31.[72]

IV.2. The door in funerary texts

Doors are frequently mentioned in the Pyramid Texts (PT), the Coffin Texts (CT) and the Book of the Dead (BD) as elements that play a role in the various stages of obtaining the afterlife:

1. the entrance of the firmament, which on earth could be the doors of the purification house and where in fact the voyage to the afterlife starts (Figure 5.22).[73]

'The doors of the horizon are opened, its bolts are drawn back' (PT, § 194).

> *'Stand at the doors of the horizon, open the doors of the firmament ...'* (PT, § 255).
> *'....receive your bread which does not grow mouldy and your beer which does not grow sour, and stand at the doors which keep out the plebs.* (PT, § 655).
> *'O, N, stand at the doors which keep out the plebs. There...'* (CT I, § 290).
> *'Opened for me are the double doors of the sky.'*
> (BD, 26 b A § S 1)

The entrance of heaven or the horizon appears to be either a double door or two separate doors, which would be in accordance with the depiction given in the chapel of *Mrrw-kꜣ.j* at Saqqara.[74] However, in a later period the plural was interpreted as the entrance of heaven having two doors that turned in the middle of the opening, and thus forming the eastern and western door between the sky and the land.[75]

This connection of the double door with the sky and the land is evident in:

[68] The sign has a strong resemblance with the hieroglyph Gardiner O31 as given in Fischer, *Varia nova*, page 96, Figure 5.

[69] Hannig, *Handwörterbuch*, XIV, 127.

[70] Petrie, *Royal tombs I*, Plate XVIII(4).

[71] Andelković, *Political organization*, Figure 3.1 (page 25).

[72] Petrie, *Royal tombs I*, Plate XV (16, 17).

[73] Brovarski, *Doors of Heaven*, 107 – 8. In the mastaba of *Mrrw-kꜣ.j* at Saqqara the coffin of the deceased is transported to the western side of the river to a landing place that is closed with doors (Duell, *Mereruka II*, Plate 130). Brovarski, *Doors of heaven*, Figure 1, proposes to interpret the construction of the landing place with the two separate doors as *ꜥꜣ.wy pt* and to translate that as 'the doors of heaven',which is in accordance with the text of PT § 194 and § 255.

[74] Brovarski, *Doors of Heaven*, Figure 1.

[75] Bruyère, *Sennedjem*, 31 – 2, Plate XXV (19th dynasty). The idea of a real double door with a middle post is visible in Perrot, *Histoire*, Figure 86 (page134), 11th dynasty) and in the house model of *Mkt-Rꜥ* (PM, I/1, 359 – 64).

'Opened for me are the double doors of the Sky; opened for me are the double doors of the earth. Opened for me are the bolts of Geb;...... ' (BD, 68 R § P 5)

2. as part of the celestial barks:

'....the doors of the night-bark shall not be opened to him; the doors of the day-bark shall not be opened to him.....' (PT, § 485).
'Open to him, double doors of the night bark; open to him double doors of the day bark.' (BD, 130 R § S)

3. according to § 1361 doors are present in the entrance of the tomb, but other spells state that these are in the burial chamber too, while the equivalence of the sarcophagus or coffin and Nut is quoted in PT § 616.[76]

'...the doors of the tomb are opened for you, the doors of Nut are opened for you'. The tomb is opened for you, (PT, § 1361).
the doors of the tomb chamber are thrown open for you... (PT, § 1909).

Figure 5.22 The double door of the entrance to the place of the afterlife (early 19th dynasty).

4. the coffin has doors (see section III.3 of this chapter):
'The tomb is opened for you; the doors of the coffin are drawn back for you....' (PT, § 2009).

5. the observation that mention is made of 'doorkeepers of the cemeteries' may indicate the existence of the doors of heaven, the doors of the purification room *ibw n wʿb*.[77]

'the Doorkeepers of the cemeteries, who present their beautiful faces.....' (BD, 141, R § P 1).

6. In the various hours of the different versions of The Book of the Dead doors are depicted in a number of functions:

- - blocking the way of the bark of the sun god (Figure 5.23).[78]
- - as doors of shrines.[79]
- - as doors guarding a group of gods.[80]
- - as doors opening and closing the region of an hour.

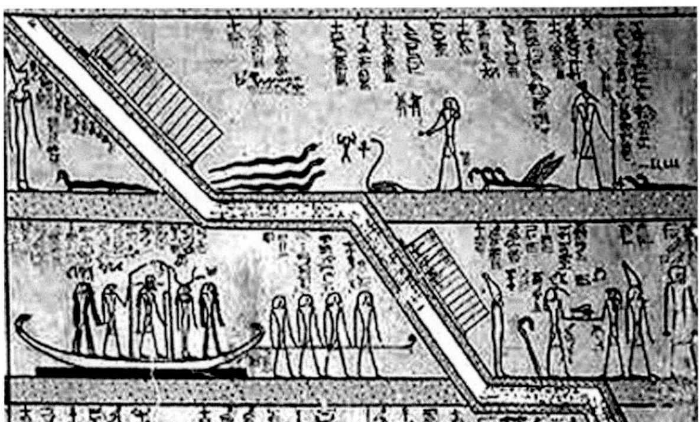

Figure 5.23 The doors obstructing the waterway in the fourth hour of the Amduat.

V. Discussion

The compilation of the various aspects of doors clearly shows their multi-functionality. Their mundane use was to close an entrance or a passage. However, for the upper social strata, the doors were also part of the program signalling the social standing of the tomb owner and his family, because the number of doors in the tomb, the door(s) being double or single, the material of which it (they) was (were) made was an indication of their wealth and consequently had a profound social impact. This was all the more visible, because, in view of the economic value of wood, the houses of those belonging to the lowest social strata probably had no doors, and they closed their houses with a mat.

76 PT § 616: .....you having been given to your mother Nut in her name of 'Sarcophagus', she has embraced you in her name of 'Coffin'.....

77 Brovarski, Doors of heaven, 108.

78 Hornung, *Amduat,* 94 – 5, 102 – 3.

79 Hornung, *Amduat,* 142 – 3, 209, 239,

80 Taylor, *Papyrus Panebmontu,* Figure 4.

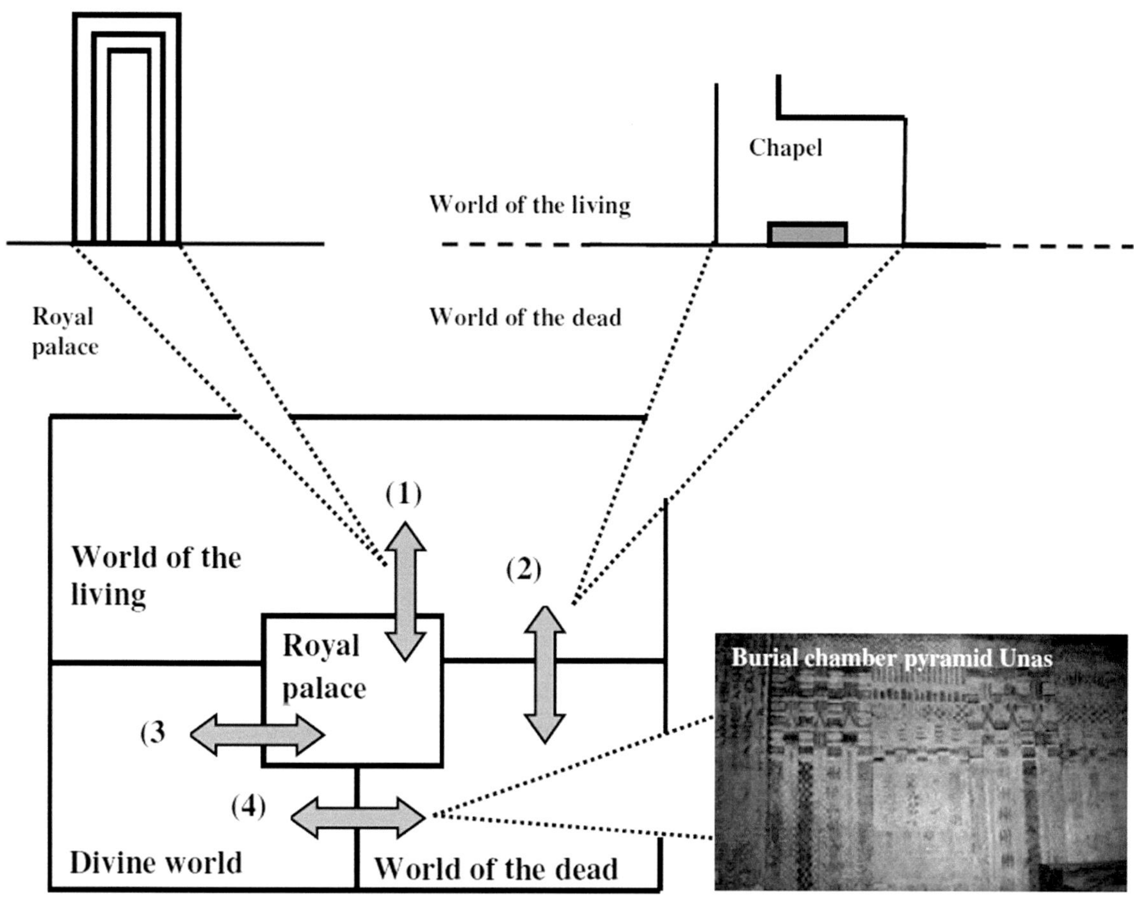

Figure 5.24 Interfaces.

Realizing the economic value that had to be invested in the production of a door made of good quality wood, this social impact also applied to the number of doors in a house or in the interior of a tomb. A residence and a tomb are to a certain degree equivalent, not only because both were seen as the abode of a person in the two different worlds, but also because both of them were divided in a number of functional units (the world outside the residence, the entrance, the private quarters of the tomb owner and his bed room). This means that both abodes must have had the same level of interest for the owner who therefore had every reason to invest the maximum financially feasible in both.

As mentioned, physically, a door is an object designed to close a passage, but closing here does not mean locking. Even Reisner's idea that the inside bolt could be closed by pulling a rope still does not lock the door. That means that placing a door in the entrance of the chapel was not only a sign of social standing, it also contained the message that the tranquillity of the tomb should not be violated, just as the message would have been in the residence of the tomb owner when still alive.

Apart from these considerations, the importance of a door was also that it was a requisite to indicate the various aspects of the interface between two adjacent worlds, the one of the dead and that of the living. For this purpose a door considered able to create a connection between these two completely different aspects was placed in the chapel.

This type of door not only marked the place where those living on earth could come into contact with the world on the other side (Figure 5.24 (2)), it also marked the interface with another world, namely the royal palace which was the place where the divine world of the king in his palace came into contact with the world of ordinary people (Figure 5.24(1)). This interface was shown in the *serekh* displaying the name of the king, and where the entrance was a niche acting as a door, just as the false door in the chapel was a niche of the same type. The increasingly lower ceiling of the entrance (see section III of this chapter) is one of the aspects of this special interface.

In the model of Figure 5.24 four interfaces are proposed of which only the numbers 1 and 2 two can be approached from the world of the living. The plan of Figure 5.24 leads to the idea that, in view of the status of the king, in the palace an identical interface between the royal palace and the divine world could have been present (Figure 5.24 (3)). In the world of the dead an interface with the divine world has been depicted in the burial chamber of the pyramid of Unas (V.9).

The observation that doors could be depicted with or without battens is not just an omission or the consequence of an aspective interpretation of the surrounding world; it is the well-thought-out representation of ideas about the underlying meaning of a door. The battens were intended to show the observer that he/she was inside the residence and looking at its entrance, whether it was a house for the living or the door of a cabinet, a naos or a tomb. Battens indicated the inside of the residence, which immediately raises the question from whose point of view this inside was determined. Although it can be observed that there was a high degree of strictness in the application of the placement and consequently the visibility of the battens on the aforementioned objects, the mere existence of that question caused an increasing dualism in their depiction.

False doors can be the actual objects but also depictions on walls or coffins and sarcophagi. On actual false doors battens are not depicted often, which would mean that they were placed on the invisible side of the door, indicating that the chapel is interpreted as the outside world while the interior of the tomb is the residence. The few false doors on which the inner-niche displays battens show that the presence or absence of battens was not of ultimate interest, [81] because both sides of the false door faced a special type of world, the inside faced the world of the dead, the outside faced the chapel which was a kind of 'twilight zone' between the worlds of the living and the dead. In this twilight zone both the living and the deceased could co-exist (see Figure 14.2).

Observation shows that in later periods the visibility of battens could not always be brought into line with the original ideas about their placement. Possibly the presence of battens was increasingly used to just indicate, in case of doubt, that the object depicted was a door, and that the original non-physical meaning of battens had lost importance.

Late in the Old Kingdom the depiction of a ritually significant door in the burial chamber appeared on the inside or the outside of the coffin, but at the same time in some tombs it appeared on the walls of the burial chamber itself, although less frequently than on coffins. Possibly this is subject to a chronological development, at first in the form of a painted compound *serekh* type decoration in the burial chamber of Unas (V.9); somewhat later it was used in a more door-like form in the burial chamber of the tomb of *Mrrw-kꜣ.j* (PM, III/2, 525 – 34) date: VI.E), and still later, exceptionally, in the form of a real monolithic false door in the burial chamber of *Ꞽnty* (date: VI.M) at Abusir. In this tomb the increasing freedom of movement of the *k3* is shown through a direct connection between the chapel and the shaft. This increasing mobility of the *k3* could be the result of the introduction of the cult of Osiris, which claimed that the *k3* of the deceased was reborn and could go to the Field of Rushes or the Field of Offerings, and thus was no longer confined to the tomb.[82]

The possible chronological development of the presence of a false door on the walls of the burial chamber that might be deduced from the data is only indicative because it is based on a relatively small number of tombs. Dawood states that there are only small developments discernible in the burial chamber, notably in architectural design the introduction of the stone lined burial chamber during the early 4th dynasty, and the introduction of decoration on the walls late in the 5th dynasty.[83]

[81] Borchardt, *Denkmäler I*, Plates 1425, 1442, 1455.; Duell, *Mereruka II*, Plates 105a, 107.

[82] Roeten, *Osiris*, 148.

[83] Dawood, *Burial chamber decoration*, 108 – 11.

Chapter Six
Doors, False Doors and Porticos

I. Introduction

In the literature it has always been and still is stated that the false door is the permanent point of contact between the world of the living and the world of the dead, and because the (non-royal) dead was 'living' in the interior of his tomb,[1] it was thus a point of contact with the deceased. The presumption that the deceased is still alive has been put into words in an utterance from the Pyramid Texts:

> '..... *you have not departed dead, you have departed alive.......'* (PT, § 134)

The aim of this part of the study is to find arguments that support the hypothesis that the false door is more than just a point of contact with the deceased; it is also a point of contact with the world he/she is living in.

The false door was the place where offerings were deposited and through which the deceased could enter into the chapel to partake of them.[2] The false door was thus a door uniquely for the benefit of the deceased, the only one who had the power to go through it, although in a magical way.

However, for the Egyptians there were several ways to come into contact with the inhabitants of the world of the dead. One of them was by means of a letter written to the *ꜣḫ* (spirit) of the deceased.[3] This contact was exclusively with deceased members of the direct family (parents, husband, wife, etc.).

> *How are you? Does the Great One look after you according with your wish? Behold, I am the one you loved on earth. Exert yourself on my behalf and speak up for my name. I did not distort any utterance before you, (but) I preserved your name on earth. Keep disease away from my limbs. O, may you be glorious for me (and) before me so that I may see in my dream how you are exerting yourself on my behalf.*
>
> Wente's stele (Michael C. Carlos Museum Nr. 2014.033.001; FIP).[4]

Another means of contact was based on the partial similarity of death and sleep, which were experienced as two states of existence, as two different, yet closely related, worlds.

> *'Turn about, turn about, O, sleeper, turn about in this place......'* (CT I, 306 (spell 74))

If this inference was combined with the similarity of dreaming and the waking state, the conclusion was that during sleep it would be possible to come into close contact with the other world,[5] while this state could also be used to make contact with the deceased in answer to a letter that had been sent.

Figure 6.1 The entrance of the chapel of *Mr-ꜥnḫ.f* (PM, III/1, 278-9) (Hassan, *Giza III*,Plate VII-1); (Figure 6.5-III).

In view of the fact that these forms of contact were considered possible, it must have been feasible for the ancient Egyptians to interpret the contact in front of the false door not only as the deceased coming to

[1] LÄ, VI, 659 – 76, s.v. 'Totenkult, Totenglauben', Part B.

[2] Wiebach, *Scheintür*, 63 – 6. Later in the Old Kingdom occasionally a false door was represented in the burial chamber either as an object (Bárta, *Inty*, Figure 9; Bárta, *Afterlife*) or as a depiction painted on the wall.

[3] Troche, *Letters to the dead.*

[4] 'Stela of Nebetiotef and Letter to the Dead from Merirtyfy to Nebetiotef,' *Michael C. Carlos Museum Collections Online*, accessed September 15, 2018, http://carlos.digitalscholarship.emory.edu/items/show/6914.

[5] LÄ, VI, 745 – 9, s.v. 'Traum', Part A.

the world of the living, but also as the deceased thus opening the way for the living to contact the world on the other side. Some false doors actually show the tomb owner standing in the opening of the door and presenting himself to the world of the living.[6]

The conclusion is that the door, which essentially only notified the existence of a passage for the deceased, had been conceived in a way that indicated that it was interpreted as more than a place of transit intended solely for the deceased. This means that two types of doors were involved in the totality of the mortuary rituals:

- the door in the entrance of the chapel and the doors in the passages between the various rooms in a multi-roomed tomb.
- the false door, which is actually also an entrance.

II. Entrances

II.1. Entrances into chapels

II.1.1. Predynastic period

The simplest chapel entrance possible consists of two jambs supporting a lintel. As already discussed in this study, the Egyptian convictions about after-life required that the name of the deceased would be remembered and this ensured that at least on the lintel the name and possibly some titles of the deceased were mentioned. The early conviction that the deceased lived in the tomb is visible in the close resemblance between the entrance of a predynastic residence found as a house model in el-Amrah and the later developments that eventually led to the true false door (Figure 6.3).[7] The same type of door construction is depicted on a seal dating to the first dynasty, showing a building that resembles the *Pr-wr* (sign O 19), but is the aspective rendition of the *pr-nw* shrine (figure 6.2).[8]

II.1.2. Dynastic period

In the course of time the decoration of the entrances in the tomb became more extensive and other elements were added, but indicating the identity of the tomb owner remained the main purpose of the entrance. In the course of time the main purpose of the lintel became the display of the offering formula and the door jambs and the door roll in the entrance became more important as a place to show name and titles of the tomb owner.

Figure 6.2 Detail of an ivory tablet of king Hor-Aha (I.1). Petrie, *Royal tombs II*, Plate X(2) (for whole tablet: Figure 5.3).

Figure 6.3 Clay model of a predynastic house (Capart, *Primitive art*, Figure 159).

Figure 6.4 The entrance of the chapel of the tomb of *Ḥwtȝ* (PM, III/1, 279); Hassan, *Giza III*, Plate XVIII;[9] (Figure 6.5-II).

However, apart from the 'normal' entrances (Figure 6.5-I), there are some tombs that have a portal of which the design indicates that they convey more than just the idea that a visitor can use it to enter into the chapel.

[6] Der Manuelian, *Redi-nes*; Simpson, *Gmast 2*, Plate XXIX.

[7] Capart, *Primitive art*, Figure 159; Randell, *El Amrah*, 42, Plate X-2.

[8] Petrie, *Courtiers*, Plate III(10).

[9] Harpur, *DETOK*, Figure 22 (page 457); Hassan, *Giza III*, Figure 39, Plate XVIII.

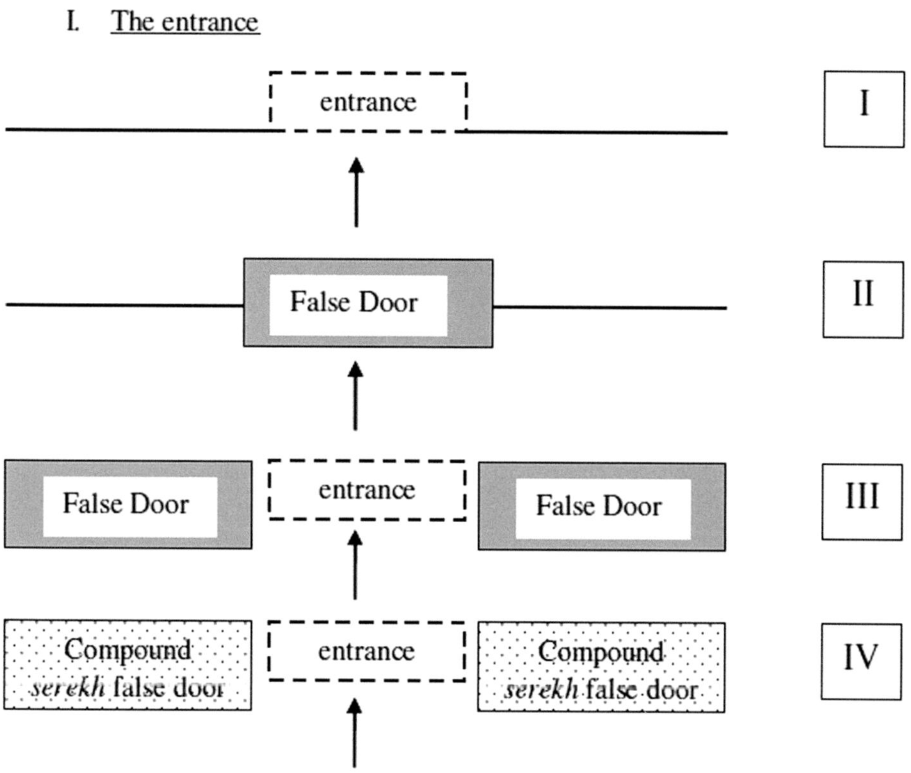

I. The entrance

entrance
I

False Door
II

False Door
entrance
False Door
III

Compound *serekh* false door
entrance
Compound *serekh* false door
IV

Figure 6.5 The configurations of the chapel entrance.

The following configurations are confined to the entrance of the chapel:

1. The door jambs of the entrance of the tomb of *Mr-ʿnḫ.f* (PM, III/1, 278-9) (Figures 6.1 and 6.5-III) are true false doors,[10] both the false doors and the entrance are spanned by an architrave. Both entrance thicknesses represent the tomb owner with his wife receiving visitors and a son facing his parents. The situation in the chapel gives the impression that the decoration was not finished, and it cannot be determined whether the placement of a false door against the western wall was intended.
   Inside a chapel an identical arrangement can exist on its western wall,[11] and in that case the space between the two doors normally was taken up by depictions of the tomb owner, either sitting at the offering table or standing or sitting with members of the family.[12]
2. The entrance of the tomb of *Ḫwfw-ḏd.f* (PM, III/1, 219) (Figures 6.7 and 6.5-IV) has been placed between two *serekh* false doors, and for the door jambs of the entrance of the mastaba of *Sšꜣt-ḥtp* (PM, III/1, 149 – 50) the same type of decoration is used (Figure 6.6).
3. The entrance of the tomb of *Ḫwtꜣ* (PM, III/1, 279) consists of two uninscribed door jambs, supporting the complete paraphernalia of a true false door (Figures 6.4 and 6.5-II).

It is evident that the entrance represented in Figure 6.5-II is not a real entrance but the magical entrance of the false door placed on the eastern exterior wall of the tomb.

II.2. Entrances inside the chapel

During the excavation of the chapel of *ꜣḫtj-mrw-nswt* (PM, III/1, 80 – 1) a statue of the tomb owner was found near the false door in the chapel (Figure 2.2). Next to the portico entrance of the tomb of *Sšm-nfr* [IV] (PM, III/1, 223 – 6) obelisks and statues had been placed,[13] this corroborates the hypothesis that the entrance of the chapel and the false door are equivalent, and that by entering the chapel the visitor comes into a zone between the two separated worlds.

In the chapel itself the situation is different and next to one or two true false doors against the western wall

[10] The same design has been used for the entrance of the chapel of the tomb of *Jy* (Kanawati, *Conspiracies*, Figures 2.9 and 2.10).

[11] Hassan, *Giza VII*, Plate XIX.

[12] Roeten, *Decoration*, 126 – 30.

[13] Giza Archives, AEOS_II_5279.

(Figure 6.9-V), which is the most common feature in the chapel; other arrangements of elements are possible:

1. In the mastaba of *Kꜣpj* the western wall of the recessed chapel has two true false doors and the wall between them is decorated with a *serekh* false door design (Figure 6.9 -VI).[14] The upper architrave extends over both true false doors, thus making the three of them into one cultual unit. This design, but without the architrave over the whole constellation, is also placed on the western wall of the chapel of *Kꜣ.j-swḏꜣ* (PM, III/1, 156; G 5340).[15]
2. In the mastaba of *Nj-mꜣꜥt-Rꜥ* (Roth, *Gmast 6*, Plate 90; G 2097) on the western wall a *serekh* false door is flanked on both sides by a design of antae of the panelling of the palace-façade (Figure 6.9 -VII).[16]
3. Another type of this design consists of two real palace façade panels bordering a *serekh* false door with a deep decorated niche *(Ḫbꜣw-škr,* PM, III/2, 449 – 50; FS 3073; Bárta, *Abusir XIX*, Plate 32).
4. In the rock-cut tomb of *Ḥmt-Rꜥ* (PM, III/1, 243-4; G 8464) the true false door has a palace façade panelling on both sides.[17]

Figure 6.6 The entrance of the mastaba of *Sšꜣt-ḥtp* (PM, III/1, 149 – 50);[18] (photo author); (Figure 6.5-IV).

5. The rock-cut tomb of *Jwn-Mnw* (PM, III/1, 237; G 8080) has an undecorated interior portico chapel with an architrave supported by two pillars. The western wall has a *serekh* type false door flanked by palace façade panelling. The *serekh* type false door is a real opening into an unfinished room that originally might have been planned as the chapel (Figure 6.8 (top)).[19]
6. The temple of the queen's pyramid III-c of the pyramid of Menkaure (IV.5) the entrance into the chapel is flanked by two compound *serekh* false doors (Figure 6.8 (under)).[20]

Figure 6.7 The entrance of the chapel of the tomb of *Ḫwfw-ḏd.f* (PM, III/1, 219) Junker, *Giza X*, Figures 23, 24; Plate IVa; (Figure 6.5-IV).(Photo author).

Other combinations do occur as in the chapel in the mastaba of *Ptḥ-ḥtp* [II], (PM, III/2, 600 – 5, plan LX, 20, 22). Against the south side of the western wall a true false door is placed, while the northern door is of the *serekh* type; in between the two doors an offering table scene is surrounded by offerings, offering bearers and an offering list.[21]

In Figure 6.9 items VII and VIII show that a true and a *serekh* false door are functionally identical, because both can serve as a passage, a conclusion that is in line with the conclusion reached in chapter V, section III.1 that the two types of false doors are based on the same fundamental idea.[22] The configuration of Figure 6.5-III and the western wall of the chapel with the two false doors united by an architrave (Figure 6.9-VI) are each other's equivalent.[23] In the chapel the combination Figure 6.9-VI serves as an entrance into an environment

14 Roth, *Gmast 6*, 99, Plate 53b/c, 54, G 2091.

15 Junker, *Giza VII*, Figures 68 and 69, Plate XXXVa.

16 Roth, *Gmast 6*, Plate 90. It has to be taken into account that a palace façade panelling is an item of decoration and *not* a false door.

17 Borchardt, *Denkmäler I*, 1380.

18 Kanawati, *Giza II*, Plate 41.

19 Reisner, *Giza I*, Figure 127.

20 Reisner, *Mycerinus*, Plan IV.

21 www.osirisnet.net Akhethotep and Ptahhotep (II), page 3.

22 This conclusion is corroborated by the false door in the tomb of *Pḥn-wj-kꜣ.j* (PM, III/2, 491 – 2). This door has two jambs on every side of the central opening, the outer one being a jamb of 'standard' design, the inner one of *serekh* design (LD, *II*, 48).

23 Hassan, *Giza V*, Figure 126.

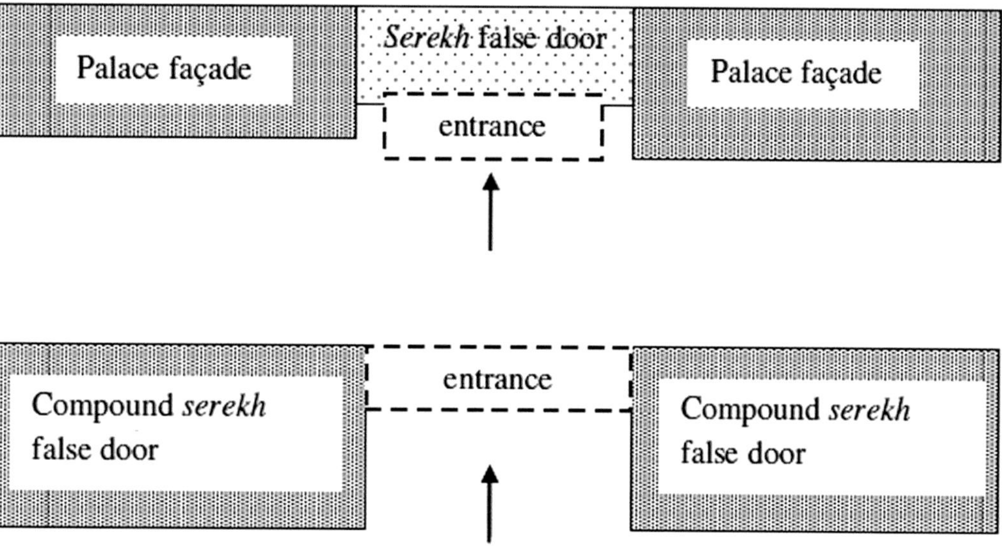

Figure 6.8 Divergent configurations of interior chapel(?) entrances.

II. The false door(s)

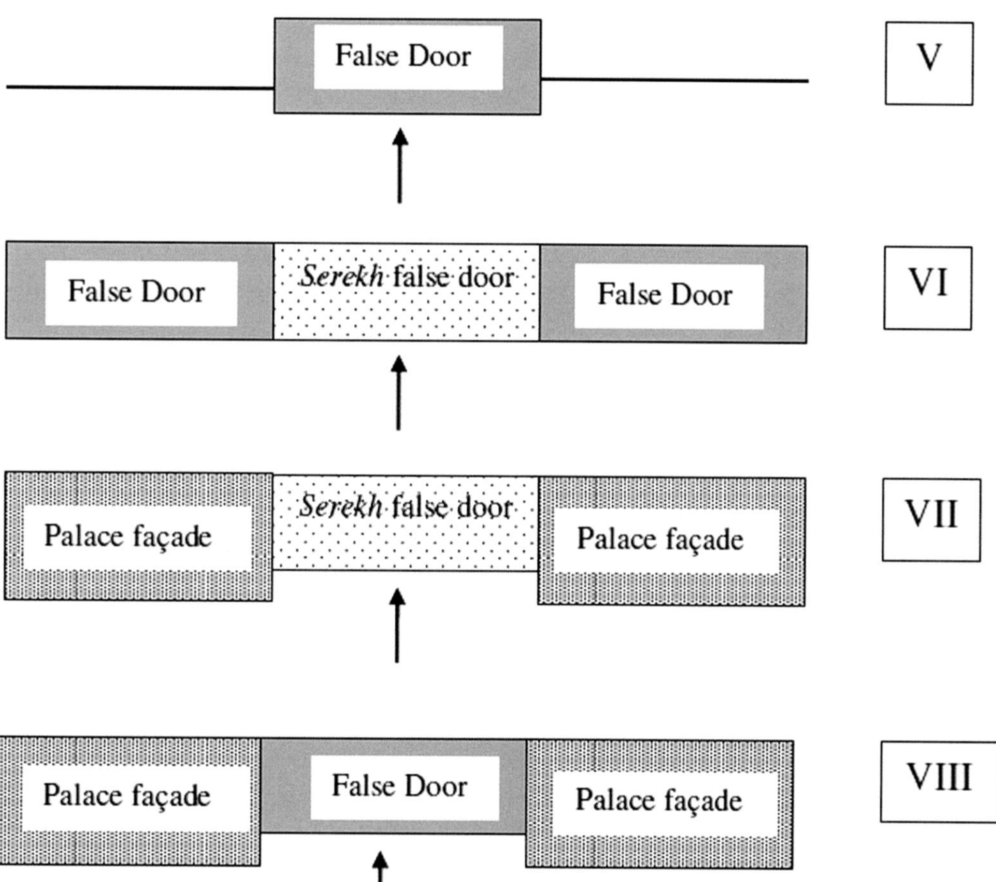

Figure 6.9 The configurations on the western wall of the chapel.

with a completely different meaning;[24] consequently, the same must be valid for the combination 6.5-III, which is used as the entrance into the chapel itself, and which means that on doing so the visitor comes into the same transitional world (Figure 14.2).

In some rock-cut tombs in the central field of the Giza Plateau chapels have been hewn out in the quarry walls in which the situation on the western wall differs in one aspect from the arrangements that are shown in Figure 6.9.

The decoration of the western wall of the chapel of *Nb-m-ꜣḫt* (PM, III/1, 230 – 2) consists of a central *serekh* false door flanked by two niches with two true false doors in each of them.[25] This is an arrangement that is equivalent to the one in Figure 6.9-VI, except that the magical inner passage of the *serekh* false door here is the real opening of a small niche of which Jánosi states that a statue was placed in it.

In these examples the entrance configurations clearly indicate that by passing through them the visitor not only entered into the chapel, but also into a world that differed from the outside world whence he came. This world was *not* the world of the dead, but it was a transitional world that differed from the outside world in so far that in some tombs the visitor was asked in a text, specially placed near the entrance, to be pure of body when he/she intended to enter into the chapel.

> *The unique friend, much loved, steward of the palace, chief of the king's barbers, ritualistic priest, Ṯjj, he says: All people who will enter into this (my) tomb of eternity unclean because they have eaten of the abominable things which repel a mind which has arrived in the necropolis, not being pure at the appropriate time, as they must be to penetrate into the god's temple........*
>
> Entrance passage of the mastaba of *Ṯjj* (PM, III/2, 468 – 78).

Although the number of tombs that have chapel entrance configurations that differ from the 'standard' (6.5-I) is small, the mere fact that these forms exist proves that, within the total context, their underlying considerations were within the span of mortuary convictions and were accepted as such.

II.3. Serdab 'entrances'

Without going further into religious backgrounds, a serdab is a place where one or more statues of the tomb owner are placed, sometimes accompanied by those of members of the family and servants. In most tombs

Figure 6.10 Reconstruction of the serdab room in the tomb of *Sšm-nfr* [II] (PM, III/1, 146 - 8) Junker, *Giza III*, Figure 34.

these serdabs are rooms completely closed to the outer world, although in some tombs the interior is exposed by way of a squint.[26]

In the mortuary monument of *Sšm-nfr* [II] (PM, III/1, 146 – 8; G 5080) south of the main body of the mastaba a hall had been constructed that was especially meant for serdabs. In the walls of this hall several spaces had been constructed that served as serdabs, each one of them being closed with a dummy door (Figure 6.10). The battens of the doors were directed to the hall, a situation that closely resembles the circumstances during the transport of statues as part of the funerary ceremonies and that have been discussed in chapter III.[27] The placement of the doors and the statues in relation to each other is identical and here too indicates that on opening the door the tomb owner is invited into the world of the living in order to receive offerings.

Serdabs are often placed in the close vicinity of the chapel, either south or west of it,[28] and the monuments of both *Sšm-nfr*'s are in accordance with this, while in some of the tombs the serdab next to the chapel is connected to it by means of a slit.

In the southern wall of the chapel of *Ṯntj* [I] (RC-tomb, eastern escarpment Giza Plateau),[29] a door has been cut, with its battens visible and embedded in a palace façade

---

[24] Hassan, *Giza II*, Figure 237.

[25] Jánosi, *Giza*, Figures 90, 91.

[26] Junker, *Giza III*, 199; Figure 36. The mastaba of *Sšm-nfr* [III] (PM, III/1, 153 – 4; G 5170) has a room surrounded by three large serdabs, each of them having several squints. A famous serdab with a replica of the original statue in it is situated next to the chapel in the tomb of *Ṯjj* (PM, III/2, 468 – 78) at Saqqara.

[27] Fischer, *Varia nova*, Figure 12.

[28] Warden, *Serdab*, in Figure 4 three types of serdab placements are close to the chapel (A, B and E). In Chart 2 (page 480) these three types make up for 89% of the serdabs included in the catalogue of Table 1.

[29] LD, *Textband I*, 86.

panelling.[30] The excavation report states that the door has two false doors next to it, but in reality the door is flanked on both sides by palace façade panelling.

III. False door versus portico

III.1. The transformation from a false door to a portico entrance

A group of chapels with another form of entrance are the ones with a portico (see Chapter IX), which cannot be considered to be just the result of a wish to build an entrance that distinguished itself from the others. It not only stresses the house concept of the tomb, but it also has a special meaning within the context of the chapel and its two types of entrances (the entrance into the chapel and the false door(s)). This is evident in the chapel of *Mrsw-ꜥnḫ* (PM, III/1; 269 – 70) where the false door is constructed in the form of a portico,[31] with the false door placed in the middle entrance between the pillars and the figures of the tomb owner on them directed toward the door (due to the fact that there is no real room behind the door, the definition given in table of Figure 9.1 for this situation is 'portico chapel'. Although this false door configuration appears to be unique, the fact that it exists shows its acceptation within the mortuary traditions.

Figure 6.11 False door in the chapel of *ꜣḫtj-ḥtp* (PM, III/1; 284); Hassan, *Giza, I*, Figure, 142; Plate L.

Because the deceased is supposed to live in the tomb, a portico can be seen as the earthly realisation of the front of the imaginary house of a member of the higher social stratum.[32] The number of tombs that really have a portico is relatively small;[33] which is surprising in view of the large quantity of tombs that can be ascribed to persons who were socially important enough to qualify for this type of house.

Even if a tomb does not have a real portico or has a portico that does not give access to a room behind it, the false door, which is the entrance into the house of the deceased, is present, whatever its form.

A further study of the structure and decorative directionality of false doors indicates that they can easily be converted into a portico entrance.

The schematic representation of the false door of *ꜣḫtj-ḥtp* (PM, III/1; 284) (Figure 6.11) can serve as an example of this transformation. Although the total design of the offering place in this chapel is of a certain complexity and has a striking resemblance with a portico entrance, the design of the false door itself is basic. It consists of two jambs on both sides of the door opening, two architraves and a panel.

This not too complicated door design can itself be 'translated' into a portico with two pillars and a simple shallow recess in the western wall (Figure 6.12).[34]

The conclusion is that this door, and with it all the false doors of this simplified design, can be traced back to a single recessed niche situated in the back wall of a portico, acting as the entrance into the interior of an elite residence, preceded by two pillars. In the same way the three-jamb false door can also be transformed into a portico entrance, giving rise to a portico of which also the side walls are decorated (Figure 6.13).

III.2. The false door and the house model

The close connection between the false door and the portico entrance is apparent in the crude clay models of the front of elite residences that have been excavated in the cemetery of Rifeh, and which W. M. Petrie called 'soul houses'. In this study they will be referred to as 'house models', and they can be dated to the First Intermediary Period and the Middle Kingdom.[35] These

30 Kormysheva, *Lepsius,* Figure 11. Figures 8 and 11 show that a palace façade panelling has been placed on the western wall embedding both false doors; on the southern wall a door is surrounded by what appears to be a palace façade panelling, probably indicating a serdab. In Figure 11 in front of the southern wall two pairs of holes in the floor indicate the presence of now lost offering basins; if these were meant for offering rituals in front of the false doors, the basins are strangely displaced with respect to them. The latter observation makes it more likely that the basins were meant for offering rituals in front of the door, forming a virtual connection between the serdab and the chapel.

31 Another example of this type of design of the western wall is the chapel of *Dꜣg* (PM, III/1, 271).

32 Junker, *Giza VI*, 84 ; Hayes, *Scepter I*, Figure 169.

33 For a catalogue of tombs with this type of entrance see Chauvet, *Portico-chapels*, 297 – 311.

34 Another example of this type of false door is that of *Mṯṯj* (PM, III/2, 646 – 8), MET (New York), 64.100 (Kaplony, *Methethi*, Figure 9).

35 LÄ, II, 1067 – 8, s.v. 'Hausmodelle'. Petrie, *Gizeh and Rifeh*, 16 dates the models from the 6th dynasty to well into the 12th dynasty. The model house that had been found in el-Amrah and that can be dated to the predynastic period (Nagada II), can be interpreted as

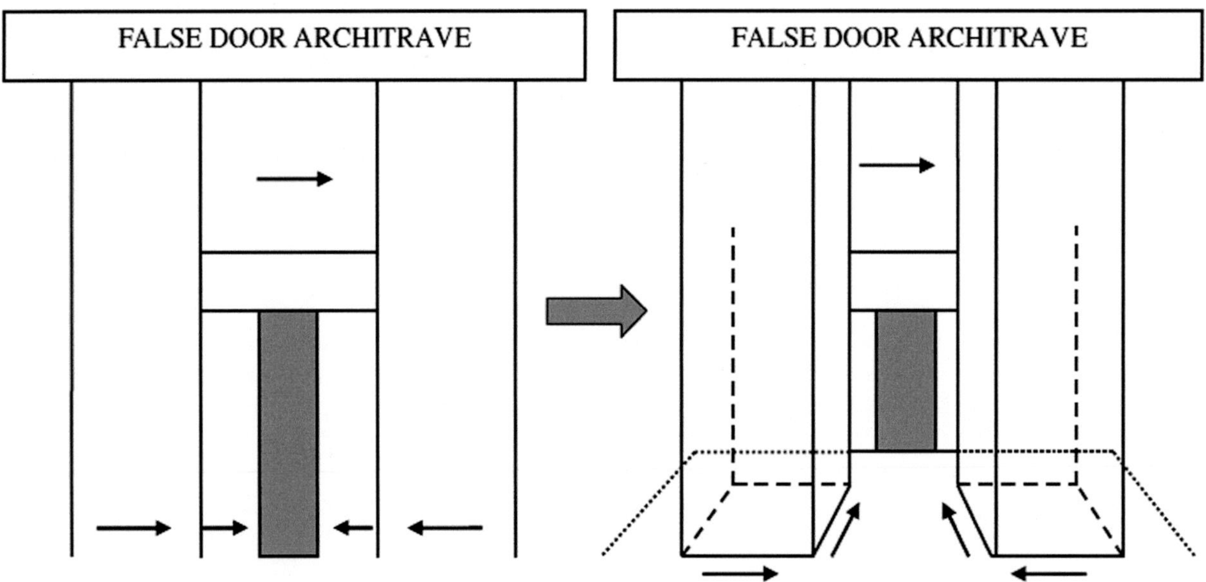

Figure 6.12 The transformation of a standard two-jamb false door into a portico entrance.

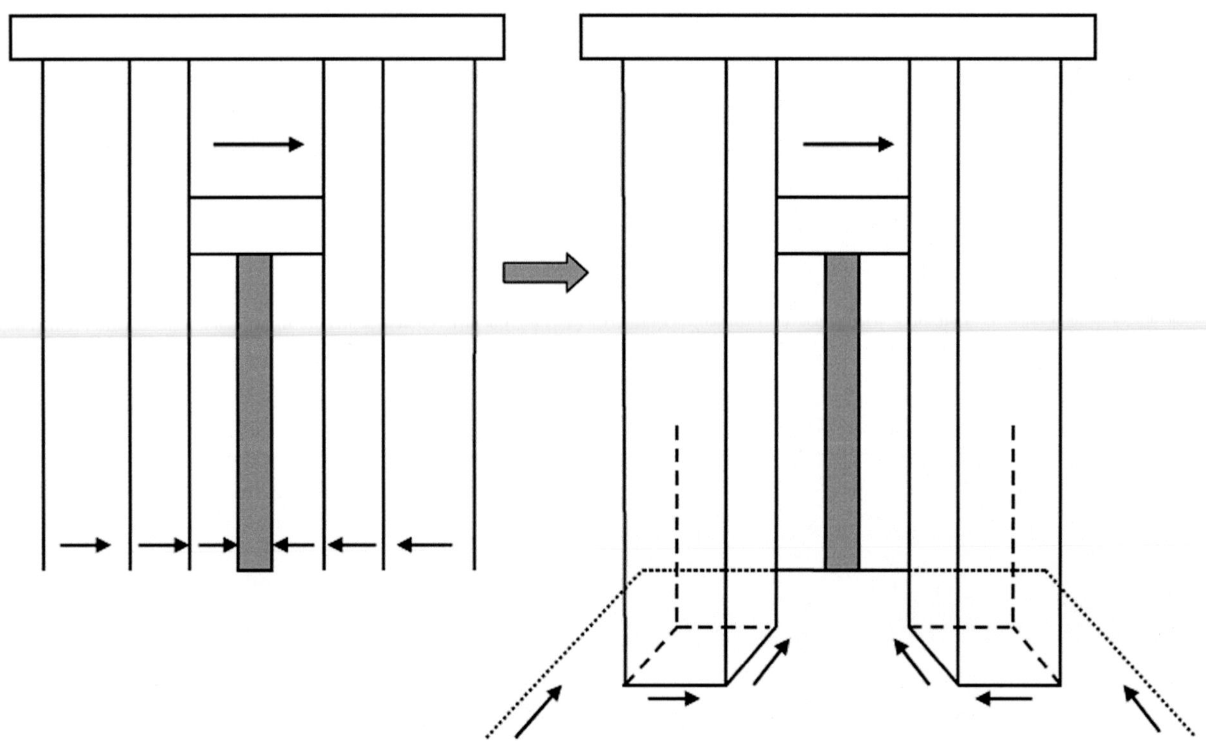

Figure 6.13 The transformation of a three-jamb false door into a portico entrance.

models have been excavated at El-Kab and Ballas too;[36] they come in the form of an offering tray (British Museum, EA 32610) or as a residence with a pillared portico (KMKG, E.3175). In the second group most of these models have the pillared portico entrance depicted with a libation basin in front of it, sometimes the holes for posts supporting a type of roof over the basin are evident (Figure 6.14).[37] The entrance into

the representation of an abode for the *k3* of the deceased, while the models from the later period show the inviting function that they have performed.

[36] Quibell, *El Kab*, Plate V(4); Petrie, *Naqada, Ballas*, Plate XLIV(4)

[37] Petrie, *Gizeh and Rifeh*, 15, Plate XV. The basin and the poles are interpreted as the presentation of a water tank with its sun shade.

the dwelling is normally closed and represented as a door made of vertical boards scratched in the clay; [38] however, there are also models in which the door is open and shown hanging next to the entrance.[39]

The excavation report of Flinders Petrie states that the models were found standing at the level of the grave-pit, at its northern side and with the opening of the model in the direction of the deceased.[40]

The excavator also remarked that the site in which they were found was particularly beneficial for maintaining this type of artefact. It is clear that this observation does not prohibit the possibility that these artefacts originally could have been included in older or contemporaneous cemeteries too, but the circumstances being less favourable there, they did not 'survive' the devastations caused by time.

Similar models have been found by Quibell in El-Kab, and apparently based on the remark 'They are only known in the Middle Kingdom,...', the excavator dated them to the 12th dynasty.[41]

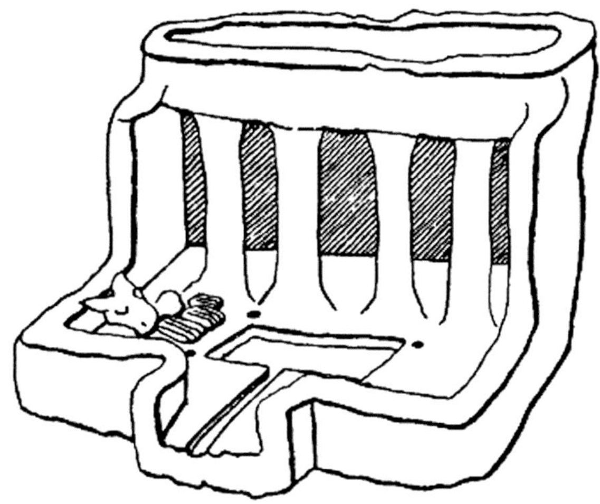

Figure 6.14 A "soul-house", from Kuentz, *Bassins,* Figure 10 (after Petrie, *Gizeh and Rifeh,*Plate XV).

The chronological development of the use of the portico as an architectural element in the design of the tomb is shown in Figure 6.15.[42]

This diagram shows that in the period V.L a marked decline occurred in the use of the portico entrance in the Memphite necropoleis. The diminution in the number of portico entrances might be attributed to the growing influence of the Osiris cult, which meant that from the period V.L on the tomb was to a decreasing degree seen as a house for the *k3* of the deceased. Due to the consideration that it is unlikely that in the course of the First Intermediate Period the spread of the Osiris cult had yet reached the provinces, the conclusion is that the emergence and spread of the Osiris cult cannot be directly involved in the appearance of house models as grave goods. This is supported by the observation that, although the diagram in Figure 6.15 shows a decline for the Memphite area, the use of the portico entrance was continued in the provincial necropoleis.[43]

> *'That they were not oftener placed on the east side, and facing the east, like the ordinary tables of offering of earlier times, shows how greatly they had departed from the original conception, and how they had become dwellings for the soul rather than places of sacrifice for the living.'*
>
> W. M. Flinders Petrie,'*Gizeh and Rifeh*' (London, 1907), 15.

Within the interconnectivity network that has been developed in this study this citation would mean that, in this type of poor graves; the house model represented the portico entrance of a residence and thus served as a false door. This, due to this equivalence of the portico and the false door, and contrary to what is concluded in the citation, enabled the visitors to contact the *k3* of the deceased and to bring offerings. This conclusion is supported by the observation that a basin with a spout and piles of food stuff was depicted (Figure 6.14).

However, regarding the house models, the following considerations have to be taken into account:

- To my knowledge, house models have not been excavated in the Memphite necropoleis.
- The diagram in Figure 6.16 shows that in the period V.L the use of the Memphite necropoleis began to decline.
- This type of tomb has also been constructed in provincial cemeteries and can be dated to a period well after the apparent disappearance of the portico entrance in the Memphite area.

That such a tank would be placed in the courtyard is plausible, but it would not be standing in front of the main entrance of the residence. In the model in the Museum of Brussels (KMKG no. E 3176) the tank is depicted standing at the side of the courtyard. This means that in the model the lowered section of the floor of the courtyard has another meaning than just a water reservoir.

38 Petrie, *Gizeh and Rifeh,* Plate XVIII, nr. 107.

39 Petrie, *Gizeh and Rifeh,* Plate XVIII, nr. 80.

40 Thus placing the house with its closed side against the prevailing wind.

41 Quibell, *El Kab,* 18, Plate V(4).

42 This diagram is based on the catalogue given in Chauvet, *Portico-chapels,* 297 – 311.

43 11th dynasty, El-Tarif; 17 – 21th dynasty, Beni Hassan.

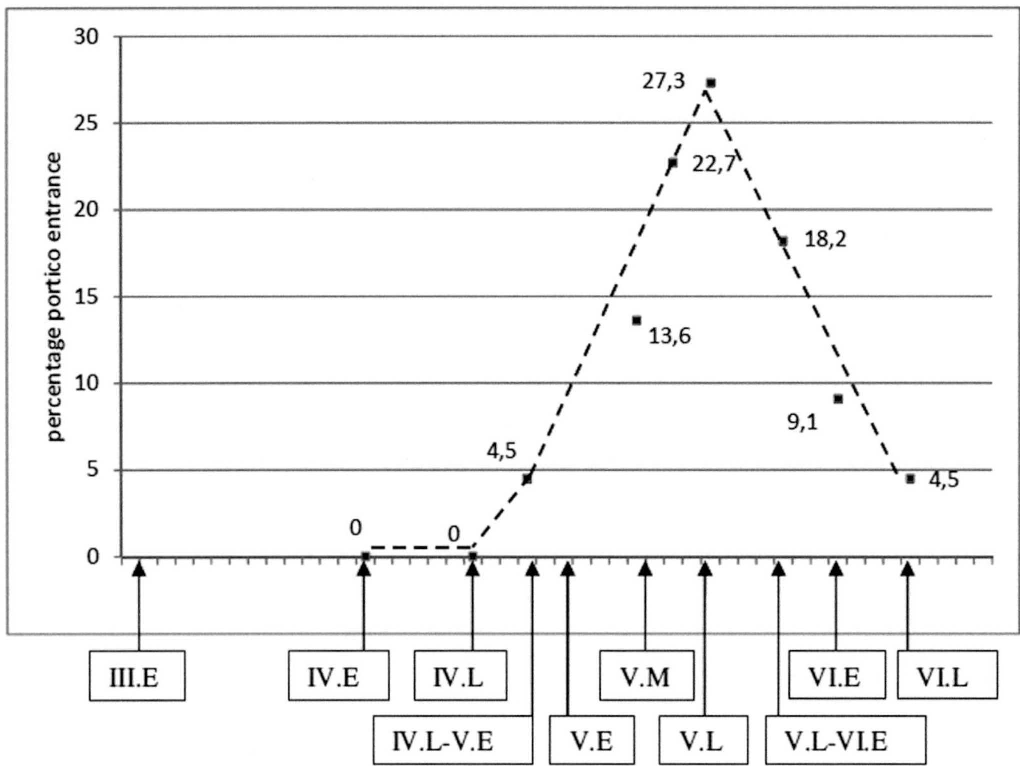

Figure 6.15 The chronological development of the use of the portico entrance in the Memphite necropoleis.

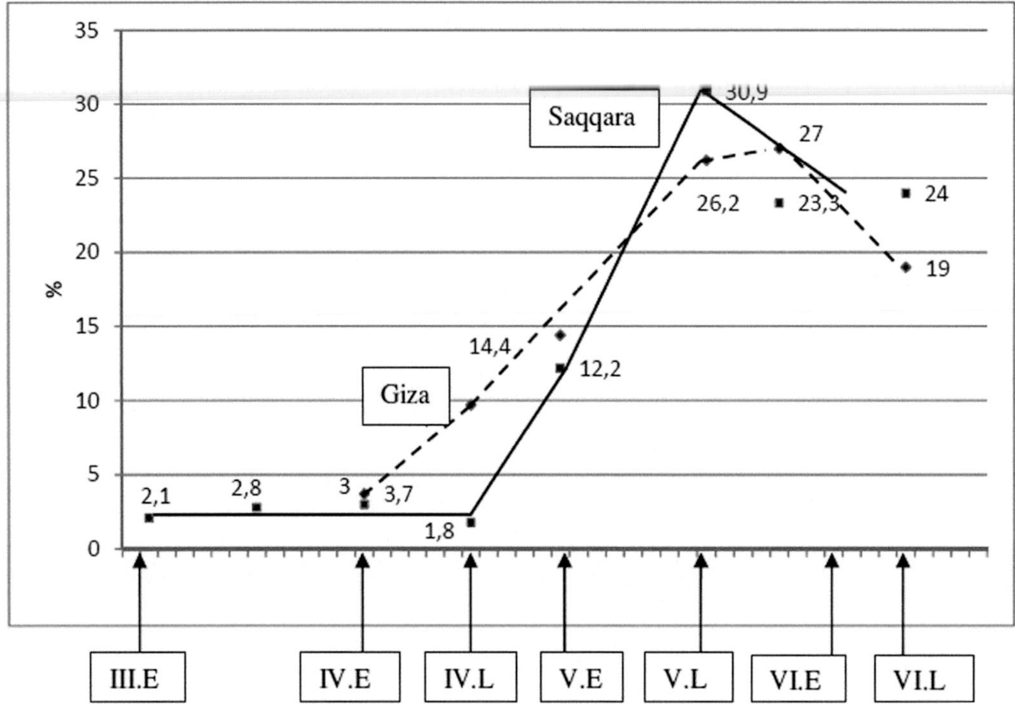

Figure 6.16 The chronological development of the occupation percentage in the necropoleis of Giza and Saqqara (from PM, III/1 and PM, III/2).

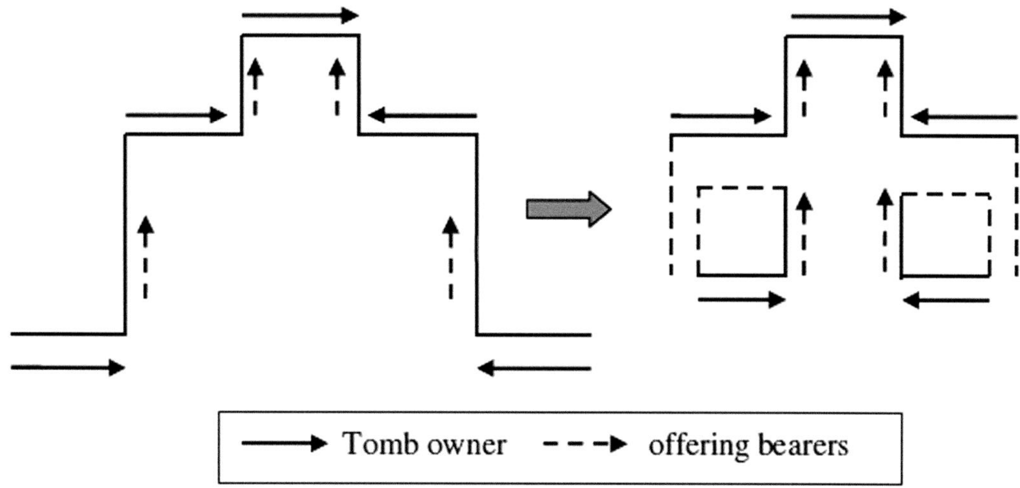

Figure 6.17 Transformation of the double niche of *Jj-nfr* (PM, III/2, 894; IV.E).[47] (ratio of the dimensions according to Alexanian, *Netjeraperef*, Figure 20).

- Already in the course of the 6th dynasty the administrative and governmental power of the nomes under their respective nomarchs belonging to rich and influential families, started to grow. Increasingly they were buried in the necropoleis of their capitals, buried within their own funerary customs and in tombs with their own architecture.

The seemingly sudden and one-time appearance of the house models would indicate that they cannot be placed in the (hypothetical) line of a chronological development that runs from the portico tombs in the Memphite area to the provincial necropoleis.

Bárta proposes to explain such a sudden appearance with a mechanism borrowed from evolutionary biology and called 'Punctuated Equilibrium'.[44] This mechanism is based on the premise that development does not necessarily follow a smooth, uninterrupted line, but that a set of observations indicating shifts can also be explained by a chain of steady states connected by points of sudden change. Such a point in the flow of time acts as the direct cause of the 'sudden' occurrence of a whole set of consequences.

The proposed disruption of the steady state would be initiated by the sudden strong tendency of the 6th dynasty kings to marry members of provincial families, and the concomitant increase of the latter's local power. This in turn led to provincial autonomy in important cultural expressions, one of them being mortuary architecture.[45] In the provinces the portico-colonnade design of the tombs of their rulers increased in importance and was in fact taking over the line of development of the cemeteries of the Memphite area. The house models found in Rifeh could have been a secondary effect of this.

The conclusion as to whether or not a disruption of steady state or a continuous flow is the prime operator here depends on the appearance of contemporaneous house models in other cemeteries than that of Rifeh.

IV. The niches

IV.1. General considerations

The niches in the chapel of *Ḥsjj-Rʿ* (PM, III/2, 437 – 9; date III.E) can be interpreted as double recessed with the tomb owner appearing on the wooden panels that were placed in the recess at the back that served as the magical door opening (see Figure 7.3).

The southern niche of the mastaba of *Nṯr-ʿpr.f* in Dahschur (mastaba II/1) has one more recess than the niche represented in Figure 6.17, and would be a 'triple recessed niche', yet, it is interpreted as a double niche because the first recess is separated from the two inner niches by means of a small step;[46] in addition, the dimensions of the front niche are out of proportion with those of the other niches. The configuration can be interpreted as an 'open space' with a step leading to a double recessed niche.[47]

The offering places in the mastabas of *Nfrj* (PM, III/1, 50 – 1) and *Nj-ḥtp- Ḫnmw* (PM, III/1, 50), although both

[44] Bárta, *Punctuated equilibrium.*

[45] Papazian, *Eights dynasty*, 410.

[46] Alexanian, *Netjer-aperef*, Plate 8b.

[47] Alexanian, *Netjer-aperef*, Figure 20.

[48] Alexanian, *Netjer-aperef*, Plate 14 – 6.

Reign	Without cavetto cornice		With cavetto cornice	
	Two-jamb	Three-jamb	Two-jamb	Three-jamb
Sneferu				
Khufu				
Radjedef				
Rakhaef				
Menkaure				
Shepseskaf				
Userkaf				
Sahure				
Neferirkare				
Shepseskare				
Raneferef				
Niuserre				
Menkauhor				
Djedkare				
Unas				
Teti				
Userkare				
Pepy I				
Merenre				
Pepy II				

Figure 6.18 The chronological development of the types of false doors (from Wiebach, *Scheintür,* Table I)

dating from a later period (PM: V.M or later),[49] are double recessed niches with a decoration that has the same directionality as that in Figure 6.17.[50]

Discussing the basic ideas concerning the chapel in the tomb the conclusion has been that in fact it is a transitional world between those of the living and the dead, while in most cases the false door could be translated as a portico entrance into the residence of the deceased elite tomb owner (Figure 6.21). Because a portico entrance has a courtyard in front of it, the purpose of the chapel can be considered to be that of a courtyard. The resemblance between the chapel and the courtyard goes even further because both of them have depictions of the inviting tomb owner on the entrance thicknesses.[51]

Without going into the reliability of the dating system described by Rusch,[52] it can be concluded from the scheme of false door forms that can be designated,[53] that the two-jamb false door is introduced in the middle of the 4th dynasty, while the three-jamb door is introduced around the middle of the 5th dynasty. In Figure 6.18 the chronological development of the types of false doors is represented.[54]

49 Harpur, *DETOK, Nfrj* V.8L – 9M this is corroborated by the length of the loaves as recalculated from Abu-Bakr, *Giza,* Plate XXXI (Roeten, *Osiris,* Figure 59); *Nj-ḥtp- H̱nmw* V.6 – VI. For the latter the date given by Harper and PM is not in accordance with the dating criteria as given in Roeten, *Osiris.* The length of the loaves is 10%, indicating that their length had been reduced possibly due to the text that was placed above them. The number of loaves is eight, indicating IV.E at the latest. The woman is holding the lotus which indicates a period up to V.L (the loop in the stem has no dating significance (Harpur, *DETOK,* 134)). This means that a date of V.L might be proposed, which would make the two tombs contemporaneous.

50 Abu-Bakr, *Giza,* Plates VIII, XXIX; Cherpion, *Mastabas,* Plate 4.

51 For the courtyard of a portico entrance see Ṯtw (PM, III/1, 66 – 7) in Simpson, *Gmast 4,* Plate 11.

52 Rusch, *Grabsteinformen.* Wiebach, *Scheintür,* 19 – 21.

53 Wiebach, *Scheintür,* Table I, Plates I and II.

54 Examples of three-jamb false doors are: *Kꜣ-gm-nj* (PM, III/2, 521 -5); *Mmrw-kꜣ.j* (PM, III/2, 525 – 34), both in the Teti-cemetery at Saqqara. In the mastaba of *Kꜣr* (Bárta, *Abusir XIII*) the false door in the first chapel he had constructed is a two-jamb door without a cavetto cornice. Once promoted to the vizierate, he had a second chapel constructed in the mastaba, also equipped with a two-jamb false door but this one *with* a cavetto cornice (Bárta, *Abusir XIII,*

The cavetto cornice is introduced in the later part of the 5th dynasty and has no obvious influence on the portico interpretation of the two- or three- jamb false door.[55] The introduction of the cornice and moulding together with the three-jamb door might have to do with the growing wealth and hereditary power of certain families visible in the large mastabas around the pyramids of the last kings of the 5th dynasty and the first king of the 6th dynasty. In the later periods of the Old Kingdom the false doors became more complex, an example being that the false door complete with cavetto cornice was placed in an enveloping stone edge that resembled a naos.[56]

This also means that the later, more and more complex forms of the elements of the false door around the central door opening still do nothing more than stressing the presence and place of the single recessed entrance, and as a side-effect, showing the wealth of the tomb owner and the family.[57]

IV.2. The single recessed niche

The single recessed niche is a form of niche that cannot itself be transformed into a portico, thus indicating that it is the 'ultimate' and basic entrance; while this transformation into a portico is already feasible with the next step in the development, the double recessed niche (Figures 6.17 and 6.21).

Apart from the fact that this type of niche represents a phase in the development of the design of the offering place,[58] the single recessed niche certainly cannot not be interpreted as an offering place for the lowest social classes (Figure 6.19), as its design was also used in early elite tombs. However, the material used for the construction of the niche certainly gives an indication of the social class of the deceased and her/his family.[59] An example are the niches of *Shrj* (PM, III/2, 490; date IV) and *Ṯtj* (PM, III/1, 302; date V or VI),[60] which both were executed in stone with relief decoration.[61]

The one-jamb false door and the single recessed niche are closely connected, and both remained in use; in this the economic decline that took place throughout the Old Kingdom and that had started already during the early dynastic period in all probability has played a role.[62]

The importance of the single recessed niche is underlined by the development of the chapels of the elite mastabas in the necropolis of Maidum which culminated in the installation of cruciform chapels, but ended, possibly due to royal intervention, with the reinstatement of the single recessed niche.[63]

Figure 6.19 Lower social class mud-brick mastaba with some single recess false doors (Junker, *Giza IX*, Figure XIXc).

IV.3. The shaft niche of ꜣIntj at Abusir

During the excavation of the mastaba of *ꜣIntj* at Abusir a connection was found between a double recessed niche that was placed at the top of the burial shaft and a door, giving access to the chapel and situated nearly at the same level as the niche. In front of the southern wall of the chapel two pairs of holes in the floor indicate the presence of now lost offering basins; if these were meant for offering rituals in front of the false doors, in that case the basins are strangely placed with respect to them. This makes it more likely that the basins were meant for offering rituals in front of the door,[64] which

Figures 5.3.1. and 5.3.9.). This might indicate that the cavetto cornice had a connection with the wealth and the social status of the family. According to Figure Annex 9 the introduction of the cavetto cornice can be dated around the reign of Teti (VI.1) and this is acceptable within the chronological concordance of the false doors with and without cavetto cornice in the mastaba of *Kꜣr*.

[55] Concerning the function of the addition of the cavetto cornice several hypotheses have been forwarded; a discussion of these is beyond the scope of this study.

[56] Borchardt, *Denkmäler I*, Plate 14 (no. 1395) and Plate 18 (no. 1409).

[57] The false door in room A 8 of the mastaba of *Mrrw-kꜣ.j* (PM, III/2, 525 – 34) has a torus moulding (Duell, *Mereruka I*, Plate 62). The cornice is no longer present.

[58] Der Manuelian, *Wadi cemetery*, Figure 11 (Giza archives photos C10392 and C10391)). In a later period in the same cemetery the mud-brick mastaba with a double recessed southern niche and a single recessed northern niche appeared.

[59] Handoussa, *Abu Bakr cemetery*, Figure on page 36. The tomb was a small mud-brick construction, the burial was contracted and without grave goods, a basin was placed in front of the two narrow niches.

[60] Cherpion, *Mastabas*, Plates, 24 and 32. For the niche of *Ṯtj* the number of loaves indicates a date of IV.M or later, and their length indicates a date IV.L-V.E (Roeten, *Osiris*, Figures 47 and 55).

[61] Cherpion, *Mastabas*, Plate 24; there dated to the middle 2nd dynasty.

[62] Roeten, *Economic decline*.

[63] Reisner, Tomb development, 222.

[64] Bárta, *Afterlife*, 5, Figures 1 and 2. In Bárta, *Inty*, Figure 2 the stele in the shaft has been added in the plan.

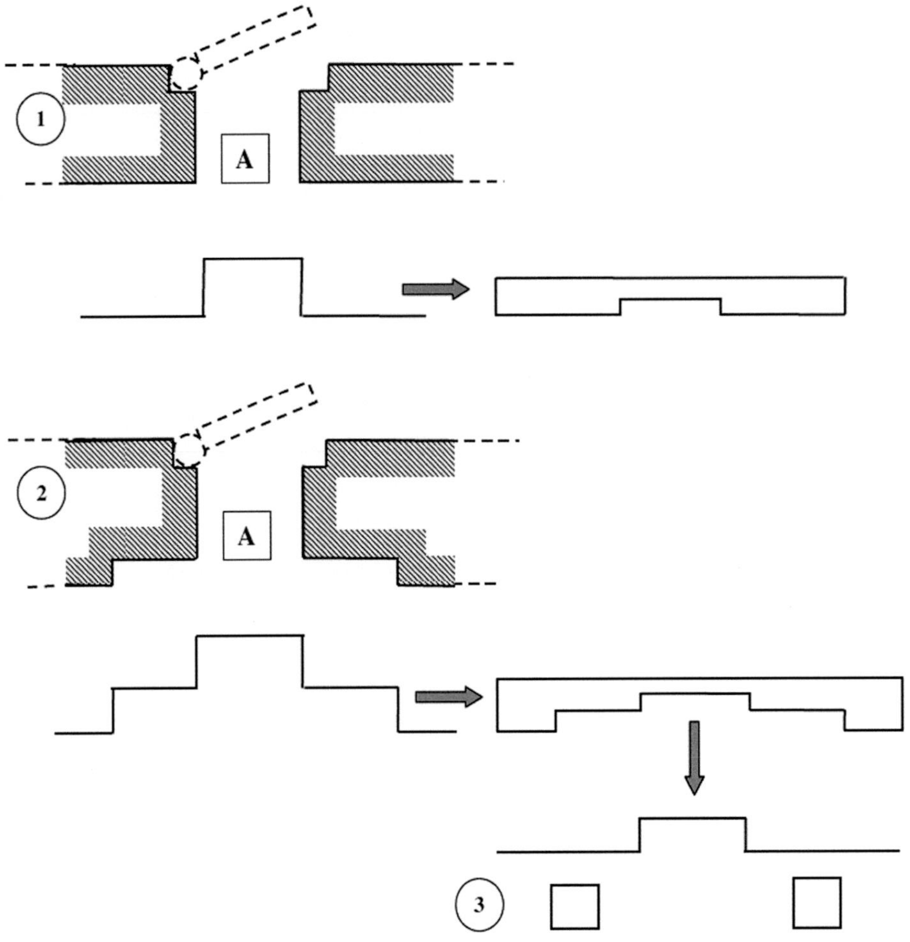

Figure 6.20 The transformation of the chapel entrance.

suggests this door was more important than the false door against the western wall. Furthermore, inside the burial chamber a false door facing the entrance had been placed against the sarcophagus. The explanation given by the excavators is that this unprecedented situation is a necessity for the soul of the deceased to reach the other parts of the mortuary monument, and that the false door has been placed against the sarcophagus in order to enable the *k3* to go in and out of it.[65]

Although the false door placed against the sarcophagus could be seen as the precursor of the ones that were painted on coffins in a later period (and during a short period on the western wall of the burial chamber), a few arguments can be considered against this:

– It does not explain the sudden necessity of a connection between the shaft and the chapel, because either it raises the question of why a long existent idea of communication within the mortuary monument had to be converted to physical reality. Would this imply that until the 6th dynasty the *k3* of the deceased would have been locked up in the burial chamber? That in its turn would make the presence of the offering place and the chapel in the superstructure needless.
– Neither does it explain why for a longer period of time it was so important that the burial chamber was close to the offering place in the chapel, in some tombs even at the expense of long underground corridors.[66] Yet the close vicinity of the chapel and the burial chamber was not an absolutely binding rule.
– It does not explain whether the 'real' false door still had the function of a passage for the *k3* of the deceased, or both doors in the chapel had this function. Neither does it explain whether or not offerings were brought to both doors.

All three niches in this tomb are double recessed, and can be either an offering place or a passage (Figure

[65] Bárta, *Funerary rites*, 21 – 2.

[66] Mastaba of *Q3r* (Bárta, *Abusir XIII*, Figure 5.2.2.

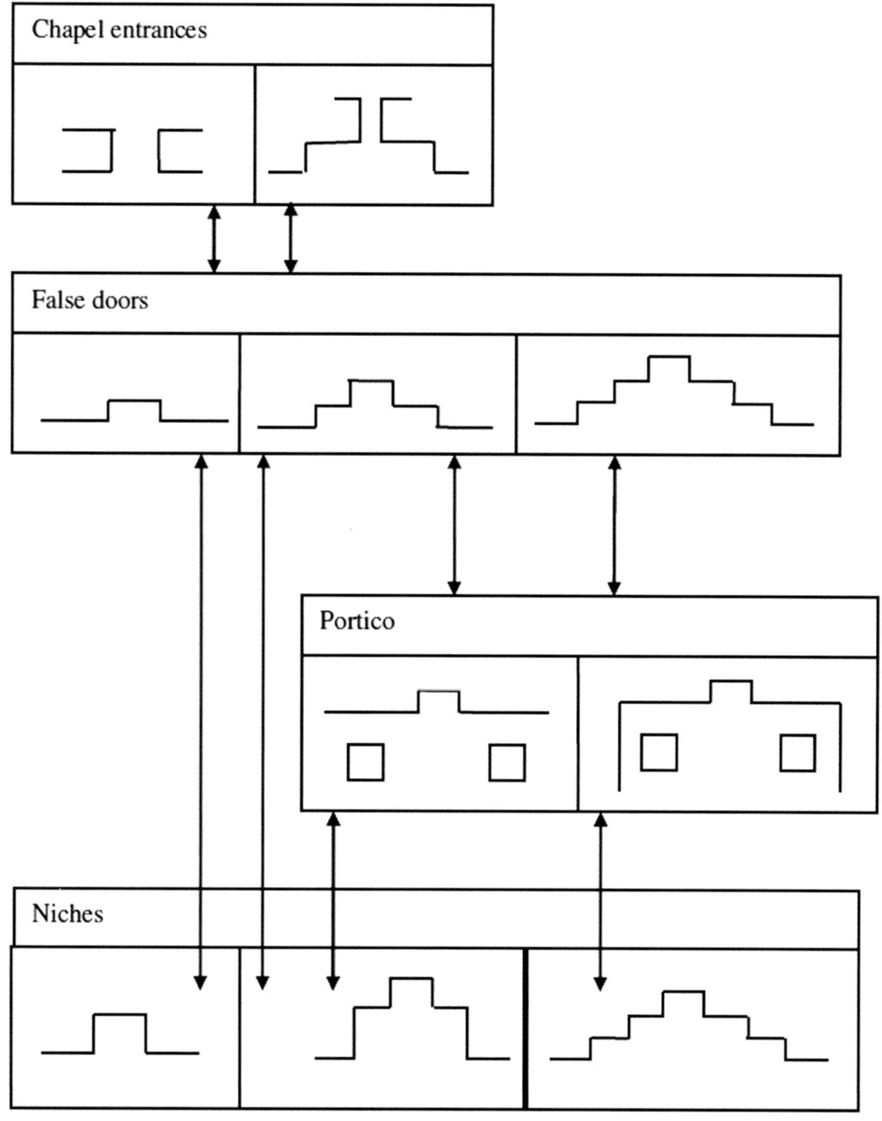

Figure 6.21 The connections between the various types of real and imaginary entrances.

6.21). An important point is that the niche in the burial chamber has all the features of a false door but on the panel no offering table scene has been depicted,[67] meaning that it does not have the function of a place for offerings, but is just a passage.

The conclusion is that the cultic ensemble burial chamber ↔shaft ↔ chapel contains a total of three entrances of which only the two in the chapel are offering places too.

The false door in front of the sarcophagus is an entrance and can be translated into a portico, which would make the inner space of the sarcophagus the residence of the *k3* of the deceased.

In the burial chamber of some tombs false doors were represented:

- In the tomb of *Jnw-Mnw* a *serekh* type false door with cavetto cornice, torus moulding and a double door with battens has been painted on the western wall of the burial chamber.[68]
- In the tomb of *Nmty-m-ḏr.f* (PM, III/2, 687) offerings and a false door with a double door with bolts is present in the burial chamber.[69]
- On the eastern and western wall of the burial chamber of *Ppj* (PM, III/2, 677) *serekh* type false

[67] Bárta, *Afterlife*, Figure 4 shows no human figures have been included in the text (even the determinative in the name of Osiris has been omitted).

[68] Kanawati, *Teti cemetery VIII*, Plates 32 and 55.

[69] Rosso, *Vipère sans tête*, Figure 2.

doors have been painted, both of them with the depiction of a double door in the entrance.[70]

The depiction of a false door in the burial chamber is in fact only one facet of a development in which the burial chamber became somewhat more involved in the total mortuary picture.

The chronological development of the number of tombs with a decorated burial chamber is given in Figure 5.19; the curve shows that toward the end of the 6th dynasty the number increased markedly, but this development reverses at the start of the Heracleopolitan period.

The number of different decoration themes that were initially placed on the walls, and contained scene from daily life and sailing ships, was shortly afterwards curtailed to only those that were more connected with the sustenance of the *k3*.[71]

V. The entrance again....

The standard entrance into an interior chapel has a strong resemblance with a plain niche, thus underlining that this entrance does not give access into just some space, but that it is an entrance into a room with a special cultual meaning. This entrance can be:

1. A construction of two jambs supporting a lintel, the whole design being flush with the surface of the wall of the tomb (Figure 6.20(1)).
2. The same construction as described in item 1, but now placed in a shallow recess in the wall (Figure 6.20(2)).

VI. Discussion

Most of these entrances can be closed with a door that falls into rebates, and, certainly with a closed door, the resemblance of the entrance corridor with the basic single recess is even stronger. The similarity to the entrance of a chapel with a niche and in this way with the central opening of a false door is strengthened in the entrance of the chapel of *Nj-wḏ3-ptḥ* where a stele with the standing tomb owner facing right has been placed over the entrance.[72] The image of the tomb owner is sometimes depicted as appearing in the central recess of a niche or of a false door, either in a two-dimensional or a three-dimensional representation.

In view of the subject of this chapter, this means that the entrance of the chapel resembles a niche with the tomb owner depicted in the central recess which in its turn can be translated into a false door (Figure 6.20(1/2).

At first the entrance into the chapel was an offering place in the form of a niche or a false door; later, the door part has been turned into a real opening.

With this the situation in the portico chapel of *Ḥsj*, as given in Figure 9.8, has returned.

From the open space in front of the entrance of the chapel (= the yard in front of the portico) the visitor goes to the entrance (= the visitor steps into the portico itself), and by way of the corridor goes to the chapel (= the visitor either goes into the chapel behind the portico or stops in front of the false door).

The introduction of the interior chapel ended the function of the niche as a door of the (imaginary) house of the deceased,[73] but the door-function was reinstated when the shallow recess around the entrance into the chapel was introduced, because in that way the portico was added to the tomb.

The result is that the plain entrance 'translates' into a one-jamb false door, a type of false door that cannot be modified into a portico entrance, while the recessed entrance construction translates into a two-jamb false door, which can be modified into a portico entrance.

70 Dawood, *Decoration burial chamber*, Figure 1.

71 Kanawati, *Giza I*, 18 – 21; Dawood, *Burial chamber decoration*, 110.

72 Abu-Bakr, *Giza*, Plate LVII-A.

73 LÄ, V, 563 – 74, s.w. 'Scheintür', there 566.

ENTRANCES

(photo author)

Chapter Seven

The Chapel and its Elements

I. The tomb

In general two main types of tombs can be distinguished:

- The mud-brick or stone built 'free-standing' mastaba (e.g. the mastabas in the cemeteries around the pyramid of Khufu (IV.2)).
- The rock-cut tomb (e.g. the rock-cut tombs in the escarpment of the Khufu-Rakhaef quarry).

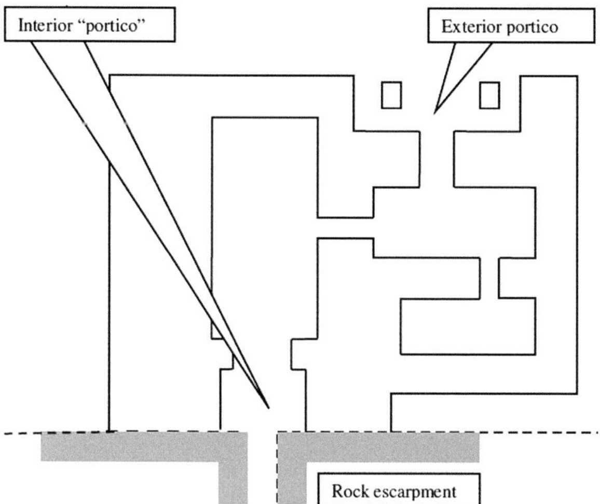

Figure 7.1 The exterior part of the semi rock-cut tomb of *Ny-ʿnḫ-H̱nmw* and *H̱nmw-ḥtp* (PM, III/2, 641 -4).

Sometimes the tomb had the form of a mastaba which was built against a rock escarpment and part of the interior room(s) was cut out in the rock (Figure 7.1), thus forming a 'mixture' of the two main types of tombs.

II. The chapel

II.1. The development of the chapel

Because, as already discussed, the main purpose of the chapel is securing the sustenance of the *k3* of the deceased, the most important part of the tomb has always been the place where magical contact between the world of the living and the world of the dead was possible and where the offerings for the *k3* of the deceased could be brought. At first this was an open place in front of the wall of the tomb where the deceased was 'looking'; as early as the cemetery of Tarkhan (late Nagada III) this place was protected by a low wall that turned the place into an open-air chapel (Figure 2.1).[1]

At the end of the 1st dynasty the offering place at the eastern wall was constructed somewhat deeper in the body of the tomb, the result being a niche that protected the offering place to a certain extent, while a wall or an open-air chapel in front of the entrance of the niche provided some privacy.[2]

By the later part of the 2nd dynasty some tombs had an interior cruciform chapel,[3] a type of interior chapel that was used over a long period in the necropolis of Saqqara.[4] It is in this period that increasingly the exterior chapel was roofed over, which might also indicate that the walls of this type of chapel were decorated.

Somewhat later another form of chapel was developed by building a wall parallel to the eastern wall of the super-structure of the mastaba, thus forming a corridor-chapel alongside this wall. This chapel could be an open air chapel, although for the sake of protection the chapel undoubtedly would be roofed over by stone slabs, wooden boards or a mud-brick vault. This type of chapel predominated in the archaic cemetery of northern Saqqara.

An example is the tomb of *Ḥsjj-Rʿ* (tomb S 2405; date: III.E; PM, III/2, 437–9); the excavation report mentions a wooden roof protecting the paintings on the eastern wall of the corridor and on the western wall the wooden boards with the reliefs depicting the tomb owner (Figure 4.2).[5]

The western wall of the chapel of this tomb is an example of the use of two sets of three plain compound

[1] In Tarkhan the deceased were lying on their left side with the head to the south and their face to the west. It is for that reason that the chapel is situated at the western wall of the tomb, and furthermore at the south end of the wall in order to have the openings in front of the face of the deceased.

[2] Clark, *Tomb security,* Figure 132 (page 102).

[3] Reisner, *Tomb development,* 264.

[4] Reisner, *History mastaba,* 581.

[5] Quibell, *Hesi,* Plate I. Reisner, *History mastaba,* 581 calls the palace facade panelling of the western wall of the corridor-chapel accidental because it would be the result of a series of reconstructions of the tomb. These wooden board with relief decoration would be the oldest known relief decoration together with the stele on the northern door jamb of the chapel in the tomb of *Ḥtpj* (Abusir, tomb AS 20) (Bárta, *Journey,* 117).

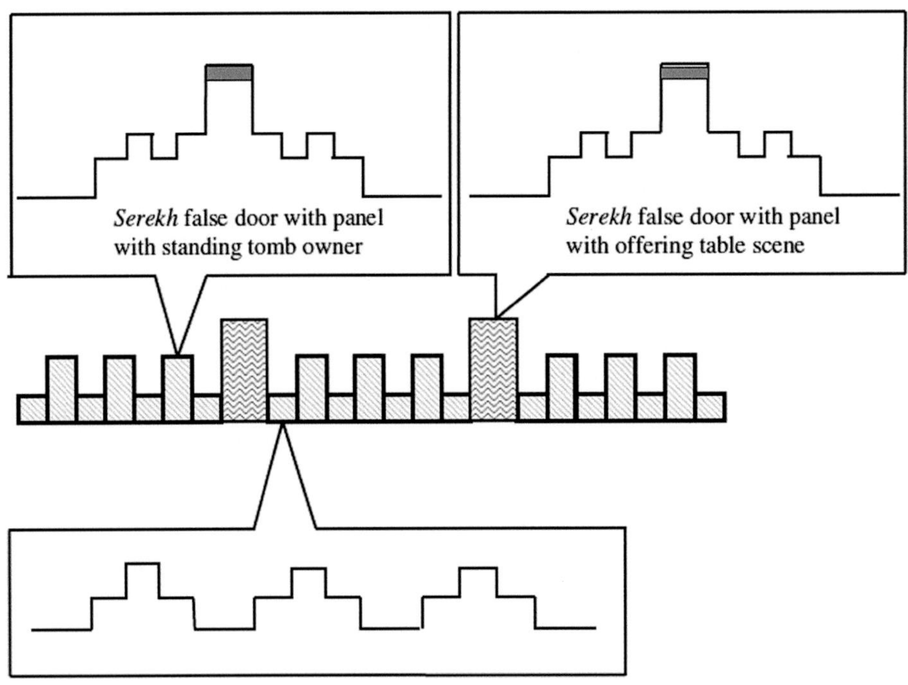

Figure 7.2 The panelling of the western wall of the corridor chapel of *Ḥsjj-Rꜥ* in the Archaic Cemetery of northern Saqqara.

niches flanking an offering place in the form of a *serekh* false door. The chapel has eleven of these *serekh* false doors in its western wall (Figure 7.2) and although only five of these wooden stelae have been recovered *in situ* by Mariette and one by Quibell,[6] the archaeological context in and around the other niches as described by Quibell was such that it can be assumed that a stele had been placed in every one of these niches.[7] On each of the six stelae that have been excavated a depiction of the tomb owner has been carved, five of them showing the tomb owner standing and the sixth depicting the tomb owner sitting at an offering table with an offering list in front of him.[8]

On all these stelae the tomb owner is oriented to the right. It cannot be determined anymore in which of the niches the stele with the offering table scene had been placed.

Based on the description given by Quibell though, it appears that the panel with the offering table scene was originally placed in one of the first five niches. In chapter V (Figure 5.13) it has been noted that the design of the compound *serekh* false door is based on a preference for three elements in a group and this leads to a possible placement of the panel with the offering table scene in the fourth niche from the south.[9] If this is combined with the consideration that over the course of the second dynasty the eastern wall of a tomb lost all of its panelling except two special 'panels' that remained, it can be hypothesized that this means that since in this period the panelling was still present on that wall, there must have been two niches that had a special significance.

If this consideration is introduced in the western wall of the chapel in Figure 7.2 there must have been a second niche with a panel with the offering table scene. In this figure it is evident that the proposed place of the second niche gives a symmetrical design of which every aspect is based on groups of three elements, while the two main offering niches concept has been adhered to.

A further development of this type of corridor is used in the somewhat later chapel of *Ḫꜥ-bꜣw-skr* (PM, III/2, 449 – 50, date: III.L – IV.E). This tomb has a long corridor with niches of which two open into cruciform chapels.[10] The western wall of both chapels consists of a decorated niche flanked by palace façade panelling.[11] Finally the corridor disappeared and the chapels were

---

6 Borchardt, *Denkmäler I*, Blad 25-7; Quibell, *Hesy*, Plate VII[3].

7 Quibell, *Hesy*, 4. Here it is also reported that the five stelae that had been removed by Mariette stood in the five southern niches, the sixth stele was decayed and the stele in the 11th niche has been removed by him, while of the other five he found the decayed remains.

8 Borchardt, *Denkmäler I*, Blad 25 (1426).

9 This preference for units of three identical items is already visible in the wall of Shunet el-zebib at Abydos where a unit of three plain single niches is followed by one plain compound niche (Figure 5.12).

10 Reisner, *Tomb development*, Figure 158. Mariette, *Mastabas*, 71 does not give the corridor in the plan.

11 Reisner, *Tomb development*, Figures 158 and 162.

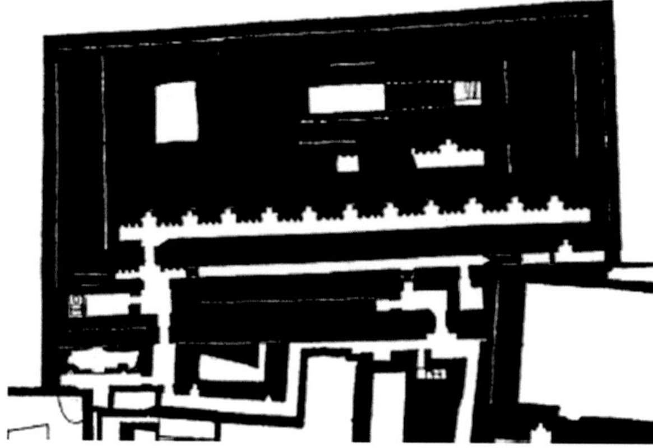

Figure 7.3 The tomb of *Ḥsjj-Rʿ* in the Archaic Cemetery of northern Saqqara.

simplified culminating in the cruciform chapels in the tombs of *Nfr-mꜣʿt*, (PM, IV, 92-4; dating: IV.E) and *Rʿ-ḥtp*, (PM, IV, 90-2) in the Northern Cemetery of Maidum.[12] In this chapel the wall with the false door niche had no panelling anymore, and due to the innovations introduced by Sneferu (IV.1) these chapels were simplified even further into exterior niches with two stelae in front of them.[13]

Early in the 4th dynasty the L-shaped chapel was introduced in the mastabas around the pyramid of Khufu (IV.2) on the Giza Plateau. This type of chapel is common in the necropoleis of Giza and less so in those of Saqqara.[14]

II.2. The functions of the chapel

The functioning of a chapel is basically twofold and can be divided in a cultic function and subsidiary functions (Figure 7.4), the latter are not directly involved in the cult itself but are necessary for the proper cultic functioning of the chapel as a whole.

The cultic function can be actively carried out in the form of bringing offerings to the chapel and depositing them in a place that is specially equipped for this, or passively by the representation of sustenance connected decorative themes on the walls of the chapel.

The subsidiary functions consist of the signalling, the inviting and the unifying functions. The first two functions are mainly connected with the entrance of the chapel but also with the part of the western wall of the chapel visible from outside the tomb; the latter consists of smaller decorative themes placed in the open spaces between the major themes (the offering table scene, the depiction of the tomb owner standing or sitting), thus not only strengthening the active or passive cultic impact of the walls, but also making a meaningful connection between two major themes.[15] Yet, this connection was not always made, an example of the tomb owner sitting without any apparent form of contact with the activities elsewhere on the wall is found in the chapel of *Jjmry* (PM, III/1, 170 – 4; LD, *II*, 52).

For the inviting function two entrance elements are the most important; firstly, the text on the architrave invites passers-by to bring offerings or to pronounce the offering formula, and, secondly, the tomb owner depicted on the door jambs and looking in the direction of the entrance and in that way inviting visitors in.[16]

Of the themes mentioned in Figure 7.4 only the subsidiary functions can be placed on the elements of the entrance; the main function is confined to the chapel itself.

An important aspect of the functioning of the chapel is the directionality of the themes; the viewing direction of the depiction of the tomb owner or the direction of movement of a row of offering bearers or priests is meant to support the basic function of an architectural element of the entrance. The viewing direction of the tomb owner who is depicted on the entrance thicknesses and is looking to the outside world can be explained as looking to the rising sun, but it is far more plausible that the tomb owner is inviting passers-by to enter into the chapel. This statement is supported by the viewing direction of the tomb owner on the door jambs. The offering bearers on the entrance thicknesses who are walking toward the entrance of the chapel itself are expressing and supporting a purpose signalling function.

III. The entrance of the chapel

III.1. Introduction

At first the entrance into the chapel was an offering place in the form of a niche (false door), of which later

[12] Harpur, *Maidum*, 5 (Figure 10). For the successive changes in the form of the chapel see Figures 38 and 61.

[13] Alexanian, *Netjeraperef*, Plate 8b.

[14] Harpur, *DETOK*, 63 – 4; Roeten, *Economic decline*, Figure 90 (page 85).

[15] An example of a unifying theme is visible on the eastern wall of the chapel of *Rʿ-ḫʿf-ʿnḫ* (PM, III/1, 207 – 8) where the tomb owner is standing inspecting scribes at work and animals being driven in his direction. The connection between the two themes is made by a servant holding up a sun-shade (LD, *II*, 9). There are examples in which a child standing in front of the tomb owner and holding his staff forms the unifying element (LD, *II*, 22a).

[16] The inviting function of the depiction of the standing tomb owner on the door jambs is in some tombs reinforced by the gesture of the raised hand (Bárta, *Afterlife existence*, Figure 2). In Harpur, *DETOK*, 129 this gesture is explained as pointing to text that has been placed in front of the tomb owner.

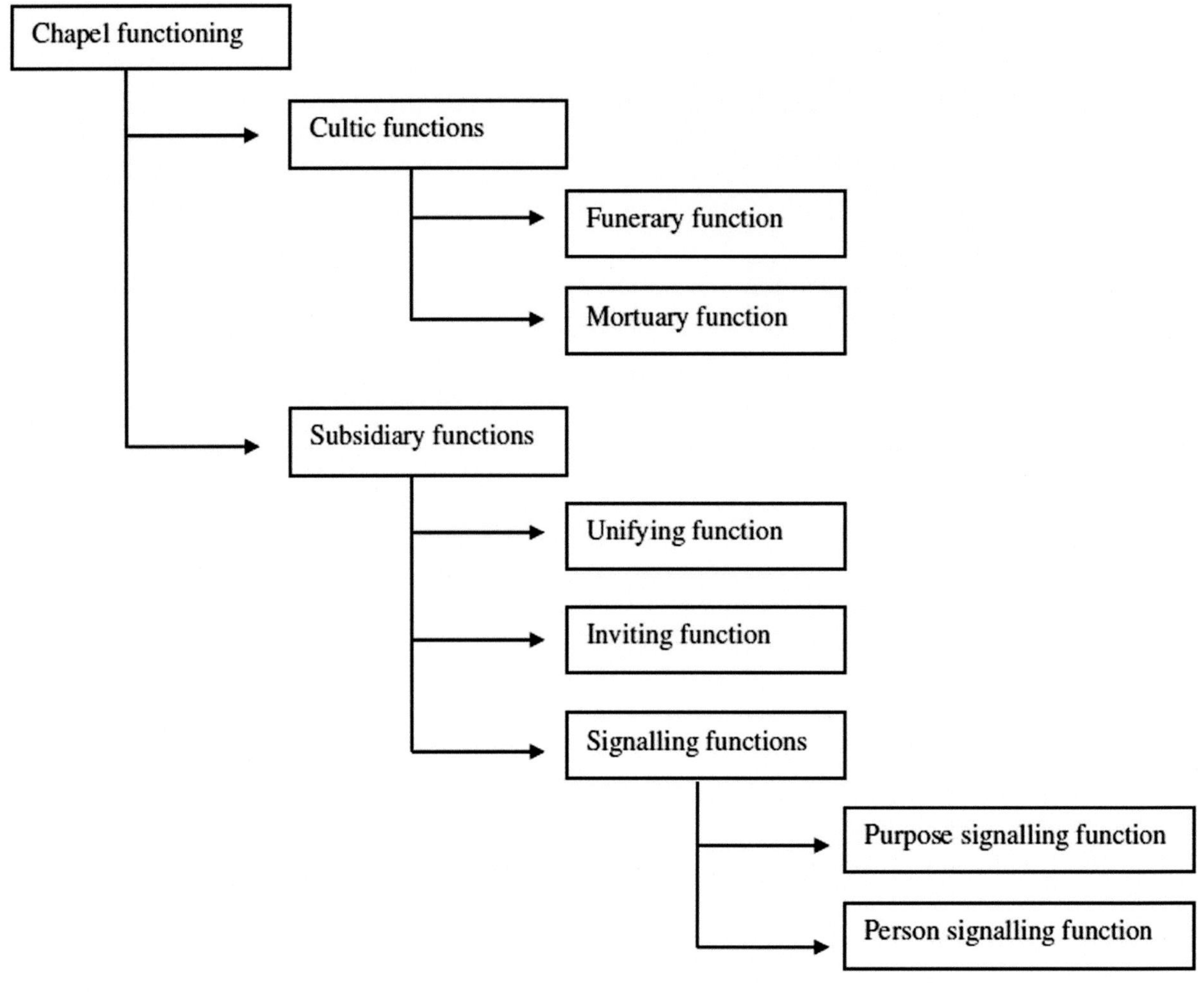

Figure 7.4 The various functions of the elements of a chapel.

the door part was turned into a real opening, and some chapel entrances still retain that idea (Figure 6.4).[17]

The entrance of the chapel consists of four architectural elements (see Figure 7.5), and in this study the following names will be employed for its constituent elements:[18]

- The door jambs.
- The architrave.
- The door drum.
- The entrance thicknesses.

Often the various functions of the chapel and its entrance elements necessitated the presence of decoration. For the application of decoration others than painted on the walls, the carving of stone was necessary. For this three techniques can be distinguished:[19]

- Bas relief: the depiction was cut out in the stone, and was made deep enough to enable the addition of details in the figure.
- Raised relief: around the depiction the stone was taken away.
- A technique with which the contour and some details of the decoration theme were hacked away, thus leaving a rather thin line of various depth.

Later in the Old Kingdom a convention developed that for decoration or texts on parts of the architecture that were exterior or considered as such sunk relief was used, while raised relief was preferred for the interior parts. That this tradition took hold only later in the Old Kingdom is visible in the mastabas of the cemeteries around the pyramid of Khufu at Giza. There the

[17] Hassan, *Giza III*, Plate XVIII.

[18] In the literature there is some confusion about the name of the various elements of the entrance: lintel versus architrave, door jamb – pilaster , entrance thickness – door jamb (Roth, *Gmast 6*, Plate 67a), door lintel – door drum.

[19] LÄ, V, 224 – 9, s.w. 'Relief'.

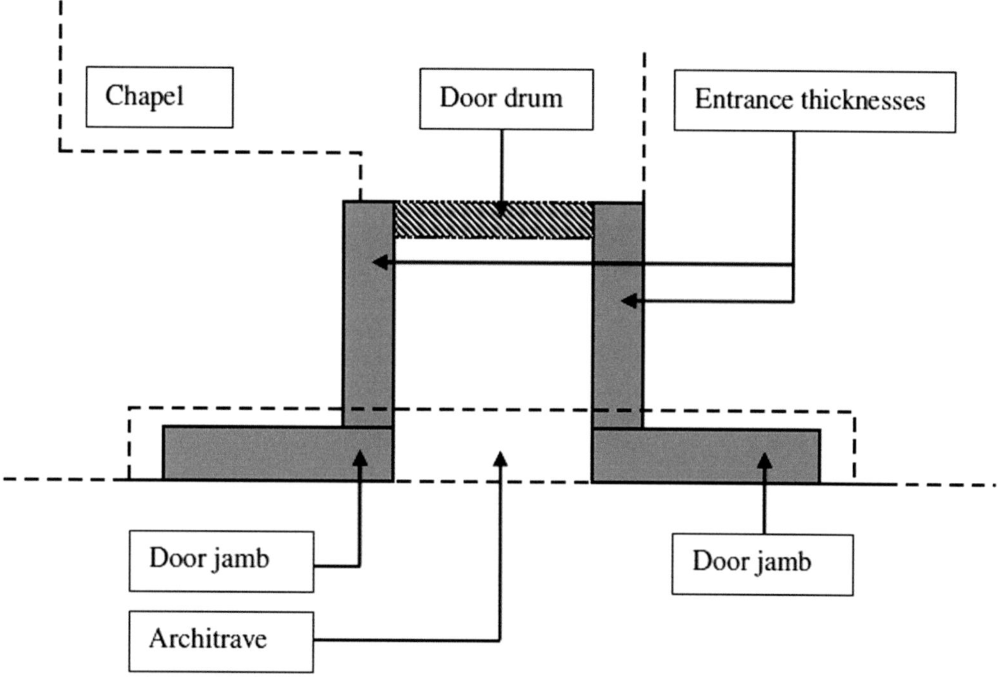

Figure 7.5 The basic plan of the entrance of a chapel without a recess.

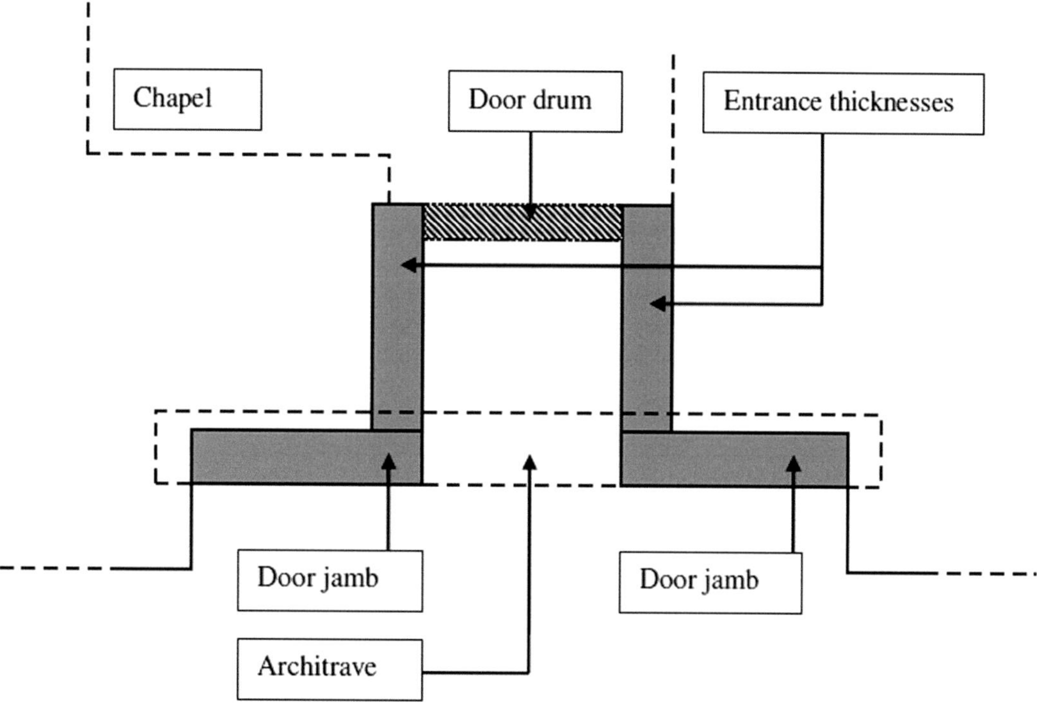

Figure 7.6 The basic plan of the entrance of a chapel with a recess.

decoration of the walls of the corridor into the interior chapel, which is, based on the location of the door closing the chapel, clearly part of the exterior world, is executed in raised relief, and not in sunk relief.[20]

As already mentioned the basic purpose of the chapel is to create a place that enables contact between the world of the living and the deceased who is in the world of the dead, and where, by way of magic based on ritual the *k3* of the deceased could receive sustenance. This sustenance could be active or passive,[21] but it is also of the utmost importance to attract the attention of passers-by and 'convince' them to enter (in modern parlance: the 'machinery' to get the would-be customer inside), and to utter an offering formula which provided sustenance for the deceased in a magical way. In some tombs this desire, which was sometimes accompanied by threats, was expressed in a text placed on a wall near the entrance.

The texts on the architrave over the entrance often show only the name and titles of the tomb owner, as on the architrave of the portico chapel of *Ṯtw* (PM, III/1, 66 – 7):

> *'The overseer of the pyramid town Akhet-Khufu, Supervisor of funerary priests of Akhet-Khufu,*
> *king's liegeman of the palace, one well provided before Osiris, Tjetu'.*
>
> *Dunham, Gmast 4, 8.*

Sometimes more text is added, an example of this can be found on the edge of the roof and the wall south of the above mentioned portico-chapel of *Ṯtw* (Figure 9.6).

> *'.....the king's liegeman [of the palace] Tjetu; whom Anubis loves, whom Osiris loves, whom*
> *the king and their god love are those who will say bread and beer for the owner of the tomb*
> *from what is in your hand(s); if there is nothing in your hand(s), say with your mouth and offer with your hand(s).*
> *I am beloved of my father, one praised of his mother, I am.....'*
> *....for any man who shall take away or who shall displace a block of stone in this tomb,*
> *I shall be judged with (him) in the tribunal of the great god.....*
>
> (Tomb of *Ṯtw* (PM, III/1, 66-7), from Simpson, *Gmast 4*, 8 [left])

The stating of name and titles and the asking of daily offerings can be accompanied by the request to bring offerings on special festive days, with a specification of the type and quantity. An example of this is the architrave over the façade of the tomb of *Jdw* (PM, III/1, 185 – 6; G 7102), giving name, titles, the *ḥtp di nswt* formula for the king, Anubis and Osiris, the wish to be buried in the west and to walk on the ways there, the hope that offerings are brought during certain festival days and on a daily basis, followed by a list of the festivals.

> *'..........May he be glorified very greatly by lectors and embalmers, at the New Year's festival, at the Thot festival, at the first of the year, at the Wag-feast, at the feast of Sokar, at the great festival, at the fire-lighting festival, at the Sadj festival, at the coming forth of Min, at the half-month (and) month festivals, at the seasonal feasts, at the beginning of all decades, at all great festivals, and throughout the course of everyday......'*
>
> *Simpson, Gmast 2,* 21.

Because often the chapel was closed with a door, in most cases the passer-by could not enter and therefore purpose from the start of the 4th dynasty on, an offering formula was placed on an external architectural element of the the tomb with the intention that the passer-by would utter the formula and in this way sustain the *k3* of the deceased.[22]

This offering formula could be on the architrave over the entrance of the chapel, on the entrance thicknesses, on the door jambs or on a line of roofing blocks as on the portico of the tomb of *Ṯtw.*

Another theme that was connected with the sustenance of the *k3* of the deceased was the offering table scene; this theme not only could be placed on the walls of the chapel or on the false door, but also on the entrance elements, and on any element with a surface large enough to accommodate it. An example of this can be seen in the chapel of *Ḥtpj* (Tomb AS 20 at Abusir), a chapel with small entrance thicknesses and three doors that all opened into the chapel; consequently, not enough wall space was left open to accommodate the offering table scene and it was decided to place this scene on the right door jamb of the entrance.[23]

The offering table scene was placed on some entrance thicknesses of tombs in Giza (Figure 3.7), but the placing of the theme on this element stopped at the start of the middle period of the 5th dynasty (V.M).[24] In the necropolis of Saqqara this theme is not placed on

[20] Der Manuelian, *Gmast 8*, Figure 13.29. This could be a consequence of reasoning that the visibility of a depiction outside was enhanced by the light of the sun, but that the corridor into the chapel could not be reached by direct light.

[21] In case of active sustenance of the *k3* of the deceased offerings are placed in front of the false door, while passive sustenance takes place through magic.

[22] LÄ, IV, 584-6, s.v. ' Opferformel '.

[23] Bárta, *Hetepi*, Plates 10 and 18.

[24] Roeten, *Decoration*, Table XII.1.Ann. (page 384).

any of the elements of the entrance. Harpur suggests that this might be due to the fact in Giza in the period V.M the offering table scene changed into the depiction of the tomb owner standing and when at the end of the 5th dynasty the necropolis of Saqqara became the main burial place, the decorative tradition of Giza was superseded.[25]

The change from sitting to standing depiction of the tomb owner might be attributed to a change of religious and funerary ideas, but the proposal of Harpur that the depiction of the standing tomb owner takes up less space is much more realistic. This reduction of space is, as already proposed, inherent to a strong diminution of the surface of the mastabas that started in the necropolis of Giza at the beginning of the 5th dynasty.[26] During this decrease of the surface of the mastaba the total surface of the chapel did not change appreciably,[27] and this leads to the conclusion that the length of the corridor to the interior chapel decreased constantly. When Saqqara became the most important necropolis of the Memphis area, the reduction of the area of the mastabas, which had already set in when the necropoleis of Giza was still the royal burial ground, continued and early in the 5th dynasty the surface of the walls of the corridor became too small to accommodate the offering table scene anymore.[28] The loss of this scene on the entrance thicknesses and its replacement by the standing tomb owner meant that the purpose signalling function of the entrance was curtailed, thus emphasizing the signalling function of the tomb owner.

III.2. The types of entrances

This section deals with the entrance of the chapel itself and not with eventual constructions placed in front of it. The purpose of the latter could be to give additional information to the visitor in the form of an offering formula, an appeal to the living (request and/or threat) or an autobiography.

The most obvious architectonic differences between the various chapel entrances can be divided into two main types:

1. The entrance is flush with the wall of the tomb in which it is placed (Figure 7.5), or is placed in a shallow entrance niche (Figure 7.6).[29]
2. The entrance is a portico with or without pillars (Figure 7.7).[30]

The first type has several possible constructions:

3. The entrance is placed between two door jambs which may or may not be provided with decoration.
4. The entrance is placed between two *serekh* false doors that are placed on the door jambs (*Ḫwfw-ḏd.f*; GIIS; PM, III/1, 219; Junker, *Giza X*, Figure 23, Plate IVa) (Figure 6.6).[31] This type of entrance decoration has also been employed in the mastaba of *Sšt-ḥtp* (PM, III/1, 149-50).[32]
5. The entrance is placed between two false doors and over the entrance is a statue of the tomb owner (*Mr-ʿnḫ.f* PM, III/1, 278-9; Hassan, *Giza III*, Plate VII(1) (Figure 6.1)).
6. The entrance to the rock-cut tomb of *Ny-wḏꜣ-ptḥ* (PM, III/1, 62-3) has no doorjambs but has a stele showing the striding figure of the tomb owner with his name and a title over him.[33]
7. The entrance to the rock-cut chapel of *Ḫwtꜣ* (PM, III/1, 279) has no decorated door jambs, but over the entrance two architraves have been placed with a false door panel between them (Figure 6.4).[34]

Although the appearance of the two types of false doors is totally different, the placement of the entrance of the chapel between two *serekh* false doors or between two true false doors is basically identical. Each of the two *serekh* false doors left and right of the entrance is a false door off its own, as can be seen in Junker, *Giza X*, Figure 24. The situation is the same when the entrance is placed between two true false doors (Figure 6.1).

However, the situation given in Figure 6.4 is completely different because here the entrance of the chapel is the middle (door) part of a true false door, which would mean that the visitor entering the chapel traverses the place where the world of the living and the world of the dead meet, and a possible but unlikely conclusion could be that this gives the chapel behind the false door a different status than the chapel without this type of entrance. This possibility is unlikely because a living human being cannot physically enter into the world of the dead.

[25] Harpur, *DETOK*, 53.

[26] Roeten, *Economic decline*, Figure 69 (page 58).

[27] Roeten, *Economic decline*, Figures 70 and 71 (pages 59-60).

[28] Roeten, *Economic decline*, Figure 132 (page 125).

[29] The northern and southern wall of a shallow entrance niche can be decorated too, and in that case these two walls are interpreted as door jambs.

[30] The portico is discussed in chapter IX.

[31] Another example is the entrance of the chapel of *Sšt-ḥtp* (PM, III/1, 149-50; Junker, *Giza II*, 174).

[32] Kanawati, *Giza II*, Plate 41. Junker, *Giza II*, 174 states that the decoration of the two door jambs together form one false door. This would mean that the visitor while entering the chapel traverses the place where the world of the living and the world of the dead meet.

[33] Abu-Bakr, *Giza*, Figures 91, 92; Plate LVII (left).

[34] Hassan, *Giza III*, Plate XVIII.

It can also mean that the entrance of a chapel can be considered as the start of a zone of overlap of the two worlds, whatever its design.

The second type of entrance, the portico, can be with pillars (Figure 7.7),[35] or without pillars,[36] although the latter type is rare.[37]

Figure 7.7 Pillared portico of the tomb of *Ptḥ-ḥtp* [I], (PM, III/2, 596-8: date: V.L) (Photo author).

Figure 7.8 Door jambs of the mastaba of *Mrrw-kꜣ.j.* (PM, III/2, 525–34).

IV. The elements of the entrance

IV.1. The jambs of the entrance

These two vertical surfaces on either side of the entrance itself could be used as the most important 'bill-boards' to attract the attention of the passer-by. Due to lack of space the number of themes on the door jambs is limited. Harpur mentions the following themes (some sub-groups are assembled in one group):[38]

1. Tomb owner, standing alone or with member(s) of the family.[39]
   - An example of the tomb owner standing alone with name and titles is found in the tomb of *Kꜣ-gm-nj* (PM, III/2, 521-5), and in Roth, *Gmast 6,* Plates 67a and 67b.
   - The door jambs of the tomb of *Mrrw-kꜣ.j.* (PM, III/2, 525–34; Photo: www.wikipedia; Mereruka, Saqqara) show the tomb owner with members of his family (Figure 7.8). The text on the jambs consists of the name and titles of the tomb owner. In the case of *Mrrw-kꜣ.j*, his wife *Wꜥtt-ḫt-ḥr* is standing in front of him while smelling a lotus flower and looking in the same direction as the tomb owner.[40]
   - It is also possible that the accompanying member of the family is looking at the tomb owner,[41] or standing behind the tomb owner, looking in the same direction.[42]
2. Tomb owner seated alone or with member(s) of the family (Figure 3.6). There are two examples of the sitting tomb owner in the form of statues placed at both sides of the entrance.[43]
   The tomb owner is sitting with name, titles and sometimes a text over him/her (*ꜥnḫ-m-ꜥ-ḥr*, PM, III/2, 512-5).[44] Harpur claims that the sitting tomb owner is common on the entrance thicknesses, and that the appearance of the sitting tomb owner on the door jambs of the entrance can be dated to the start of the 6th

[35] The pillars of the portico entrance in Figure 7.7 are anepigraphic due to time and human intervention. The pillars of the portico of *Nj-ꜥnḫ-H̱nmw* and *H̱nmw-ḥtp* (PM, III/2, 641-4) are inscribed with names and titles (without depiction of the tomb owners), while those of the portico of *Ṯjj* (PM, III/2, 468-78) carry a depiction of the tomb owner with his name and titles.

[36] An example of this type is the entrance of the tomb of *Rꜥ-špss* (PM, III/2, 494-6; plan XLIX, a more recent and more complete plan of the tomb can be found in EA, 44 (2014), 8-9). The northern wall of the portico is decorated with the tomb owner and a son standing in a canoe in the marshes (LD, *II*, 60 [right], on the northern door jamb the tomb owner is fowling accompanied by his wife and a son (LD, *II*, 60 [left]).

[37] Harpur, *DETOK,* 50 states that very few subsidiary figures are depicted on the jambs of the entrance, except in portico entrances.

[38] Harpur, *DETOK,* Table 4.7 (pages 307 -9).

[39] A special sub-group is the tomb owner depicted as a corpulent man.

[40] Harpur, *DETOK*, 49.

[41] LD, *II*, 18.

[42] Junker, *Giza III*, Figure 14 (page 129).

[43] Harpur, *DETOK*, 50 – 1.

[44] Capart, *Rue des tombeaux II*, Plates XX-XXII.

	Type of decoration (Harpur, *DETOK*, Table 4.8)	percentage
VI.1.1	Tomb owner, standing alone or with member(s) of the family	66
VI.1.2	Tomb owner seated alone or with member(s) of the family	12
VI.1.3	Tomb owner sitting at the offering table	0 [1]
VI.1.4	Subsidiary figures	22

Figure 7.9 The decoration themes on the door jambs in the necropoleis of Giza and Saqqara.

dynasty.[45] It has already been remarked that in the necropolis of Giza from the middle of the 5th dynasty on, the sitting tomb owner is no longer depicted on the entrance thicknesses.[46]

3. To my knowledge the on this moment only existing example of the tomb owner sitting at the offering table was found in the tomb of *Ḥtpj* (AS 20, Abusir).[47]
4. Subsidiary figures.

The percentage of the type of depiction is gathered in the table of Figure 7.9:[48]

It is evident that on this element of the entrance the tomb owner is either with or without other persons mainly depicted in a standing position, understandable in view of the restricted area available for decoration. This might also be the reason that the offering table scene is not placed on this entrance element.

An example of an offering formula on what can be interpreted as the door jambs is found in the tomb of *Sḥtpw* (PM, III/1, 222, in plan XXXI items 1a/b).[49]

Some entrances do not have decoration other than statuary, which is only another way of depicting the tomb owner (*Sšm-nfr* [IV], PM; III/1, 223 - 6). Later entrance jambs show the tomb owner standing with a text not only giving the name and some titles but also with a statement that the tomb owner had the tomb constructed out of his/her own funds and/or a threat against anyone who tries to do evil, or wants to enter in an impure state. An example of this is the decoration of the entrance of the mastaba of *Ḥtp-ḥr-ꜣḫtj* (PM, III/2, 593-5).[50]

(1) *The judge, the speaker of Nekhen, Ḥtp-ḥr-ꜣḫtj, he says: I made this my tomb as my rightful property. Never did I deprive any person of anything.*
(2) *As to any person, who made something for me in it, they worked, whilst they prayed very much to the god for me; and they made this*
(3) *for bread, beer, for clothes, for oil, for barley and emmer, very much. Never did I do anything*
(4) *by means of violence against anybody. The god loves righteousness. I am a revered one near the king,*
(5) *A venerated one near the great god,*
(6) *The judge, the speaker of Nekhen, the president of the hall,*
(7) *he who is over the secrets of the great house,*
(8) *The priest of Maat,*
(9) *The revered one near the great god,*
(10) *Ḥtp-ḥr-ꜣḫtj*

(Left entrance door jamb tomb of *Ḥtp-ḥr-ꜣḫtj* (PM, III/2, 593-5), after Mohr, *Hetep-her-akhty*,34)

(1) *The judge, the president of the hall, Ḥtp-ḥr-ꜣḫtj , he says: I made this my tomb on the west side in a clear place where there was not yet*
(2) *a tomb of any person, in order that the property of one who has gone to his k3 might be protected. As to all those, who shall enter*
(3) *this my tomb in their impure state and who shall do something evil against it, I shall be judged with them on account of it*
(4) *by the great god. I made this my tomb because I was a revered one near the king who delivered the sarcophagus to me.*

(Right entrance door jamb tomb of *Ḥtp-ḥr-ꜣḫtj* (PM, III/2, 593-5), after Mohr, *Hetep-her-akhty*,35)

IV.1.1. The chapel of Htpj at Abusir

The entrance of the chapel of *Ḥtpj* at Abusir (tomb AS 20) is exceptional in that an offering table scene has been placed on the northern door jamb.[51] This feature

[45] Harpur, *DETOK*, 50.

[46] Roeten, *Decoration*, Table XII.1.Ann. (page 384-7).

[47] Bárta, *Abusir XIX*, Plate 10.

[48] Theme VI.1.1 is a combination of Harpur, *DETOK*, Table 4.8 items D, CD, W, SW and s/d; theme VI.1.2 is a combination of SD, W, S, W and s/d.

[49] Junker, *Giza XI*, Figure 34.

[50] Leyden Museum (RMO), no. F.1904/3.1.

[51] Bárta, *Abusir XIX*, Plate 10 gives a photo of the total situation.

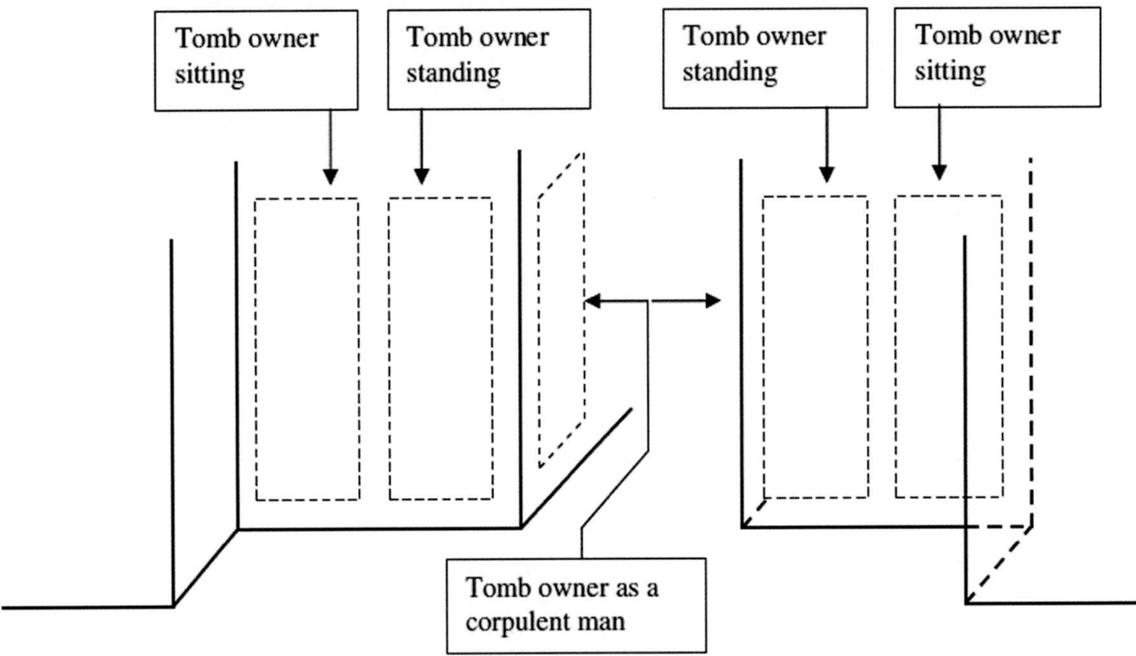

Figure 7.10 The entrance of the mastaba of *ʿnḫ-m-ʿ-ḥr* (PM, III/2, 512 – 5).

has not been repeated on the southern door jamb, only a sketch of the striding tomb owner facing toward the entrance with three (smaller) figures in front of him are placed there (Figure 4.9). Both depictions of the tomb owner are looking in the direction of the entrance, which causes that the orientation of the person in the offering table scene to be inverted from the usual direction. The offering table scene can be seen as an example of the tomb owner seated, which, in this period (III.L – IV.E), was extremely rare on the door jambs of chapel entrances.[52]

IV.1.2. The mastaba of ʿnḫ-m-ʿ-Ḥr in the Teti cemetery

On the door jambs on both sides of the entrance of the mastaba of *ʿnḫ-m-ʿ-ḥr* (PM, III/2, 512 – 5) the tomb owner is depicted both seated *and* standing, while on the narrow entrance thickness he is shown as a corpulent man standing and looking in the direction of the outside world (Figure 7.10).[53]

IV.2. The architrave over the entrance

The pictorial development of the architrave is discussed by Harpur and needs no further comment.[54]

The texts on the architrave can range from the mentioning of name and titles,[55] the offering formula, and an offering formula followed by the request of offerings being brought on all festivals (see below). The placing of this formula on the architrave was so that it could be recited by a visitor or a passer-by thus performing the offering for the deceased in a magical way.[56]

(1) *A boon which the king gives and Anubis, foremost of the divine booth, that he may be buried in the necropolis of the western cemetery having aged very gracefully.*

(2) *And that an invocation offering (of bread, cattle, and fowl) comes forth for him on the opening of the year, the Thot festival, the first of the year, the Wag festival, and every festival; the overseer of the six tenant farmers of the great house, custodian of the containers of the royal degrees, the weeb-priest of the king, the supervisor of weeb-priests, tenant farmer, counsellor, the priest of Khufu, Iasen; his beloved wife, Merytot[es].*[57]

(Tomb of *Ỉꜣsn*, (PM, III/1, 82), from Simpson, *Gmast* 4, 17 |left])

[52] Harpur, *DETOK*, 50-1 ; Roeten, *Decoration*, Table XII.2.Ann (page 388).

[53] Capart, *Rue des tombeaux II*, Plates XIX – XXIV.

[54] Harpur, *DETOK*, 44-8.

[55] Petrie, *Medum*, Plates IX and X.

[56] LÄ, IV, 584 – 6, s.v. 'Opferformel', there 586.

[57] The title 'weeb-priest' has been taken over from the original texts of Simpson; the orthography of this title is now interpreted as *wʿb*, wab-priest (Jones, *Index I*, 368 [1360]).

The oldest appearance of the offering formule is on the false door in the chapel of the tomb of *Rˁ-ḥtp* at Maidum (PM, IV, 90-1, date: III.L – IV.E), but in this formula the king is not mentioned

> *A boon which Anubis gives that he comes as a possessor of reverence, to the west....*

Later it was employed to ask boons from more than one party; the first is a request for offerings from the king *ḥtp dj njswt;* the second a request for offerings from Anubis *ḥtp dj Inpw*.[58] The latter was later increasingly replaced by Osiris. In some offering formulas mention is also made of a "great god".[59]

Junker gives the tomb of *ꜣḫj* (PM, III/1, 137; date: temp. Menkaure (IV.5)) as an early Gizean example of the offering formula on the architrave over the entrance; in this text gifts are requested from the king and Anubis; in addition, in this tomb the offering formula was also placed on the architrave of the false door.[60]

An exemple of this text on the entrance thicknesses has been found in the entrance of the exterior chapel of *Ḫwfw-ḫˁ.f* [I] (PM, III/1, 188-90; dating PM: IV.2-IV.5; dating Harpur, *DETOK,* 269[183]: IV.4).[61]

Bárta mentions that the earliest offering formulas were randomly placed in the chapel, but that later in the 4th dynasty the place of the offering formula was bound by fixed rules.[62]

Figure 7.11 Southern entrance thickness and door drum of the family mastaba of *Kꜣ-m-nfrt* (PM, III/1, 263-5), Hassan, *Giza II,* Figures 116 and 118, Plate XXXVI(1).

Because the exterior offering place was the facsimile of a door a door drum was present too, which showed the name of the tomb owner and sometimes one or more titles,[63] the presence of the latter not only depended on the length of the name and the title but also on the design of the false door.[64] When the offering place became invisible from the outside, the entrance was constructed in strong resemblance to the door form of the offering place (Figure 7.11), which might indicate that this door was considered to be an entrance into a world that differed from the world outside the chapel, but was not equal to the world of the dead behind the false door in the chapel. This hypothesis is corroborated by the fact that texts on the door jambs asked visitors to enter but demanded their cleanliness.

> *The unique friend much loved, steward of the palace, chief of the king's barbers, ritualistic priest Ty.*

He says:

> *All people who will enter into this (my) tomb of eternity unclean because they have eaten of the abominable things which repel a mind which has arrived in the necropolis, (not) being pure at the appropriate time, as they must not penetrate into the god's temple, a judgement will be uttered against them because of it by the great god.........*
>
> (Tomb of *Tjj* , PM, III/2, 468-78; 1E in plan XLVIII; date: V.L).

IV.3. The door drum

That the entrance into the chapel at the end of the corridor was considered to be a door is made clear by the presence of a door drum which was inscribed with the name of the tomb owner and one or more of his titles (Figure 7.11). In this figure the titles are (after Hassan, *Giza II,* 110):

---

58 Junker, *Giza I,* 238.

59 Kayser, *Mastaba,* 41.

60 Junker, *Giza I,* 238.

61 Simpson, *Gmast 3,* Plates XVa and XVb.

62 Bárta, *Opferformel,* 3 gives as the oldest known offering formula is placed in the inner niche of the false door in the chapel of the tomb of *Rˁ-ḥtp,* (PM, IV, 90-2) in the Northern Cemetery of Maidum (Harpur, *Maidum,* 112) (date Harpur, *DETOK,* 279[620]: IV.1-2).

63 The 'real' false door (Normal-Scheintür) was introduced during the 4th dynasty (LÄ, V, 563-74, s.v. 'Scheintür').

64 With title: Cherpion, *Mastabas,* Plate 24; without title: ibidem, Plate 33.

> *The sole confident, the director of the palace, the exempted, the administrator of the 'Bat', the director of 'the black vase', the administrator of the navy, the overseer of the canals (?) Ka-em-nefert.*

Other titles could be mentioned on the entrance thicknesses. This passage from the entrance corridor into the chapel was often closed with a door (Figure 4.10) as is indicated by a pivot hole in the pyramid complex of Djoser (III.2); although the doors there were facsimiles in stone, the photo shows that movable doors already existed in that period.

In some tombs next to name and titles the depiction of the tomb owner was placed on the door drum.[65] In the case of W^{c} (PM, III/1, 210) the tomb owner is shown seated together with his wife.[66]

The entrance thicknesses constitute the most decorated part of the entrance of the chapel and for a more profound study of the functioning of this element a method will be used that was originally developed for the study of the interaction between the themes on the walls of the chapel. The methodology and the result of applying it to the decoration themes of the entrance thicknesses will be discussed in chapter XI.

65 Harpur, *DETOK,* Table 4.6.

66 LD, *II*, 93a.

Chapter Eight

Decoration Directionality in Entrances and Chapels

I. Introduction

In a chapel the direction of the decoration can be divided in that of the direction of the depictions of the tomb owner, and the direction of the depictions of members of the family and of servants. The direction of the main figures determines the total functioning of the two types of entrances that are the subject of this study, namely niches (false doors) and real entrances.

II. Of niches and cruciform chapels

Basically there are two types of niches, the single and the double recessed one (Figure 5.12). They can be placed either in the eastern (exterior) wall of the tomb (mastaba II/1 at Dahshur) or in the western wall of an interior chapel (*Mṯn*, (PM, III/2, 493 – 4).

Very early double recessed niches include the ones in the corridor chapel of *Ḥsjj-Rˁ* (tomb S 2405; date: III.E; PM, III/2, 437–9). The niches have a wooden plate as back panel on which the tomb owner has been depicted either striding or sitting (Figure 4.2).[1] The excavation report does not mention the existence of decoration on the sides of the niches, although the drawing made of one of them does not rule it out.[2]

An example of a single recessed niche within a more complex surrounding has been found in the tomb of *Ḫˁ-bꜣw-Skr* (PM, III/2, 449 – 50) (Figure 8.1).[3] This is a single niche flanked by palace façade panelling of plain compound niches. On the back panel the tomb owner is sitting at an offering table looking to the right; on the side walls the tomb owner is looking toward the outside world (this shallow recessed niche has been placed in the western wall of a cruciform chapel).

The double recessed niche has more decoration room available and in some tombs servants are added to the figures of the tomb owner and the texts, and on the walls of the niche in the cruciform chapel of *Mṯn*, (PM, III/2, 493 – 4; date: IV.1-2) (Figure 8.5) depictions of the tomb owner, priests and some offering bearers have been placed.[4] In Figure 8.2 the form and the decoration directionality of the niches in the tomb of *Jj-nfr* at Dahshur are given. On the back panel of the southern niche the tomb owner is striding to the right, while on the back panel of the northern niche the tomb owner is sitting, also facing right.

Figure 8.3 gives the seemingly more complex,[5] but only partly preserved, niche of *Nṯr-ˁpr.f* .

If the tomb owner is depicted on the recess back wall in a standing or sitting position without further elements of a false door present, this indicates that the whole niche is considered as a false door.

It is evident that a figure on the back wall of the niche could be either sitting or standing but it was preferentially directed to the right,[6] the same direction as on the panel of the later false doors. This direction is possibly chosen because it is the direction that gives the least problems with conventions concerning hands holding status symbols.[7] In the tomb of *Jy* (PM, III/2, 565) the female tomb owner is depicted in the niche of the false door, looking to the right, but in accordance with the conventions she is standing with both feet together, and without paraphernalia of status.[8]

In the niches of the early 4th dynasty the subsidiary figures are already directed to the back wall of the niche, the place that can be interpreted as the passage between the world of the living and the dead, and this tendency remained present in the later niches (the place where the transitional zone between the world of the living and the world of the dead begins has been marked with a hollow arrow (Figure 8.4)).

In the niches of Figures 8.2 and 8.3 the directionality of the depiction of the tomb owner is identical. The direction of the other depictions is nearly always mirror symmetrical on equivalent walls. In the cruciform

---

[1] On the boards that have been excavated the tomb owner is looking to the right.

[2] Quibell, *Hesy*, Plate V.

[3] Borchardt, *Denkmäler I*, no. 1385; Bárta, *Abusir XIX*, Plates 32 – 4.

[4] Harpur, *DETOK*, Plan 2 (page 378).

[5] In reality the outer step is not part of the niche itself, but a small platform in front of the niche.

[6] An example of a false door with the figure of the tomb owner directed to the left is of *Snj-wḥmw* (PM, III/1, 75, G 2132) were in the central niche offering bearers and the wife of the tomb owner are directed to the right (MFA, Boston, 27.444).

[7] For an example of this see Alexanian, *Netjeraperef*, Plates 17a and 18d. This hypothesis is supported by the problem that is visible in the way the arms of the figure at the right side of the offering table are rendered on the false door panel of *Sšmw* (PM, III/1, 164) (Junker, *Giza IX*, Figure 15).

[8] Petrie, *Memphite chapels*, Plate II.

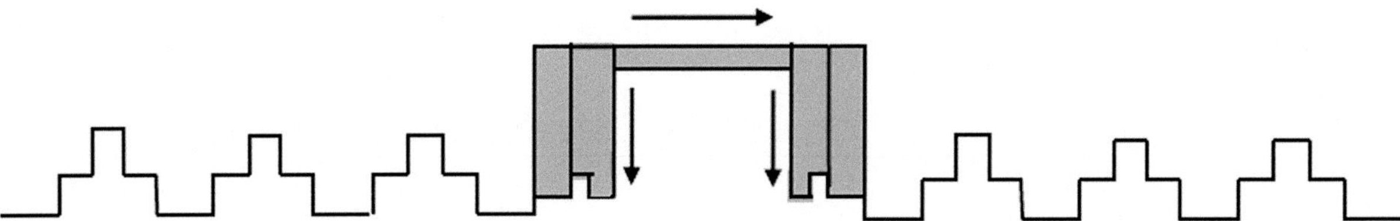

Figure 8.1 The niche in the chapel of *Ḫʿ-bꜣw-skr* (PM, III/2, 449 – 50, date: III.M – IV.E) (after Reisner, *Tomb development,* Figure 158).

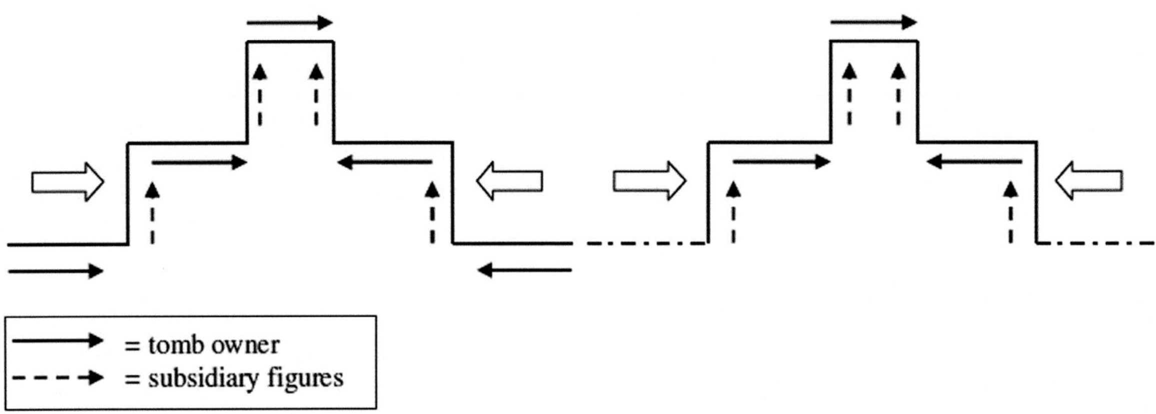

Figure 8.2 The southern niche (left) and the northern niche (right) of the tomb of *Jj-nfr* (PM, III/2, 894, date: IV.E).

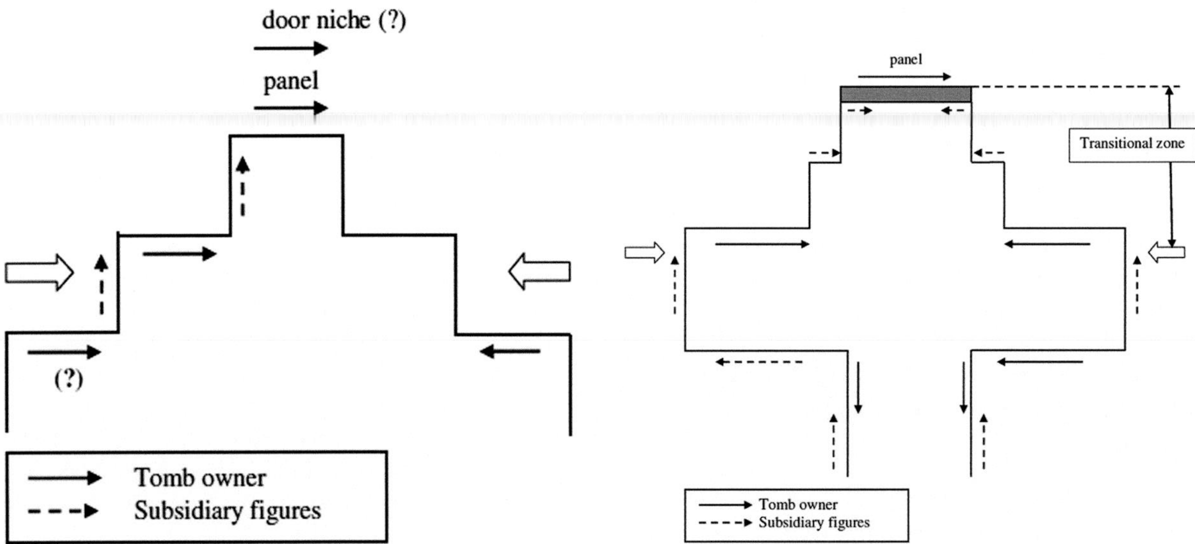

Figure 8.3 The southern niche of *Nṯr-ʿpr.f* (Alexanian, *Netjer-aperef,* 52 – 62; date: IV.E).

Figure 8.4 The cruciform chapel of *Rʿ-ḥtp* (PM, IV, 90 – 2), date: IV.1-2.

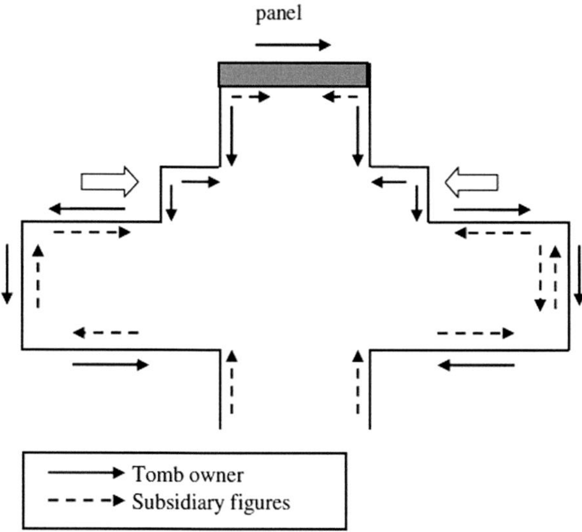

Figure 8.5 The cruciform chapel of *Mṯn* (PM, III/2, 493 – 4), date: IV.1-2.

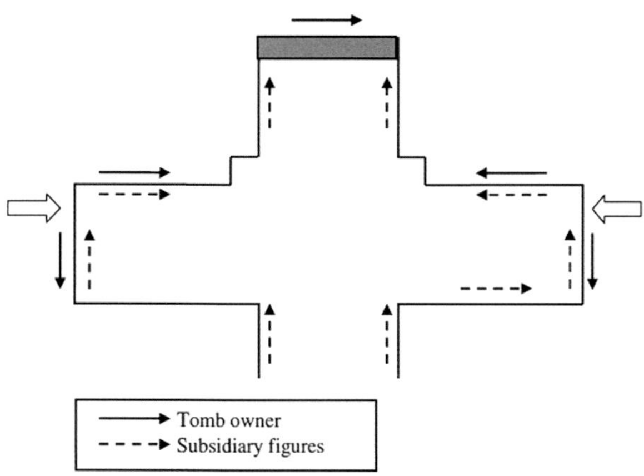

Figure 8.6 The cruciform chapel of *Sḫm-kꜣ.j* (PM, III/1, 221 – 2; date: V.L – VI.E).

chapels of Figures 8.4, 8.5 and 8.6 no further overall rules can be discerned.

The cruciform chapel can be interpreted as a transitional form between the niches and the modified cruciform chapel with a false door, while as a further step in the development of the latter chapel the transformation into the L-form chapel with the entrance in the northern or southern part of the eastern wall can be proposed. Because the niche in the western wall became increasingly shallow, it became part of the false door (see Figure 6.21). During this transformation the depiction of the tomb owner striding or sitting in the central niche of the false door became rare.[9] In most cases the niche remained empty, and if a design was placed there, it mainly was a text or a decoration representing a door.[10]

In a few tombs the tomb owner is represented in the niche of the false door as a standing half-statue or sculpted in a full frontal standing pose.[11] indicating that the right looking depiction of the tomb owner in the central niche is meant to represent the deceased coming through the door as is really the case in the mastaba of *Mrrw-kꜣ.j* in the Teti-cemetery of Saqqara. In all probability statues would have stood in the deep false door niches of the twin-mastabas in the Eastern Field at Giza.[12]

During the transitional period (dynasty IV) in the few existing cruciform chapels, in addition to the movement of the subsidiary figures, three major movements of the depiction of the human figures can be distinguished in the transitional zone:

- Depictions of the tomb owner directed toward the central niche are placed on the walls that are visible from the entrance of the chapel. This movement is continued in later periods on the posts of the false door.
- The tomb owner is directed toward the entrance,[13] possibly to invite and welcome visitors. In the later interior chapel this movement remained visible on the entrance thicknesses in the form of the tomb owner sitting or standing, and only later standing, inviting and receiving visitors (Figure 8.7).
- Subsidiary figures are moving toward the back wall of the niche.

In later periods all three movements remained in use:

- The subsidiary figures directed to the interior of the chapel were placed on the entrance thicknesses and initially also on the posts of the false door.[14]
- The tomb owner directed toward the central niche is continued on the posts of the false door.

9 The false door of *Nfr* (PM, III/2, 639 – 41, plan LXV(6); date: V.M-L) and other false doors in the tomb.

10 The central niche of the false door of *Snj-wḥmw* (PM, III/1, 75; G 2132) depicts several registers of offering bearers directed to the right; the tomb owner is depicted looking to the left. The false door of *Ἰpity* (PM, III/2, 897) has no jambs and depicts the tomb owner sitting at the offering table looking to the *left* and surrounded by text (Borchardt, *Denkmäler I*, Plate 41 (1486).

11 Borchardt, *Denkmäler I*, no. 1447; Der Manuelian, *Redi-nes*, Figure 4.6.

12 Jánosi, *Giza*, 293 – 4.

13 Harpur, *Maidum*, Figure 69 shows the same decoration directions as the niche in infra Figure 8.7.

14 On the door jambs of the false door the themes family, offering bearers and priests started to disappear in the period V.E, a development that ended in period V.L (Roeten, *Decoration*, Diagrams VIII.2.Ann., VIII.5.Ann. and VIII.6.Ann. (page 401 – 3)).

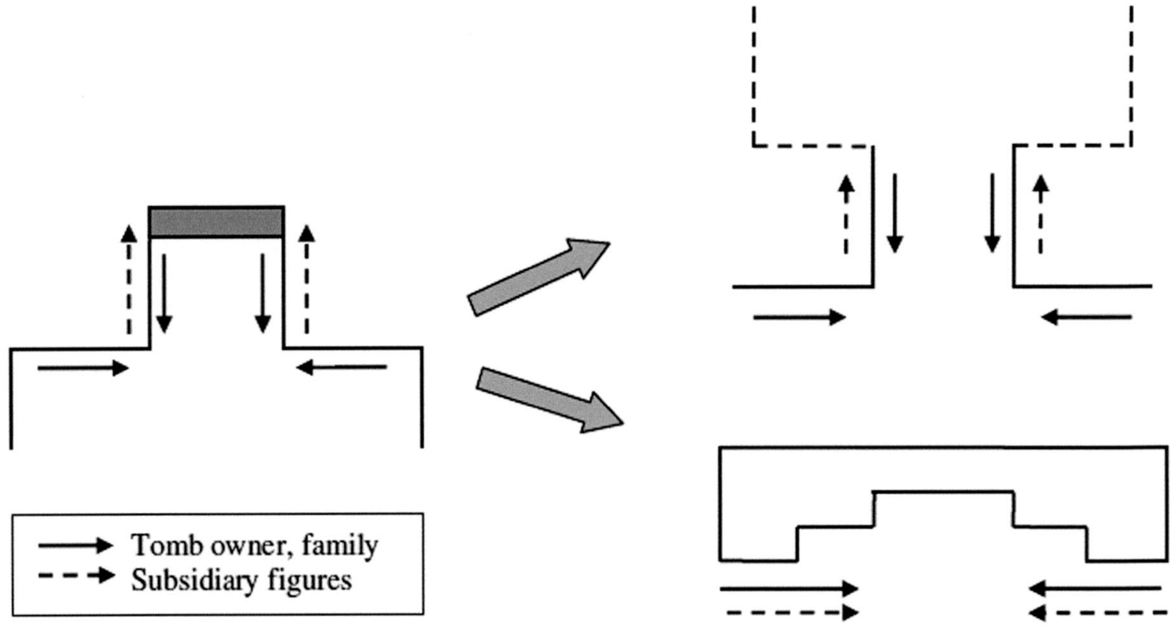

Figure 8.7 Decoration direction equivalence between niche, entrance and false door.

- The tomb owner directed toward the entrance is continued on the entrance thicknesses.

In the diagram of Figure 6.21 the result of the various discussions about possible connections between niches, entrances and false doors has been shown and will be discussed again in chapter XIV. These links between the decorative themes of these architectural elements corroborate the proposed connections between these elements.

Because the portico chapel is a different type of entrance, its decoration directionalities will be discussed in a separate chapter.

III. The entrance thicknesses, the northern and the western wall of the chapel

In L-shaped chapels that have their entrance in their eastern wall, the northern wall and the northern part of the western wall could have a connection with the entrance thicknesses. The directionality of the decorative themes on the other walls of the chapel is beyond the scope of this study.

In five tombs in the Gizean necropolis the depiction of the standing tomb owner (theme 1) has been placed on the western wall opposite the entrance of the chapel. For all five chapels the directionality of these representations is towards the false door(s) (Figure 8.8), thus guiding visitors in that direction. A special case can be found in the tomb of *Mr-jb.j* (PM, III/1, 71 – 2) where the tomb owner is sitting at the offering table over the false door that has been placed on wall section 3 opposite the entrance of the chapel, thus guiding visitors to the main false door.[15]

This theme was placed on this section of the western wall during the period V.E – V.L,[16] a relatively short period which probably ended because the importance of the actual bringing of offerings diminished at the end of the 5th dynasty. In these chapels the offering bearers in front of the standing tomb owner were directed in his/her direction and not in the direction of the false door.

The tombs gathered in Roeten, *Decoration,* Table XIII.1.Ann. (page 389 – 90) show the placements of decoration themes on the northern wall of the chapels, from this table the themes with the tomb owner (themes 1, 2 and 3) are gathered in Table IX of this study. All the depictions of the tomb owner are directed toward the entrance of the chapel. This means that, due to the light that is scattered into the entrance corridor of the chapel, the depiction of the tomb owner on the northern wall has an inviting function. The fact that the visitors on entering the chapel proceeded toward the western wall and then were faced with the depiction of the tomb owner on section 3 of the western wall which was looking in the direction of the false door, means that the presentation of the tomb owner, although placed there for a short period, guided the visitors

15 Der Manualian, *Gmast 8*, Figure 4.56.

16 Roeten, *Decoration,* Diagram IV.1.Ann. (page 397) and Table VI.1.Ann. (page 375 – 6).

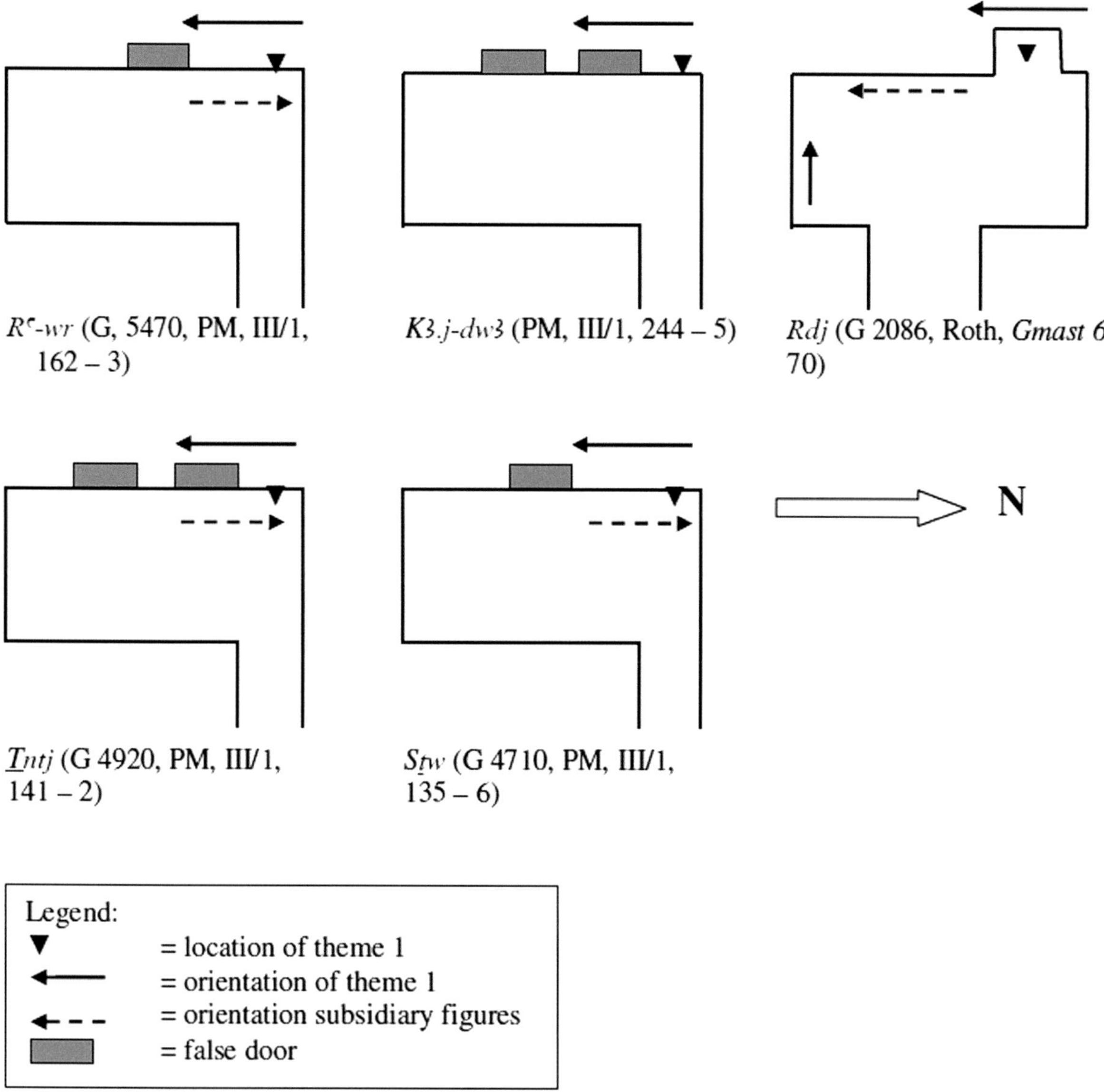

Figure 8.8 The direction of the representation of theme 1 (the tomb owner standing) on the western wall in front of the entrance.

further toward the false door too. The depiction on this part of the western wall must have been visible from the outside and consequently had an inviting function too.

IV. The connection between the niche and the entrance of the chapel

Figure 6.21 shows the connection between the various elements that are directly or indirectly linked with an entrance. For the niches and the chapel entrance the connection is that a plain single niche leads to a chapel entrance without a recess, while a plain compound niche is connected with a recessed entrance. As is shown in Figure 8.7, when this type of chapel transformed into the chapel with a false door on the western wall, it was the configuration of the deepest step of the original niche that later became the design of the false door and the chapel entrance.

Chapter Nine
Portico Chapels

I. Introduction

Chapels could be exterior or interior; in both cases the marker of the offering place was placed either against the real eastern wall of the tomb or against the western wall of the interior chapel which acted as a facsimile of the eastern wall of the tomb.

Some of these porticos are in fact chapels themselves because there is no interior chapel (*Ṯtw* (PM, III/1, 66 - 7), and the ground-plan of the portico chapel can be considered as an intermediary form of the two types of chapels.[1] The portico is in fact the transitional zone between the court-yard (the outside world) and the false door against the back wall of the portico. This makes the depiction of the tomb owner on the pillars supporting the roof equivalent to the inviting representation on the door jambs of a normal entrance.

Other porticos are a way in to an interior chapel that could be closed by means of a door (Figure 9.1).[2] In chapels of that design the portico cannot be interpreted as a transitional zone; it is an entrance, because the transitional zone is in the chapel behind the portico.

The portico could be constructed as the entrance of a mastaba (G 2001, Figure 9.6) or as the entrance of a rock-cut tomb,[3] although the latter is rare.[4]

The number of tombs with this type of entrance is small.[5] Based on the architectural surrounding, Reisner distinguishes three types of portico chapels:[6]

- The portico is situated at an open court (G 2001, Figure 9.6).
- Alongside a N-S corridor (G 4513, Reisner, *Giza I*, Figure 185).
- Opening on a street between mastabas (G 2414, Reisner, *Giza I*, Figure 187).

Chauvet distinguishes two types determined by the presence/absence of a chapel and a door (Figure 9.1).

In many of the chapels the decoration consists of an architrave with an offering formula and pillars with presentations of the tomb owner accompanied by his name and titles, while the walls remained undecorated.[7] That the portico entrance has a special meaning is evident in the chapel of *3ḫtj-ḥtp* (PM, III/1; 284) where the false door is constructed in the form of a portico entrance (Figure 9.2), with the door between the two pillars and the figures on them directed toward the false door (Figures 6.12 and 6.13).

The design of this false door goes even further, while the entrance of the tomb of *Ḫwt3* (PM, III/1, 279) (see Figure 6.4) looks like a false door that invites the visitor to enter the world of the deceased, but a false door as in Figure 9.2 can be converted into a portico that invites the visitor to enter into the chapel (Figure 9.3).

II. The decoration of the portico chapel

The decoration themes in this type of chapel are inventoried according to the list given in Figures 9.4 and 9.5,[8] and the results are gathered in Table III. There are in total 15 decorated tombs with this type of entrance and there are 70 occurrences of themes.

- The tomb owner with or without family, with or without offering table (themes 1 - 6), represents 24% (= 17) of the total occurrences. Of these 17 occurrences four are representations of the offering table scene, which is 24% (or 6% of the total occurrences), while the two portico-chapels (13 and 15) both have the scene on the walls. The possible conclusion is that the offering table scene is of minor importance in the entrance-porticos (in only two of these 13 entrance-porticos is the table scene present, which is 15%), possibly because the offering

[1] Junker (Junker, *Giza VI*, 82) considers the form of the portico as a facsimile of the porch and reception room of an Egyptian house for the well-to-do (Petrie, *Gizeh and Rifeh*, Plate XV). Another example is the model found in the tomb of *Mkt-Rᶜ* (PM, I, 359 - 64; 11th-12th dynasty) (MET, DP350593).

[2] Kanawati, *Teti cemetery V*, 18. Chauvet, *Portico-chapels*, 261.The entrance-portico can be equipped with an offering place in the portico (see the tomb of Hesi).

[3] The tomb of *Jn-k3.f* (PM, III/1, 214 - 5; date: V; G 9090; Hassan, *Giza IX*, 21 - 6) is rock-cut and has a two-pillared portico. The columns bear a text on the outside that is directed toward the entrance of the chapel; the walls of the portico are not decorated. A relatively recent discovery is the rock-cut chapel of *Jḫj* (Kuraszkiewicz, *Ikhi*). In the hewn-out opening in front of the entrance of the tomb a two-pillared portico had been constructed of plates of limestone, thus covering up the irregularity of the exposed rock.

[4] Jánosi, *Giza*, In Figure 108 in court D of the tomb of *Jwn-Mnw* (PM, III/1, 237) two pillars have been proposed that are doubtful because, apart from the lack of necessity to roof over this court, the many openings leading from the court would make roofing it over difficult.

[5] This is the same for the mortuary temples of the king and members of the royal family. An example is the entrance of the pyramid temple of *Ḫnt-k3w.s* [II] at Abusir (Verner, *Abusir III*, Figure 3a).

[6] Reisner, *Giza I*, 285.

[7] For a catalogue of tombs with a portico and a brief summary of its decoration see Chauvet, *Portico-chapels*, 297 - 311.

[8] Data from Chauvet, *Portico-chapels*, 297 - 311.

Interior chapel	Door between portico and chapel	Portico chapel	Entrance portico
X	X	---	X
---	---	X	---

Figure 9.1 The types of porticos depending on the presence/absence of a chapel and its door as defined by V.Chauvet (Chauvet, *Portico-chapels*, 261).

Figure 9.2 False door in the chapel of *ꜣḫtj-ḥtp*(PM, III/1, 284); Hassan, *Giza, I*, Plate L

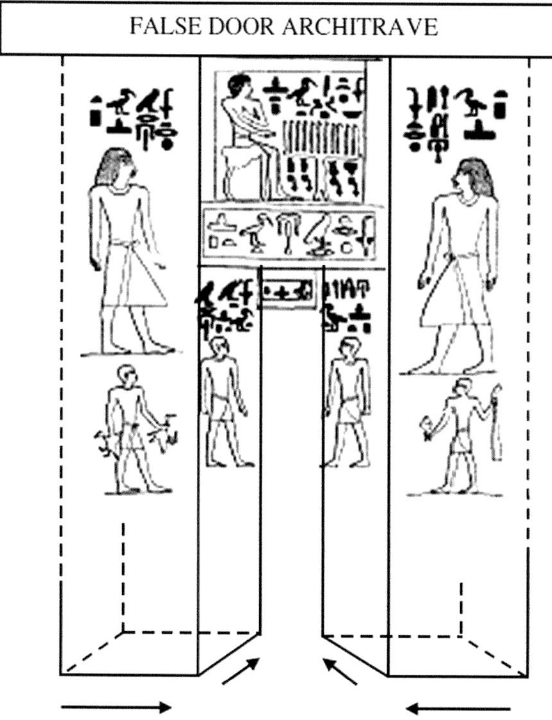

Figure 9.3 False door *ꜣḫtj-ḥtp* (PM, III/1; 284) transformed into a portico entrance.

scene is present in the chapel itself. The main function of this type of portico is thus person signalling and not purpose signalling.

- The two real portico-chapels (no. 13 and 15) both have an offering table scene, while theme 7 (= priests) only has one occurrence (in the portico-chapel of no. 15), although it might be possible that in the other portico-chapel (no. 13) the depiction of priests once was present, which leads to the conclusion that these portico-chapels were meant for cultic purposes.

The themes can be assigned to two groups: the themes with a person signalling function and the themes with a purpose (cultual) signalling function.

The person signalling themes are: Figure 9.4.

The purpose signalling themes are: Figure 9.5.

In Table III the FO percentages of the two groups have been gathered (grey columns),[9] and the result corroborates the conclusion already proposed that in the entrance-porticos the person signalling function is more important than the purpose signalling function (person signalling = 63%).

III. Discussion of some porticos

III.1. The portico chapel of Ṯtw (G 2001)

The chapel of *Ṯtw* (PM, III/1, 66 – 7; PM date: V-VI; VI.L (Simpson, *Gmast 4*, 7); VI (Harpur, *DETOK*)) is a two-pillared portico with three false doors against its western wall and no interior chapel at its western side.[10] After the termination of the construction, the northern entrance between the pillars has been closed up by a

[9] The percentages in the grey columns are determined in the following way: for a tomb of the total number of crosses the percentage in each of the two groups is calculated.

[10] Dating based on the number of loaves on the offering table that has not been placed on the panel of the false door (14 loaves) (Roeten, *Osiris*, Figure 47), the length of the loaves (38%) (Roeten, *Osiris*, Figure 59) and the surface of tomb and chapel ($28m^2$, $5m^2$) (Roeten, *Economic decline*, Figure 63) the best date is dynasty VI.

theme	description
1	The tomb owner alone (standing or sitting)
2	The tomb owner with adult man or woman
3	The tomb owner with child(ren)
10	Attendants including scribes, rendering of accounts, dancers, clappers, musicians
12	Text other than names and titles
15	Boat scenes other than funerary
16	Marsh(scenes (fish-spearing, fowling)
18	Members of the family not in direct contact with the tomb owner

Figure 9.4 The person signalling themes in portico chapels.

theme	description
4	The tomb owner alone in offering table scene
5	The tomb owner in offering table scene with adult (man or woman)
6	The tomb owner in offering table scene with child(ren)
7	Priests
8	Personified estates
9	Offering bearers
11	Butchery scene
13	Transporting statues, funeral scenes
14	Piles of offerings
17	Agriculture (including marsh-activities like fording)

Figure 9.5 The purpose signalling themes in portico chapels.

wall.[11] Offering table scenes have been represented on the three walls of the portico;[12] the false door of the tomb owner is placed against the western wall in the north-western corner. On the northern wall, next to the false door, the wall is decorated with an offering list, the tomb owner is represented in an offering table scene, and the lowest register shows some offering bearers. It is possible that the wall, which partially screens the portico from the courtyard, has been erected in order to obtain, in view of the openness of a portico-courtyard combination, at least for the offering place of the tomb owner, some privacy during the rituals for the sustenance of his *k3*.[13] This possible explanation is supported by the fact that the false door of the tomb owner has been placed completely off centre.

However, the directional program in Figure 9.6 enables another explanation based on the fact that the entrance into the courtyard is at the eastern side of the northern wall of the courtyard, a location that gave the visitors, before entering into the portico,[14] the possibility of seeing the whole length of the text above the entrance

[11] The statement that the wall is of a later date than the tomb itself is based on the observation that this screening wall is placed partly in front of the northern framing text of the portico (Simpson, *Gmast 4*, Figure 13; Giza Archives, photo A532_NS). Another argument is the difference in construction quality that is plainly visible in the photos taken after the clearing of the portico and the courtyard (Simpson, *Gmast 4*, Plate XIIIb/c; Giza Archives, photos A532_NS and A531_NS; although the construction of this wall differs strongly from that shown in Chauvet, *Portico-chapels*, Plate 13).

[12] Simpson, *Gmast 4*.

[13] Chauvet, *Portico-chapels*, 294.

[14] Chauvet, *Portico-chapels*, 294, following the text on the architrave would indeed lead to the text at the left side of the portico, but that would keep the visitor from entering the portico between the southern wall and pillar, thereby having the possibility to pass in front of all the false doors before entering the portico part reserved for the tomb owner.

in one glance, a text which was written in one line both on the architrave and on the edge of the roofing blocks.[15]

Because in the first construction phase the screening wall was not present and the figures on the eastern side of the pillars and on the western wall were all looking at the offering place of the tomb owner, the visitor entered between the northern wall and pillar. On returning from the offering place the figures on the back side of the pillars indicated to the visitor to pass before the false door of a woman who was probably the wife of the tomb owner.

After the screening wall had been placed, the visitor could still read the architrave over its full length, but, in order to reach the chapel of the tomb owner, he or she had to pass between the two pillars, thus facing the false door of the wife (?) and turn right while being invited in by the figure of the tomb owner on the western side of the northern pillar.

Whatever the solution, the importance of the tomb owner is evident from the unilateral orientation of the persons presented on the various architectural elements.[16] The screening wall formed a narrow east-west (!) oriented chapel that was entered from the south and in which a false door was placed against the western wall (Figure 9.6). Nowhere in the decoration of this small (private) chapel was another person than the tomb owner depicted. Upon leaving the chapel the decoration on the reverse of the pillars guided the visitor out of the portico. The direction of the various presentations of the tomb owner on the pillars indicates that the situation without the screening was the original intention and that the installation of the screening wall disturbed the underlying idea of these images.

The direction of the persons represented on the sides of the pillars poses some problems:

- The standing figure on the western side of the northern pillar is facing south and not, as the other figures on the pillars, north. Giza Archives, Giza Archives Photo A5695_NS shows that the sceptre is visible in front of the legs and the hand is the closed right-side hand of a person walking to the right. An explanation could be that the figure was deliberately placed in this way, at first in order to convey visitors to the middle exit, and later to receive visitors coming to the chapel of the tomb owner.
- The figures on the front side of the two pillars are both walking to the right and have the sceptre in front of their legs and the closed side of the hand holding it is visible (Giza Archive photo A531_NS), which indicates that they were depicted according to the convention.[17]
- The only figure that has been depicted not in accordance with the convention is the figure on the western side of the southern pillar (Giza Archives, Photo A5698), who is walking to the left with the staff and the baton holding as if walking to the right.

What also stands out is that on the panel of the southern false door that was re-dedicated from a woman called *Nb.t* to *Msnj*, a son of the tomb owner, it remained visible that the original female owner had been depicted smelling the flower of a water lily (Giza Archives, photo A5654_NS). At first sight it seems remarkable that on the panel of a false door, the place where the depiction of the person involved had the most magical significance, so little effort has been made to take away this detail.[18] Later in the Old Kingdom the depiction of a male person smelling the flower had become more frequent, and if the date of the tomb is VI.L as given by Simpson is correct,[19] the chronological development of the male and female gestures involving the flower of the water lily indicates that in that period the smelling gesture was already quite 'normal' for male persons.[20]

In view of the connection between the increasing smelling of water lily flowers by male persons and the emergence of the cult of Osiris, it is possible that this detail was deliberately not removed.

III.2. The portico chapel of ꜣḫtj-mḥw (G 2375)

The entrance of the mastaba of *ꜣḫtj-mḥw* (PM, III/1, 87; date: VI (PM); VI.3-4? (Harpur, *DETOK*) is a portico-chapel (Figure 9.7). During the excavation of this tomb G 2375 an intrusive tomb G 2375a was found that had been constructed to the right side of the portico. This tomb had been built after the termination of the cult for the deceased in mastaba G 2375, as its construction made going into the portico impossible. As in the mastaba of *Ṯtw* the visitor enters the courtyard in the north-eastern corner, and this gives him/her the possibility

[15] Simpson, *Gmast 4*, Plate XIVa.

[16] Simpson, *Gmast 4*, Figure 14. The inside face of the southern pillar shows the person walking to the left. In that case the baton-carrying hand would be depicted with the open side visible with the sceptre hidden behind the legs, while the stave carrying hand would be closed; it is obvious that here a mistake has been made that is later (partly) corrected by taking away the sceptre over the legs (Giza Archives photo A5698-NS).

[17] Simpson, *Gmast 4*, Plate XVI/c and page 8. Giza Archives Photos A530P, A531P, A5695 and A5698.

[18] Roeten, *Osiris*, Table VIII.

[19] *Gmast 4*, 7. Based on the surface of the tomb (Roeten, *Economic decline*, Figures 56, 60 and 63), the number and the length of the loaves (Roeten, *Osiris*, Figures 47and 59) a date VI.M - VI.L is probable.

[20] Roeten, *Osiris*, Figure 113 gives 80% for the period VI.M – VI.L.

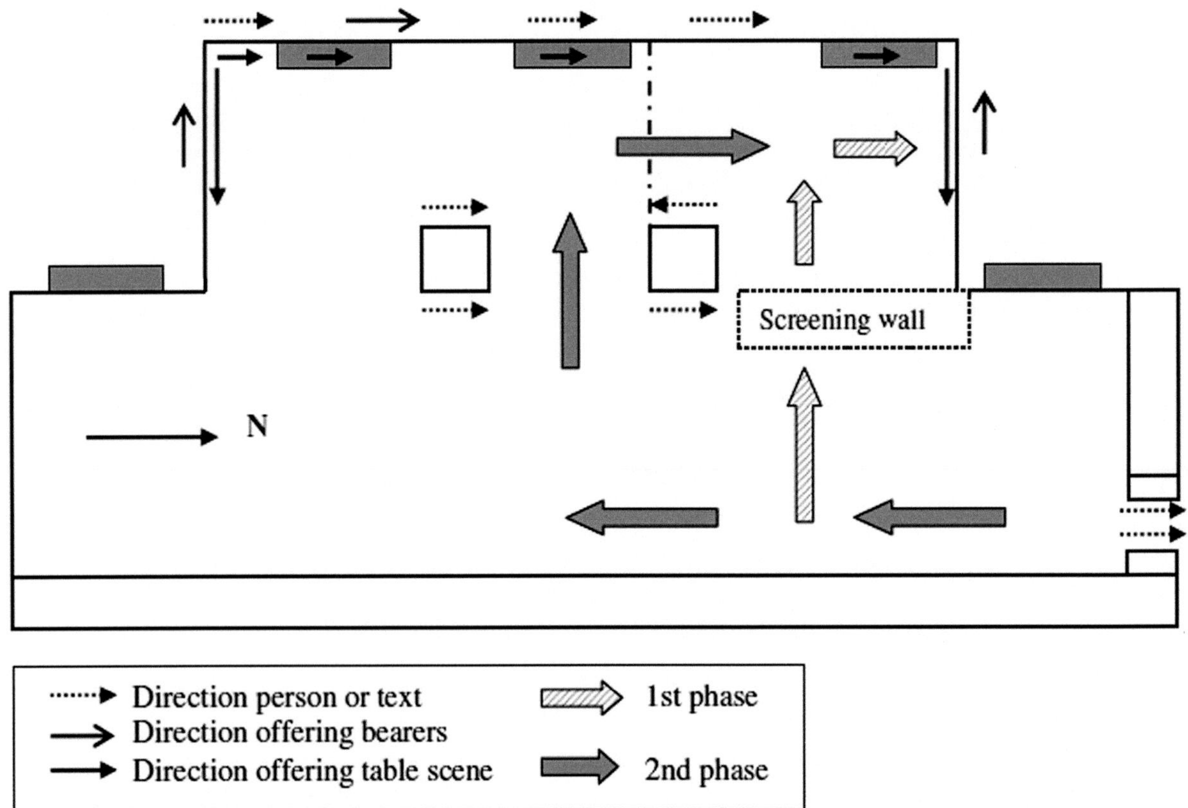

Figure 9.6 Decoration direction diagram portico-chapel of *Ṯtw* (G 2001).

to look at the text on the architrave without following it to the end (the text is read from right to left).

The portico chapel of *3ḫt-mḥw* differs from that of *Ṯtw* (section I.1) in that it is dedicated to one person. The decoration of the northern and southern separation walls is not identical. The northern wall shows the tomb owner with family and servants fishing in the marshes, thereby moving in the direction of the false door, while on the southern wall the tomb owner is standing together with family and looks at how the animals that are intended as offerings are being led. The direction of the decoration of the pillars is such that the visitor is guided between the pillars toward the false door.

III.3. The entrance portico of Hsj [21]

The portico of *Hsj* is an 'entrance-portico' with, at the northern side of the portico, an extra false door dedicated to the tomb owner. The basic idea of the portico itself is identical with the one of *Ṯtw*, except for the separating wall that has been constructed later in the chapel of the latter. The recess in the passage between the portico and chapel gives the impression that it could be closed, and this might explain the presence of the false door in the portico itself. However, whether the recess at the end of this passage could be closed or not remains a problem, because, although a pivot hole has been found in the ceiling, both walls of the recess are decorated, and no floor pivot or bolt hole has been found.[22]

In this portico it is clear that the orientation of the non-textual decoration on walls and pillars was aimed at receiving the visitors and after that guiding them to the chapel. In the orientation of the decoration in the portico itself there is no specific indication of a preference to lead the visitors to the false door there. If the door into the interior chapel was closed, the false door in the portico,being an east-west oriented facsimile of the north-south oriented main chapel,[23] became the offering place. Apart from the false door, one of the decorative themes on the western portico wall showed a convoy of two ships sailing south and a third much smaller boat faring in the same direction. In the literature these decoration themes have been interpreted in a funerary context. Apart from the older interpretations, like a pilgrimage to, in this case,

[21] According to Kanawati, *Teti cemetery V,* Plate 47door-rebates are present at the chapel side of the corridor between the portico and the chapel; in the text no mention is made of the presence of door-pivots.

[22] Kanawati, *Teti cemetery V,* 18.

[23] The surface of the interior chapel is 50% of the surface of the portico, while the ratio L:W is about 1:3 for both of them.

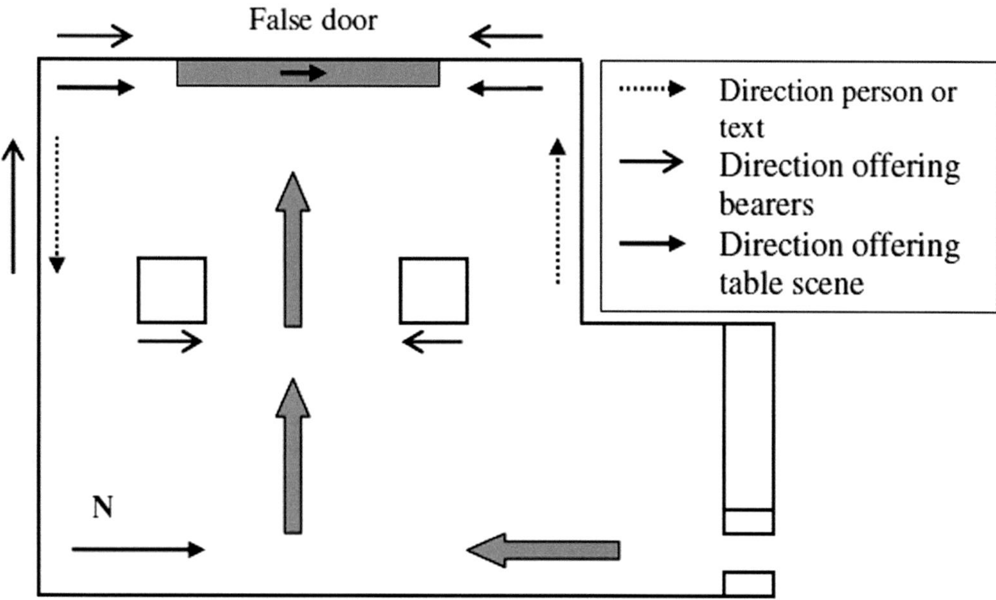

Figure 9.7 Decoration direction diagram portico-chapel of *ꜣḫt-mḥw* (G 2375).

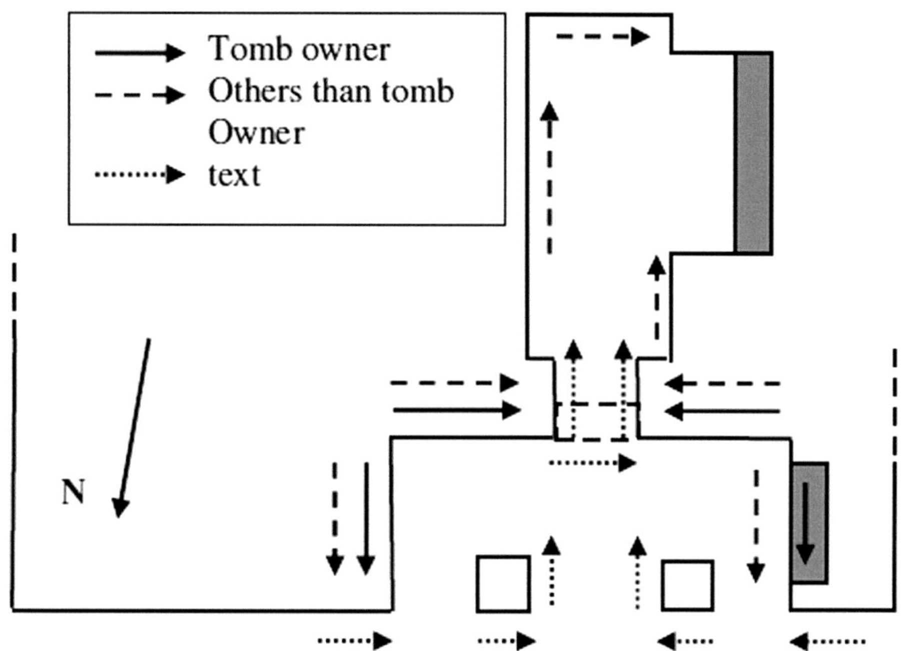

Figure 9.8 The portico-chapel of Hesi (date: VI.1) (schematically after Kanawati, *Teti cemetery V*, Plate 47; Chauvet, *Portico-chapels*, Plate 10).

Abydos, other propositions have been put forward, such as a journey to the sanctuaries of the great gods in the canal of the West,[24] all of them being funerary and connected to the after-life. However, there is another possible explanation; the first two ships just show the tomb owner on one of his voyages necessary for some of the offices he held, and the scene is nothing more than the presentation of an aspect of his daily life.

III.4. The porticos of Nj-ꜥnḫ-ḫnmw & ḫnmw –ḥtp[25]

According to the table in Figure 9.1 the type of entrance as shown in Figure 9.9 makes it an entrance-portico.

[24] Kanawati, *Teti cemetery V*, 33.

[25] PM, III/2, 641 – 4 (V.6-7).

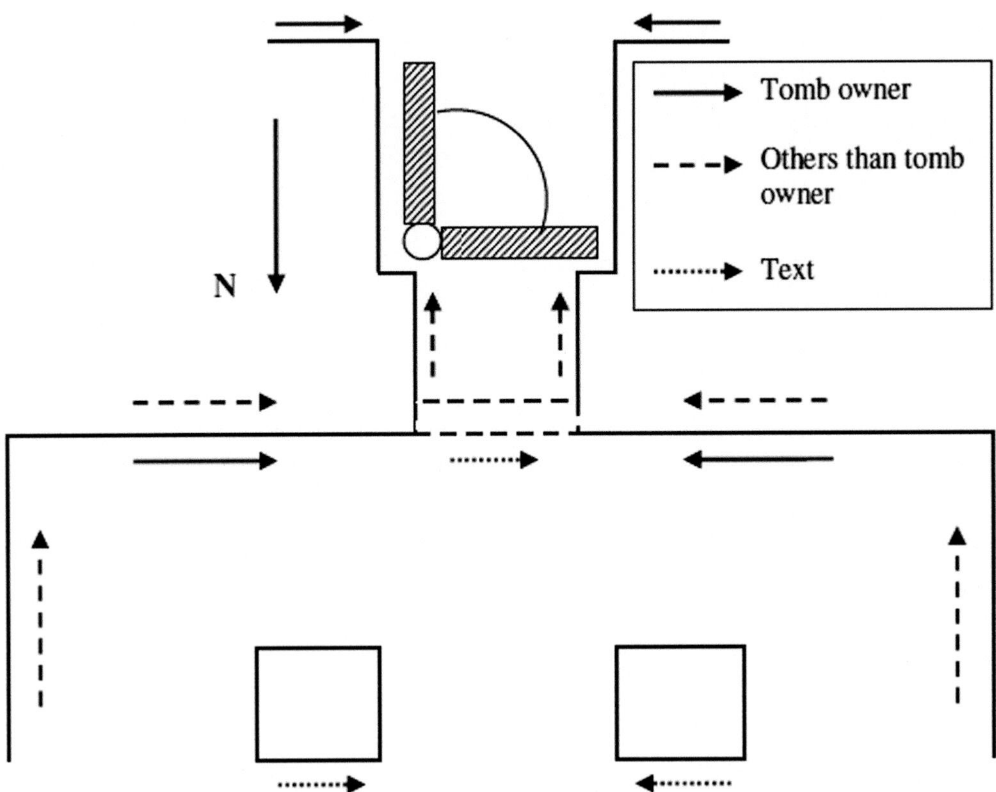

Figure 9.9 The first (exterior) entrance-"portico" of the tomb of *Nj-ʿnḫ-H̱nmw* and *H̱nmw-ḥtp*.

Because this tomb is partly built as a mastaba and partly rock-cut, the consequence is that the cult chapel has no direct connection with the portico. The plan of the tomb (PM, III/2, plan LXVI) shows that in reality in this tomb two porticos are discernible.

The portico in Figure 9.9 (further called the 'exterior portico') gives access to the mastaba part of the tomb (the width of the portico is 3.75m) and is a pillared portico. The second portico gives access to the rock-cut part of the tomb and is at 2.25m is less wide than the first (Figure 9.10). This entrance is not a portico in the direct sense, but the pilasters can be interpreted as such, because on these pilasters only the depiction of the tomb owner and text is placed, as is the case in the other porticos.

The larger width of the southern wall of the first portico makes it possible to place a major scene between the two sitting tomb owners over the architrave; however, the depiction consists of piles of offerings and a small butchery scene, and is nearly identical with the equivalent scene in the interior portico where some offering bearers are placed between the two sitting tomb owners. The southern wall of the exterior portico provides enough space to place the fishing and fowling scenes on both sides of the entrance.

The interior portico was initially planned as the main entrance of the tomb, and it was foreseen as a 'normal' entrance consisting of two door jambs, an architrave and two entrance thicknesses, each of them provided with the decoration that was customary for these elements. This made the original entrance exclusively person signalling.

In the second construction phase a vestibule was placed in front of the original entrance, which created extra space over the door. This space was filled with the offering table scene of the two tomb owners, priests, offering bearers and offerings, while the side walls were filled with the tomb owner receiving persons leading animals meant as offerings, thus giving the portico a purpose signalling function next to the person signalling one.

During the second construction phase of the tomb an exterior entrance in the form of a portico was added. The roof was supported by two pillars stating names and titles. Over the entrance, offerings, butchery and the offering table scene were depicted which gave it a purpose signalling function. The only person signalling functions were the two marsh scenes showing the two tomb owners in the activity of spear fishing and fowling, accompanied by their names and titles, servants and members of the family.

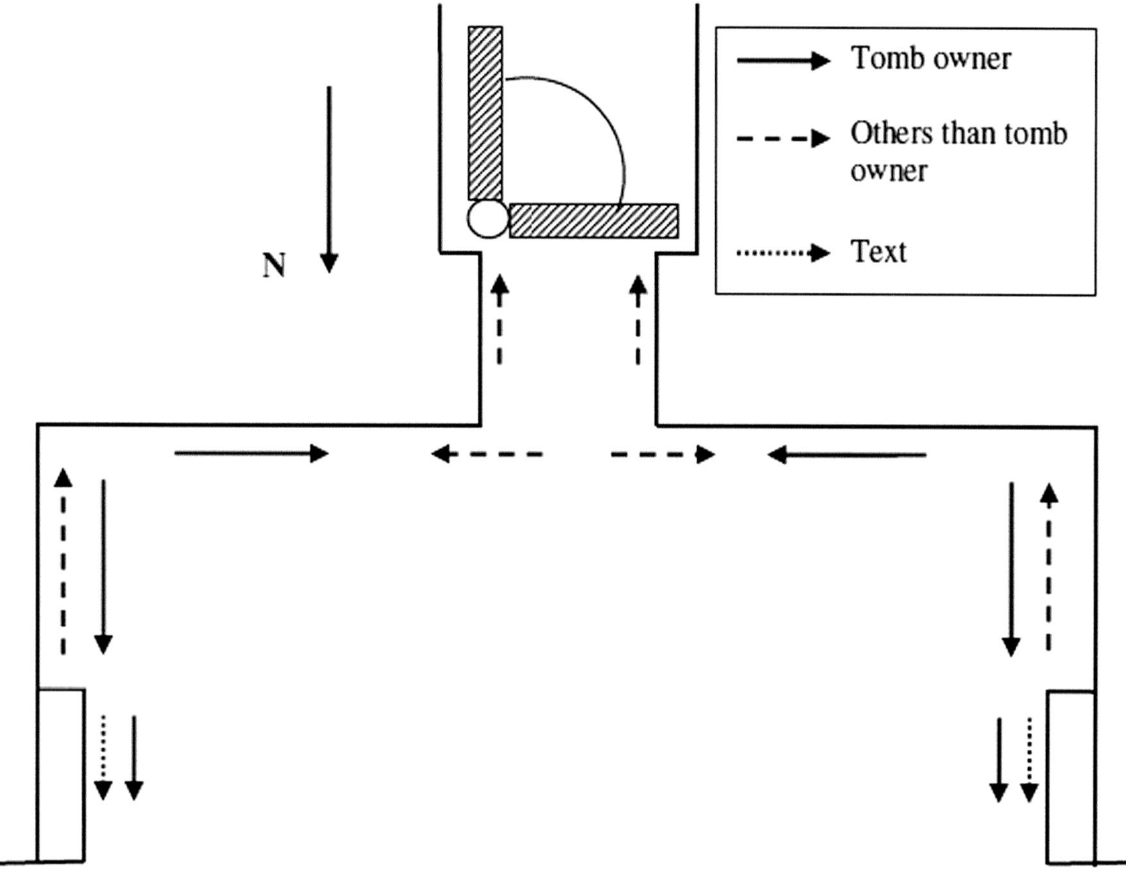

Figure 9.10 The second (interior) entrance-“portico” of the tomb of *Nj-ʿnḫ-H̱nmw* and *H̱nmw-ḥtp*.

	Person signalling									Purpose signalling									
entrance	1	2	3	10	12	15	16	18		4	5	6	7	8	9	11	14	17	13
exterior					x		x	x		x						x	x		x
interior	x	x	x							x			x		x		x		

Figure 9.11 The decoration themes on the walls of the porticos in Figures 9.9 and 9.10.

From Figure 9.11 it can be concluded that the basic ratio of person and purpose signalling themes is equal for both porticos although their respective catalogue of themes is not completely identical, which might indicate a change in the concept of the decoration of the entrance of the tomb.

III.5. Special cases......

III.5.1. Mrrw- kꜣ.j

The mastaba of *Mrrw -.kꜣ.j* (PM, III/2, 525 – 34; date: VI.1) in the Teti cemetery is one of the exceptionally large tombs that were built in the early years of the 6th dynasty. Room A 13 in this mastaba is a hall with a roof supported by six decorated pillars (Figure 9.12). In the northern wall an ‘entrance’ with a striding statue of the tomb owner was constructed.

Standing between pillars 2 and 3 and somewhat south of them,[26] the ensemble resembles the pillared entrance of an elite residence with the owner of the house coming out of the door to meet the visitor(s), and in that respect resembles the portico tomb of *N-sḏr-kꜣ.j* (PM, III/1, 72). The passage could be closed with a double door of which the lower pivot holes are still

[26] Duell, *Mereruka I*, Frontispiece.

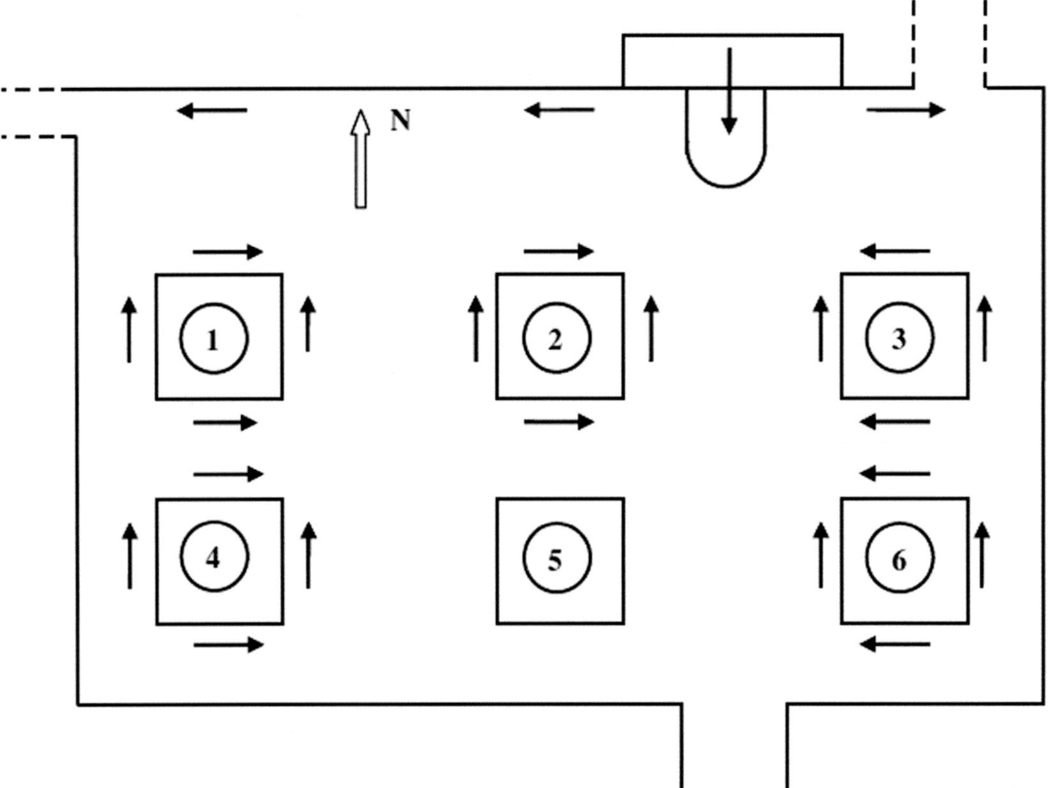

Figure 9.12 Plan of room A 13 in the mastaba of *Mrrw-.kꜣ.j*.

visible (the pivot holes at the top are lost, and the top of the door has been reconstructed).[27] In accordance with the portico entrances discussed, the directionality of the decoration on the six pillars is centred on the door with the statue of the tomb owner; on the northern wall the presentations of the tomb owner are directed away from the door which is in accordance with coming out of the door and walking away into the world of the living.

Although there are three passages connecting the hall with other rooms, its ground-plan plainly shows that the main entrance was situated in the southern wall and that the area between that entrance and the door in the northern wall was the most important part of the room.

Originally this hall was the end point of the interior structure of the mastaba; the corridor to the west leads to a complex of store rooms; the corridor to the north leads to the superstructure of the tomb of the son *Mrj-ttj*, which was added in a later phase of the construction of the mastaba. The conclusion is that this hall was intended as a major cultic space of the mastaba of *Mrrw-kꜣ.j* and his wife and that the tomb owner is represented as coming through an entrance in the northern wall of the tomb (later the superstructure of the tomb of the son was constructed against this wall).[28] The presence of the staircase with offering table in front of the door of appearance carries the message that the tomb owner is not only coming forth out of the world of the dead but also that the world he was living in as a deceased person lies on a higher plane of existence than the world of the living.

III.5.2. Kꜣ.j-m-ḥst

The mastaba of *Kꜣ.j-m-ḥst* (PM, III/2, 542 – 3) was constructed in several phases. At first the mastaba had a plain façade; in a later stage the tomb owner had a pillared hall constructed against the original eastern wall.[29] This hall was probably covered with a vaulted

27 Duell, *Mereruka II*, Plate 147.

28 The tomb owner coming from the north fits perfectly in the probable lay-out of an elite residence. The prevailing wind was from the north, which made that the private quarters of the tomb owner were situated in the direction of the northern side of the house (Roth, *Social change*, Figure 2 (Khentkawes)). The public entrance and the public part of the residence would then be at the southern side, the former provoking the necessity and presence of the portico. The situation with a double row of pillars in the portico is not represented in the collection of 'soul-houses' that have been excavated by W. M. Flinders Petrie (Petrie, *Gizeh and Rifeh*), but is visible in the house model of *Mkt-Rꜥ*.

29 McFarlane, *Kaiemheset*, 23 – 9.

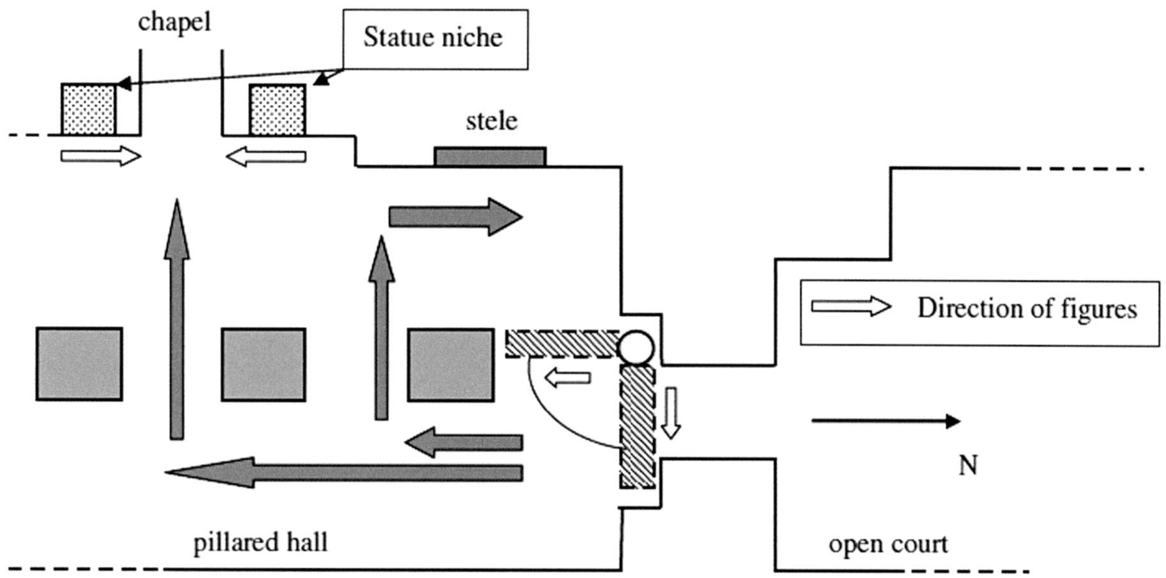

Figure 9.13 The pillared hall, the chapel entrance and the open court of the chapel of *K3.j-m-ḥst* (after McFarlane, *Kaiemheset*, Plate 40).

roof and consequently is not a portico according to the strict interpretation of the definition.[30] Nevertheless the tomb and its hall are included in the discussion because the directionality of the complex as a whole has a strong resemblance with the situation in the portico of *Ṯtw* (G 2001) (Figure 9.6).

The door from the open court into the pillared hall has a decoration that is directed to the left when the door is closed, and therefore has a signalling function, and by looking towards the opening side of the door possibly an inviting function. On opening the door not only did its decoration guide the visitor in, but it also closed the passage between the wall and the northern pillar, thus converting the northern half of the hall into a small chapel with a(n) (anepigraphic) but possibly somewhat later stele against its western wall. When the door was opened the situation resembled that in the portico of *Ṯtw* (G 2001) (Figure 9.6) where the stone wall created the same small chapel with a false door against the western wall.

Because the pillars have no directional decoration (anymore) the depiction of the tomb owner together with his wife and the statue niches grouped at both sides of the chapel entrance are the only guiding and inviting items that have been found.

This resembles to a certain extent the situation in the chapel of *Ḫww-wr* (PM, III/1, 254 – 5) where a deep niche with a false door is flanked by niches with statues of the tomb owner,[31] while over the three niches a cavetto cornice has been placed. The figures of the tomb owner are clearly inviting visitors to enter into the niche with the false door, and this would mean that the figures are in fact the depictions normally placed on the door jambs flanking the entrance. This consideration makes the niche with the false door the chapel, and thus the transitional zone.

III.5.3. Ptḥ – špss

During the three phases of the building history that resulted in the final plan of the mastaba of *Ptḥ – špss* at Abusir (PM, III/1, 340 – 2) several entrances were constructed.[32] Some of these entrances are to a certain degree problematic unless it is realized that, during the successive phases of the construction, the social status of the tomb owner was on a constant upward trend.

The construction of the mastaba started with the 'initial mastaba' of which the dimensions were in accordance with the conventions that existed for tombs of high officials.[33] The plan of the rooms inside the superstructure was consistent with the interior of the tombs in the nearby, nearly contemporaneous 'Cemetery of nobles',[34] and the somewhat later tombs in the 'family cemetery of Djedkare' (Figure 9.14).[35]

30 McFarlane, *Kaiemheset*, 27.

31 LD, *II*, 44.

32 Krejči, *Abusir XI*, Figure I.12.

33 Roeten, *Economic decline*, 110.

34 Krejči, *Abusir XI*, Figure 3.2.

35 Verner, *Abusir VI*, Figure G1.

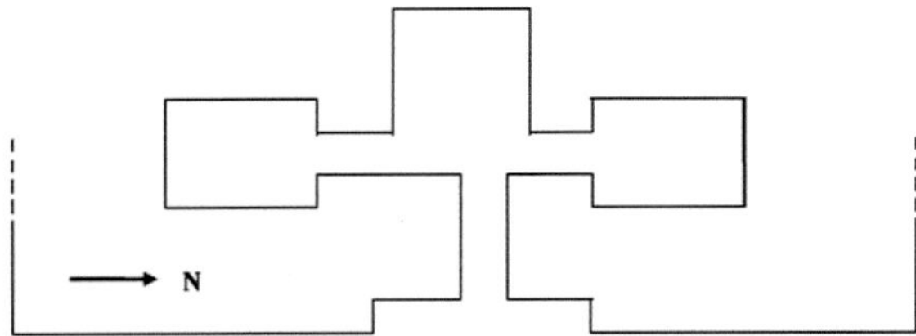

Figure 9.14 Ground-plan of 5th dynasty Abusir mastabas (schematically after Verner, Krejči, *Abusir VI,* Figure G1).

The design of the entrance is completely different from that of non-royal tombs of that period (Figures 9.14 and 9.15), but it shows a likeness to the entrance of the royal mortuary temple where the causeway reaches the vestibule of the pyramid temple.[36]

The reports of the excavations do not mention a reconstruction of the entrance, so it is probable that the entrance was designed in this way from the start of the construction of the mastaba.

This entrance never lost its importance because, once the pillared court constructed, the effigies of the tomb owner that were placed on the pillars directed the visitor towards that entrance. That the design of this entrance is based on a tendency to incorporate royal mortuary architecture can be seen from the following observations:

- In the ground plan of the mastaba of the first building-phase, as shown in Figure 9.14, the basic design of the interior rooms is recognizable, although the two rooms next to the vestibule have been lengthened in the E-W direction. This makes the offering rooms (rooms 25 and 28 in Krejči, *Abusir XI,* Figure 1.12) resemble the offering room in royal mortuary temples.[37]
- Although it is evident that the tendency to incorporate royal mortuary architectural elements in his tomb was present from the very beginning of its construction, it became even more pronounced during the second building phase. In this phase a building was constructed against the northern side of the east wall of the initial mastaba that had no direct connection with it (it was only during the third building phase that this became the sole entrance into the complex, but still without making a connection with the initial mastaba).[38] In this building a room with statue niches, preceded by a room with two pillars and statues of the standing tomb owner, was constructed.[39] Seen from the outside, this must have looked like the pillared court in the mastaba of *Mrrw-.k3.j* (Figure 9.12),[40] although the directionality of the decoration in the pillared court might lead to the conclusion that it was originally meant as a portico.
- In the third building phase a second portico was added in front of the first one, thus not only giving a view similar to that of the pillared court of *Mrrw-.k3.j* upon entering, but also a view similar to that when entering the peristyle court of a royal mortuary temple.[41]

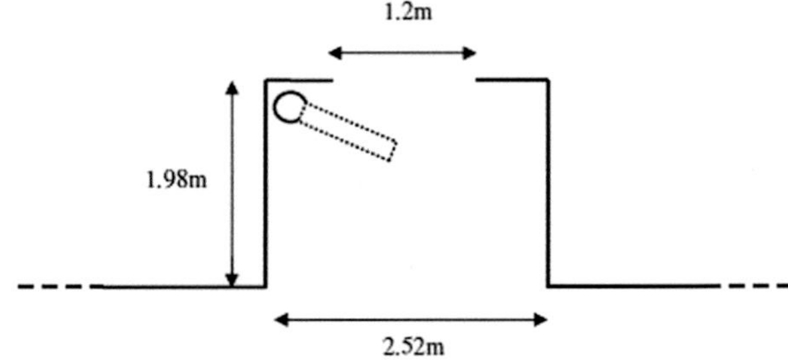

Figure 9.15 The entrance of the initial mastaba (schematically).

Architectural elements that direct the gaze to the centre of cultic importance had already been used in royal mortuary architecture, and the result of the second building phase created a situation that resembled this. In later periods traces of this tendency to represent social status and a place within royal circles by incorporating royal mortuary architectural elements are still visible in the mastabas of *Mrrw -.k3.j* (PM, III/2, 525 – 34) and *K3-gm-nj* (PM, III/2, 521 – 5). Both mastabas have boat pits and a narrow east-west directed chapel, while in the mastaba of *Mrrw -.k3.j* the pillared court still directs the gaze of the visitor to the niche with the striding tomb owner.

[36] Stadelmann, *Pyramiden,* Figures 53, 61.

[37] Stadelmann, *Pyramiden,* Figures 28, 32, 53; Krejči, *Abusir XI,* 81.

[38] There are some architectural aspects in this building that give the impression that it was meant as a (much smaller) facsimile of the valley temple in the royal mortuary complex. Some of these aspects are:
- When entering the pillared portico is the first roofed over space (Stadelmann, *Pyramiden,* Figures 53, 55).
- The narrow corridor between the first and second room.
- The two portico entrances/exits.

[39] Morgan, *Ptah-chepsés,* Figure 2 (room B).

[40] Balík, *Ptahshepses,* Figure 3.

[41] Balík, *Ptahshepses,* Figure 5.

Chapter Ten

The Themes of the Decoration

I. Introduction

In order to enable the *k3* of the deceased to have an after-life it needed sustenance, and a place where it magically could take the essence of it.[1] This eventually developed into a chapel with a false door in front of which offerings could be placed. Many of these chapels had decoration on one or more of its walls. As early as the predynastic period, decoration was used in a mortuary context; an example is tomb 100 at Hieraconpolis that had two walls in the burial chamber that bore painted decoration. The tomb has been dated to middle Naqada II, and the main-stream scholarly opinion is that the scenes depicted on the wall indicate that it must have been the burial monument of a predynastic ruler (Figure 10.1).[2]

Decorating the walls of an offering place developed further until finally the walls of the now mainly interior chapels were covered with it.

Apart from the meaning and importance of every one of the decorative themes, there are several roles that can be assigned to the decoration as a whole. The basic intention could be magical, and in view of that some scholars propose that the decoration was meant to show the tomb owner, whose *k3* had free access to the chapel, the life he had led while still alive. Yet, in my opinion the latter hypothesis is basically invalid for two reasons: the first being that the tomb owner did not need to be reminded how his life on earth had been, he had been at the centre of it, and the second being that this could indicate that the afterlife was less joyous than life on earth. Because he had died in the conviction that a better and grander life awaited him, there was little call for a look back at the life that had been. It is more likely that it was meant to show illiterate visitors the social status and the professional occupations of the tomb owner, because, from their emic point of view, they must have been able to interpret the symbolism of the decorative themes.

A more plausible reason for the presence of the themes could be that part of the decoration was meant as a magical means of giving sustenance to the *k3* of the deceased, examples of such themes being agricultural scenes and the production of bread and beer.

II. The decorative themes, preliminary considerations

The decorative themes that are the subject of this part of the study are placed in tombs in the major necropoleis of the Memphite area, Saqqara, Abusir and Giza.

The necropolis of Abû Rawâsh consists of a group of (sub) necropoleis in the vicinity of the pyramid of Radjedef (IV.3). Renewed excavations revealed that of these cemeteries cemetery F can be dated to the reign of that king.[3] Although PM, II/1 claims that the tombs of cemetery F are dated to the 5th dynasty or later, these dates are based on information that can be considered to be outdated or misinterpreted.

Consequently this cemetery can be seen as a part of the Giza cemetery because of the Old Kingdom funeral traditions of the early 4th dynasty (late in the reign of Khufu (IV.2) or the reign of his successor Radjedef (IV.3)), that can be found in the architecture and decoration of the tombs that make up the cemetery.[4]

A distinction is made between a 'normal' entrance with door-jambs and a portico entrance in which the jambs are placed deeper in the tomb complex and are roofed over; one of the reasons for this distinction is that in portico entrances some decorative themes are employed that are not used in the other type of entrance (an example is the decoration theme depicting the tomb owner hunting in the marshes, which can be found in portico entrances on both sides of the door into the chapel (for example in the portico of the chapel of *Nj-ˁnḫ-H̱nmw* and *H̱nmw-ḥtp* (PM, III/2, 641-4)), but not in the other types of entrances.[5]

In the tables that are made to indicate the presence or absence of the decoration themes on the various elements of the entrance every theme is specified by a numeral preceded by an abbreviation which specifies the element (D = Door jamb (tables I, IV), E = Entrance thickness (table II, V)). The numeral stands for one type

1 See chapters XII and XIII.

2 Payne, *Tomb 100;* Adams, *Protodynastic,* 36-40; Monnet Saleh, *Tomb 100.*

3 Baud, *F 19,* 18-23.

4 Baud, *F 19,* 29-30.

5 Harpur, *DETOK,* 52. Sometimes the scenes were placed on the walls of the chapel (Fowling: G 6020; Weeks, *Gmast 5,* 41, Plate 33; spear fishing: Hassan, *Giza V,* 267).

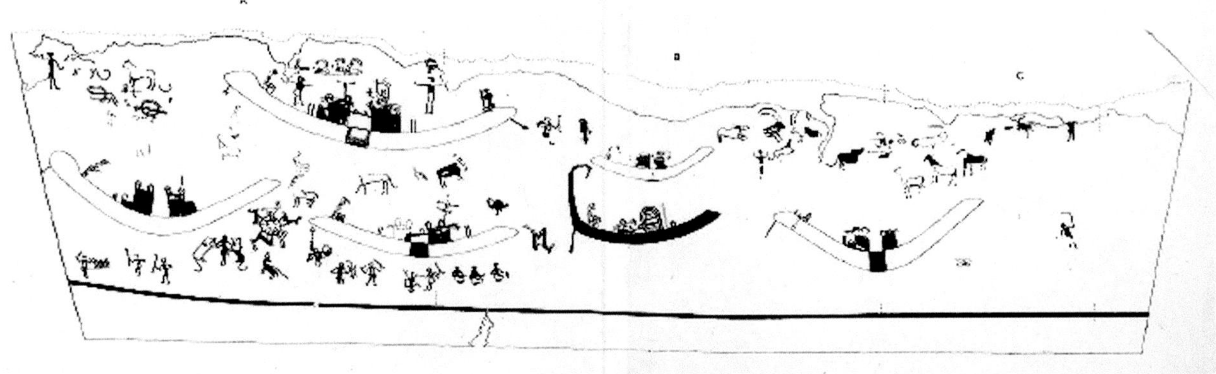

Figure 10.1 The decoration of the south-western wall of tomb 100 at Hierakonpolis (from Quibell, *Hierakonpolis II,* Plate 75).

of theme regardless of whether it is present or not on the element.

In Roeten, *Decoration,* in the tables given for the presence or absence of themes on the walls of the chapel, the possible presence of minor themes is added as an option. Compared to the walls of the chapel, those of the entrance thicknesses are small, so that the presence of several strong space engaging themes could not be supposed. The consequence is that next to the main theme of the tomb owner only the much smaller subsidiary figures could have been present. A differentiation has been made between the various subsidiary figures. In a part of the wall where the decoration is only partly present, but where a subsidiary figure could be placed, this figure will not be included in the catalogue, because due to the differentiation the type of subsidiary figure cannot be determined.

In the tables of the decoration themes on the door jambs and the entrance thicknesses a significant portion of the themes will be present in a low percentage. These themes are not included in the further considerations.

Although the total of decorative themes can be interpreted as a unit with the cult for the deceased in order to sustain his *k3* as its sole purpose, it is evident that the scenes can be divided into a number of groups and that each of these groups serves a specific purpose (Figure 7.4). The themes can be divided into

- The large group of scenes from daily life, including the daily life of the tomb owner and that of the servants.
- The group of mortuary and funerary themes, of which the most important is the tomb owner sitting at the offering table.
- The small group of rare themes.

A unifying function can be attributed to some small themes; examples are the offering bearers and the personified estates, which in their long rows connect several main themes.

II.1. The scenes from daily life

Some of the scenes on the walls of mortuary chapels have long been described as reflecting the daily life of pharaonic Egypt. The first one to closer study this group of themes more closely was P. Montet in his study 'Les scenes de la vie privée...... '.[6] In this study, which is not conclusive (see PM, III/1, 355-8 and PM, III/2, 903-7), it is evident that the whole group of scenes can be divided in a few main-themes which in turn can be sub-divided into details of the whole activity. The division made by Montet is not completely identical to that in Porter & Moss. The themes that can be considered to be the most important are the following:

- The tomb owner inspecting various activities while standing or sitting alone or with members of the family with/without attendants.
- Hippopotamus hunt, fowling and fish spearing in the marshes, rattling papyrus.
- Marsh scenes and activities like fishing, fowling, harvesting papyrus or lotus, jousting sailors.
- Hunting in the desert.
- The tomb owner being carried in a palanquin.
- Agriculture, cattle breeding and bird cultivation, harvesting various products.
- Horticulture, grape harvest and the production of wine.
- Various crafts.
- Food production including the baking of bread and the brewing of beer.
- Medical and paramedical procedures.
- Market scenes.
- Ship construction and naval activities.
- Music, dance, sports and games.
- Attendants, scribes, rendering of accounts.

[6] Montet, *Vie privée.*

The majority of the themes given in the list above show the everyday Egyptian toiling to earn his daily living and are indeed themes from daily life. In most of these themes, if the tomb owner is depicted, it is in an inactive role. Only in a few of the scenes can the tomb owner, although a member of the highest social stratum, be observed to be 'actively' engaged. These scenes are:

- Fowling and fish spearing in the marshes including the rattling of papyrus stems.
- The deceased being carried in a palanquin.
- Hunting in the desert.
- Games.

In this list the rattling of papyrus and the playing of games like *senet* are the only themes that describe an activity which is exclusively done by the tomb owner and members of his family and that is not also being done by servants on a production scale.[7]

In the themes of fish-spearing, fowling and hunting in the desert, the tomb owner is engaged in an activity that can also be done by servants, although in that case they are in a provider role, and not working in the sportive way shown by the tomb owner. A possible interpretation of these scenes given by some scholars is that the tomb owner wanted to show that he also could provide sustenance, but it is more likely that he just wanted to demonstrate that he was (or had been) fit enough to do this type of sport. Another explanation is that, due to the presence of the wife, both scenes are connected with rebirth through the woman; an argument against this supposition is that she is not always present in these scenes.

In the scenes in which people are performing for the tomb owner (dancing, making music and singing), which can be done by professionals but also by members of the family, the tomb owner can be inactively watching and listening or actively playing a board game during the performance of the dancers and musicians.[8]

Many of the other activities in this list are controlled by overseers or estate managers, with the latter giving a conclusive rendering of accounts to a physically inactive tomb owner who is either sitting (Simpson, *Gmast 3,* Plate XVII, Figure 29) or standing (Dunham, *Gmast I,* Plate IIc, Figure 3b).[9]

As a consequence of this rendering of accounts a sub-group of themes exists in which certain persons are led in front of the tomb owner or are being punished (Figure 10.3).[10] For reasons that might be connected with the increasing negative influence of climate change, this type of scene appears on the walls of the chapel relatively late in the Old Kingdom (V.L).[11]

Figure 10.2 *Mrrw-k3.j* painting (PM, III/2, 525–34; after Duell, *Mereruka, I,* Plate 7).

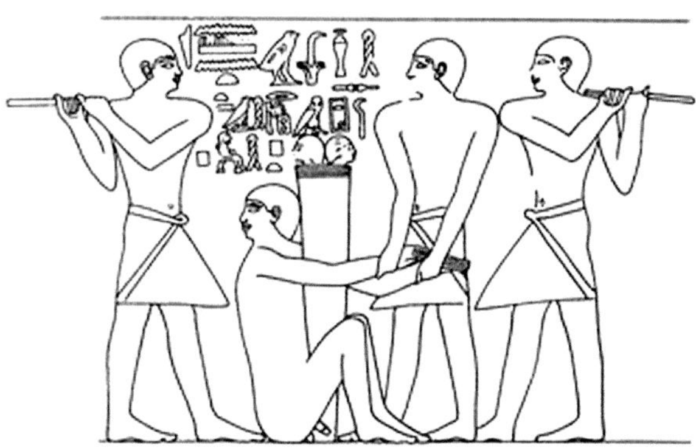

Figure 10.3 A person being punished (chapel of *Mrrw-k3.j* (PM, III/1, 525 – 34); after Duell, *Mereruka, I,* Plate 37).

II.2. Funerary and mortuary decorative themes

The following themes can be considered to be funerary or mortuary themes, thereby fulfilling a different role than being a representation of daily life:

[7] Woods, *Rattling papyrus.*

[8] Kanawati, *Giza I,* Plate 32.

[9] Der Manuelian, *Presenting scroll.*

[10] In the tomb of *3ḫtj-mrw-nswt* (PM, III/1, 80-1) the leading of these persons in front of the tomb owner is done by his brothers (www.giza.fas.harvard.edu/ancientpeople153/intro/).

[11] Roeten, *Economic decline,* Table .04.1.

- The tomb owner sitting at the offering table, alone, with members of the family with or without attendants and priests.
- Butchery scene.
- Various stages of the funeral showing the priests and the rites they perform.
- Rows of offering bringers and personified estates.
- Piles of offerings.

II.3. Other groups of themes

II.3.1. Rare themes

In some chapels scenes are placed that belong to the group of scenes that are rarely used:

- The tomb owner is depicted in the act of painting the seasons (*Ḫntj-k3.j*, PM, III/2, 508-11 and *Mrrw-k3.j*, PM, III/2, 525-35 (Figure 10.2)).
- In the chapel of *Ptḥ-ḥtp* (PM, III/2, 653 – 4), it appears that, in view of the wig, it is a woman that is acting as a helmsman on a ship.[12]

Figure 10.4 The feeding of a puppy. Tomb of *Rˁ-špss* (PM, III/2, 494 – 5).

- The force-feeding of hyenas in room IV of the tomb of *K3-gm-nj* (PM, III/2, 521 – 5).
- In the tomb of *Ḫww-wr* (PM, III/1, 254 -5) the tomb owner is sitting in a palanquin that has been placed on the back of two donkeys.
- In the chapel of *K3-gm-nj* (PM, III/2, 521 – 5) a man is depicted mouth to mouth with a porkling(?), possibly bringing milk(?) into the latter's mouth.[13]
- Attacking a city in the tomb of *K3.j-m-ḥst* at Saqqara.[14]
- The dressing of hair or a wig in the tomb of *Ptḥ-ḥtp* (PM, III/2, 600 – 4).[15]

II.3.2. and further.....

In the chapels texts are placed in the form of the name and titles of the tomb owner, names and often titles of members of the family, and of priests, certainly when they are relatives or friends. On the door jambs or entrance thicknesses autobiographical texts and warnings could be placed. Most scenes on the various walls are provided with captions explaining the activities displayed.

Other texts state that the king either gave important elements of the tomb (the false door in the case of *Nj-ˁnḫ-sḫmt* (PM, III/2, 482-3),[16] or even gave the whole tomb (*W3š-ptḥ*, PM, III/2, 456);[17] there are also examples of the king giving land or the right to share offerings from the mortuary temples of royalty.[18]

III. Connections between the themes and the functions of the chapel

Decoration themes that are placed on the various elements of the mortuary monument have a strong connection with the function of that element and are also interacting between each other. These connections and interactions are given in Figure 10.5 and in this figure the tomb owner has been placed as the focal point.

IV. Some further considerations

The mortuary tradition as it existed in its entirety in pharaonic Egypt was based on the desire of the Egyptian to obtain eternal life once death had separated him from the world of the living. In order to achieve this goal several steps had to be taken in which the lector priest played a major role,[19] but of which a small number of steps could already be taken by the tomb owner while he/she was still alive.

---

[12] LD, *II*, 103b.

[13] In El-Tayet, *Rashepses*, 291 – 3 is stated that the feeding of the porkling is in fact the feeding of a puppy, which is far more probable also because of the strikingly short distance at which a (female) dog is depicted in a higher register.

[14] McFarlane, *Kaiemheset*, 33 – 4, Plates 2a and 38.

[15] Davies, *Akhethotep I*, 9, Plate XXXb.

[16] Breasted, *Ancient records*, 108-9.

[17] Breasted, *Ancient records*, 111-3; Alexanian, *Tomb and social status*.

[18] The endowment of land in Breasted, *Ancient records*, 93; the right to share in the offerings in Breasted, *Ancient records*, 77-8.

[19] Forshaw, *Lector*, 83 ff..

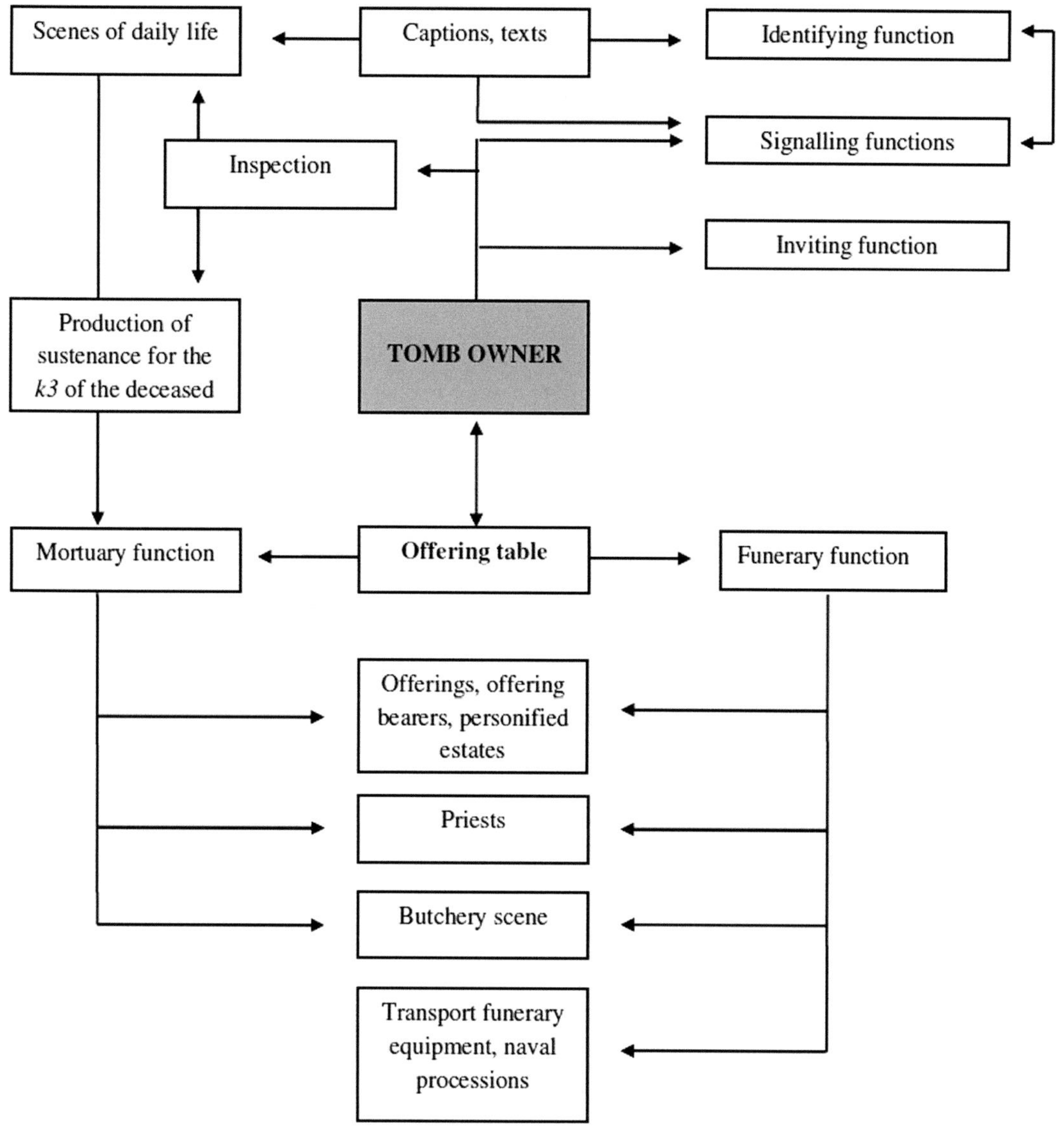

Figure 10.5 The connection between the decoration themes and the functions of the chapel.

Except for accidental or sudden death usually the tomb owner had already started the construction of his tomb during his life time, including the production of part of his burial equipment, of which the rest could be made during the embalming period in the embalmers tent.[20]

The organization of the daily offerings that had to be brought before the false door in the chapel was also part of the measures that could be taken by the tomb owner during his life-time.[21]

These measures were meant to secure the 'eternal' continuation of the daily mortuary cult, but proof of the tomb owner also taking measures about the persons involved in the various phases of the funeral itself like priests, mourners, dancers, bearers, etc. are less obvious.

Sometimes the scene of the tomb owner being carried in a palanquin is interpreted as the depiction of a visit to the construction site of the tomb, and in some cases this is indeed stated by the caption that goes with the theme, but without this caption the scene could also be interpreted as the tomb owner travelling for the functions he held. Most of the travelling would have been done by ship, but in order to go from the ship to the place where he had to be undoubtedly a palanquin was needed.

The transition from life to death and obtaining a life after death has several aspects which directly influenced the way the Egyptians dealt with death as a physical phenomenon, from preparing the body for

[20] Forshaw, *Lector*, 87.

[21] Alexanian, *Tomb and social status*, 2. Breasted, *Ancient records*, 91-3.

'eternity' followed by the prosaic disposing of the body in a tomb; a short time later, the second function of the tomb became apparent, that of being the focus of the daily mortuary cult meant for the supply of sustenance for the *k3* of the deceased. Some of the aspects of bringing of the body to the tomb were important enough to warrant in a few tombs the depiction of some of its stages, although during the Old Kingdom the dead body was never shown,[22] and certainly not the various stages of the mummification.[23]

Figure 10.6 Detail of a funerary scene (Tomb of *Dbḥnj, (*PM, III/1, 235-6); detail Hassan, *Giza IV,* Figure 122).

During the whole process priests performed acts that had been laid down already many centuries ago. The final stages of the funeral ceremony took place in the vicinity of the tomb, and part of it even seems to have taken place on the roof of the tomb (Figures 10.6 and 10.7). For a mastaba this would be a logical place and would require the presence of a path leading to its top. This implies that the ramps that have sometimes been found next to mastabas were not only used to transport the sarcophagus to the opening of the shaft to the burial chamber,[24] but also to perform rituals in front of statues of the deceased.[25]

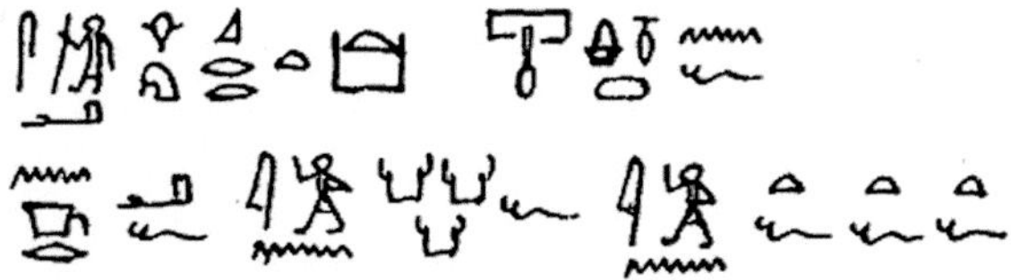

Figure 10.7 K. Sethe, *Urkunden des Alten Reichs*, vol I, 190, 9-10; Mariette, *Mastabas,* 195. Chapel *Tp-m-ʿnḫ* (PM, III/2, 483).

sʿḥʿ r-tp ḳrtt prt-ḫrw n.f nḏr ʿ.f jn k3w.f jn jtw.f[26]

'...causing to stand on the roof; an invocation-offering is made to him; his hand is grasped by his *k3*'s and his fathers'

(Forshaw, *Lector,* 91).

Due to the fact that most rock-cut tombs have the shaft entrances in the interior of the chapel, this ceremony would not be applicable. Yet in the rock-cut tomb of *Dbḥnj* (PM, III/1, 235-6) a decoration has been found that seems to indicate the presence of a ramp and a ceremony on the roof of the tomb.

Hassan interprets the ramp and the construction at the right side of the third and fourth register from above in Figure 10.6 as the embalming house, with a statue in a naos standing in front of the entrance, and the doorway under the ramp as a less conspicuous rear exit. An argument that can be put forward against this interpretation is the presence of the row of stands and vases at both side of the 'rear exit' and the row of offering bearers on the ramp. The whole theme of Figure 10.6 is a problem, because on top of the escarpment no trace of a mastaba-like structure has been found.[27] A possible explanation is that the last part of the road that the procession to the tomb had to go was rather steep and was shown as what looks like the ascent of a

[22] There is one item of decoration that is possibly an example of the mummy of the deceased lying on a bed in a ship (Altenmüller, *Mehu,* Plate 19a).

[23] OEE, Oxford Expedition to Egypt, Scene-details Database 15.7 mentions 21 examples of the displaying of mummification and funeral procedures of which 15.7.9 and 15.7.10 are directly involved with the mummification tent, but no further details are shown.

[24] Alexanian, *Netjeraperef*, Figure 15; Reisner, *Estate stewards,* Figure 3 (page 32).

[25] Junker, *Giza XI,* Figure 89. The entrance to the burial chamber was on the top of the mastaba, but because the excavation reports never mention the presence of statues in a burial chamber (in the burial chamber of the tomb AC 33 of *K3-jr.s* which is discovered in October 2018 at Abusir, a statue of the sitting tomb owner has been found standing in front of the sarcophagus) , this makes the actual presence of a statue on the roof illogical. An explanation would be that in reality the statue is the mummy of the deceased, but convention prevented the recognizable depiction thereof.

[26] Forshaw, *Lector,* 91.

[27] Hassan, *Giza IV,* 163.

ramp, followed by the depicted rituals in the courtyard in front of the entrance of the tomb.

Other decorative themes can also be interpreted as part of the funerary rites such as the performing priests, and the long rows of offering bringers and sometimes personified estates bringing the things that have to be placed in the tomb in order to give the deceased all that is necessary for a continuation of life in the realm of the dead.[28]

A special theme is the offering table scene that not only can be interpreted as part of the funeral, namely as a depiction of the deceased taking part in the funeral meal, but it can also be seen as the deceased taking part in the offerings that have been laid down in front of the false door. In that case it is part of the mortuary cult for the deceased.

The relative scarcity of the depiction of the more specific funerary themes in the chapel could have been caused by the primary function of the chapel being to receive the daily offerings and to keep the memory of the deceased alive. This also resulted in themes with both a mortuary and a funerary function being present in all chapels (in Figure 10.5 offerings, offering bearers and personified estates, priests and butchery scenes).

[28] In the necropolis of Giza the theme of the offering bearers (offering bearers and personified estates) is present not only on the western and eastern wall of the chapel, but also on the entrance thicknesses. On the western wall from V.M on this theme is no longer present, and on the eastern wall it disappears in the course of the Old Kingdom (Roeten, *Decoration,* Diagrams IV.6.Ann. and XV.5.Ann.). In Saqqara the theme is present on the entrance thicknesses.

Entrances and Decoration

Entrance into the tomb of Inty at Abusir.
(From: M. Bárta and V. Dulíková, 'The Afterlife Existence Captured in Stone', in P. Jánosi and H. Vymazalová (eds), *The Art of Describing. Studies in Honour of Yvonne Harpur* (Prague, 2018)).
(With the kind permission of Prof. Dr. M. Bárta; Czech Institute of Egyptology, Charles University, Prague)

Chapter Eleven

The Door Jambs and the Entrance Thicknesses

I. Introduction

Both the door jambs and the entrance thicknesses can be decorated. An inventory of the decoration themes on the entrance elements of a chapel is given in figure 11.1.[1]

In the course of this study different groups of themes will be taken together, their choice being determined by the by the type of research that is foreseen.

II. The door jambs

The door jambs are the parts on both sides of the entrance of the chapel. Sometimes they are narrow and carry just the name and some of the titles of the tomb owner and sometimes they carry text (Figure 3.3). The door jambs of some tombs are decorated with, apart from the afore mentioned themes, also other themes, although the number of decorative themes that can be placed together is small (Figure 7.8). Together with the architrave, they were the first elements to be seen; consequently the themes placed on these elements had a signalling and identifying function.

In Tables I and IV the doorjambs decoration is gathered for the necropoleis of Saqqara and Giza.

The table clearly shows the difference between the door jamb decoration of the tombs in Giza and those in Saqqara; except for themes 1, 2, 3 and 9 the catalogues of themes do not show an overlap. This difference can be explained by the fact that during the 4th dynasty the necropolis of Giza was the main Memphite burial ground, while during the 5th and the 6th dynasty this role was taken over by the necropolis of Saqqara.

- It is observable that themes 1, 2 and 3 (the tomb owner with either an adult or a child) are all three present in Giza with the same degree of importance. This is in contrast to Saqqara where the tomb owner standing alone (theme 1) was the most important, followed by the tomb owner with a child (theme 3). The latter cannot be explained by the decrease in tomb dimensions that took place during the Old Kingdom.
  Although the dimensions of the tomb decreased over the course of the Old Kingdom, the space available on the door jambs was not automatically affected by this development. The observation that the choice in auxiliary themes in Saqqara was twice that of the tombs in the necropolis of Giza might lead to the conclusion the door jambs were not subject to a reduction in space. Because it is highly improbable that the door jambs increased in size, the increase in number of themes could be explained by assuming that possibly the size of the themes had been diminished, or that a less voluminous theme was chosen. The standing tomb owner with staff and adult behind him takes up more space than the tomb owner with a child, because the latter could be depicted between the tomb owner and his staff, thus requiring only a little extra space due to the position of the staff being a bit further to the front.
- In Saqqara theme 12 (texts other than name and titles) is important, while in Giza this theme is not in use, indicating that these sorts of texts were placed on the door jambs only later in the Old Kingdom.
- The main themes in Giza are typically connected with the bringing of actual offerings to the chapel, while in Saqqara, thus in a later period, the emphasis was not only on the magical sustenance (offering bearers, piles of offerings, butchery), but also on the showing the social importance of the tomb owner during his life-time (attendants, texts).
- Tables I and IV show that both in Saqqara and Giza the depiction of offering bearers (theme D9) is no longer placed on the door jambs of the entrance after the end of the 5th dynasty, and the same development takes place on the jambs of the false door in the necropolis of Giza.[2]

III. The entrance thicknesses

These thicknesses are the walls of the corridor leading into the chapel. The decoration placed on it had a signalling, an inviting and possibly a guiding function. The corridor was still part of the outside world because at the end of the corridor a door drum was placed over the entrance, thus indicating that at that place the transition from the outside world to the world of the chapel was made.

[1] Where possible this numbering of the themes will be maintained.

[2] Roeten, *Decoration*, Diagram VIII.5.Ann. (page 402).

number	Decoration theme
1	The tomb owner alone (standing or sitting)
2	The tomb owner with adult man or woman
3	The tomb owner in direct contact with children
4	The tomb owner alone at the offering table
5	The tomb owner at the offering table with adult (man or woman)
6	The tomb owner at the offering table with children
7	Priests
8	Personified estates
9	Offering bearers, including the leading of animals
10	Attendants including scribes, rendering of accounts, dancers, clappers, musicians
11	Butchery scene
12	Text other than names and titles
13	Funerary scenes (e.g. the transport of statues)
14	Piles of offerings
15	Boat scenes other than funerary
16	Marsh-scenes (non-agricultural activities like fish-spearing, fowling, rattling papyrus)
17	Agriculture, including marsh-activities like cattle fording
18	Members of the family not in direct contact with the tomb owner

Figure 11.1 Decoration themes on the entrance elements.

This architectonic element was subject to the decreasing tomb dimensions that took place during the Old Kingdom.

The difference in function between the door jambs and the entrance thicknesses is plainly visible in the tombs in the necropolis of Giza.

In Tables II and V the FO values are determined and gathered in the table in Figure 11.3.

- Because of the slightly larger space that is available on the thicknesses of the entrance, the number of decorative themes that is placed on them is larger than on the door jambs.
- The values for the themes 1, 2 and 3 are virtually identical for the necropolis of Giza, but in that of Saqqara there is a marked tendency to depict the tomb owner either alone or with a child in physical contact, as is the case on the door jambs too.
- The tendency to depict the tomb owner either alone or with a child but rarely with an adult is apparent in Saqqara for both the door jambs and the entrance thicknesses. The value for the Giza necropolis indicates that in tombs that can be dated to early in the Old Kingdom more space was available on both elements of the entrance.
- In Giza theme 12 (texts) is not present on both elements, while texts are present on the door jambs in Saqqara. This means that the placing of text on either the door jambs or the entrance thicknesses is a development that is strongly tied to the later period in which the necropolis of Saqqara had become the main burial place.

		Giza	Saqqara
1		45	61
2		45	11
3		45	32
7		14	
9		14	11
10			11
11			11
12			21
13			4
14			7
17			4
18		5	
total		6	10

Figure 11.2 The FO values of the themes on the door jambs in Giza and Saqqara. (the numbering of the themes is according to Figure 11.1).

		Giza	Saqqara
1		39	52
2		33	5
3		40	27
4		7	
5		1	
7		20	9
8		1	7
9		23	32
10		8	14
11		2	11
12			7
13		1	14
14		1	5
15			5
18		1	
total		13	12

Figure 11.3 The FO values of the themes on the entrance thicknesses in Giza and Saqqara. (the numbering of the themes is according to Figure 119).

– The theme that shows the tomb owner sitting at the offering table (theme 4 – 6) is present in the tombs of Giza but no longer in those of Saqqara. This development can be explained by the decreasing space that is available on the entrance thicknesses, a development caused by the decrease in tomb dimensions.

IV. The main themes

IV.1. The determination of the main themes

The themes can be divided into groups in different ways, depending on the subject of the study at hand. An example is that the group 'attendants' can be subdivided in scribes, dancers, musicians etc. Another example is the division as given in Harpur, *DETOK*, 310 – 3 where the term 'subsidiary figures' is used for a larger group of secondary figures.[3]

The following subjects can be studied:

1. The chronological development of the themes most frequently present on the entrance thicknesses in the necropoleis of Saqqara and Giza (Tables I, II, IV and V).
2. The various interactions between the themes on the entrance thicknesses, either positive or negative (Figure 11.9).
3. Due to the small number of tombs per period, the chronological development of the themes on the door jambs is too unreliable and is not included in the study.
4. For the same reason, the interactions between themes can only be studied on the entrance thicknesses. The choice of the different themes is based on considerations that reflect the probability and the logic of such an interaction.
5. The interaction between the different themes on the entrance thicknesses and the themes on the chapel wall that is closest to the entrance of the chapel (Table VII).

The information that can be obtained is gathered from the available excavation reports of the above mentioned necropoleis, of which the necropolis of Saqqara is the worst reported, and for that reason will have to be excluded from some studies.

In Tables I, II, IV and V the decoration themes on the entrance door jambs and the entrance thicknesses have been gathered for the necropoleis of Giza and Saqqara.

In these tables the themes are designated either with a D or an E meaning respectively 'door jamb' and 'entrance thickness'; the number that follows refers to the theme as mentioned in Figure 11.1.

In that figure the description of the theme 'text' (D-12 and E-12) means texts other than name, titles or offering formula, because the name and titles are 'automatically' present due to the signalling function of the chapel entrance, while the offering formula is frequently placed there with the aim of inciting the passer-by to utter this formula and thus magically give sustenance to the *k3* of the deceased, particularly if the chapel is inaccessible because of a closed door.

In some tombs cattle or other animals are walking in the direction of the chapel without visible guidance; taking into account that they are in fact guided by persons that are not depicted, this theme is interpreted as 'offering bringers' (D-9 and E-9).

IV.2. The chronological development of the main themes

In order to determine whether there is a difference in the extent the various decoration themes are used on these walls, the two largest necropoleis of the Memphite area to which, Giza and Saqqara, are studied separately.

[3] In Table 4.8 of Harpur, *DETOK* (page 310 – 3) the following dates are not included in the determination: III, IV, V, VI, V-VI; this makes the number of tombs in the Giza necropolis that are accepted 78 and in the Saqqara necropolis 46.

	Type of decoration (Giza cemeteries)	percentage
11.4/1	Anubis/offering list	5.1
11.4/2	Dragging a statue	1.3
11.4/3	Journey to the west	2.6
11.4/4	Butchery scene	3.8
11.4/5	Tomb owner sitting at the offering table	9.0
11.4/6	Tomb owner standing alone or with member(s) of the family	61.5
11.4/7	Tomb owner seated alone or with member(s) of the family	29.5
11.4/8	Subsidiary figures	35.9

Figure 11.4 The decoration themes on the entrance thicknesses in the necropolis of Giza.

	Type of decoration (Saqqara cemeteries)	percentage
11.5/1	Anubis/offering list	2.1
11.5/2	Dragging a statue	14.5
11.5/3	Journey to the west	4.2
11.5/4	Butchery scene	18.8
11.5/5	Tomb owner sitting at the offering table	6.3
11.5/6	Tomb owner standing alone or with member(s) of the family	60.4
11.5/7	Tomb owner seated alone or with member(s) of the family	12.5
11.5/8	Subsidiary figures	47.9

Figure 11.5 The decoration themes on the entrance thicknesses in the necropolis of Saqqara.

For a preliminary study the decorative themes as given by Harpur (*DETOK*, 310 – 3) are used.

From the two tables it is evident that in both necropoleis the main themes are the tomb owner standing (11.4(6) and 11.5(6)) and subsidiary figures (11.4(8) and 11.5(8)), while in the necropolis of Giza the depiction of the seated tomb owner (11.4(7)) is an important theme (29,5%), while on the cemetery of Saqqara this theme (11.5(7)) has lost most of its former importance (12.5%).

The difference in percentages between themes 11.4(7) (29.5%) and 11.5(7) (12.5%) in both necropoleis is due to the decrease in tomb surface that was already going on in the 4th dynasty in the necropolis of Giza,[4] a development that continued in the 5th and 6th dynasty when the necropolis of Saqqara became the main Memphite burial ground. Already in the necropolis of Giza this provoked a shift in the use of the spacious theme of the seated tomb owner (11.4(7) – 11.5(7)) to the theme of the standing figure (11.4(6) – 11.5(6)).

The chronological development of the various themes is given in Figures 11.6 (subsidiary figures), 11.7 (standing tomb owner) and 11.8 (seated tomb owner). In these diagrams curves are introduced that represent the calculated best fit, but the extrapolations of these lines have no archaeological meaning.

The themes 11.4(6)/11.4(8) and 11.5(6)/11.5(8) are, based on the percentages, obviously the main themes.

The themes in the entrances of the tombs in the necropoleis of Saqqara and Giza as given in Figures 11.4 and 11.5 differ so much in percentage values that it must be concluded that the two necropoleis had different traditions, as far as the less important themes are concerned.

Due to a longer interruption in the employment of Saqqara as the main necropolis, the number of tombs with decoration on the walls of the entrance thicknesses is relatively small and spread over the various periods of the Old Kingdom in such a way that a long period remains without sufficient and adequate information. Consequently only the entrance thicknesses of tombs

[4] Roeten, *Economic decline.*Figures 67and 69.

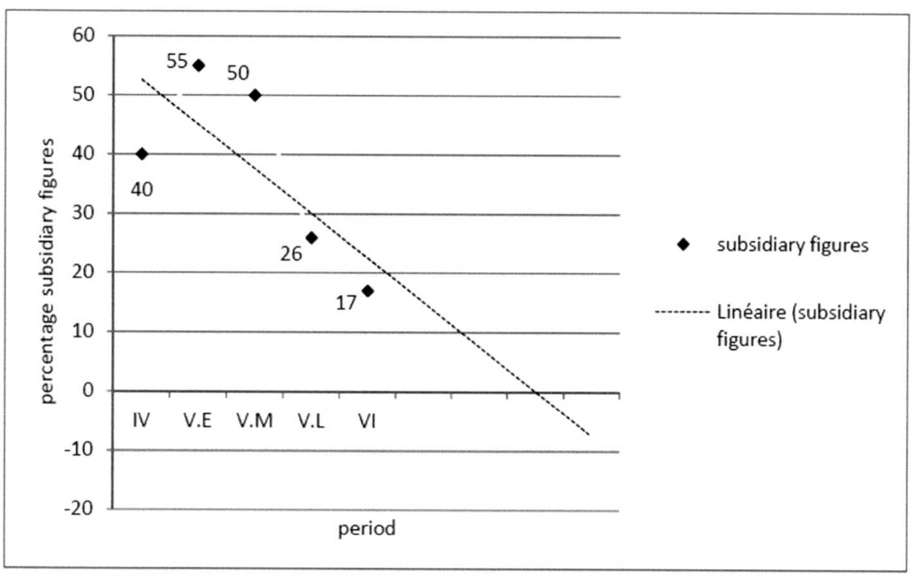

Figure 11.6 The chronological development of the percentage of subsidiary figures in the necropolis of Giza (after Roeten, *Decoration*,Table XII.1.Ann (page 384 – 5)).

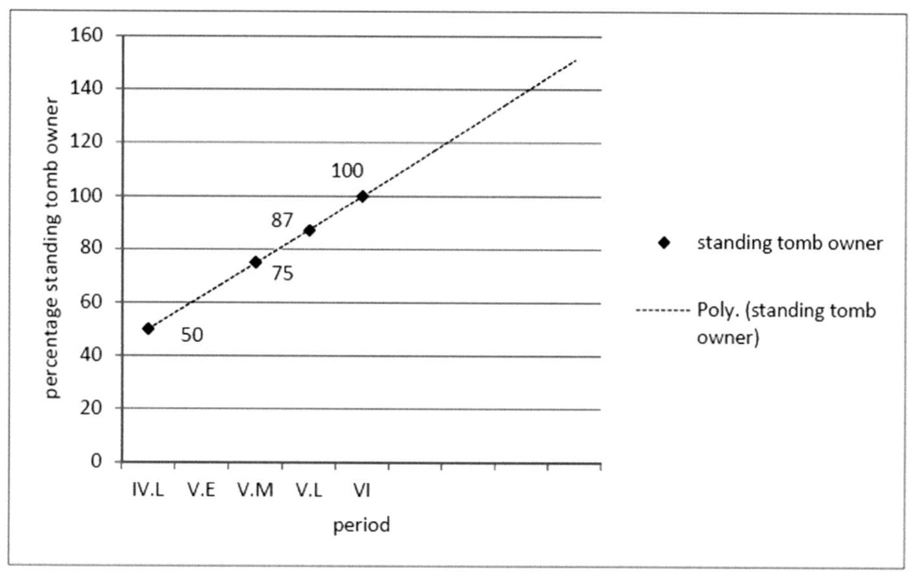

Figure 11.7 The chronological development of the percentage of the tomb owner seated in the necropolis of Giza (after Roeten, *Decoration*,Table XII.1.Ann (page 384 – 5)).

in the necropolis of Giza can further be studied with an acceptable degree of reliability.

The chronological development as shown in the curves of Figures 11.6 and 11.7 shows a positive connection between the subsidiary figures and the sitting tomb owner.

Because the group of subsidiary figures consists of a number of themes, the above given conclusion is in itself of little significance. In section V of this chapter some of the themes of this group are studied more closely.

In Figures 11.6 -11.8 the influence of the decreasing dimensions of the tomb and thus the entrance thicknesses is evident, and in the next section the interaction of these themes is studied using an adapted methodology.

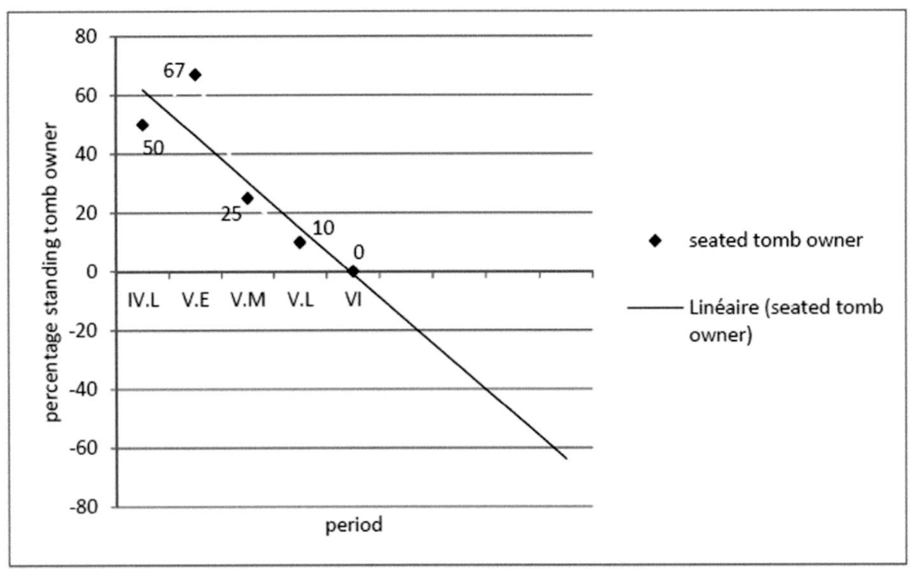

Figure 11.8 The chronological development of the percentage of the tomb owner standing in the necropolis of Giza (after Roeten, *Decoration*,Table XII.1.Ann (page 384 – 5)).

V. The interactions of themes

V.1. Methodology

Interactions between themes are either associations (positive interactions) or dissociations (negative interactions). Between some themes no interaction at all exists; this can be caused by an extremely strong dissociation or a lack of 'overlap' in time. Therefore criteria have been developed by which such an association or dissociation can be reliably determined, described and even quantified. Although the author developed a complete methodology in order to quantify the various aspects of the interactions between decorative themes,[5] only the part of the method in which the type of interaction is determined is necessary to describe adequately those interactions important for the study at hand.

1. The frequency of occurrence (FO) of the themes, and its derivative FO/chronological period are defined.
2. The chronological development of the themes on the entrance thicknesses are described by means of chronological orderings and/or diagrams.
3. The co-occurrence of themes on the two walls is given as 'co-occurrence percentage' (CP), a criterion which can also be expressed as CP/(chronological) period. A derivative of the CP value of a theme is the 'co-occurrence percentage surrounds discrepancy' (CPSD) value that pertains to it. This CPSD value quantifies the degree of association or dissociation between themes, information that will not be used in this study.

V.1.1. The 'frequency of occurrence' (FO) of the themes

On an architecturally *and* decoratively completely finished *and* preserved wall the presence or absence of a theme is unambiguous in the sense that it was *intentionally* chosen or not from the repertoire of the themes available (and permissible?) at that time.[6] However, a wall may be architecturally completely preserved and yet be incomplete in decoration, indicating that its decoration remained unfinished.[7] It is also possible that the wall may have been partially destroyed. Therefore, although the reasons for the absence of a theme on the wall are the following:

1. The theme has never been placed on the wall, as on an unfinished wall.
2. The theme has been lost, as on a finished wall that has been (partially) destroyed.

there is no certainty as to which of the following categories apply:

1. It was planned, but not placed there because the wall was never finished.

[5] Roeten, *Decoration*, Chapter III (page 55 – 96)

[6] The availability of themes and the way in which they were chosen is beyond the scope of the present study.

[7] An example can be found in mastaba G 6040 (*Špss-kꜣ.f-ꜥnḫ*, PM, III[1], 175; Weeks, *Gmast 5*, plates 35-7).

2. It was never chosen, the hypothesis here being that the tomb owner had, within limits, the option of choosing among the decorative themes him/herself.[8]
3. It was originally placed on the wall, but subsequently lost due to the destruction of a section of the wall (however, in some cases it is possible to create a reliable reconstruction of the missing section of the wall, in which case the wall is included in the catalogue as complete).[9]

These arguments make it necessary to distinguish between certainty and uncertainty in the presence or absence of a theme. In the two compilations of Table VIII-1 and Table VIII-2 certainty in presence is marked with 'x', and certainty in absence is marked with '-'. Uncertainty in presence or absence is marked as 'o'.[10]

These compilations the tombs have been ordered chronologically, and a division into chronological periods has been made in the table.

The FO value is calculated with the following formula: FO (%) = 'x'. 100 / 'x' + '—'

The FO values calculated in both are a measure for the degree of employment ('the popularity') of the themes over the whole of the Old Kingdom, but they give little information about its chronological development over the successive periods. In order to determine this FO values of the themes are calculated for each period (this is called the FO/period). With these results it is possible to make a FO/period versus period diagram of the chronological development of each theme.

V.1.2. The 'co-occurrence percentage' (CP) of themes

In a compilation of themes their presence can be stated not only for each tomb but also for each of its decorated walls. It is evident that several themes can be placed together on a wall and in order to quantify this phenomenon the term 'co-occurrence' is adopted.

The co-occurrence of themes can be determined in tables such as the compilations given in Tables I, II, IV, V. Co-occurrence can be determined between themes on the two thicknesses, and on the thickness itself.

An example of the first possibility that can be determined from Table VIII-1 is the co-occurrence between the standing tomb owner (theme 1) on the northern and southern entrance thicknesses. On the northern wall the theme is placed 17 times and on the southern wall 18 times. This means that the maximum number of co-occurrences is 17; the number of co-occurrences is 16, which gives a CP of 94%.

An example of the other type of co-occurrence can be determined in Table VIII-2 between themes 4 (offering bearers) and 5 (priests).

On the northern thickness theme 4 is placed 20 times and theme 5 8 times, the maximum number of co-occurrences is 8 and this occurs 0 times, the CP value is 0%.

On the southern thickness the values are 23 for theme 4 and 5 for theme 5; the CP is 60%.

It is evident that a CP > 0 can only be found between themes that overlap in time, but the observation CP = 0 does not indicate that the two themes do not overlap in time; it is also possible that two themes cannot be together in the same architectural element. The latter observation either can be due to the size of the two themes in relation to the available space or to a convention-based incompatibility.

V.1.3. The determination of association or dissociation between themes

This determination is made using the FO and CP values that can be calculated from a compilation of decorated elements in a catalogue of decorated tombs as given in Tables VIII-1 and VIII-2. The seven themes are placed in the diagram according to an increasing total FO value, and for every interaction in these two figures the CP value is calculated and placed in the diagram (Figures 11.11 and 11.12).

Based on the expectation that there is a direct connection between high CP values and high FO values, it is evident that the most reliable conclusions can be drawn from CP values derived from two themes with a high FO value. However, sometimes two themes have a much lower CP value than could be expected from the FO values of the interacting themes.

Consequently, if both themes have a high FO value, the observed low CP value of their interaction is embedded in an area where the CP values normally are high(er). An example is the low CP value of the interaction of themes 4 (offering bearers) and 5 (priests) on the northern entrance thickness in Figure 11.11(CP value = 0%) which is embedded in a field of higher CP values. This is a situation that indicates a possible dissociation between the themes.

Between two themes a positive interaction (an association) is also possible; in that case the CP value

[8] Staring, *Personal choice*, 269.

[9] Cf. on this also Walsem, van, *Iconography*, 44 - 6 and 60 - 1.

[10] The reason(s) for the incompleteness of the themes (either unfinished or partially destroyed) is not given in the tables, because this criterion is not important for the study at hand.

1	Tomb owner standing alone or with members of the family	4	Offering bearers or estates
2	Tomb owner sitting alone or with members of the family	5	priests
3	Tomb owner sitting at the offering table	6	Scribe(s)
		7	Butchery scene

Figure 11.9 Compilation of themes relevant for the determination of association and dissociation.

has to be higher than an expectation based on the surrounding field, and if this positive interaction is between two themes with low FO values, the higher CP value will be embedded in a surrounding field of lower CP values. An example is the interaction between themes 3 (tomb sitting at the offering table) and 5 (priests) on the northern entrance thickness (CP value = 80%).

VI. The interaction between main themes and subsidiary figures

The term 'subsidiary figures' as used in Figure 11.6 actually includes several types of attendants:

- Offering bearers (including personified estates)
- Priests
- Scribe(s)
- Butchery scene as a group of attendants.

Members of the family or acquaintances of the tomb owner are not included in this group

Possibly the strong interaction between the seated tomb owner and the subsidiary figures is not caused by all types of subsidiary figures. This means that relevant interactions between the depiction of the tomb owner and the different types of subsidiary figures have to be determined.

The following themes might show an interaction:

In order to quantify the possible correlations between the various themes depicted in this area of the chapel, the methodology developed for the interior walls of the chapel has been employed for this area of the chapel too (see section II of this chapter).[11] The following considerations have to be taken into account:

- Only the CP based correlations of themes that are depicted on the same entrance thicknesses are compared.

CP(%)	
theme	CP (%)
1	94
2	78
3	75
4	70
5	40

Figure 11.10 The CP values (%) of the interactions between the same themes on the two thicknesses.

- The CP values of correlations between themes 1-3 are meaningless because the joint appearance of two or more of these themes on *one* entrance thickness is virtually impossible, due to lack of space (This assumption is corroborated in Figures 11.11 and 11.12 where both on the southern and the northern thicknesses the interactions 1↔2, 1↔3 and 2↔3 have CP = 0%).[12]
- The northern and southern thicknesses are studied separately due to a degree of asymmetry in the decoration of the two walls (Figure 11.10).
- Persons accompanying animals are considered as offering bearers.
- On the entrance elements of some tombs persons carrying offerings have the designation *ḥm - nṯr*; in that case they are entered in the table as priests and not as offering bearers.
- On the entrance thicknesses of the chapel of *Jj-mrjj* (PM, 170 - 4) a man carrying an oar is followed by a man leading a calf, which has more the appearance of a detail of the transport of cattle by ship than the leading of cattle to the tomb; consequently the scene is not considered as theme 4 (offering bearers).[13]

[11] Roeten, *Decoration,* xiii - xvii and pages 55 - 96 for the methodology and the definitions of the various terms used therein.

[12] An example of the double placement of themes 1 and 2 is on the door-jambs of the entrance of the chapel of *ʿnḫ-m-ʿ-ḥr* in the Teti cemetery.

[13] Weeks, *Gmast 5,* Plate 25.

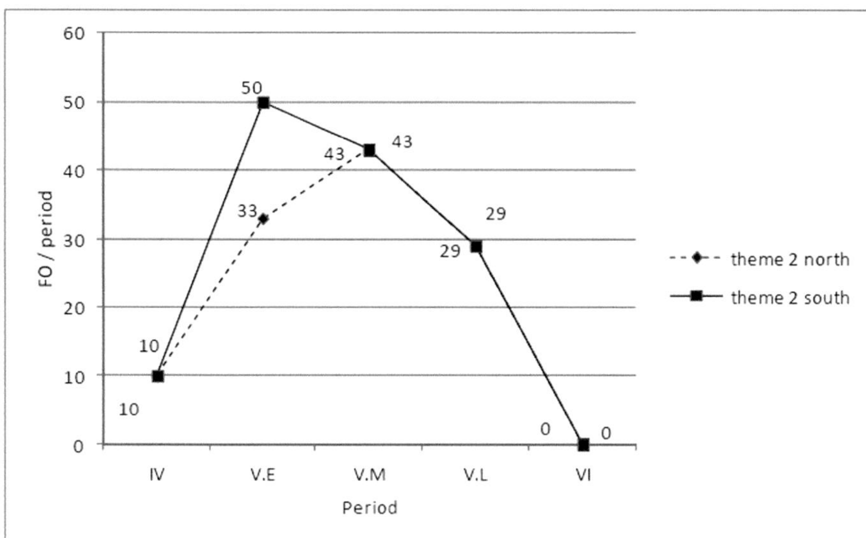

Figure 11.21 FO/period curves of theme 2 (sitting tomb owner) on the northern and southern thicknesses.

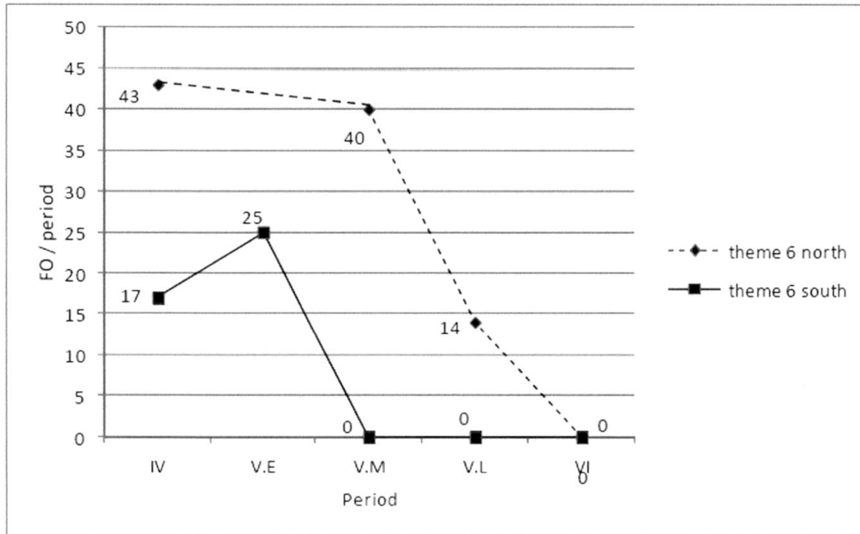

Figure 11.22 FO/period curves of theme 6 (scribes) on the northern and southern thicknesses.

- Because the butchery scene (theme 7) is seldom depicted on the entrance thicknesses no chronological development can be determined, although a strong association between them can be discerned on both thicknesses (Figures 11.11 and 11.12).
- It can be observed that the offering table scene (theme 3, Figure 11.19) only has an association with the priests (theme 5, Figure 11.18), while the offering bearers (theme 4, Figure 11.17) increase in importance in the period that the offering table scene starts to disappear from the thicknesses. This indicates that the basic function of these two walls changed from mainly purpose signalling (showing the necessity of the actual bringing of offerings to the place where the tomb owner could benefit from them) to exclusively inviting.

In view of their chronological development, the themes on the entrance thicknesses can be divided in two main groups:

1. The group of themes that have a decreasing presence on the thicknesses, which are the themes 2 (sitting tomb owner without offering table), 3 (the tomb owner sitting at the offering table), 5 (priests) and 6 (scribes). The butchery scene might belong to this group, but this is doubtful because of a discrepancy in FO/ period values between the southern and the northern thickness (see Figure 11.15) linked to low FO values (3% and 6% in Figures 11.11 and 11.12).
2. The group of themes that have an increasing presence; these are theme 1 (the standing tomb owner) and theme 4 (the offering bearers).

VII.1. The themes of group 1.

An association is apparent between the chronological development of the priests on the entrance thicknesses (theme 5, Figure 11.18) and the priests on the jambs of the false doors (Figure 11.20). On both elements the presence of the theme starts to decrease in the period V.E-V.M and disappears completely in V.L (Figure 11.23).

This development of the presence of priests on the two elements has a strong connection with the decrease of the presence of the offering table scene on the entrance thicknesses that disappears from there at the end of period V.M (Table V, Figure 11.23).

The offering table scene does not disappear from the false door as a whole because it remains in use on the panel that is placed over the simulacrum of the entrance part of the false door, while its presence on the western wall of the chapel increased.[16]

Although it has been pointed out in this study that the two passages were based on the same idea, a difference is discernible between them. On the false door the table scene is placed nearly exclusively on the panel and never on the door jambs.[17] In the entrance of the chapel the table scene can be placed on the thicknesses *and* on the architrave over the entrance,[18] the latter being comparable with the table scene on the panel over the entrance of the false door. This indicates that the function of the table scene on the entrance thicknesses is different from that of the table scene on the false door.

In view of the fact that on the false door the table scene remains and the priests disappear, while on the entrance thicknesses both disappear in the same period, indicates that the priests on the false door jambs enacted magically a ritual function in the actual bringing of offerings and had no direct connection with a offering table scene either on the panel or on the false door jambs. The disappearance of both the priests and the table scene on the entrance thicknesses indicates a direct connection between them on that element. There are two possible explanations about the purpose of the themes there. The proposition that the themes were meant as a replacement of the false door in case the door of the chapel itself was closed has already been rejected as improbable. It is more likely that the themes were meant to show the purpose of the chapel and invite the passer-by to enter and to bring offerings to the false door. The moment the actual offering was no longer the main purpose of the chapel and as the activity all but disappeared, the themes were no longer necessary on that element,[19] and were replaced by an increasing number of servants bringing offerings (theme 4) into the chapel.

The observation that both theme 2 (the tomb owner sitting) and theme 3 (the tomb owner sitting at the offering table) start to disappear in period V.E might be explained by presuming that this is solely provoked by the decreasing availability of space on the thicknesses. However, there is a large discrepancy in the period of their total disappearance (theme 3, the offering table scene, in period V.M (Figure 11.19), and theme 2, the sitting tomb owner, in period VI (Figure 11.21). This means, while both figures are depictions of the sitting tomb owner, it is not just the lack of room that is the main cause of the decrease of the presence of the offering table scene. In view of the chronological development of theme 2 (the tomb owner sitting) it is plausible that part of the decrease of theme 3 is due to that, but there is a second development that causes the disappearance of this theme to be faster than can be due to the reduction in available space. This accelerated disappearance is most likely caused by the change in mode of sustenance of the *k3* of the deceased which took place in the period V.E-late – V.L-early.[20]

In an earlier chapter the equivalence of the entrance of the chapel and the false door therein has already been discussed, and the curves of the offering table scene (theme 3) and the priests (theme 5) on the entrance thicknesses are compared with that of the priests on the jambs of the false door. The fact that the southern and northern thickness curves of a single theme show sufficient congruence, the mean value of the two FO/ period points is determined and introduced in the diagram of Figure 11.23. It is evident that the diagram corroborates the equivalence between the two entrances.

VII.2. The themes of group 2.

The chronological development of the two themes placed in this group is shown in Figure 11.25. It is evident that the curves show, in the second half of the Old Kingdom (V.L – VI), a strong connection in their chronological development. The development of this connection coincides with the change in mode of sustenance of the *k3* of the deceased. In order to determine the possible connection between the developments of the decoration on the entrance thicknesses and the jambs

[16] Roeten, *Decoration*, Diagram IV.3.Ann (page 398).

[17] The table scene is placed on the architrave of the false door of *Jtj* (PM, III/1, 174 – 5), LD, *II*, 59.

[18] Harpur, *DETOK*, Figure 6 (page 453), Table 4.1 (page 303) ; *K3-pw-nswt* (PM, III/1, 135), Junker, *Giza III*, Figure 14.

[19] Roeten, *Osiris*, Chapter IX, Section II and Figure 108.

[20] Roeten, *Osiris*, Figure 108; Roeten, *Decoration*, Figure X.6.

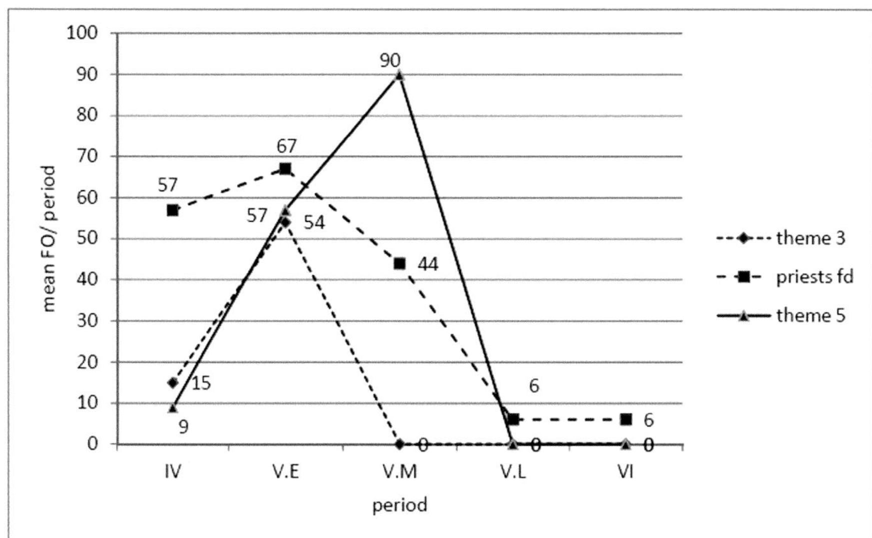

Figure 11.23 Chronological development of the offering table scene (theme 3), the priests on the entrance thicknesses (theme 5) and the priests on the jambs of the false door (= priests false door).

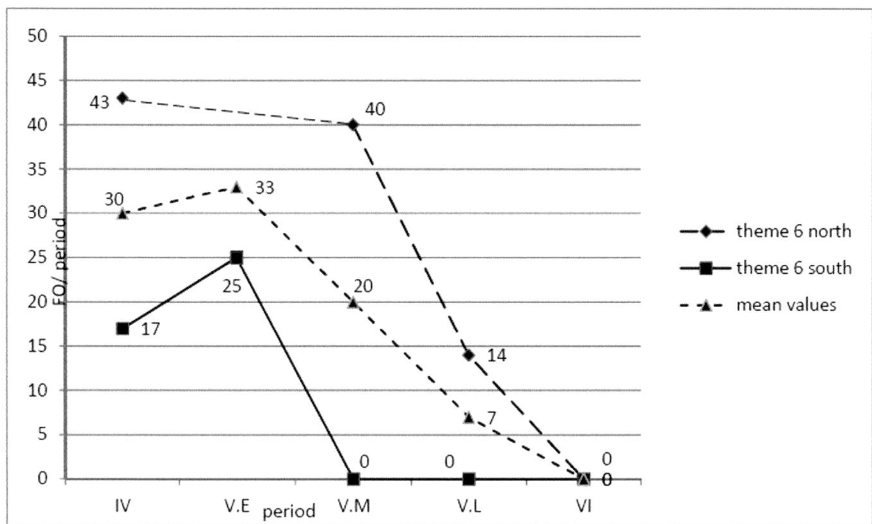

Figure 11.24 Chronological development of the scribes (theme 6) on the entrance thicknesses.

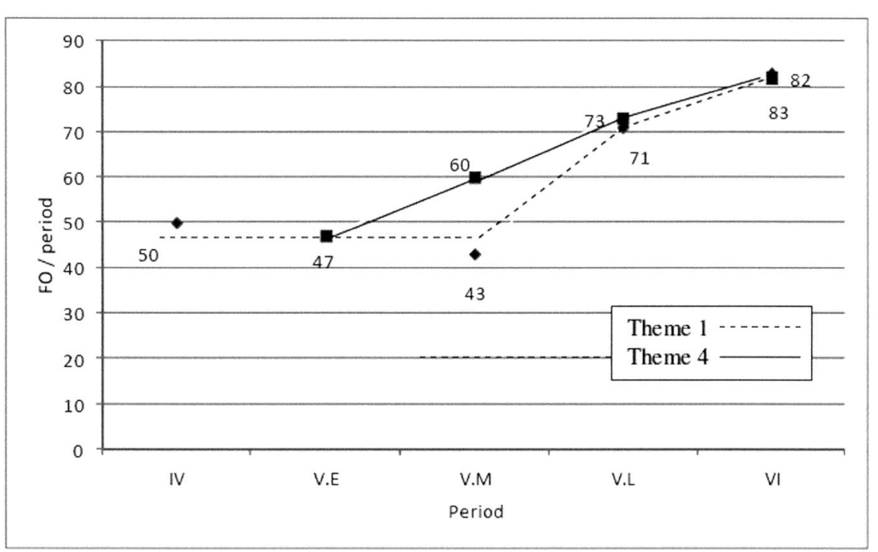

Figure 11.25 Chronological development of theme 1 (standing tomb owner) and theme 4 (offering bearers) on the entrance thicknesses (for theme 4 the mean value of the northern and southern thickness has been calculated from the values in Figure 11.15).

	IV ←→ V.E		V.L ←→ VI
	Actual sustenance	V.M	Magical sustenance
Entrance thicknesses	Table scene		----
	Priests		----
	Offering bearers		Offering bearers
	----		Tomb owner standing
Jambs false door [1]	Tomb owner standing		Tomb owner standing
	----		Offering formula
	Priests		----
	Offering bearers		----
	Family		----
	Ritual equipment		----

Figure 11.26 Development of the type of themes in connection with the change in the mode of sustenance.

IV ←→ V.E		V.L ←→ VI
Giza	V.M	Saqqara
Table scene (entrance thickness)		----
Priests		----
Tomb owner with adult		----
Offering bearers		Offering bearers
----		Tomb owner standing alone
----		Tomb owner standing with child

Figure 11.27 Development of the type of themes in connection with the change in location of the necropolis.

of the false door in the chapel, the relevant themes on the elements are gathered in Figure 11.26.[21]

In the period before the transition period V.M the decoration of the entrance thicknesses and the false door jambs differed considerably from that after this transition period.

But the same development can be discerned when the location is taken as the main feature. In Figure 11.27 the locations Giza and Saqqara are also time dependant.

It is evident that there are two developments:

a. Over the course of time the decreasing dimensions of the tombs.
b. The change in the mode of sustenance of the *k3* of the deceased.both give the same results for the entrance thicknesses; but it cannot be concluded from this observation that they are directly linked,[22] because it is possible that these are two parallel non-opposing developments.

[21] In this figure the meaning of the indication ' ---' is not that the theme is not present on the element but that it is present to a lesser extent.

[22] It must be taken into account that there is a probable connection between the development in the dimensions of the tombs and the change of necropolis.

Chapter Twelve

The Entrance Thicknesses and Chapel Walls

I. Introduction.

As a follow-up to the results obtained in chapter VIII regarding the directionality of decorative themes, in this chapter the chronological development of possible connections between themes observed on the western wall of the chapels and the decoration of the entrance thicknesses, although already partly discussed, are further studied. If the presence of such a link is established, results obtained in a previous research project set up by the author will be used in order to try to interpret them.

The working hypothesis is that the design and the architecture of the entrance of the chapel were not intended to be part of the cult itself, but rather to support and optimize the secondary conditions necessary for the functioning of the cult.

In the earlier period, not only were priests a prime necessity for an optimal functioning of the cult, but visitors too were in demand and highly regarded, because their offerings, whether spoken or in kind, constituted a welcome addition to the daily supply brought by priests.

Every part of the chapel has a function (for the various functions see Figure 7.4), and the elements of the entrance are not directly involved in the direct cultic functioning of the chapel, their main function is both purpose- and person signalling.

In most of the tombs the decoration of the door jambs is such that the signalling function is evident and can be interpreted as person-signalling.[1]

The function of the decoration on the entrance thicknesses is less straightforward; a signalling function is possible because direct or reflected light penetrates deep enough into the corridor to make the decoration there visible. But this argument makes an inviting function just as probable or even more so, since a signalling function has already been assigned to the decoration on the door jambs and the architrave. This inviting function of the decoration on the thicknesses is possible because the tomb owner is, save for a few exceptions, looking in the direction of the outside world and thus at passers-by.[2]

It is possible that the part of the western wall in front of the entrance, which would be visible from the outside, has a connection with the decoration on the entrance thicknesses. In order to determine whether this connection between the decoration themes on the entrance thicknesses and on the western wall is present, the chronological developments of the following themes showing the tomb owner are studied.[3]

theme A(et):	The tomb owner standing alone.
theme B(et):	The tomb owner, sitting or standing, with wife and/or children.[4]
theme C(et):	The tomb owner, sitting or standing, with wife and/or children and/or other persons.[5]
theme D(et):	The tomb owner alone at the offering table.
theme E(et):	The tomb owner at the offering table with family.

[1] On the door jambs the figure of the tomb owner can be depicted but there can also be just text. An example of the former is the entrance to the chapel of *Mrrw-k3.j* (PM, III/2, 525-34) on which the tomb owner is depicted in a standing position, facing the entrance with above and in front of him name and titles (Figure 7.8); an example of the latter is the entrance to the chapel of *Ḫwfw-ḫʿ.f* [I] (PM, III/1, 188-90) (Simpson, *Gmast 3* Plate XVI a/b).

[2] Dodson, *Tomb*, 82 states that the tomb owner is also depicted in an outward orientation in order to watch the rising of the sun in the east (irrespective of the actual orientation of the tomb).

[3] The choice is based on the working hypothesis that the most important themes in the chapel, and the only ones capable of inviting, were the depictions of the tomb owner, and that their chronological developments would be the most informative in answering the question. The subsidiary figures were depicted in a serving function and were focused on the tomb owner and/or the chapel and not on the passers-by. The abbreviations 'et' and 'ww' mean resp. 'entrance thickness' and 'western wall'.

[4] There appears to be a close resemblance between themes B and C, yet, it is necessary to designate them differently because chronologically they do not behave in the same way. Although there does not appear to be such a different chronological development between themes D and F, for the sake of clarity a division is maintained between them.

[5] Subsidiary figures are only taken into account in the determination of the type of theme if a direct contact with the tomb owner exists. That means that a line of offering bearers walking in the direction of the cult chapel but placed beneath the effigy of the tomb owner is *not* considered as part of the whole group. But a child standing in the vicinity of the tomb owner and touching him/her is determinative for the choice of the type of theme.

theme F(et): The tomb owner at the offering table, with family and/or other persons.

theme 1(ww/nw): The tomb owner standing alone on the western wall of the chapel.

theme 2(ww/nw): The tomb owner in physical contact with members of the family, standing or sitting.

theme 3(ww/nw): The tomb owner sitting at the offering table on the western wall.

It has to be born in mind that the presence on the entrance thicknesses of themes D, E and F, depicting the tomb owner sitting at the offering table, does *not* a priori indicate a cultic function. This is contrary to its character when placed on the western and possibly southern wall of the chapel.[6]

In a preliminary study it has been determined that the themes on the western wall most likely to have a connection with themes on the entrance thicknesses are:

1. The effigy of the tomb owner standing alone (further indicated as theme 1(ww)). However, the above mentioned previous study showed that this connection only exists if the theme has been placed on the section of the western wall that is directly opposite the entrance of the chapel.
2. The theme of the tomb owner sitting at the offering table (further indicated as theme 3(ww)) always played a major role in the cultic function of the funerary monument.[7] Not only was it placed on the panel of the false door, but during the 4th and the first part of the 5th dynasty it was also frequently placed on the southern wall of the chapel. Placement on this wall fell into near disuse during the middle part of the 5th dynasty and henceforth the theme was, except for its placement on the panel of the false door, almost exclusively placed on the western wall (see Table VII and Figure 12.1).

The cult chapels with decorated entrance thicknesses are compiled for the necropolis of Giza and the themes placed on them are determined according to the above given list and gathered in Table VII.[8]

II. Conclusions from Table VII.

1. If in the list of tombs given in Tables VIII-1 and VIII-2 a compilation is made of the orientation of the depiction of the tomb owner on the thicknesses, it shows that the main orientation is in the direction of the world outside the cult chapel.[9]
2. Table VII gives the impression that on the southern wall of the chapel theme 3(ww) (the offering table scene) disappeared at the start of period V.M, and 'shifted' to the western wall. However, from the values from Roeten, *Decoration* are gathered in Figure 12.1 it is clear that originally both themes were present on their respective walls and remained there,[10] but that both of them show a marked chronological development. Some points of the curve of theme 3(sw) are somewhat problematic, but nevertheless the curve shows a marked decreasing tendency from V.E on.
3. From the end of period V.E onward themes with the tomb owner at the offering table (themes D, E and F) are no longer placed on the entrance thicknesses (Figure 12.2), while the increasing tendency of theme 3 on the western wall continues (Figure 12.1). This means that, due to the change in the mode of sustenance of the deceased, the purpose signalling function of the table scene was no longer necessary on the thicknesses and this development was strengthened by the decreasing dimensions of the tombs.
4. Early in the Old Kingdom the offering table scene could be placed on four locations: the panel of the false door, the western wall, the southern

[6] Until early in the 5th dynasty the table scene on the walls of the chapel and on the false door originally had a purpose-signalling function; after the change of mode of sustenance only the table scene on the false door retained its original function. The scene on the southern wall of the chapel shifted to the western wall and became part of the decoration for the magical mode of supplying sustenance.

[7] LÄ, V, 1128-33, s.v. ‚Speisetischszene'.

[8] Only the thicknesses of the entrance to the funerary construction have been included. That means that in e.g. G 2370 (*Snḏm-jb,*(PM, III/1 85-7, plan XXVI)) no. 1-i and 1-j are interpreted as such, while 13-a and 13-b are rejected.

[9] In the necropolis of Giza 5 examples of tombs can be found with the owner entering *into* the chapel (Harpur, *DETOK,* 53, note 49, gives 6 examples, but the tomb of *Ỉpi* is situated in the necropolis of Saqqara). It is possible that the reason for the inversion of the orientation is that a building or a courtyard used to be in front of the entrance to the chapel, which has disappeared in the course of time. On the entrance thicknesses into this building or into the courtyard, which is a passage from exterior to interior, the tomb owner was depicted in the normal outward directed orientation; on the entrance thicknesses of the passage into the chapel proper, the orientation could then be inverted, because it was not the main exterior-interior passage. An example of this is the cult chapel of *Mrrj-Rꜥ-nfr* (*Qꜣr*) (PM, III/1, 184-5). In that tomb on the entrance thicknesses of the passage between the open court and room III (PM, III/1, plan XXX) the orientation is outward. On both entrance thicknesses of the passage between rooms III and IV a male person, acting as a lector priest, stated by the texts to be the tomb owner himself, is walking *into* the offering room.

[10] Roeten, *Decoration* Diagrams IV.3.Ann. and XIV.3.Ann..

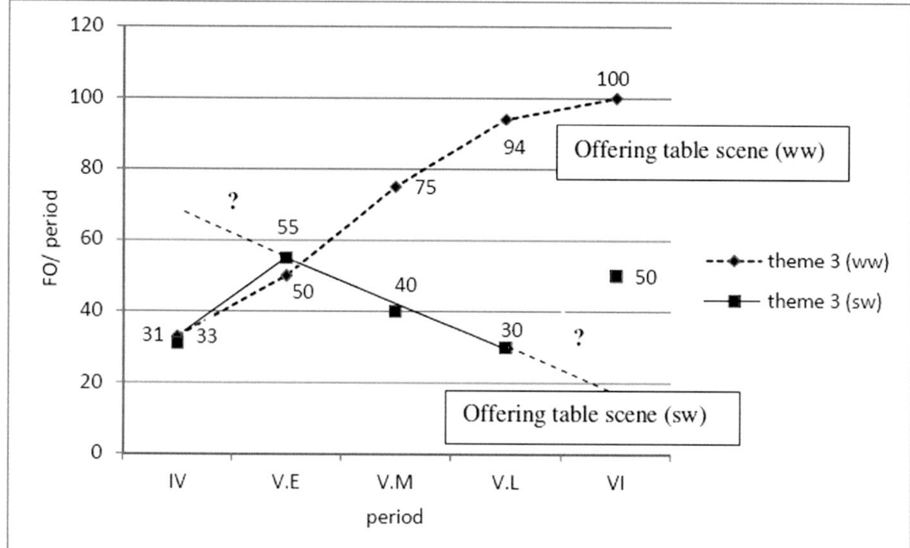

Figure 12.1. The chronological development of theme 3 (the offering table scene) on the southern and western wall of the chapel (after Roeten, *Decoration*, Diagrams IV.3.Ann and XIV.3.Ann).

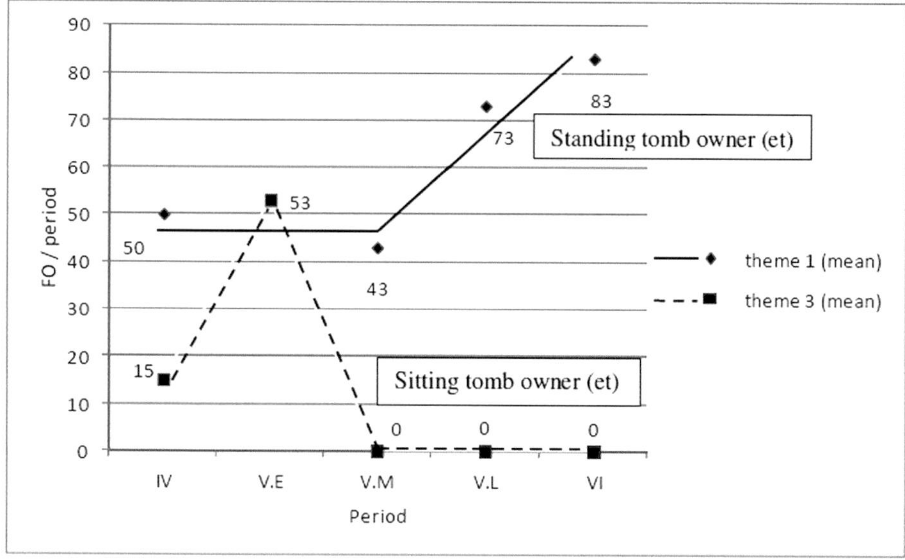

Figure 12.2 The chronological development of themes 1 and 3 on the entrance thicknesses.

wall and the entrance thicknesses. From the 5th dynasty on the scene began to be concentrated on the western wall while the scene remained on the panel.

5. From the second half of the period V.M depictions of the tomb owner in a seated position are rarely placed on the entrance thicknesses any longer. From then on the tomb owner is depicted there as a standing person (Figure 12.2).[11]

6. After the disappearance of the table scene from the entrance thicknesses (late V.E), for a short period theme 1(ww) is introduced on the section of the western wall opposite the entrance of the chapel.[12] However, from period V.L on this theme

[11] Harpur, *DETOK*, 53 specifies that the tomb owner was depicted in a standing posture from V.6 (V.M – V.L) on, a statement corroborated by the result obtained from Table VII.
In Junker, *Giza VI*, 36 and 38 this is explained by the premise that if a table scene or a depiction of the sitting tomb owner has been placed on the entrance thicknesses, an extra building (antechamber) was constructed in front of the entrance to the chapel. This turned the passage between the antechamber and the chapel into a passage similar in cultic meaning to the entrance in the false door. Normally offerings were laid down in front of the false door in order to be consumed by the deceased, and now the same could be done in front of the equivalent depictions on the entrance thicknesses. However, further study makes this explanation untenable, although the decoration scheme of many entrance door jambs has a strong resemblance with the decoration of a false door. Another explanation could be that the sitting tomb owner acted as the ideogram (A 50, (*šps(w)*) (Hannig, *Handwörterbuch*, 1293). The disappearance of this type of depiction could be due to the increasing importance of the magical supply of food for the *k3* of the deceased and the concomitant decrease in the necessity of showing the tomb owner as a 'revered person' (also see LÄ, VI, 711-26, s.v. 'Toter am Opfertisch', 711).

[12] The role of theme 1 on this section of the western wall is to all probability a guiding one, the signalling and inviting function having

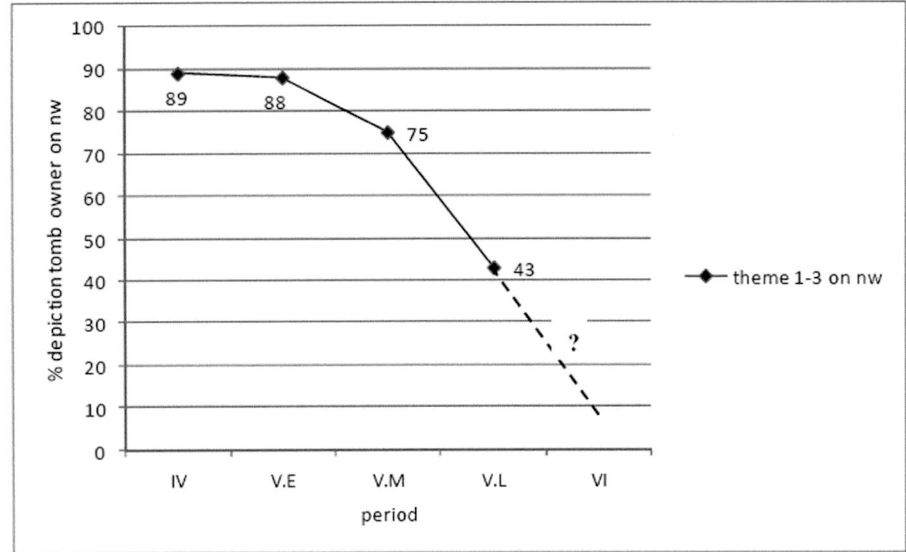

Figure 12.3 The percentage of tombs with themes 1-3 on the northern wall of the chapel.

disappears again from this section of the western wall.[13]

7. After the disappearance of theme 1(ww) from the western wall, the signalling role on the entrance thickness is further performed by the themes A(et) (tomb owner alone) and B(et) (tomb owner with family, preferentially a child).[14]

III. The northern wall of the chapel

In chapter VIII the interaction between section 3 of the western wall and the entrance has been discussed (Figure 8.7), but due to the observation in Table IX that the depictions of the tomb owner placed on that wall are exclusively looking in the direction of the entrance, possibly the northern wall of the chapel could also play a role in the total inviting and guiding function of the decoration. In Table IX the tombs with the tomb owner presented in themes 1 – 3 have been gathered.[15] The chronological development of these themes shows that from period V.M on the presence of these themes decreased markedly.

The table also shows that the purpose signalling theme 3 (tomb owner at the offering table) is rarely placed on this wall and that for that theme no chronological development is discernible.

IV. Discussion

The results obtained are compiled in a schema comparing the various chronological developments (Figure 12.4). In this schema two chronological developments can be distinguished, that are the result of two different causes. The first cause is the change in the mode of sustenance:

1. The table scene is placed on the western and southern chapel walls (Figure 12.4 - 1) and on the entrance thicknesses (Figure 12.4 - 3) →
2. On the southern wall the table scene is replaced by offering bearers (theme 1a) and piles of food offerings (theme 1b).
3. On the western wall of the chapel (Figure 12.4 – 3) the importance of the table scene increases (theme 3(ww)).
4. The table scene (Figure 12.4 - 2) disappears from the entrance thicknesses.
5. The depiction of the tomb owner on the northern wall (Figure 12.4 – 9, Figure 12.3) is directed toward the outside world, an observation that

been exerted on the entrance thicknesses by themes B and C.

[13] In Table VII only 4 tombs have the tomb owner depicted on wall section 3 in front of the entrance of the chapel, and in all of them the tomb owner is directed to the south, thus guiding visitors toward the southern false door. This theme lost its significance during the period that the magical mode of sustenance became the main constituent (Roeten, *Decoration,* Figure X.6 (page 209)), indicating that the guiding function was no longer necessary.

[14] This inviting function of major standing and sitting figures of the tomb owner is also mentioned in Harpur, *DETOK,* 53. On the western wall theme 2 (the tomb owner with members of the family) is the main theme during the early years of the Old Kingdom, and it has a guiding role, first on wall part 3 and for a short period on wall part 2 (Roeten, *Decoration,* Figure XI.9). When theme 1 takes over the guiding role on section 3 of the western wall, theme 2 retains, as a scene from the profane life of the tomb owner, its guiding function on wall part 2. On wall parts 2 and 3 theme 2 is often accompanied by personified estates and scribes, and this indicates that, even as a group out of the profane familial and professional life of the tomb owner, it can have a guiding role. Yet, on the entrance thicknesses theme B (tomb owner with family) is mostly accompanied by attendants and/or priests and hardly ever by offering bearers and/or scribes, thus indicating that it is *not* identical with the guiding group of theme 2 on wall parts 2 and 3.

[15] This table is derived from Roeten, *Decoration,* Table XIII.1.Ann. (page 389 – 90). The tombs that do not have themes 1 – 3 on the wall are nevertheless included because they are decorated with one or more other themes.

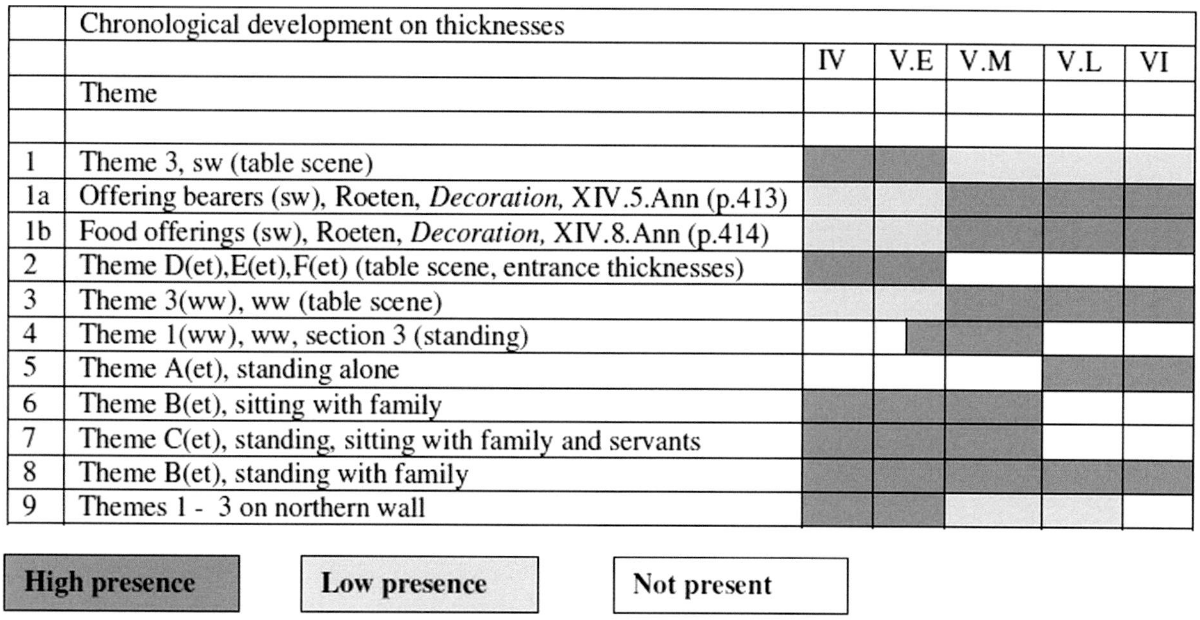

	Chronological development on thicknesses					
		IV	V.E	V.M	V.L	VI
	Theme					
1	Theme 3, sw (table scene)					
1a	Offering bearers (sw), Roeten, *Decoration*, XIV.5.Ann (p.413)					
1b	Food offerings (sw), Roeten, *Decoration*, XIV.8.Ann (p.414)					
2	Theme D(et),E(et),F(et) (table scene, entrance thicknesses)					
3	Theme 3(ww), ww (table scene)					
4	Theme 1(ww), ww, section 3 (standing)					
5	Theme A(et), standing alone					
6	Theme B(et), sitting with family					
7	Theme C(et), standing, sitting with family and servants					
8	Theme B(et), standing with family					
9	Themes 1 - 3 on northern wall					

High presence **Low presence** **Not present**

Figure 12.4 Chronological development of themes on chapel walls and entrance thicknesses.

can be explained with the inviting function of the theme, although it is placed further into the chapel complex.

6. Beginning from period V.M the presence of the depiction of item 5shows a decreasing tendency. This development can be explained by the change in the mode of sustenance of the *k3* of the deceased that became apparent in that period.[16] This development made the presence of inviting images in the chapel itself no longer necessary.

The second cause is the decreasing surface of the entrance thicknesses and the subsequent decrease in use or the disappearance of certain themes thereon:

- The standing tomb owner with family (Figure 12.4 - 8) remains on the thicknesses →
- The sitting tomb owner with family (Figure 12.4 - 6) disappears →

7. The table scene (Figure 12.4 - 2) disappears from the entrance thicknesses.

The smaller theme of the standing or sitting tomb owner alone (Figure 12.4 - 5) appears →The standing or sitting tomb owner with family and with and servants (Figure 12.4 - 6, 7) is too big and disappears.

The observation that theme B(et) (Figure 12.4 - 8) (the tomb owner standing with family) remains on the thicknesses during the whole period under study makes the placement of theme 1(ww) (Figure 12.4 - 3) on the western wall opposite the entrance into the chapel apparently superfluous. This theme was originally placed there in order to guide the visitors to the southern false door,[17] but because the importance of the false door diminished, the guiding theme and, with it, its guiding function disappeared from the chapel. The chronological development of themes 1 (Figure 12.4 – 4) and A (Figure 12.4 – 5) is such that while theme 1 disappears from the western wall, the same type of depiction is henceforth placed on the entrance thicknesses as theme A (tomb owner standing alone), but now with a person signalling and inviting function instead of a guiding one. The only connection between the developments on the two elements is the change in the mode of sustenance of the deceased; this causes the table scene to shift from the southern to the western wall. This change in mode and the concomitant appearance of the table scene on the western wall itself was probably not connected with the disappearance of the table scene from the entrance thicknesses.

This provoked the start of a change in the function of the entrance thicknesses which, finally, changed from purpose and person signalling to only person signalling and inviting.

The continuing decrease of the surface of the tombs had little influence on the surface of the chapel;[18] consequently no reaction to this development is identifiable there.

[16] Roeten, *Decoration*, Figure X.6 (page 209).

[17] The 4 times that theme 1 is placed on wall section 3 the tomb owner is depicted in a standing position (Table VIII).

[18] Roeten, *Economic decline*, Figure 68 (page 58).

However, due to the decreasing length of the corridor leading to the chapel, a marked reduction of the surface available for decoration on the entrance thicknesses took place. This reduction led to the disappearance of the decorative themes that took up more space, such as the tomb owner sitting with family with or without servants. Even the standing tomb owner, if accompanied by family and servants, was too large for the entrance thicknesses. An observation that corroborates this development is that either theme A (tomb owner standing alone) or theme B (tomb owner standing / sitting with family) are depicted on the thicknesses (Table VII).[19]

Until the end of period V.E theme B (tomb owner with family) could be placed either sitting or standing; from that period on, the tomb owner was depicted on the entrance thicknesses only in a standing position, sometimes with a child.

The consequence is that from the start of period V.M the whole series of decoration designed to attract the attention of a would-be visitor, to induce him to enter into the chapel and to guide him to the offering place, was abandoned.

1. The only functions aimed at passers-by that remained were person signalling and inviting, both functions being confined to the entrance thicknesses.
2. The presence of the table scene increased on the western wall, its role being limited to supporting the magical mode of sustenance.
3. Although the decoration pertaining to the signalling and inviting function of the entrance was of no direct importance to the sustenance of the *k3* of the deceased, it could not be abolished because it was this type of decoration that made sure that the deceased remained part of the social constellation of which he once had been a member.[20] Another reason that the signalling and inviting function could not disappear was that the sustenance of the *k3* was not completely independent of the bringing of real offerings and the recitation of the offer formula.

The idea that the table scene in the corridor acted as a kind of false door with an offering place in front of it, if the access into the chapel had been closed, has already been discussed and rejected (Figure 13.18).

[19] The only exception being the tomb of *Jdw* (PM, III/1, 185 -3). Simpson, *Gmast 2*, Figure 34.

[20] Assmann, *Tod, jenseits*,15.

Offering Places

(photo author)

Chapter Thirteen

Offering places

I. Introduction

From the start of the 3rd dynasty onward a dichotomy in tomb architecture became apparent between that intended for the king and that for non-royal persons, a difference not only in dimensions, but also in total lay-out of the mortuary complex. However, the bringing of offerings remained of the utmost importance, both for a king and for a private person,[1] and in both types of tombs facilities had to be present that enabled the living to bring offerings for the deceased.

In the little that remains of the total architecture and lay-out of both royal tombs and non-royal of the 1st and the 2nd dynasty some indications can be found concerning the presence of a place of worship and offering. In tomb V at Abu-Ghurab a double recessed niche is located at the end of a corridor chapel.[2]

The earliest royal tombs at Abydos give the impression that no persons were intended to enter any part of the royal mortuary complex (at first there was not even an entrance into the burial chamber, later, after the introduction of access, once the burial had ended the entrance was closed with portcullises).

The lack of an apparent offering place for the royal tombs of this period could be a result of time and other destructive influences, because the chapel of the tomb of the first dynasty king Den (I.5; PM, V, 83-5) consists of a subterranean, thus less exposed, room that could be reached by means of a staircase (see Chapter I). This might indicate that originally all of these tombs were equipped with a chapel, although above ground. It cannot be determined whether everybody was entitled to enter the chapel in order to bring actual offerings or to pronounce ritual spells, or whether this was limited to a select group of priests, as was undoubtedly the case in royal mortuary complexes of later date.

It is certain that in accord with the dichotomy between royal and non-royal mortuary architecture all aspects of the deceased king were completely out of reach for private persons and, in view of the priestly titles, that the rituals in the royal mortuary complexes were exclusively in the hands of members of the highest social stratum. The consequence was that any worshipping or requesting contact between a private person and the deceased king or the highest members of the royal family had to take place outside the mortuary complex (see further in this chapter). Because initially the contact between royal mortuary monuments and private persons was restricted to the placing of libation basins in the vicinity of these monuments, the discussion of that is included in that of the private libation basins.

The decision to close the chapel or other interior rooms in the tombs was undoubtedly motivated by the wish to protect them from unwanted visits during the periods that they were not in use for the 'official' offering rituals and associated ceremonies.[3] The disadvantage was that this made it impossible for a passer-by to enter the chapel and place offerings in front of the false door.[4]

This might have led to the development of alternative offering places other than the offering stone or basin in front of the false door.

The more obvious of these alternative offering places would be in the corridor leading into the chapel, and a further study indicates that from the beginning of the 4th dynasty the theme of the tomb owner sitting at the offering table was placed on the entrance thicknesses of some of the mastabas in the necropoleis of Giza (Figure 3.7).[5] The use of this theme on the walls of the corridor into the chapel stopped at the end of period V.M., and the tomb owner was from then on exclusively represented there in a standing position.[6] Harpur describes this development as follows: '.....but after V.6 this posture is largely replaced by the standing man, who occupied less space.......'[7].

[1] At the eastern side of the tomb of Qa'a (I.8) a stele was found by Petrie (Petrie, *Royal tombs I*, 6) while a second one had already been found by Amélineau. Next to the stele a large quantity of stone bowls have been excavated, indicating that probably a mortuary cult had existed there.

[2] Bárta, *Serdab*, Figure 2.

[3] Lauer, *Saqqara*, Plate IX; Bárta, *Abusir XIX*, Plate 13 (in this chapel it is probable that doors were placed directly in front of the false door too), apart from the observation that the chapel itself could also be closed.

[4] In the large mastabas of the Teti cemetery at Saqqara bringing an offering in front of the false door by a casual passer-by would have been less obvious because they were usually placed deep in the interior of the mastaba (*Kꜣ-gm-nj* and *Mrrw-kꜣ.j*).

[5] Harpur, *DETOK*, 53 indicates that the representation of the sitting tomb owner hardly exists in the necropolis of Saqqara.

[6] Roeten, *Decoration*, Table XII.1.Ann. (page 384 ff.).

[7] Harpur, *DETOK*, 53.

In view of a previous study of the author, to this observation the remark can be added that the change from the sitting to the standing figure might be caused by an increasing lack of space on the entrance thicknesses, which is due to the constantly decreasing dimensions of the mastabas over the course of the Old Kingdom.[8]

If indeed the offering table scene on the entrance thicknesses was introduced as a replacement for the statue(s) in the exterior chapel, which itself can be interpreted as a substitute for the offering place that had been moved into the interior chapel, then as to the question of whether or not offering basins or stones have been found *in situ* inside the corridor into the interior chapel, the following two considerations can be taken into account:

1. It is certain that offerings were brought to the statue(s) in the exterior chapel, because proof of the bringing of them has been found near a platform in front of the statue of *ʿnḫ-ḥꜣ.f* (PM, III/1, 196) (Figures 13.4 and 13.5).
2. For the same reason it is certain that offerings were placed on the offering stone in front of the false door in the interior chapel (Figure 2.2).

The answer to the question is that to my knowledge there are no examples of offering stones that have been found *in situ* in front of the offering table theme on the entrance thicknesses, which might be due to the exposed placement of the scene, but it has to be taken into account that placing an offering stone in the corridor in most cases made the access to the chapel difficult.

An intermediary solution would be to transform one or both of the door jambs into an offering place by marking it with a stele presenting the tomb owner sitting at an offering table, accompanied by his name, titles and an offering list. This situation has been found in the mastaba of *Ḥtpj* (Abusir, tomb AS 20, date: either III-IV.E,[9] or III [10]);[11] there this type of stele had been placed against the northern door jamb of the entrance of the chapel; the part of the corridor in front of the entrance could be closed with doors at the northern and southern side of the entrance recess (Figure 4.9).

Another solution to the problem would be placing the offering equipment in the vicinity of the entrance into the chapel, all the more because the door jambs very often carried a depiction of the tomb owner.[12]

There is a possibility that as early as the reign of Unas (V.9) installations for cultic libations were placed in front of the entrance of the mastaba of *H̲nwt* (PM, III/2, 623-4).[13]

Archaeological evidence shows that offering basins were placed around the pyramids of queens of Pepy II (VI.4).[14] The same evidence has been found around the pyramids of some of the queens of Pepy I (VI.2); here a preference to place them in front of the entrances of the temenoi of the pyramids has been observed, possibly because the name and the representation of the owner of the pyramid were given on the posts and the architrave. Lehner remarks that in Jéquier's excavation report of the pyramid complex of *Wd̲b.tn*, one of the queens of Pepy II (VI.4), it is mentioned that not only basins but also offering tables were found just outside the entrance in the wall around the pyramid complex.[15]

II. Offering places in front of statues in an exterior chapel

II.1. In royal mortuary complexes

II.1.1.The chapel of mastaba S 3505 at Saqqara [16]

In the early-dynastic cemetery of Saqqara, mastaba S3505, dated to the end of the 1st dynasty, has at its northern side a construction that can be interpreted as an exterior chapel (Figure 3.2). In the remnant of this construction the bases of two wooden statues representing a striding male have been found in a niche in a room that was floored with stone tiles (Figure 13.1). These statues would be visible to someone going in the direction of the big room at the end of the corridor and could have served as a place to see the image of the tomb owner and possibly to bring some offerings. Because this whole construction was at the northern side of the mastaba, it can also be interpreted as a

---

[8] Roeten, *Economic decline,* Figures 67and 69.

[9] This date is corroborated by Roeten, *Economic decline,* Table X.1 (page 141) where the surface of $1154m^2$ places this tomb in the period III.L – IV.E..

[10] Bárta, *Abusir XIX*, 56. The date III – IV.E is supported by the consideration that already in the 3rd dynasty the statue(s) started to be withdrawn from the exterior chapel in the direction of the mastaba core and also in serdabs in the interior of the core luminal to the surface and already early in the period IV.E the offering table scene was placed on the entrance thicknesses (Roeten, *Decoration,* Table XII.1.Ann. (page 384)). The asymmetrical arrangement of the loaves cannot be used as a dating criterion; neither can the number of loaves on the offering table (Roeten, *Osiris,* Figure 47).

[11] Bárta, *Abusir XIX,* Figure 2.21.

[12] Giza archives Photo B10774 shows these pieces of equipment in front of the entrance of the chapel, which has been walled up undoubtedly to turn the chapel into a serdab.

[13] Dobrev, *Tables d'offerande,* 146.

[14] Jéquier, *Pyramides reines,* 57; Jéquier, *Oujebten,* 25 – 31.

[15] Lehner, *Shareholders,* 250.

[16] This tomb is included in this section due to the ambivalent character of its dedication.

precursor of the northern chapel of the royal mortuary monuments of the 3rd dynasty.

Figure 13.1 Statues in the northern temple of mastaba S 3505.

II.1.2. The pyramid complex of Djoser (III.2)

At the northern side of the step pyramid of king Djoser (III.2), east of the northern temple a small building with two open dummy door-leaves has been constructed, in which a statue of the king (Cairo Museum, JE 49458) was placed. In Figure 13.2 the path leading to the entrance of that temple is indicated and it shows that the entrance had been placed in such a way that a person headed there inevitably had to pass in front of the statue.[17] Probably offerings were deposited in front of the northern wall of the building.[18] This situation is identical to that in the exterior chapels of *ʿnḫ-ḥ3.f* (PM, III/1, 196, section II.2.1.) and *Ḥsjj-Rʿ* (PM, III/2, 437 - 9; section III.1) where the statue of the tomb owner is standing next to the path to the cult chapel.

Stadelmann states that, based on the length of the court, the temple should have been twice as large in northerly direction and that the planned entrance was further to the north of this court. This would make the statue redundant in its present place while direct passing in front of the statue would not be necessary. In that case the building with the statue would probably have been placed further to the north against the eastern wall of the temple, although it is possible that the entrance would have remained in its present place. This way of placing a serdab at the north side of a mortuary monument was used in only one private tomb in the Memphite necropoleis, this being the mastaba of the dwarf *Pr-n(j)-ʿnḫ* that has been excavated in the vicinity of mastaba G 1457 (PM, III/1, 64) and that can be dated to the 4th dynasty.[19] The presence of standards in front of the aperture of the serdab in the tomb of the dwarf corroborates the previously mentioned possibility that this might also have been the case in front of the serdab of Djoser.

In the mortuary complex the remains of a statue depicting the king and the base of another statue of him but now standing on rekhyt birds and bows (Cairo, Museum, JE 49889) have been found,[20] on the front side of the base the name and titles of the non-royal person *Jm-ḥtp* were mentioned.[21] The literature is unclear about the place where the statue was found. According to Verner the excavator found it in hall B of Figure 13.3, together with fragments of other statues.

According to Sourouzian the statue base was found south of the colonnade, and it is possible that the chapel with the winding corridor that opens into the colonnade was meant (C in Figure 13.3).[22] Because the niche for the statue was placed at the end of a winding corridor, a common type of construction in this mortuary complex, the statue would be present but not directly visible, but the chapel cannot be interpreted as a serdab because it can be entered.

The Porter and Moss Topography states 'Found in colonnade and nearby', which indicates that the excavator has not been precise about the find spot.[23] This information makes it possible that the statue was found in the vicinity of the receiving part of the complex, and the most likely places would have been the entrance hall B or the winding chapel C halfway connected to the southern side of the colonnade.

Of the two possibilities the proposition that the statue had been standing in the entrance hall is the least likely for the following reasons:

- The precinct of the royal mortuary installation was not intended to receive visitors (except priests), because it was meant as a stage for the eternal life of the king, and was as such sacrosanct. Yet, in Figure 13.3 the presence

[17] The person passing must have been one of the priests responsible for the mortuary cult of the deceased king because other people were not permitted to enter the precinct or the temple.

[18] Friedman, *Djoser*, 11.

[19] Hawass, *Dwarf statue*, Plate 12. This tomb is not mentioned in Lehmann, *Serdab III*.

[20] The literature is unclear about the place where the statue has been found, Verner, *Pyramids*, 114 gives the entrance hall; Lauer, *Saqqara*, 92, gives the impression that it has been found in the hall between the court and the colonnade or just means to say 'somewhere in the complex'; PM, III/2, 407 gives 'Found in colonnade and nearby',; Lauer, *Imhotep*, 494 gives a place outside the south-eastern corner of the complex; Sourouzian, , *L'iconographie*, 149, gives 'trouvé au sud de la grande colonnade....'.

[21] Stadelmann, *Famille royale*, 174; Verner, *Pyramids*, 114 ; Gunn, *Inscriptions*, 192 - 5.

[22] Sourouzian, *L'iconographie*, 149.

[23] PM, III/2, 407.

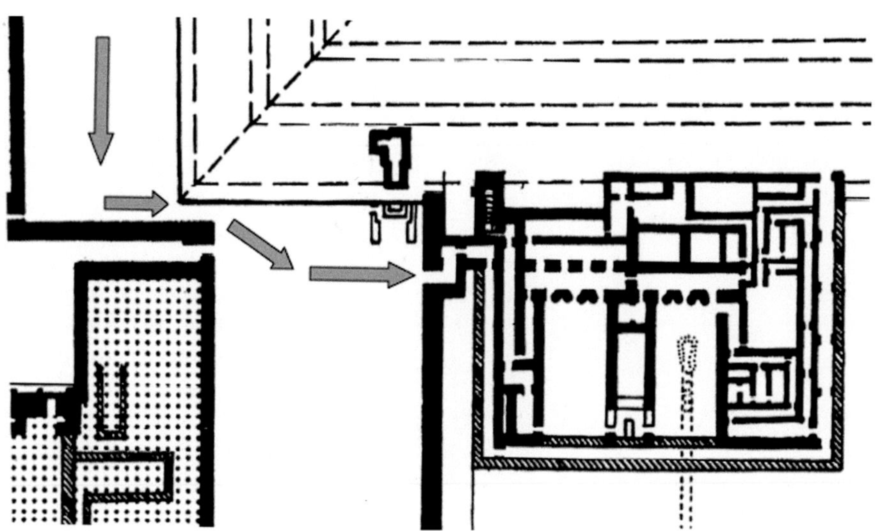

Figure 13.2 Plan of the northern chapel of the mortuary complex of Djoser (III.2).

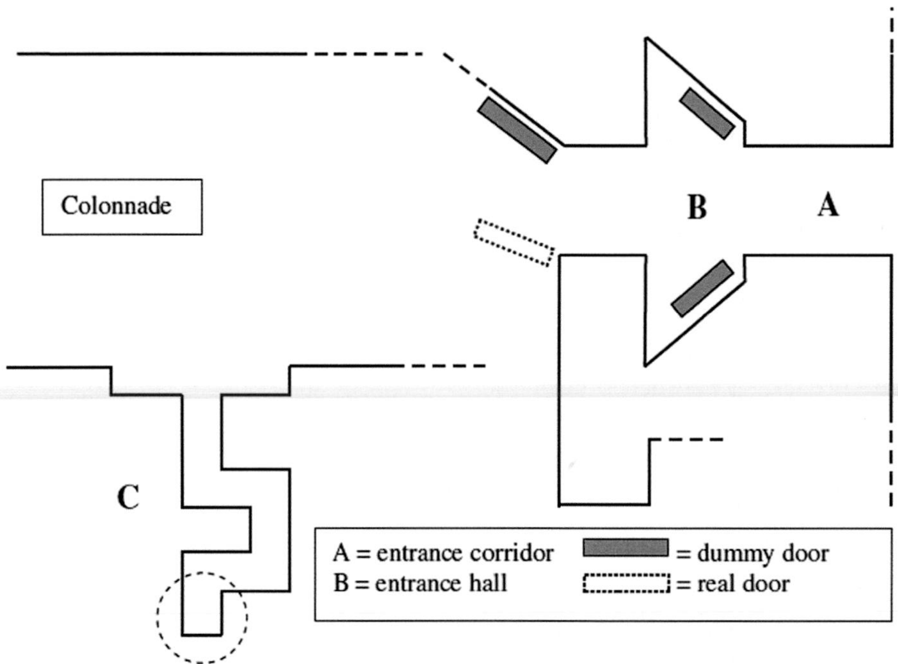

Figure 13.3 The entrance of the pyramid complex of Djoser (III.2).

of a door closing corridor A from the outside world is not likely, because in that case the king could not present himself and receive offerings. This means that visitors were entitled to enter through the corridor into the entrance hall where they were stopped by the door between hall B and the colonnade. In that case it is likely that a statue of the king with an offering table (the lion headed table JE 52519?) in front had been placed there.

– That a statue of the king would be placed in the hall awaiting rituals and offerings while on the base of the statue the name and titles of another and non-royal person are mentioned, is unlikely, however high in regard and rank that person might have been.

Consequently it is plausible that statue JE 49889 with the name of *Jm-ḥtp* on it had been placed in the chapel south of the colonnade, which would be highly honourable for the person involved without disrupting the divinity of the king. This conclusion is strengthened by Lauer's statement about the finding place of the pedestal : ' à cinq mètres au sud de l'enceinte de la

Pyramide à degrés et à quelque vingt-cinq mètres de son angle sud-est....' which is outside the complex but right in front of the chapel (the distance between the entrance of the chapel and the complex is ca. 30m). It is not possible to determine whether offerings were placed in front of this statue, but although *Jm-ḥtp* might have been highly appreciated by the king, decorum would have forbidden any form of special attention to the statue and the person.

II.2. In non-royal mortuary complexes

Over the course of the 4th dynasty the use of the exterior chapel decreased, and in the end this type of chapel was replaced by an interior chapel,[24] although exterior chapels were never completely abandoned.

Bárta proposes that statues were originally placed in the vicinity of the entrance of the exterior chapel thus enabling the placing of offerings in front of the statue (which would necessitate the presence of an offering block, a libation basin and possibly a platform).[25]

A statue served as a facsimile of the tomb owner, and could house the *k3* of the deceased. As already discussed, the *k3* could not leave the premises of the tomb, thus the observation that one or more statues could be placed in a building outside the tomb itself, means that the exterior chapel was not a construction added for grandeur and/or protection only, but that it was also part of the total mortuary monument. This statement is corroborated by the development of this type of chapel which was initially the only chapel available, a chapel originally meant for privacy and protection. It was only later that the interior chapel was introduced, thus ushering in a period of joint architectonic and ritual use, which was followed by the gradual nearly total disappearance of the exterior chapel.

The decreasing occurrence of the exterior chapel in the total offering place led to a marked increase of the introduction of the serdab, an internal room in which statues of the tomb owner, members of the family and later also those of servants, were placed.[26]

II.2.1. The exterior chapel of ʿnḫ-ḥ3.f (G 7510)

An example of a statue that had been placed in an exterior chapel but near the entrance of the interior chapel and which might have been visible from the outside,[27] has been excavated in the mastaba of *ʿnḫ-ḥ3.f* (G 7510; PM, III/1, 196; date: IV.4).[28] The mastaba has an exterior mud-brick chapel and an L-shaped interior chapel (Figure 13.4), with one false door dedicated to his wife *Ḥtp-ḥr.s* against the northern part of the western wall and a serdab behind the wall against which the southern false door would have been placed.[29]

The plan, as given by Reisner, suggests that a door had been placed in the entrance of the interior chapel, closing it in such a way that not only the entrance itself but also the door jambs were covered;[30] an argument against this is that, even with a double door, within the dimensions given in the plan of Reisner, *Giza I*, Figure 8 this is not possible; the door(s) would not completely open because the door-leaves would be too long for the corridor in front of the entrance.[31] The only possible way of closing the interior chapel would be with a door in the interior of the chapel, for which, according to the figure, the rebates were present.[32]

When the door into the interior chapel was closed, the only place where offerings for the deceased could be deposited would be the statue in the exterior chapel, which was placed there on a platform (Figure 13.5).[33]

The statue had been placed in such a dead end of the chapel that the visitor had to make a detour in order to get to it, and, in view of the rebates in Figure 13.5, the room with the statue could also be closed. But apparently that was no problem, because in front of the statue models of containers for food and drink that passers-by had left there have been excavated.[35]

In the interior chapel two false doors had been placed against the western wall.[36] Behind the southern false

[24] Reisner, *Preliminary report*, 231.

[25] Bárta, *Serdab*, 74.

[26] After the introduction of the serdab statues were also sometimes placed in the chapel itself. Examples are: *Ḥsfj* (PM, III/1, 68, G 2036, Giza Archives, photos C1024 and 1057); *3ḫtj-mrw-nswt* (PM, III/1, 80-1; G 2184; ASAE, 13-4(1914), Plate 118) (see intra Figure 2.2).

[27] The statue was a bust.

[28] Flentye, *Ankh-haf.* proposes a re-dating to IV.2 – 4.

[29] For the northern false door, see Giza Archives photo B 5761_NS. There is no opening between the chapel and the serdab; the southern offering place is a simple niche with an offering slab in front of it (Giza Archives, excavation journal, page ED25_02_226, dd. 02.07.1925).

[30] Reisner, *Giza I*, Figure 122 (page 213).

[31] Giza Archives excavation journal page ED25_02_230 (dd. 02.09.1925) shows that the pit was round with two stones in it that were lying upon each other. This could have been the basis for a door pivot support made of a harder type of stone and lying upon the other two. As already remarked, in view of the dimension of the corridor, the door had to be two-leaved.

[32] In Reisner, *Giza I*, Figure 122 (page 213) the opening of the inner-entrance of the chapel would be 1.50m, the wall north of the entrance is 1.00m wide and would be able to accommodate half a door-leaf when opened.

[33] Giza Archives, Photos B5602_NS and C10884_NS; excavation journal ED25_02_229 (date 02.08.1925).

[34] The bust of *ʿnḫ-ḥ3.f* is now in the Museum of Fine Arts, Boston, no. 27.442 (Dunham, *Prince Ankh-haf*, Plan page 43).

[35] Giza Archives, Photo C 10884_NS. Dunham, *Prince Ankh-haf*, 43; Bolshakov, *Ankh-haf.*

[36] Giza Archives, Photo A8249_NS.

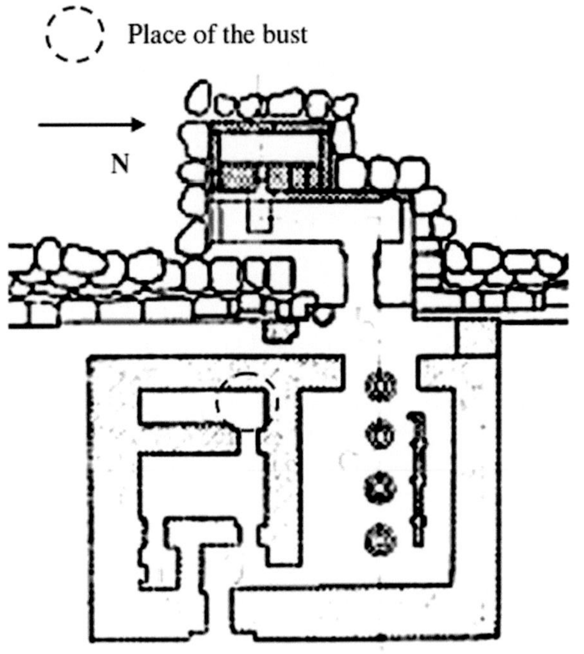

Figure 13.4 The chapels of *ʿnḫ-ḥ3.f* (G 7510; PM, III/1, 196; date IV.4) indicating the place of the bust in the exterior chapel (after Reisner, *Giza I*, Figure 8).[34]

door a serdab had been constructed that had no statue(s) in it and had no (visible) slot into the interior of the serdab.[37]

According to the plan in Figure 13.5 the dimensions of the door construction are such that it can be opened to the north without touching the platform. The observation that the statue had been nearly hidden in a small space in the exterior chapel, and not in the courtyard where it would have been plainly visible for all visitors passing by, leads to the conclusion that in this period the development had already reached the point where the interior chapel and the serdab were more important than the exterior chapel and also more important than the statue that may have been placed in it.

Possibly a stele has been excavated in the south-western corner of the court-yard. G. Reisner mentions it with a question mark and no further information about it can be found.[38]

[37] Lehmann, *Serdab III*, tomb no. G 256. Reisner, *Giza I*, Figure 122 (page 213). The state of preservation of the southern false door was such that no definitive answer can be given about the presence of a slot, neither about the statues in the serdab because in all probability they were robbed a long time ago (Giza Archives, photo A8249_NS).

[38] Giza Archives, Excavation Journal, ED25_02_232, dd. 02.09.1925.

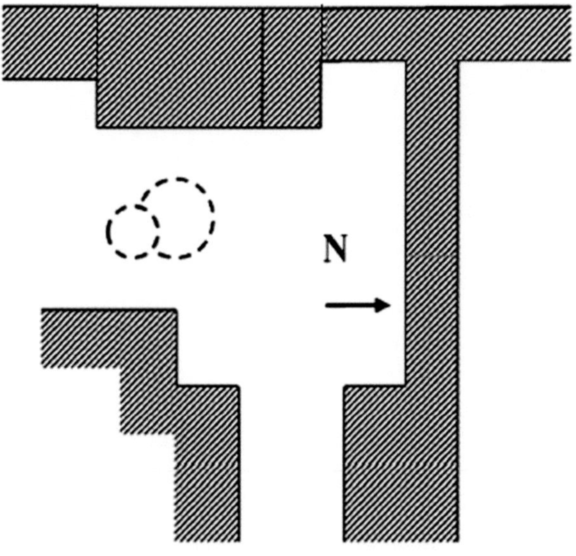

Figure 13.5 Detail room I of exterior chapel of G 7510 (after Giza Archives excavation journal page EG016997).

II.2.2. The exterior chapel of Mrs-ʿnḫ [III] (G 7530sub)

The subterranean tomb of *Mrs-ʿnḫ* [III] (PM, 197 – 9; G 7530*sub*; Giza Archives photo A 4905_NS; date: IV.M) has a courtyard in front of the entrance that could be reached by means of two stairs. Between the entrance and the southern stair is a construction of which the excavators carefully expressed the possibility that it has been used as a serdab, although they do not include the construction in their plan.[39] It is more probable that the construction was meant to accommodate statues that were plainly visible and before which offerings could be placed if the door to the chapel was closed. In that case the bench in the construction as given in Figure 13.6 could have been a platform on which the statues that were mentioned by the excavators were standing.[40]

The limited possibilities for moving around in the courtyard ensued that visitors had to pass in front of the statue(s) in the serdab, regardless which of the two stairs they used to descend to the entrance. From the situation that developed in the courtyard it is clear that the number of visitors coming from the north is less than from the south, because the whole Memphite area lies to the south of the necropoleis of Giza.

A similar situation is in all probability present in the tomb of *Ḫnt-k3w.s* (PM, III/1, 288 – 9; LG 100). The

[39] Dunham, *Gmast 1*. Plan B. The construction and the platform are visible in Dunham, *Gmast 1*, Plate 1a, Giza archives, Photo A4730_NS, in some of the photos that can be found on www.osirisnet.net (Meresankh) and in Reisner, *Meresankh*, Figure 16. It is obvious that other scholars that used the plan never included the clearly visible construction of the serdab.

[40] Flentye, *Statuary*, 139 states that the pair statue MFA 30.1456 and standing statue MFA30.1457 had been placed in this construction.

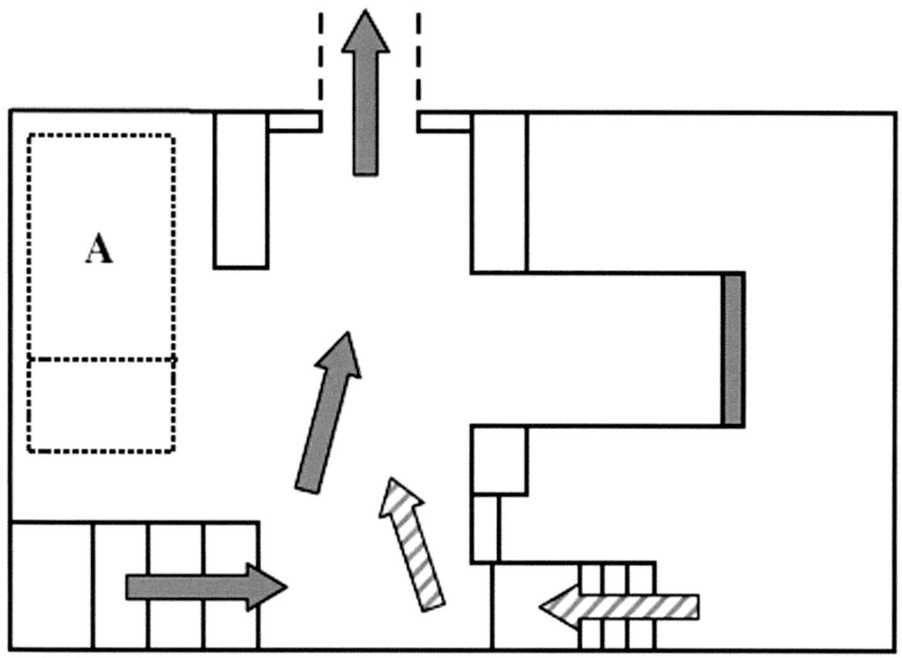

Figure 13.6 Exterior court of the chapel of *Mrs-ꜥnḫ* [III]; Giza Archives, photo A4905_NS (after Dunham, *Gmast 1,* Plan B, with construction A added).

causeway of the tomb ended in an antechamber with a naos and a statue niche.[41] Each of the two granite pillars that flanked the entrance are decorated with a plain simple niche, while in the chapel a compound *serekh* false door had been placed (Figure 13.7).[42] The pillars with the plain simple niches show that here three entrances were meant, of which one was real (a situation that has a similarity with that in Figure 6.1).

II.2.3. The exterior chapel of Ḫwfw-nḫt (G 1205) [43]

The mastaba of *Ḫwfw-nḫt* (PM, III/1, 57 – 8, date: IV.2; G 1205) is one of a group of tombs in which a special type of marker for the offering place, the slab stele, has been found. The mastaba has a mud-brick exterior chapel, originally consisting of two or three rooms, later extended to five rooms, while no interior chapel is present in the core of the mastaba.[44] The slab stele has been found embedded in the western wall of the chapel which, is not covered with a layer of mud-brick where the stele is placed.[45] In front of the slab stele is a mud-brick platform with two libation basins and two offering standards of which one is still present.[46] In

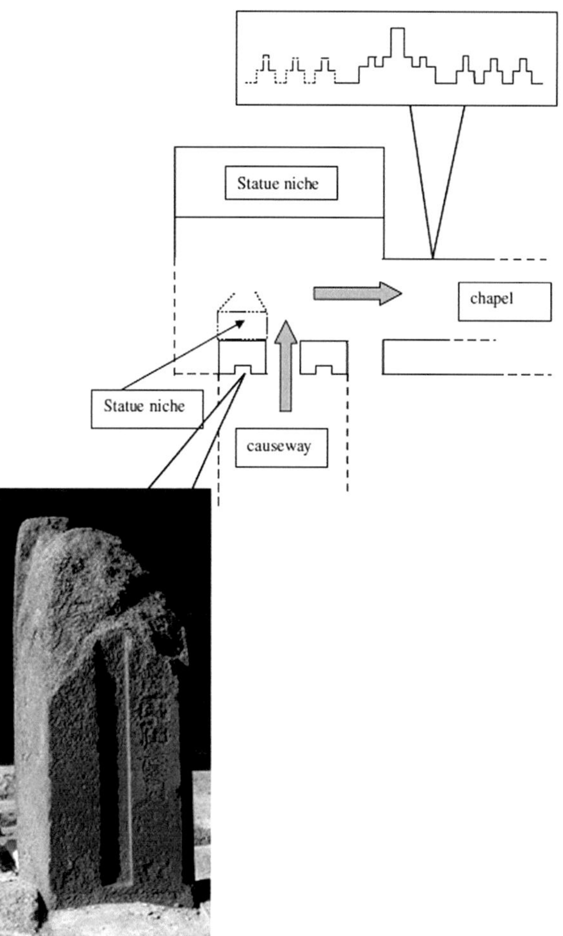

Figure 13.7 Plan of the entrance to the chapel in the tomb of *Ḫnt-kꜣw.s.*

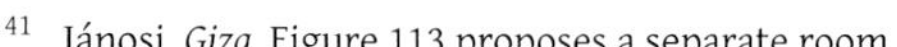

[41] Jánosi, *Giza,* Figure 113 proposes a separate room.

[42] Lehner, *Giza,* Figures 12.15 and 12.18.

[43] Reisner, *Giza I,* 392-4.

[44] Reisner, *Giza I,* Figure 95; Jánosi, *Giza,* 158-9.

[45] Der Manuelian, *Giza slab stelae,* 46 – 9; Figures 39 and 41.

[46] Der Manuelian, *Giza slab stelae,* Figure 40; Giza Archives photo B10770. In this photo an offering standard is lying partly over the platform in front of the stele; its original place being the round spot

view of one of the explanations which proposes that the introduction of the slab stele was imposed from above, thereby prohibiting the presence of any other subject of an offering ritual, the presence of a statue would be impossible.[47]

Nevertheless, in the extended chapel a platform for a statue was found in the south-east corner of the offering room.[48] The construction history of the chapel indicates that this platform was built during or after the enlargement of the chapel, which might indicate that the stricter rules about chapel decoration that developed from the reign of Sneferu (IV.1) on and that found their culmination in the first decades of the reign of Khufu (IV.2) had already slackened somewhat. This is corroborated by the observation that in the exterior chapel of *ꜥnḫ-ḥꜣ.f* (G 7510; PM, III/1, 196; date: IV.4) one or more statues had also been placed.

The only difference being that in the chapel of *ꜥnḫ-ḥꜣ.f* the statue could be seen from the outside, while in the chapel of *Ḫwfw-nḫt* there were two possible places for a statue. One is that there was a platform in the far south-east corner, in which case the statue would be hidden and be invisible even from the entrance giving direct access to the offering place (Figure 13.8). The other possibility was on the platform directly next to the offering place (which would explain the second offering basin); a statue placed there would be more visible from the outside.

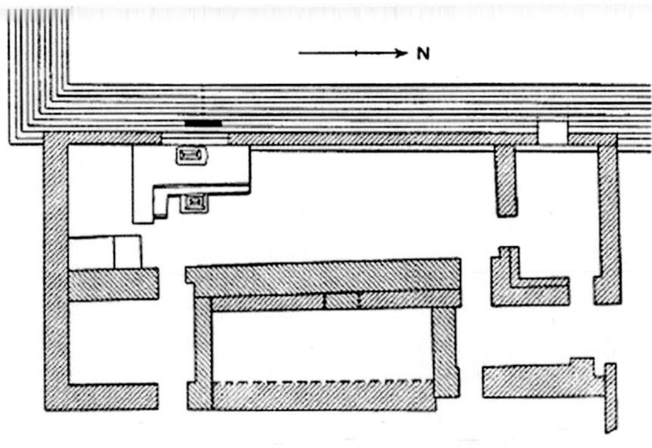

Figure 13.8 The chapel of mastaba G 1205 (Jánosi, *Giza*, Figure 16).

II.2.4. The chapel of Nfr (G 1207)

The mastaba of *Nfr* (PM, III/1, 58; IV.2 or later; G 1207) has a mud-brick exterior chapel and no interior chapel. Like in the chapel of mastaba G1205, a slab stele has been installed in the western wall which was, in this case, covered with a layer of mud-bricks.[49]

Reisner indicates that it is likewise possible that the slab stele had been installed in the stones of the core and that, as a second step, a mud-brick wall had been placed around the stele.[50] The opening in the mud-brick layer against the western wall is wider than the slab stele itself, which could lead to the conclusion that the possibility of a false door being removed in order to place the slab stele cannot be excluded. However, as can be seen in Giza Archives photo B10764_OS it is evident that it was foreseen that a layer of plaster would be applied to the mud-brick wall, and that enough space was left open between the thickness of the mud-brick layer and the slab stele that the plaster layer could fill that up.

Flentye suggests that it is possible that on the platforms in the vicinity of the slab stele that have been found in some chapels in the G 1200 cemetery statues might have been placed;[51] on these platforms the placing of offering stands is also possible, but less probable. The more probable place for the offering stands is next to the focus of the cult. This can be seen in the chapel of mastaba G 1205 where a slab stele had been placed with an offering-platform in front of it; in photo B10770 of Giza Archives it is evident that at both sides of the stele offering stands had been standing,[52] and in the chapel of *Mrj-ḥtp.f* (PM, III/1, 127) a libation stone has been excavated with three of the four offering stands still present.[53]

If a form of offering place together with a platform had been present in the chapel prior to the placing of the slab stele, in view of the supposed 'intolerant' character of the imposed change, it is improbable that, once the stele placed, one or both of the mud-brick platforms that were possibly present in the chapel would still serve as a base for a statue.[54]

in the photo right of the libation basin on the platform. Offering stands like this were placed on both sides of the basin. It is possible that on the E-W oriented platform next to the stele another statue had been placed.

47 Here a statue is considered as a subject of an offering ritual; the offering standard is considered to be a tool for the ritual.

48 Reisner, *Giza I*, Figure 95, room a. Jánosi, *Giza*, states that the platform certainly has served as the basis for a statue, but argues, in accordance with Reisner, that it was constructed after the extension of the chapel had taken place (Reisner, *Giza I*, 393).

49 Reisner, *Giza I*, Plates 13c-e; Der Manuelian, *Giza slab stelae*, Figure 48. The 'scar' in the western wall shows that the slab stele was placed on one of the rows of core stones and partly let into the row on top.

50 Reisner, *Giza I*, 187.

51 Flentye, *Statuary*, 128.

52 Der Manuelian, *Giza slab stelae*, Figure 40.

53 Junker, *Giza I*, Plate VIIIb.

54 Whether this 'intolerant' character is a reality or not is still not clear; there are scholars who claim that tomb owners who belonged to the highest social stratum like *Ḥm-jwnw* and *Kꜣ.j-wꜥb* could have large quantities of statues in their chapels, thus acting against the generally applicable rules laid down by the king, while those of lesser standing had barren chapels except perhaps for a slab stele This

The possibility that prior to the placement of the slab stele a false door had been present appears to be supported by the observation that in the vicinity of the slab stele the mud-brick cover of the western wall is interrupted over its whole height, thus giving the impression of a false door with a panel above.[55] However, a solution is that once the chapel had been built, a slab stele was placed at once; but, because the idea of the false door was not abandoned, a mud-brick wall was placed around the stele, leaving the semblance of a false door intact. Even if this apparent 'imitating' of the false door was intended,[56] it was not an innovation, since this type of false doors existed from early in the Egyptian history. Figure 2.1 represents the plan of a tomb in the cemetery of Tarkhan that can be dated to the transition from the predynastic period to the first dynasty; in the chapel are two openings that had the form of slots.[57]

If the slab stele was placed directly after the mastaba had been assigned, it is possible that platforms were constructed that could accommodate offering stands at one or both sides of the stele.

II.2.5. The chapel of Nfrt-kȝ.w (G 7050)

The stone exterior entrance building of *Nfrt-kȝ.w* (PM, III/1, 182 – 3; date: IV.4; G 7050) has a platform straight in front of the entrance (Figure 13.9),[58] clearly in order to receive visitors. Possibly an offering place had been made next to a statue, thus turning the room into an exterior chapel in front of the L-shaped interior chapel.

It is impossible to obtain certainty in this matter, not only because the state of conservation of both ritual elements of the mortuary monument and the visibility of the entrance of the exterior part make it highly unlikely that a statue that might have been standing there would have been preserved, but also because the reporting about this place leaves something to be desired.[59]

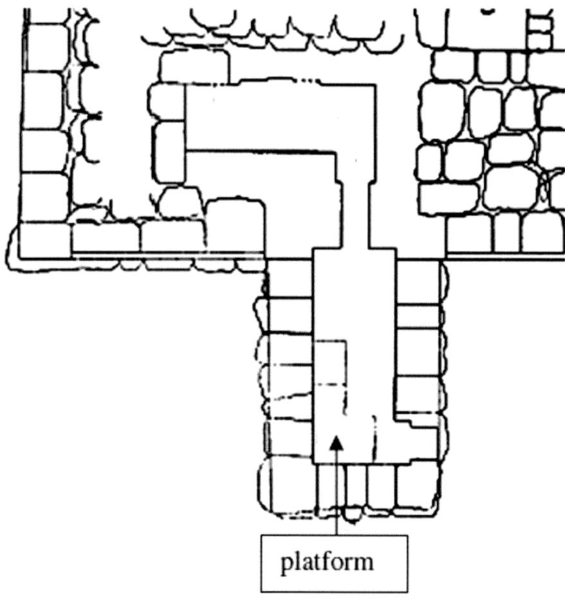

Figure 13.9 Chapel of the mastaba of *Nfrt-kȝ.w* (PM, III/1, 182 – 3; date: IV.4; G 7050), detail of Reisner, *Giza I*, Figure 10.

II.2.6. The chapel of Ḥm-jwnw (G 4000)

In the necropolis of Giza mastaba G 4000 of *Ḥm-jwnw* (PM, II/1, 122 – 3; date: IV.2) has a chapel corridor with two false doors in it. According to Junker, the excavator, the mastaba was been built in several phases, many of which were not entirely in accordance with the line of development that were in force in the early years of the reign of Khufu (IV.2). In order to explain this Junker assumed that the tomb owner was so high ranking within the echelon of the royal family that he was at liberty to do this.[60]

Over the course of time scholars have added so much information and have expressed so many opinions that a further discussion of the development of the monument is beyond the scope of this study. The door in passage between rooms A and B in the mud-brick chapel(?) east of the entrance of the corridor chapel is, however, of interest and within the scope of the study.

In the south-eastern corner of room B a stone basin is situated of which the form shows that it was not constructed for libation offerings. Because this part of the building is in fact the anteroom of the chapel, this basin could have been placed there in order to provide

argument is not strong since close family of *Ḥm-jwnw* had the chapels of their mastabas closed up in the early years of the new development (for a discussion see Stadelmann, *Strenge Stil*); Jánosi, *Giza*, 293.

55 Der Manuelian, *Giza slab stelae*, Figure 48. This situation has been found in the chapels of a number of other tombs (G 1227, Giza Archives photos B10786 and C12815; G 1235, Giza Archives photo C11398; G 2120, Giza Archives photo A7992).

56 Bolshakov, *Man and double*, 38 mentions the tomb of *Ḥm-jwnw* (G 4000) as an example where (uninscribed) false doors have been placed.

57 Petrie, *Tarkhan II*, Plate XII (right, top and middle).

58 Reisner, *Giza I*, Figure 10 (page 48). The plan of the exterior chapel shows that the entrance probably could be closed with a door. In Figure 13.9 it is not clear whether the two squares west of the 'platform' are places meant for other ritual activities or whether they are part of the tiling of the floor (in Giza Archives, plan EG021327 all the tiles in the room are given; also see Photo A4285). Giza archives Photo A4539 shows that one of these stones further to the west is higher than the surrounding tiles.

59 In the diary pages no mention is made of a platform, the only information about this is found in Reisner, *Giza I*, Figure 10.

60 Junker, *Giza I*, 134.

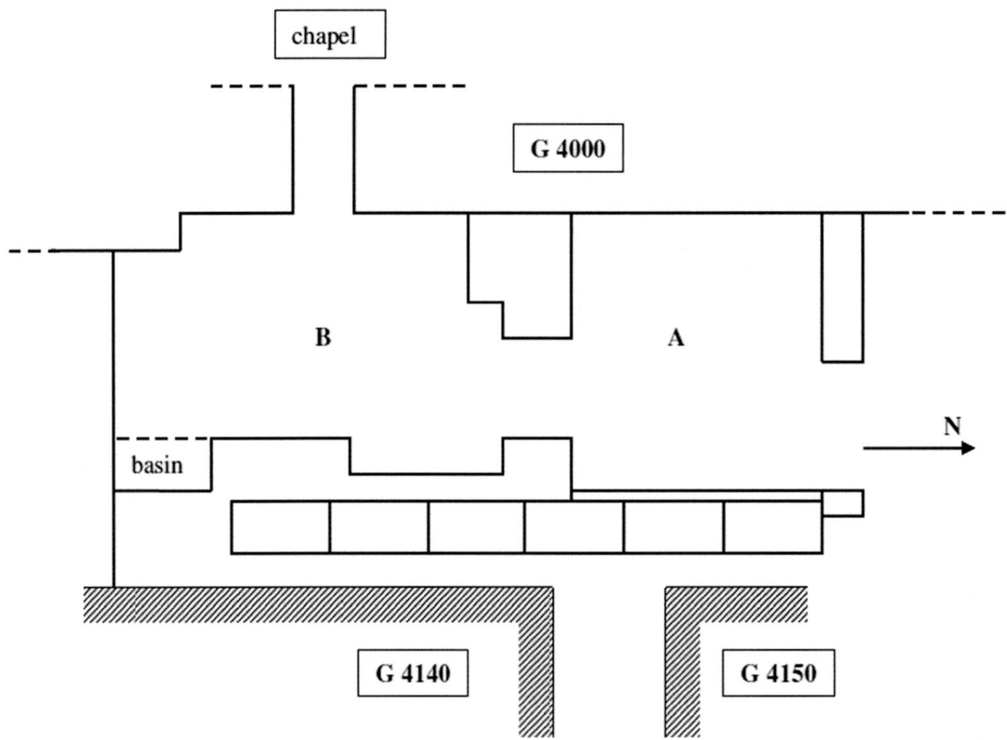

Figure 13.10 Mastaba G 4000, the building in front of the entrance of the chapel (schematically after Reisner, *Giza I*, Figure 121).

water needed for the rituals but also to pour residual water away.[61]

It is also possible that this water was meant for purification before entering the chapel, although it is more likely that, due to the inherent increasing impurity of the water left there, the priests brought water for the ritual cleaning and libations themselves.[62] That cleanliness was a prerequisite is evident from the text that was placed at the entrance of many tombs of later date, although there is no direct proof of the same type of requirements in the earlier years of the Old Kingdom; the presence of the basin might be seen as circumstantial evidence.

> *As for all people who will enter this tomb in a state of impurity, after they have eaten the abominations which the glorious spirit who has gone to the necropolis abominates, without removing their impurity, as they should purify themselves for the temple.....*

Part of the text on the inner-architrave in the chapel of the tomb of *Mrf-nbf* (Saqqara-west). www.osirisnet.net (merefnebef).

III. Offering places in front of statues in the interior chapel

Possibly due to experience of the vulnerability of statues standing in an exterior chapel that is practically open to the outside world, the emergence of the interior chapel ensured that the statue was increasingly placed in its interior. Tombs have been excavated in which one or more rooms are present in which clearly statues had been placed and that had no connection with the outside world in the form of a doorway; a room like that, can, according to the definition, be interpreted as a serdab.[63]

Serdabs that were incorporated in the prime planning of the tomb were normally relatively close to the main cult place where the offerings for the deceased were brought, thus sharing the cultic activities in the chapel.[64] In order to be closer to the entrance and the

[61] These basins have also been found in the exterior chapels of G 1223 (Reisner, *Giza I*, Plate 14c), G 4350 (Junker, *Giza I*, Figure 39) and others.

[62] It is possible that the cleaning ritual was not more than token and did not involve a real cleaning action.

[63] The serdab is a room in a mortuary structure that served to place the statues of the deceased, sometimes accompanied by statues of members of the family and occasionally statues of servants. Sometimes the serdab was completely closed; sometimes an opening to the outside world was present. Often it is stated that this narrow elongated opening (in the chapel of *Tjj* (Saqqara) the width is 10cm and its height 30cm, while it is constructed at ca. 1.60m above floor level) is meant for the living to see the image of the deceased. The main argument against this is that the serdab is a closed room and thus in complete darkness, which renders the statues invisible.

[64] In some cases the statue was placed in the chapel itself (which can be seen as a reference to an old tradition in the exterior chapels)

place of the former exterior chapel, initially a statue-room was constructed next to the corridor leading to the chapel. The statues were not always placed in a separate space; some have been found in the chapel (Figure 2.2) or in other open spaces in the tomb.[65]

Possibly as a consequence of an increasing complexity of interior chapels that started early in the 3rd dynasty, in most cases the false door was too far away from the entrance for the casual passer-by. As a solution at first a statue was placed in the exterior chapel (section II.2.1), but after the exterior chapel fell into disuse, an interior offering place closer to the entrance, and to the place of the former exterior chapel was chosen (see section III.1).

In the course of the 4th dynasty the statues were increasingly placed in a serdab.[66] While standing in the exterior chapel, the function of the statue had been twofold:

- Receiving visitors and offerings.
- Acting as a double of the tomb owner.

The increasing tendency to place the statues in interior room(s) of the tomb meant that their functions were reduced to that of sharing the cult and acting as a double of the tomb owner.

In the article by Bárta, *Serdab* the author states that the disappearance of the statues into the serdab 'robbed' them not only of their function of receiving visitors, but also of their reception of offerings.[67] The latter is contradicted by the following observations:

- Against the eastern wall of the stone-built mastaba of *Ỉḫt-nb* (PM, III/1, 57-8, G 1206) two offering basins have been found in front of the place that once had been the entrance of a chapel, a chapel that later had been converted into a serdab by closing off the entrance.[68] After the conversion of the chapel into a serdab two libation basins were placed in front of the eastern outer wall, thus enabling the bringing of offerings to the statue(s) that was(were) placed in the serdab.[69] The placement of the basins in front of the eastern wall of the tomb indicates that there was no objection against ritual activity there, and this makes it possible that the basins were also placed outside when the tomb owner was represented in the offering table scene on the thicknesses of an open entrance.
- In the mastaba of *Ṯjj* (PM, III/2, 468-78) two serdabs can be distinguished, one at the east side of the portico and one north of the interior chapel. In the portico offering bearers are depicted on the western and eastern wall, moving in the direction of the central entrance, but on the eastern wall that means that they are also going in the direction of the opening of the serdab.[70] This serdab has an opening in the pillared court too and on both sides of that slot priests are bringing offerings to it. This observation stresses the idea that there is still a connection between the serdab and the receiving of offerings. The serdab in the chapel has three openings and the decoration around the two openings nearest the false doors consists of processions of animals and offering bearers heading in the direction of *the false doors* which supports the close connection between the false door and the serdab.

Since in several tombs offering basins or blocks have been found in front of the serdab, it is evident that the statues there were receiving offerings, not only in a magical way but apparently also by means of actual offerings.

This appears not to be the case with the depictions of the tomb owner on the entrance thicknesses, where no offering basins have been found *in situ* in front of them. This may be an archaeological mishap due to the exposed position of an offering basin in this corridor where the basin would be extremely prone to theft.[71] It may also be due to the inconvenience of an offering basin standing in the rather narrow corridor.[72] An example of an offering basin standing in a somewhat wider corridor-chapel (Figure 13.12) can be found in the chapel of mastaba G 3086.[73]

(Junker, *Giza V*, 146; also see Junker, *Giza XII*, 54).

65 Junker, *Giza XII*, 54 ; Fisher, *Minor cemetery*, Plate 28. The rock-cut statues that are found in the interior walls of the chapels of some tombs can be interpreted as such.

66 Bárta, *Serdab* ,75.

67 This statement is also denied in LÄ V, 874-9, s.v. 'Serdab'.

68 Lehmann, *Serdab III*, G-72; Lutz, *Offering stones*, no. 3; Giza archives Photos A10910 and A10911.

69 Reisner, *Giza I*, 218[29]; Ibidem, Plan Cemetery G 1200; PM, III/2, 58; Giza Archives, photo A10910 and A10911.

70 Beaux, *portico*, 225.

71 It is possible that these basins were protected by their inherent mortuary character; offering basins have been found near entrances of the temenos of queen's pyramids in Saqqara-south, and these basins clearly had the same degree of exposure.

72 From Roth, *Gmast 6*, Der Manuelian, *Gmast 8* and El-Fikey, *Re'-wer* the width of the entrance of the chapels has been determined and the mean value is 0.7m, while the average width of a rectangular offering basin comes to about 0.25m (Dobrev, *Tables d'offerandes*, Figures 10b, 12-14, 16-17).

73 Lehmann, *Serdab III*, G 165. The mean width of a corridor chapel is about 70cm, the width of a small libation basin is 20-25cm, and this means that passing was possible but not too easy, all the more so because offering stands were placed at both sides of the basin. Fisher, *Minor cemetery*, Plate 20.

although several examples of basins in that type of chapel are known (Figure 13.18).

The mastaba of *Mddj* (PM, III/1, 98; G 3093) has a corridor chapel with a western wall that can be interpreted as a recessed palace facade.[93] The niche opposite the recess at the southern end of the corridor has been closed off with a false door,[94] in front of which a libation basin is standing.[95] In the narrow northern end of the corridor another basin standing in front of a niche has been found.[96]

In the necropolis of Abusir a new type of tomb was excavated in 2017: the chapel had several niches in the western wall and in front of these mud-brick enclosures had been constructed that cannot be interpreted as the openings of shafts, but which must be classified as an offering area that took up nearly the whole width of the corridor chapel.[97]

V.2. Standing in the exterior chapel

In the exterior chapel of mastaba G 7650 (PM, III/1, 200) a basin was standing against the southern wall of the chapel; the way it is placed clearly shows that this is not the result of being thrown out of the interior chapel during the pillaging of the tomb (Giza Archives, photo A8251_NS).[98] The form of the basin (deep with small, anepigraph rims) indicates that this basin was not intended for offerings but served another purpose).

In the exterior chapel of mastaba G 1223 (PM, III/1, 59) the basin is placed in a corner facing the entrance and is surrounded by white-washed walls (Giza Archives, photo B12975_OS), thus demonstrating that the placement of the basin was intentional and ritually important and because of that had to be pure.[99]

In the chapel of the mastaba of *Ḫwfw-snb* [I] (PM, III/1, 152 – 3) a large libation basin had been placed in the south-eastern corner of the recess for the possible reason that the serdab was constructed on the other side of the wall (Figure 13.15).[100] More probable is that this basin was foreseen as a reservoir for water needed for the rituals. The same could be the case in the mortuary construction of *Sšm-nfr* [III], PM, III/1, 153 – 4).[101]

Junker proposes that the basins that were not placed in the direct vicinity of a kind of offering place served to collect excess water from the libations in the chapel. In some cases this seems logical,[102] certainly when the basin has a drain that brings the excess water outside the chapel.[103]

In the chapel of mastaba G 4350 (PM, III/1, 126; Reisner, *Giza I*, Figure 97) the basin in the offering room is lying next to the path leading to the offering place. In a small ante-room (c) north of the chapel this path goes in front of a niche which might have been intended for a statue, although there is no indication of a base for it, thus serving as an offering place.[104] If that is really the case, the basin in the north-eastern corner of the offering room (a) could have served as a place to get rid of the excess water of the offering rituals, and moreover has the design for it.[105] In this chapel another feature is that against the eastern wall of the chapel and in front of the slab stele the print of a piece of offering equipment, giving the impression of a basin with a somewhat wider rim, is visible in the floor. A libation basin could be placed there without being an obstacle because the distance between the platform and the eastern wall is ca. 1.20m and in the photo it is visible that enough room is available.

V.3. Standing in the area around the tomb

After their death, some private persons not only had their mortuary cult, but also gained a special interest that was probably based on their social and/or familial importance, obtaining a special status that can be described as 'deified', although most of them never became more than a local god. Examples of private persons that obtained that status are *Ḏdf-ḥr* (PM, III/1,

[93] Reisner, *Giza I*, 279 gives 1.10m as the width of the corridor, which makes placing mortuary equipment like basins and standards more possible.

[94] Fisher, *Minor cemetery*, Plate 44 shows that the false door is dedicated to the tomb owner and his wife.

[95] Ibidem, Plate 24, Plate 23 shows that a life-size statue of the tomb owner stood at the left side of the false door; probably the libation basin served both persons. Lehmann, *Serdab III*, G 166.

[96] Fisher, *Minor cemetery*, Plate 20 (G 3086 (= Fisher G 2086); Lehmann, *Serdab III*, G 165.

[97] Odler, *Tomb Abusir*, Figure 7.

[98] Reisner, *Giza I*, Figure 9. In the photo it is visible that the surrounding of the basin had been plastered white, indicating the ritual importance of the basin.

[99] Reisner, Giza I, Figure 16. Kurasziewicz, *Practical, ritual*, 533 – 4.

[100] , Junker, *Giza VII*, 117 ff..

[101] Junker, *Giza III*, 198 and Figure 36.

[102] Junker, *Giza I*, Figure 38, where the basin is standing in a separate room (although the question arises why the priests did not get rid of the water by throwing it outside the chapel, but perhaps in a mortuary surrounding water had a special meaning). Sometimes the water was evacuated by means of a drain (exterior chapel of mastaba G 7650, Reisner, *Giza I*, Figure 9h). These drains were also in use in royal mortuary installations (Verner, *Abusir IX*, 47, 52).

[103] Of this several examples can be found, also in other cemeteries than that of Giza, one of them being in tomb F48 at Abu Rawash (Gourdon, *Djedefra*, Figure 5 and Plate 1).

[104] Reisner, *Giza I*, 189; Jánosi, *Giza*, 172 indicates that it is either the placement for a statue or for a libation basin (but why not both of them?).

[105] Junker, *Giza I*, Figure 39; Giza Archives photo AEOS_I_5947.

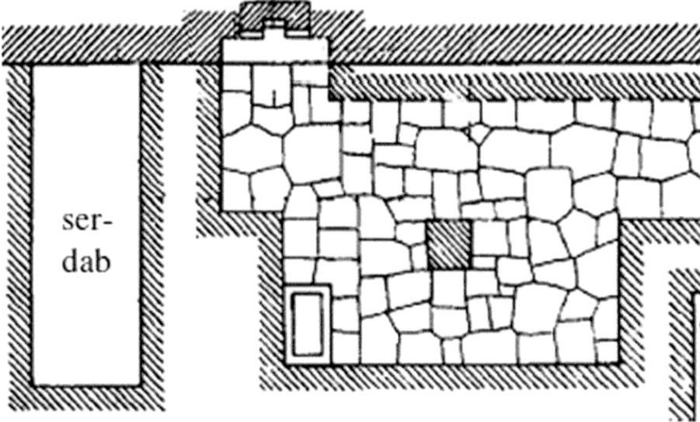

Figure 13.15 Detail of the chapel of *Ḫwfw-snb* [I] (PM, III/1, 152 – 3; S 359). Junker, *Giza VII*, Figure 43.

143), *Kꜣ-gm-nj* (PM, III/2, 521 -5),[106] and *Jsj* (PM, V, 201 – 5).

In the chapels of some private persons they were referred to with the expression '*jmꜣḫw ḫr*', 'the honored one before.....' (Figure 13.16), which entitlement was normally reserved for the god (*nṯr*), [107] the great god (*nṯr ꜥꜣ*)[108], or a god mentioned by name,[109] while also his master (the king) (*nb=f*) could be mentioned.[110] In the text on an offering basin that has been found outside the mastaba of *Jsj* the tomb owner is called 'the living god' (*nṯr ꜥnḫ Jsj*).[111]

In the chapel of such a deified person objects like offering basins and stelae were placed,[112] but there are no indications that a special cult connected to the deified status was performed, either on a daily basis or occasionally.[113]

The cults intended for most of the deified private persons extended somewhat further in time than the average mortuary cult of a 'normal' individual. However, there are exceptions to these observations:

- The cult of *Jm-ḥtp*, a high official during the reign of Djoser (III.2) whose cult lasted well toward the end of pharaonic Egypt.

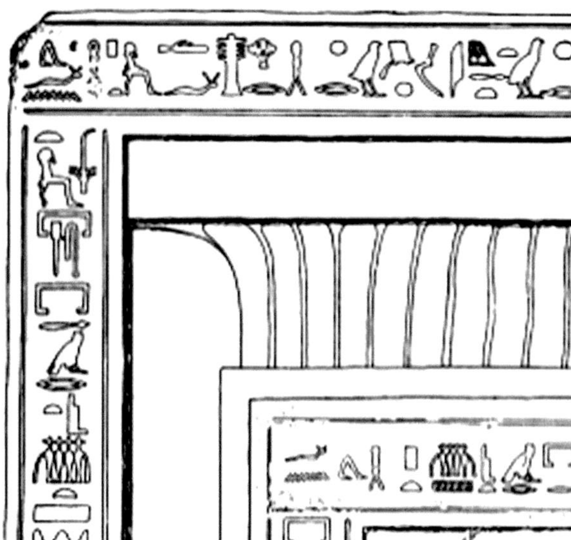

Figure 13.16 The false door of *Ptḥ-jw.f-n.f* with the dedication *jmꜣw ḫr Ḏdf-ḥr*. (PM, III/1, 143). From Junker, *Giza VII*, Figure 8.

- *Ḥkꜣ-jb*, who was nomarch of the first nome of Upper-Egypt during the later part of the Old Kingdom, whose cult lasted until the end of the Middle Kingdom.[114]

V.3.1. The mastaba of ꜣḫtj-ḥtp at Saqqara

In the necropolis of Saqqara, during the excavation of the mastaba of *ꜣḫtj-ḥtp* (PM, III/2, 634 – 7; V.L-VI.E;[115] chapel Louvre E 10958), a large quantity of small offering basins was found that had been placed against the eastern wall of the mastaba, not far away from the entrance of the chapel (see dotted circle in Figure 13.17).[116]

The flat rectangular stones were hollowed out, had a wide rim and some of them were inscribed with a text and thus were basically meant for offerings, either liquid or solid. The presence of these items of ritual equipment combined with the texts that some of them bear,[117] might indicate that they were used for the cult of the tomb owner, although his name is not mentioned. The basins can be dated to the end of the 6th dynasty or the start of the First Intermediate Period,[118] a date that is in accordance with the fact that those basins being

[106] Junker, *Giza VII*, 26. The deification of these two private persons may be based on the 'instructions' that are claimed to be of their hand (Lichtheim, *Literature I*, 5, 58 – 80). LÄ, I, 1099, s.w. 'Djedefhor'.

[107] Der Manuelian, *Gmast 8*, 76.

[108] Der Manuelian, *Gmast 8*, 317.

[109] Alliot, *Isi*, 23 (b.2) mentions Anubis. Marée, *Edfu*, 34 mentions Osiris.

[110] Der Manuelian, *Gmast 8*, 155. The text around the niche with the statue of *Mrrwkꜣ(.j)* mentions *jmꜣḫw ḫr nswt*. Mohr, *Hetep-her-akhty*, 34.

[111] Marée, *Edfu*, Figure 12.

[112] Alliot, *Divinisé;* Alliot, *Isi*, 18 – 21. LÄ, II, 1120 – 2, s.w. ' Heqaib ' there 1121.

[113] LÄ, VI, 989 – 92, s.w. 'Vergöttlichung'.

[114] At first artefacts were placed around his tomb in Qubbet el-Hawa, during the Middle Kingdom a temple for his cult was erected on the isle of Elephantine.

[115] Ziegler, *Saqqara Louvre*, 49 gives Djedkare(-Izezi) (V.8) as date.

[116] Ziegler, *Saqqara*, 278, Figure 12; Ziegler, *Akhethetep*, 379 – 80.

[117] Ziegler, *Saqqara*, 278 states that some of the basins bear the title '*k3*-priest' followed by a name. See Andreu, *Akhethetep*.

[118] Ziegler, *Akhethetep*, 379.

placed there indicate that they postdate the expiration of the mortuary cult of the tomb owner.

This placing of tokens of cultic activity outside the tomb of private persons is extremely rare, yet in a royal context it has been found more often (see section VI). This can be the result of the difference in awe that both groups evoke. A possible explanation for the scarcity of these placings in a non-royal connection is the supposition that normally, as soon as the mortuary cult for the deceased was no longer maintained, cultic activity in and around the chapel came to a halt. The fact that in the case of *ꜣḫtj-ḥtp* the cultic activity continued, although now outside the chapel, could be due to the existence of a personal veneration for a person whose name had developed a special meaning.[119]

This observation corroborates the supposition that it has to be taken into account that there is a remarkable difference between the cult for a venerated person and the mortuary cult for a deceased person. The mortuary cult was closely connected to the chapel of the deceased where contact could be made with and offerings could be made to the deceased in order to sustain his or her *kꜣ*.

Apparently for the veneration of a person (private person or a member of the royal family) this direct connection with a ritually charged place was not of the utmost importance, although it is obvious that the focus of this cult had to be in the vicinity of such a place.

In view of Junker's claim that the entrance of a chapel could be considered to be an offering place,[120] the solution would be to place a basin next to the (probably closed) entrance of the chapel. The width of the passage in front of the chapel of *ꜣḫtj-ḥtp* was 0.68m,[121] a dimension that is identical with the average size of the entrance of a non-corridor chapel, and thus can considered to be too small to place an obstacle in it. It might be for that reason that the basins have been not been placed in the entrance or in the corridor but in the courtyard which is much wider (3.64m).

The reconstruction of the chapel of *ꜣḫtj-ḥtp* shows that, within the reliability of the reconstruction of its entrance, the conclusion is that the chapel could be closed at the inside of the entrance corridor.[122] This might lead to the inference that, due to the possibility to close the door, the basins were placed outside the mastaba during the period that the cult for the deceased was still performed. The observation that the archaeological record does not show that these collections of deposited utensils are found frequently gives rise to the possible conclusion that these were placed there in order to honour a venerated person.

The small mastaba south of the courtyard (mastaba E-17) has a modified cruciform chapel with a false door against the western wall.[123] Based on the plan given by C. Ziegler (*Saqqara*, Figure 8) in front of this mastaba a courtyard must have been present too; yet, no mention is made of basins or other offering utensils being found there.

V.3.2. Mastaba Abusir AC 31

In front of the eastern wall of mastaba AC 31 in the necropolis of Abusir cultic pottery for the most part consisting of model vessels has been found. On the same side in front of the entrance of the chapel a rectangular place had been made of mud that had an altar next to it which had traces of a fire place in front of it. It is possible that it had served a cultic purpose, one of them being the burning of offerings. [124] A special place for that purpose could have been necessary because in the entrance of the chapel the rebate of a door was present.[125] The same type of rectangular place has been excavated in front of the entrance of the chapel of mastaba AC 30 of *Ḫnt-kꜣw.s* [III] at Abusir.[126]

V.3.3. The mastaba of Kꜣr at Abusir and others

The mastaba of *Kꜣr* (Bárta, *Abusir XIX*) was entered from its northern side by way of a courtyard. In this yard a basin was placed against the southern wall; the excavators interpret it as an offering basin possibly ritually connected with a serdab south of it.[127] As already discussed, the basin can also be meant for a ritual cleaning before entering into one of the chapels, or as a reservoir. The place of this basin indicates that it was originally meant for the cult of *Kꜣr*, because the entrances of the chapels of the two sons have been added at a later stage and are not aligned with it.

In the yard on the level of the floor offering stones with libation depressions were found; some were uninscribed while one bore a dedication text written on the *hetep* sign. In view of the place where these basins were found and the possibility of closing the chapel, it is

119 Lieven, *Deified humans.*

120 Junker, *Giza II*, 19, 145.

121 Determined in Ziegler, *Saqqara*, Figure 8.

122 Ziegler, *Saqqara*, Figure 11.

123 Petrie, *Memphite chapels*, 7 – 8, Plates IV, VI, XXI (Figures 18, 20, 21, 22, 24). Mariette, *Mastaba*, 423.

124 Krejči, *AC 31*, 21, Figure 11. In the necropolis west of the pyramid complex of king Djoser in Saqqara traces of small fireplaces have been found around chapels and in courtyards that had a connection with the plants and wood in order to fill jars with the ashes (Rzeuska, *Funerary customs*, 369).

125 Krejči, *AC 31*, Figure 2.

126 Krejči, *AC 31*, Figure 2.

127 Bárta, *Abusir XIX*, 57, 61.

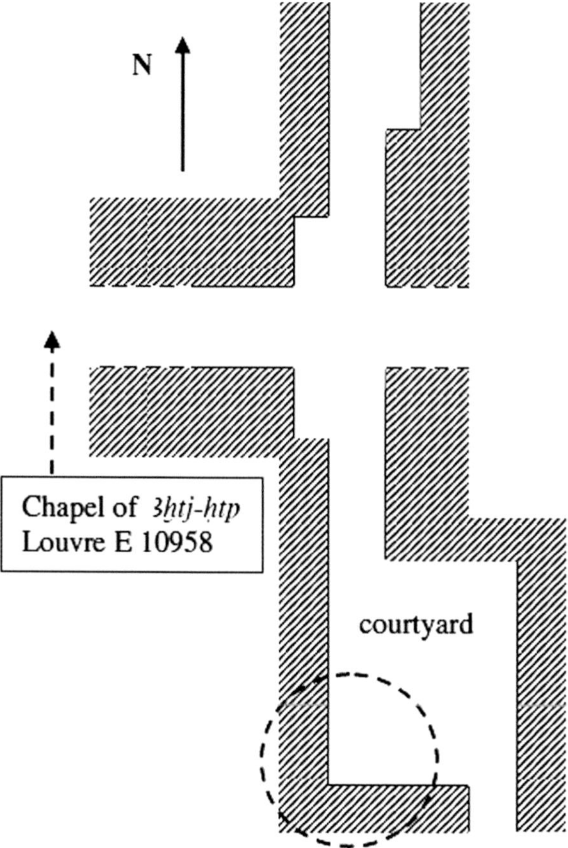

Figure 13.17 Surrounding of chapel entrance of the mastaba of *3ḫtj-ḥtp* (schematically from Ziegler, *Saqqara*, Figure 8).

possible that they were left there as token of veneration for the tomb owner.[128] The quality of the basins was such that they cannot be interpreted as being thrown out of the three smaller chapels that were adjacent to the open courtyard.

In the street between the mastaba G 2100-II of *N-sḏr-k3.j* and G 2120 tiles were placed that show hacked-out forms of libation basins.[129] This might be a sign of special devotion for one of the two tomb owners, because the same type of basins hacked out in tiles have been found in the vicinity of the queen's pyramids in het mortuary complex of Pepy [I] (VI.2).[130] However, one of the forms shows a round depression that can be interpreted as a pivot hole, so it is probable that these tiles were recuperated from another building and re-used in this street. This proposition is corroborated by the fact that for neither of the two mastabas are the basins situated in front of ritually important walls.

128 Vlćková, *Abusir south*, 165.

129 Giza Archives, photo PDM_1993.105.24.

130 Dobrev, *Tables d'offerandes*, Figure 2.

VI. Offering basins in the vicinity of the tombs of royal family

The previously stated claim that the entrance of a chapel could be considered to be an offering place is probably right for private tombs in view of the ritual equipment in the vicinity of the chapel of *3ḫtj-ḥtp*.[131] However, for royal mortuary complexes this claim has to be interpreted in a less strict sense, because it is probable that private persons were not permitted to approach beyond a certain limit, which would in the case of royal wives be the temenos closest to the queen's pyramid.[132]

This is supported by Munro who communicates in his excavation report of the twin-mastaba of *Ḫnwt* and *Nb.t* (PM, III/2, 623-5; date: reign Unas (V.9)) that installations for cultic activities have already been found in front of the entrance of the mastaba of *Ḫnwt*.[133]

VI.1. The Abusir cemetery

At the end of the Old Kingdom the cult for various kings of the 5th and the 6th dynasty have seen a posthumous veneration that lasted until the 12th dynasty;[134] this veneration not only took the form of an 'official' royal cult in the mortuary complex (e.g. Niuserre (V.6)), but also as the pious expression of the population for a king whose name has obtained a special meaning (which had already been the case for Sneferu (IV.1)).[135] This was not limited just to the kings of these dynasties; some queens were the subject of such veneration too.

The veneration expressed by the population can be determined by the presence of offering equipment *outside* the walls of the mortuary complex of the king or queen,[136] while sometimes offering basins are hacked out directly in the pavement in front of the entrance of the temple.[137] It has to be remarked that, with a few exceptions which can be attributed to disruptions by human interference, these deposits of offerings equipment are habitually placed outside the mortuary complexes.

131 Junker, *Giza II*, 19, 145.

132 Berger, *Cultes de reines*, 18.

133 Dobrev, *Tables d'offerande*, 146. Munro, *Unas-Friedhof* reports that, around the entrance of the mastaba blocks were placed in which small recesses had been made that were meant for miniature false doors.

134 Morales, *Veneration*. For some kings the mortuary cult probably continued through the First Intermediate Period into the Middle Kingdom (an example of this 'survival' is Niuserre).

135 Petrie, *Sinai*, 84, 96 - 7. In the shrine inscriptions in the temple of Hathor at Serabit el-Khadim have been found stating the honouring of Sneferu by Hatshepsut. The fact that Sneferu is mentioned here as being deified can be the result of the fact that according to Petrie this king is the first to start mining activities there.

136 Ibidem.

137 Dobrev, *Tables d'offerandes*, Figure 2.

The most 'popular' place to put the equipment was in the vicinity of the mortuary temple, but in case this was prevented by means of a temenos, a placement in front of the entrances into the mortuary precinct was used as an alternative.

Offering equipment in the form of 12th dynasty pottery cups has been found outside the entrance to the temple of the queen's pyramid Lepsius XXIV,[138] while in the temple itself the remains of an offering basin have been found.[139]

Part of the cemetery south-east of the royal pyramids, a cemetery that can be dated to the reign of Djedkare (V.8), has been used for the burial of members of the royal family. The tomb of the princess *Ḫkrt-nbtj* lies in the centre of an agglomerate of six tombs.[140]. During the first building stage a small courtyard surrounded by storerooms, an ensemble that can be interpreted as a kind of exterior chapel, was constructed in front of the entrance into the tomb. A final construction stage resulted in a second, much larger, courtyard. In the middle of this yard (anepigraphic) offering tables (platforms) have been found, artefacts that give rise to the following observations:

- The poor quality of the tables probably indicates that:
  a. The official (mortuary) cult had been ended.
  b. The popular (veneration) cult continued or started.
- The royal aura of the place still prevented the cult from taking place in the vicinity of the entrance of the chapel.

A similar and contemporaneous case has been found further south in the cemetery of Abusir where a conglomerate of tombs of lower social strata is situated to the west of the tomb of *Ftktj*. In the middle of this group of mastabas a courtyard has been placed with the main entrance from the north, which was also the only side that was not delimited by the walls of already existing monuments.[141]

This was also the sole construction that had its entrance in that direction, all the chapels of the surrounding monuments opening to the south. At the northern side of the courtyard two large and deep basins had been placed, possibly to supply water for the rituals in the chapels, but offering tables as in the former conglomerate have not been found.[142]

North and south of the causeway of the complex of Niuserre extensive lower social class cemeteries are situated which can be dated to later in his reign or just after the end of it (the cemetery of the princesses, the family cemetery of Djedkare Isesi) to the Middle Kingdom.[143] Archaeological evidence from some of these tombs indicates that king Niuserre, whose mortuary complex was nearby, was their focus of veneration.

VI.2. The pyramid complex of Pepy I (VI.2)

South of the funerary complex of Pepy I (VI.2) a number of smaller pyramids have been excavated of which some were the funerary complexes of queens.[144] In the vicinity of the funerary complexes of the queens *Ỉnnk* and *Nbw-ntj* and the funerary complex of an unnamed queen ('reine de l'ouest') offering basins have been found *in situ.* Apparently the royal connection means that, in accordance with Junker's claim, the vicinity of the complex was considered sacred enough to serve as an offering place.[145]

The reason for placing these basins there could have been personal adoration, but some of these offering basins were not only meant for the cult of the deceased, because they also served the interests of the person who supplied the offerings (LÄ, IV, 596 – 7, s.w. 'Opferumlauf'), indicating a period when there was still cultic activity for the queens themselves.

These basins were placed in front of the effigies of the queens that decorated the entrance door jambs of their funerary complex, meaning that these offering basins were placed *outside* the complex.[146] The plan of the entrance of the complex of queen *Ỉnnk* shows that the access to the complex could be closed with a two-winged door and that left and right of this access offering basins were placed.[147]

138 Krejči, *Abusir XII*, 115.

139 It is possible that the offering basin has ended up there as the result of the complex's exploitation as a quarry.

140 In total four of these six tombs were used for the burial of members of the royal family, and one used for a scribe of the royal children; the sixth tomb must already have been present when the 'mini-cemetery' for Djedkare's family was started (Krejči, *Abusir XII*, Figure B1 (page 13)).

141 Bárta, *Abusir V*, 56, 133 – 4.

142 The two large basins were standing against the southern wall, obliging the persons coming from the north in order to take water, to leave in the same direction. In a later period an opening has been made in the southern wall.

143 Morales, *Veneration*, 324 – 5 ; Daoud, *Abusir* ;

144 Dobrev, *Tables d'offerandes*, Figure 1 (page 148) ; Legros, *Cultes privés*, Figure 1.

145 Junker, *Giza II*, 19, 145.

146 Dobrev, *Tables d'offerandes*, Figure 9. For the sitting figure of queen *Ỉnnk* see EA, 8 (1996), 3-6, Figure on page 5 (top, left), and for queen *Nbw-wn.tj* the standing figure EA, 8 (1996), 3-6, Figure on page 6 (right, bottom). Berger, *Culte de reines*, 18 mentions that, although most of the deposits have been found outside the queens' complexes, a deposit of offering stones has been found inside the complex of queen *Ỉnnk*.

147 For queen *Ỉnnk*: Dobrev, *Tables d'offerandes*, Figure 8 and for the door: ibidem, Figure 9.

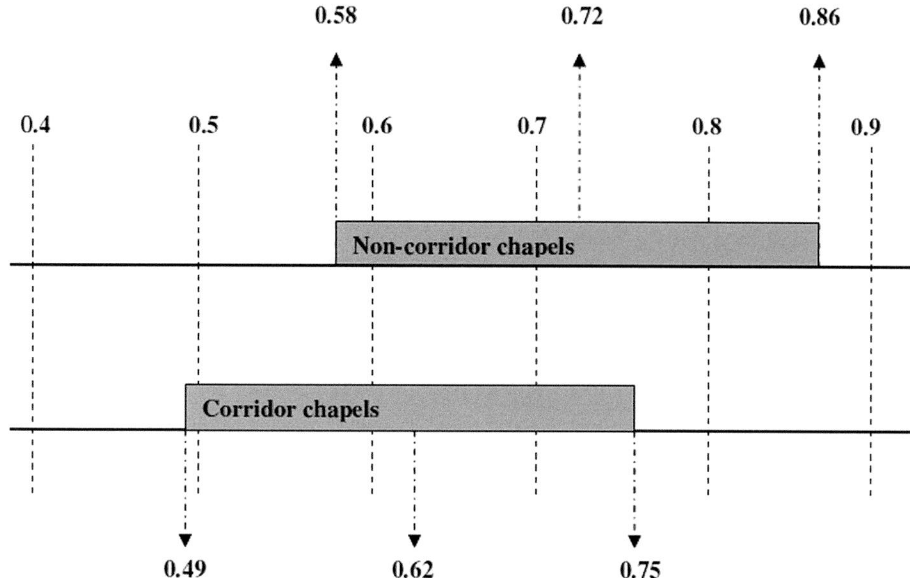

Figure 13.18 The mean values and the spread of the width of the entrances of corridor chapels and other types of chapels.

The observation that offering utensils, steles and even buildings were introduced in the area behind the temenos probably not only indicates that in later years the complex remained of special interest for those living in its vicinity, but also that the area slowly lost its protected and inaccessible royal aura.

The deposits of offering stones that have been found around the various complexes are dated late in the Old Kingdom, which leads to the question why this development took place so late.

Annex: The width of the chapel entrance versus the corridor chapel.

In Table VI of a sample of 50 chapels the width of the entrance of the chapel has been determined, and although the mean value comes to 0.72m +/- 0.14m, the standard deviation is large.

The mean value of the width of a corridor chapel *entrance* is determined at the tombs given in Harpur, *DETOK*, 92, and the mean value is 0.62m +/- 0.13m (Table VIb).

These results show that there is no significant difference between the width of the entrance of a corridor chapel and the entrance of other types of chapels.

Taking into account that the normal size of a larger rectangular offering basin comes to about 0.25-0.30m (Dobrev, *Tables d'offerandes,* Figures 10b, 12-14, 16-17; Fisher, *Minor cemetery*, Plates 46-8), the width of the remaining passage is not such that placing pieces of ritual equipment could become standard procedure. The narrowness would be even more emphasized by the presence of offering stands on both sides of the basin, as is already the case in the chapel itself (Giza Archives, Photo B11816_OS).

Chapter Fourteen

Discussion and Conclusions

The primary use of the door as a physical object is to close the chapel to visitors and intruders. The fact that the entrance into the chapel could be closed but not locked implies that the privacy of the chapel was secured by other means. This was probably based on 'respect' for the mortuary monument and its intrinsic meaning, while fear for the magical powers invested in the monument undoubtedly must have played an important role too.

Very often excavation reports state that pivots and holes for bolts to slide into have been found in openings which were thus meant for doors. Strangely enough these locking devises were on the inside of the door, and to my knowledge no means have been found to manipulate this type of lock from the outside. This would mean that everybody had the opportunity to walk 'in and out' of the interior room(s), except when a priest was performing the daily ritual which apparently was not a public affair.

The observation that increasingly threats against unclean intrusion or damage infliction were placed at the entrance might indicate that a growing lack of respect occurred in the later periods of the Old Kingdom.

This means that gradually an aspect of fear was introduced, which is strengthened by the consideration that the chapel is in fact *'a twilight zone'* (called 'transitional world' in Figures 7.1 and 14.2) between the world of the living and the world of the dead, and thus a place where it was possible to have contact with the latter. The place where this contact could be made is the false door against the western wall of an interior or exterior chapel or the eastern exterior wall of a tomb (Figure 14.2).

At first this site of offering and contact took the form of a niche, which had, together with a second niche, a special meaning within a tomb's exterior wall that was made up of palace façade panelling. The continuation of the development was that the panelling slowly disappeared but that the two 'special' niches remained on the eastern wall. Although from the 4th dynasty on this type of decoration was no longer used for mastabas, it sometimes (re)appeared on the exterior wall of rock-cut tombs.[1]

A special case is tomb LG 100 which, although sometimes called 'Giza's fourth pyramid', is not a pyramid in the strict sense of the word; in reality it is a rock-cut tomb with a mastaba built over the entrance.[2] The southern wall of the rock pedestal has been decorated with palace façade panelling but not the eastern wall, although the two offering places were situated in that wall. At the end of the causeway the entrance is between two blocks of stone that resemble a plain simple niche, while in the chapel the western wall is adorned with a *serekh* false door flanked by façade panelling in a combination of three basic units (Figures 5.13 and 13.7).

The next step in the development of the exterior chapel is that it was 'drawn' into the mass of the tomb, at first as a cruciform chapel with a palace façade panelling on the western wall, later as a niche in a wall with decoration, while the other walls of the chapel were decorated too (chapel of *Rꜥ-ḥtp* at Maidum). The cruciform chapel disappeared and was replaced by other types of chapels, the L-shaped chapel being the most commonly used.

In the cruciform chapel the basic decorative outlines of the entrance elements of the later chapels were already present in the first step of the niche, regardless of whether it was a plain single niche or a plain compound niche (Figures 8.2 – 8.5):

- The tomb owner represented in the central niche facing right, later to be replaced by a depiction of the tomb owner on the panel of the false door where he was mainly shown sitting at the offering table and also here preferentially looking to the right.
- The tomb owner on the entrance thicknesses was looking at the opening of the entrance, thus looking at the outside world and inviting passers-by to enter into the chapel.
- The tomb owner standing on the door jambs looking in the direction of the entrance of the chapel, and clearly inviting passers-by to pay attention and stop to pronounce an offering formula or to enter.

[1] The rock-cut tomb of *Kꜣj* (PM, III/1, 277), Hassan, *Giza III,* Plate XII.

[2] This feature is also apparent over the entrance of the tomb of *Mr.f-nb.f* at Saqqara. (www.osirisnet.net/popupImage.php?img=/mastabas/merefnebef/photo/merefnebef_pl_006.gif&lang=en&sw=1280&sh=1024).

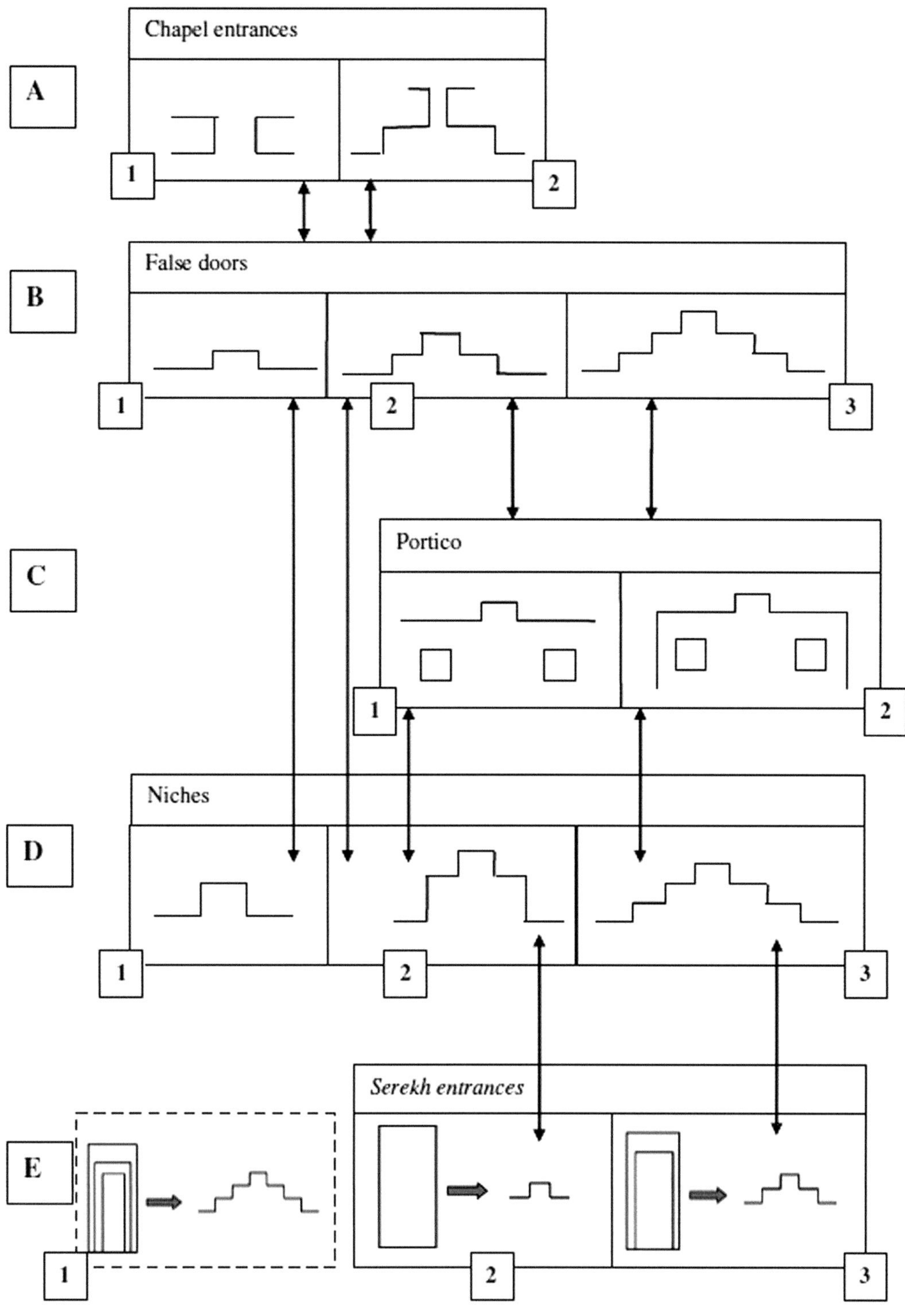

Figure 14.1 The interconnection between various architectonic elements in the chapel.

A result of the relocation of the offering place into the mass of the tomb was that the name and titles signalling function of the original offering place had to be taken over by other architectural elements. Apparently this signalling function was considered to be so important that this information was placed on several elements of the entrance. The most important element was the architrave over the entrance which not only stated name and titles but also gave the offering formula, thereby inviting the passer-by to recite it, who thus contributed to the sustenance of the *k3* of the deceased. This architrave could grow out to enormous dimensions containing a growing amount of text.[3]

[3] The length in the Saqqara tomb of *Ptḥ-špss* is 5.20m (Soleiman, *Ptahshepses*), and the lintel in the tomb of *Mrf-nbf* at Saqqara (www.

The other elements with signalling decoration and text were the door jambs, the entrance thicknesses and the roll over the door into the chapel which was located at the end of the entrance passage. It has to be realized that these four elements remained part of the outside world outside world because an eventual door was closed behind the roll over the door.

In the earlier period of the Old Kingdom the offering table scene had been placed on the entrance thicknesses, but it disappeared from there in the middle of the 5th dynasty. It is probable that this disappearance is the consequence of two parallel developments, the first being the steady decrease of the dimensions of the mastabas that took place during the course of the Old Kingdom (Roeten, *Economic decline*), thus making the available space on the entrance thicknesses smaller and the second being the change in the mode of sustenance of the *k3* of the deceased (Roeten, *Decoration*), the latter making the actual offering of sustenance and thus the presence of the offering table scene other than on the western wall less important. The change in the mode of sustenance may itself have been entirely or partly the result of the growing importance and influence of the cult of Osiris (Roeten, *Osiris,* 97).

The door itself was made of wood and the type of wood depended on the financial capacity of the tomb owner. The highest echelon could afford imported wood (Lebanon cedar); lower officials had to settle for high quality local wood. Another factor that was a benchmark for the wealth and economic power not only of the tomb owner but also of his family was the number of doors in the tomb. In the period of the reign of Teti (VI.1) multi-chambered mastabas were common among the highest social strata, and in these chapels nearly every passage could be closed with a door, the previous presence of which is detectable by means of rebates that were still visible in the passages.

Due to the nature of the material used to construct doors, the number of them found is small, not only as the result of the vulnerability of the material but also because the door also fell 'victim' to the relative scarcity of its material in Egypt, and its usefulness as a building material (e.g. for coffins) and as fuel.

The door was meant to be a device for the physically closing off an entrance, but the opening itself could be more than just a passage to another room. An example of that has been excavated in the mastaba of *Ḥtpj* (Abusir, tomb AS 20), which has a chapel that had a double door in front of the western wall, thus not just magically but literally closing the connection between the two worlds that met in the chapel (Figure 4.9). This set-up is unique because normally the passage over the offering place was intended only to be used by the deceased, which made the presence of a real door superfluous.

The two types of false doors, the real false door and the *serekh* false door, were not only used as representations of ritually important magical passages to the world of the dead, but they could also serve as real passages to rooms that might have had a mortuary importance (a palace façade panelling on the western wall of the rock-cut tomb of *Jwn-mnw* (PM, III/1, 237; LD, *I,* 29), and a false door as passage in Figure 6.4). This duality in use of these false doors led to the use of combinations of them on the walls, thus indicating that both doors were equivalent. The observation that the two types of false door could also be used as real passages to the ritually important chapel corroborates the hypothesis that the chapel was in fact another world than the outside world. This transitional world may have been experienced as so threatening that there was little urge to enter the chapel without conscious purpose, which would make the locking of doors unnecessary.

The most common material for doors was wood; only for doors of buildings meant for 'eternity' and built within a state-program could another type of material like bronze be used.

As a result of the inclusion of the chapel in the mass of the tomb, the offering place in the palace façade panelling against the eastern wall became a real opening. Depending on the architectonic design of the original offering niche the entrance of the chapel became a plain entrance (Figure 14.1 D-1 ↔ A-1) or a recessed entrance (Figure 14.1 D-2 ↔ A-2).

Another result of the introduction of the interior chapel was that the offering place was transferred to the western wall of that chapel; it must be taken into account that the design of the original niche on the tomb's eastern wall directly led to the form of the false door and the chapel entrance. The first interior chapel was cruciform with a palace façade western wall in which a deep niche formed the false door (Figure 8.1). Not only did a direct connection exist between the design of the niche and the chapel entrance, this connection was also in effect between the false door and the niche (Figure 14.1 A-1 ↔ B-1, A-2 ↔ B-2).[4]

In the design of the false door the subsidiary figures also play a role; in Figures 8.2 to 8.6 these figures move in the direction of the central niche toward the tomb owner who is sometimes standing or sitting there. On the jambs of the 'true' false door the situation is identical too because the tomb owner and/or subsidiary figures

Osirisnet, Saqqara) reaches 5.60m.

4 The connection between entrance A-2 and false door B-2 is visible in the chapel entrance of tomb AS 31 at Abusir (Bárta, *Rock-cut tomb,* 16, Figures 4 and 5).

are standing and looking in the direction of the central niche or moving toward it. The preference for this directionality can be explained with the connection that exists between a two-stepped or three-stepped false door and a portico (Figure 14.1 B-2 ↔ C-1, B-3 ↔ C-2) (Figures 6.12 and 6.13). On the pillars of the portico the figures are placed in such a way that they guide the visitor to the middle of the western wall, where either the entrance into the chapel or the false door is located. This is a further indication that the false door is in fact an entrance with pillars indicating that it is not just a place where offerings can be placed, but it is also the entrance of the residence of the deceased. This conclusion is based on the consideration that the entrance of a residence for the living is indicated in a similar manner as is visible in the house model of *Mkt-Rʿ* (Metropolitan Museum of Art, no. 20.313) and the offering place in the form of a house (Figure 6.14).

According to the scheme in Figure 14.1 the connections between the various elements can be traced back to the architectural design of the entrance of the early dynastic royal palace (E). In chapter V (Figure 5.1) it has been proposed that the faience tiling of the subterranean corridors and entrances under the southern tomb in the pyramid complex of Djoser (III.2) represents the design and look of the outer wall of the royal palace. This type of wall has not only been used in funerary constructions of the kings of the 1st dynasty, but also in the *serekh,* an identifying symbol showing the panelling of the royal palace topped by the Horus falcon and bearing the name of the king in what could be the depiction of the palace courtyard. This heraldic symbol has been used throughout the Egyptian pharaonic period.

A development of the false door is a three-jamb door that, since this type of false door cannot be deduced from one of the niches (Figure 14.1), must be interpreted as the consequence of the strong tendency in Egyptian material culture to form units of three identical items (Figures 5.13, 7.2 and 13.7). This also led to the *serekh* of Djet (I.4) with the (rare) tri-partite entrance (E-1) (Figure 5.7), a design that is not intended to give a perspective view of the entrance, but that might lead to the conclusion that the entrance became progressively lower, possibly as a means to impress entering visitors. The same design is visible on the incense burner of Qustul (Figure 5.10), but does not necessarily have the same meaning.[5]

In the scheme of Figure 14.1 the portico is a type of entrance that has a direct connection with the false door (B-2,3 ↔ C-1,2) and with the plain single niche (C-1 ↔ D-1). Because the portico together with its courtyard and the chapel can be interpreted as a house,[6] the chapel with the false door can be 'translated' as follows:

- In the house model the entrance of the mortuary monument is the entrance into the courtyard,[7] with, at the gate, the depictions of the tomb owner receiving visitors (*Ṯtw* (PM, III/1, 66 – 7); Simpson, *Gmast 4,* Plate XVa).
- The chapel itself represents the courtyard of the residence, which can be compared with the garden a visitor had to cross in order to reach the portico. On entering into the chapel very often it was necessary to change course as if provoked by the presence of a small pond in the garden (see house model of *Mkt-Rʿ* (PM, I/1, 359 – 64; 11th dynasty; also see Figure 6.14).
- The false door of the chapel can be transformed into a portico (Figure 14.1 B-2 ↔ C-1, B-3 ↔ C-2), which in the house model equates to the pillared portico which protects the door(s) into the residence. The connection between the false door and the entrance of a residence is visible in the arched top of false doors that have been described by Junker.[8] In the temple of Seti [I] (XIX.2) the back side of the niches west of the second hypostyle hall has the form of a door with a middle-pillar and an arced top.[9] The stele of *Mrt-Njt* (Cairo Museum JE 34450), that can be dated to the 1st dynasty, has the same arched top, although this stele might have served either as a person signalling artefact or as the indicator of the offering place; Junker gives arguments that these stelae served as the latter.[10]
- Normally a false door is placed at the back wall of the portico, and this door would magically serve as the entrance into the 'public' part of the residence of the deceased.
- In reality some porticos have an opening in the back wall leading into a chapel, and adopting the idea of it being a consecutive room would extend the resemblance with a residence even further. The room behind the entrance served to receive guests, thus making the (imaginary) chapel behind the portico the 'public' part of the residence of the deceased, while the (false) door(s) in it lead(s) to the private rooms of the residence.[11]

5 At first this burner was dated to the early Nagada period, but a 1st dynasty dating is in better accordance with the archaeological data.

6 Junker, *Giza II,* 105.

7 The entrance into the court of the tomb of *N-sḏr-kꜣ.j* (PM, III/1, 72) is placed at the right side of the eastern wall.

8 Junker, *Giza V,* 172 – 4, Figure 53, Plate XVIIa.

9 The decoration of the arched top of this door is adapted to the use in a temple.

10 Junker, *Giza II,* 14.

11 In some tombs the door connection is stronger, an example is the cultic centre in the tomb of *Mnnꜣ* (TT 69; PM, I/1, 134 – 9; 18th dynasty) (Osirisnet, Valley of the Nobles, Menna, page 8).

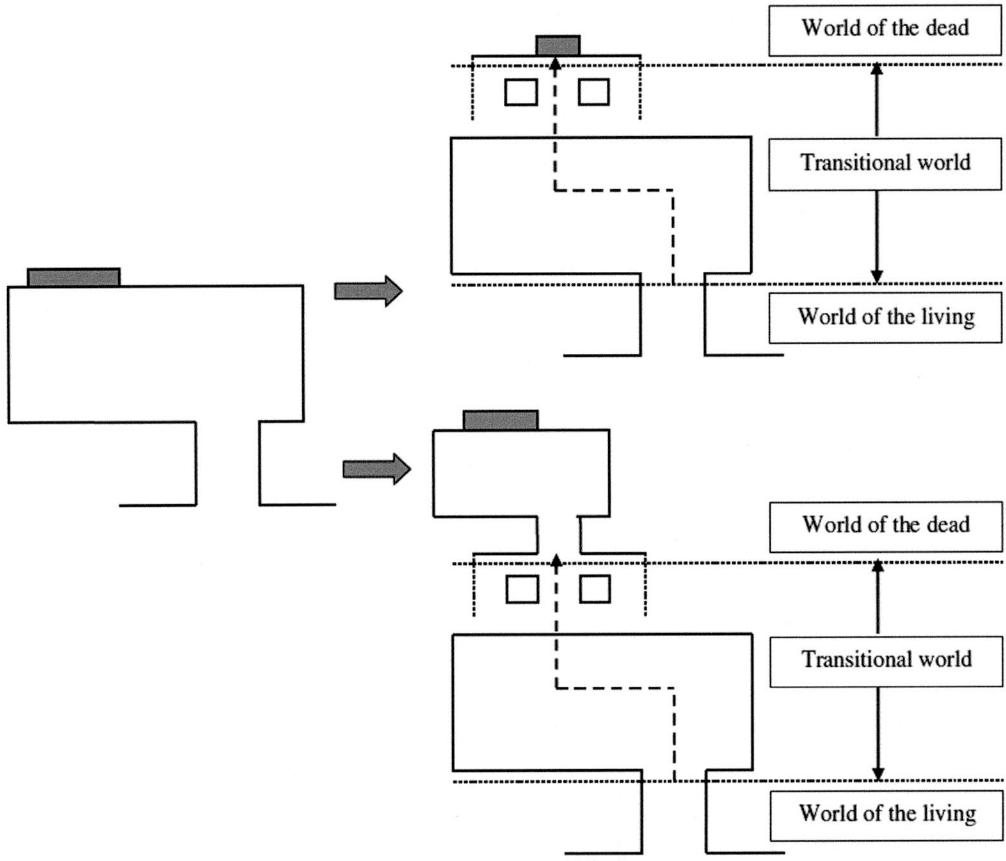

Figure 14.2 The transition between the world of the living and the world of the dead.

This re-evaluation of the design of a false door into a portico entrance, resembling the front look of the worldly house of the deceased, emphasises its entrance function from the transitional world into the world of the dead. The idea of a zone of transition between two different worlds, whereby the world at the other side is sacred and clean, is strengthened by the texts that have been placed in the entrances of some tombs stressing the necessity of cleanliness if the passer-by intends to enter the chapel. In exterior chapels or in court yards in front of the entrance of some chapels (Figures 13.10 and 13.16) basins have been found of which the form indicates that they were not meant to serve as offering basins. They could have served as basins for water for the offering rituals (libation, ritual cleansing), the latter underlining the apparent necessity of cleanliness, while the presence of draining systems points to the possibility that they were intended for excess water.[12]

The function of a chapel was to enable the sustenance of the *k3* of the deceased; at first this was done mainly by way of the bringing of offerings with a small contribution of magical sustenance. During the period V.M-V.L the magical mode of sustenance started to play a bigger role, finally becoming the most importan way of supplying support for the after-life of the deceased. This development could have been a result of noticing that the daily bringing of offerings nearly always stopped after a relatively short period, an exception being the somewhat longer lasting service for a locally venerated person. An argument against this is that if this were the case this development would undoubtedly have started earlier in the Old Kingdom.

A more realistic reason could have been declining economic prosperity, of which one consequence was a decrease in the dimensions of the tombs. This development had no influence on the size of the chapel, and for the entrance elements only the available space on the entrance thicknesses was reduced.

Whatever reason(s) was(were) the cause of these developments, one of the consequences was that the decorative themes that were used changed, not only on the walls of the chapel, but also on some of the entrance elements.

The offering table scene on the entrance thicknesses had a twofold function. The first was purpose signalling, thus inviting passers-by to enter into the chapel and lay out some offerings on the table in front of the false door. However, since most of the richer tombs had a door that

[12] Intra Figure 13.10; Gourdon, *Djedkare*, Plate 1.

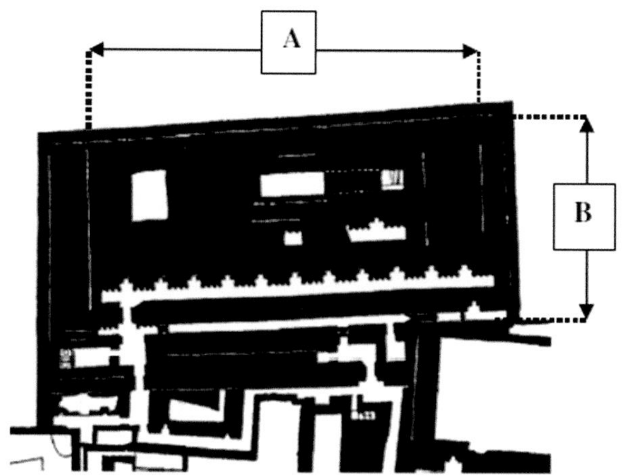

Figure 14.3 Indication of the first phase of the tomb of *Ḥsjj-Rʿ* (PM, III/2, 437 – 9).

closed the entrance of the chapel, it would have been impossible to do that there. The possibility that this could be solved by placing offerings on a stone in front of this decorative theme has the disadvantage that in a normal entrance corridor the offering stone or libation basin would make such an obstruction that passage would be highly difficult, and this possibility has been rejected, based on the annex of Chapter XIII. The inversion of the mode of sustenance made the offering table scene on the entrance thicknesses redundant (Figure 11.19); while the presence of subsidiary figures like offering bearers increased (Figure 11.17), the other subsidiary figures like priests (Figure 11.18) and scribes (Figure 11.24) disappeared, a development which also took place on the false door in the chapel. The decreasing space on the entrance thicknesses resulted in the presence of the smaller theme of the standing tomb owner with or without family increasing. The theme of the tomb owner with an adult member of the family (Figure 11.1, theme 2) is hardly present on the entrance thicknesses because it is too large (Figures 11.2 and 11.3), while the tomb owner with a child (Figure 11.1, theme 3) is better represented due to the fact that a child, represented on a smaller scale, could be placed between the front leg and the staff held by the father. This indicates that the choice of themes is dictated by their size.

The consequence of these changes in theme content was that some of the functions of the entrance elements disappeared. The original functions of the entrance elements together had been inviting, guiding, person- and purpose signalling. With the disappearance of the offering table scene from the entrance thicknesses the latter function no longer existed, and the standing tomb owner became the only inviting theme together with the depictions of the tomb owner on the chapel wall next to the entrance corridor. The guiding function of the door jambs remained, although increasingly they were used for texts. The growing percentage of offering bearers was a consequence of the change in the mode of sustenance.

The guiding function, that for a short period had been performed by the theme of the tomb owner on the western wall opposite the entrance, became redundant too and disappeared.

Another consequence of bringing the chapel into the mass of the tomb was that the cult that was performed in front of the offering place whether or not in an exterior chapel, and with it the cult for statues that were eventually placed in the vicinity of the offering place, had to be placed in the interior chapel too. Junker states that the oldest tombs in the Giza necropolis did not have a room that could have served as a serdab (while in Saqqara the tomb of *Ḥsjj-Rʿ* (PM, III/2, 437 – 9), which can be dated to period III.E, a serdab was placed in the body of the tomb, but still next to the entrance), and that later these rooms were nearly always placed behind the southern false door in the chapel. The explanation could be that, as already discussed, the statues were normally placed in the exterior chapel, but due to the introduction of the interior chapel, the statues started to be drawn into the body of the tomb. At first the statues were placed, whether visible or not, in the vicinity of the entrance, only later to be placed further in the body of the tomb, often near the chapel, sometimes with an aperture into it. Junker states that this development continued and the statues were increasingly placed in the vicinity of the shaft to the burial chamber, or in the shaft,[13] finally to end up in the burial chamber itself.[14] It is improbable that this was done in order to protect the statues against destruction and robbery; it is more likely that this ran in parallel with the introduction of decoration in the burial chamber.

[13] Hassan, *Giza V*, 46, Plate VIII.

[14] Junker, *Vorbericht 1914*, 12 – 4; a life-size statue has been found in the burial chamber of *Ḫwfw-snb* [I] (PM, III/1, 152 – 3) (Junker, *Giza VII*, 125); likewise a small wooden statue in the burial chamber of *Mrj-jb* (PM, III/1, 167 – 8) (Junker, *Giza VIII*, 140). Also see Hassan, *Giza V*, Plate IX. In October 2018 the tomb of *K3.j-jr.s* was excavated in Abusir, and in the burial chamber a granite statue of the seated tomb owner had been placed in front of the sarcophagus.

Tables

Table I. Saqqara. Themes on the entrance door jambs

Name	PM	Date	D1	D2	D3	D4	D5	D6	D7	D8	D9	D10	D11	D12	D13	D14	D15	D16	D17	D18
Wꜣš-ptḥ	456	V.E			x									x						
Nn-ḫft-kꜣ.j	580-1	V.E-V.M			x						x									
Šnnw-ʿnḫ	582	V.E-V.M	x																	
ꜣḫtj-ḥtp	627-9	V.L	x																	
Jj-nfrt	616	V.L		x																
Ḥtp-ḥr-ꜣḫtj	593-5	V.L			x									x						
Pr-nb	497-8	V.L	x																	
Rʿ-špss	494-6	V.L																	x	
Kꜣ-m-rḥw	485-7	V.L	x																	
Ḥtp-kꜣ	447-8	V.L-VI.E			x						x		x		x	x				
ḥmt-Rʿ	450	V.L-VI.E	x		x						x	x				x				
Kꜣ-gm-nj	521-5	VI.E	x																	
Kꜣ(j)-ʿpr(w)	---	VI.E	x		x															
Ššsšt	617-9	VI.E	x									x								
Kꜣ-gm-nj	521-5	VI.E	x											x						
Mttj	646-8	VI.E																		
Mrrw-kꜣ.j	525-34	VI.E	x	x																
Ptḥ-špss	460-1	VI.E			x															
Nfr-ššm-Rʿ	511-2	VI.E	x																	
ʿnḫ-m-ʿ-ḥr	512-5	VI.E	x											x						
wḏꜣ-ḥꜣ-ttj	515-6	VI.E	x											x						
Mrw-ṯtj-snb	520	VI.E-VI.M	x																	
šsšst	617-9	VI.E-VI.M	x									x								
Mrrj	518-9	VI.M	x																	
ḏwꜣ-ḥp	595	VI.L			x															
Nj-ʿnḫ-Ppj	630-1	VI.L		x	x									x						
ꜣḫtj-ḥtp	634-7	VI.L																		
Šmdntj	520-1	VI	x																	
total	**28**		**17**	**3**	**9**	**---**	**---**	**---**	**---**	**---**	**3**	**3**	**3**	**6**	**1**	**2**	**---**	**---**	**1**	**---**
		%	**61**	**11**	**32**						**11**	**11**	**11**	**21**	**4**	**7**			**4**	

Table II. Saqqara. Themes on the entrance thicknesses

Name	PM	Date	E1	E2	E3	E4	E5	E6	E7	E8	E9	E10	E11	E12	E13	E14	E15	E16	E17	E18
ꜥꜣ - ꜣḫtj	500	III.L	x[1]																	
F 3078	443	III.L									x	x[2]								
Mṯn	493-4	IV.E								x	x			x						
Pḥr-nfr	502	IV.E	x																	
ꜣḫtj-ḥtp	453	IV.E	x								x									
ḏbḥn	235-6	IV.L			x							x								
Wꜣš-ptḥ	456	V.E			x									x						
Ptḥ-ḥtp	581-2	V.E-V.M		x	x						x		x							
šnnw-ꜥnḫ	582	V.E-V.M	x							x		x								
Nfr-jrt-n.f	583-4	V.M								x					x					
Jpj	451	V.M-V.L	x[3]																	
špd-ḥtp	481-2	V.M-V.L			x						x		x							
Jj-nfrt	616	V.L	x																	
Rꜥ-špss	494-6	V.L			x						x									
Rꜥ-m-kꜣ	487-8	V.L									x		x		x		x			
Kꜣ-m-rḥw	485-7	V.L									x[4]		x							
Ḥtp-ḥr-ꜣḫtj	593-5	V.L							x		x	x			x	x				
Ḫnwt	623-4	V.L	x																	
Nbt	624-5	V.L	x																	
ꜣḫtj-ḥtp	627-9	V.L													x					
Ḫwjt	482	V.L-VI.E	x																	
Pḥnw-kꜣ	491-2	V.L-VI.E															x			
Ḥtp-kꜣ	447-8	V.L-VI.E			x				x			x								
ḥmt-Rꜥ	450	V.L-VI.E	x																	
ṯp-m-ꜥnḫ	483	V.L-VI.E									x									
Kꜣ-gm-nj	521-5	VI.E	x											x						
Nj-kꜣw-Issi	---	VI.E			x															
Nb.t	624-5	VI.E	x																	
Kꜣ(j)-ꜥpr(w)	---	VI.E	x		x															
Mrrw-kꜣ.j	525-34	VI.E	x																	
šꜣbw	460-1	VI.E		x	x															
Ptḥ-špss	460-1	VI.E			x						x									
Nfr-ššm-Rꜥ	511-2	VI.E	x								x[5]									
ꜥnḫ-m-ꜥ-ḥr	512-5	VI.E	x																	
Wḏꜣ-ḥꜣ-ttj	515-6	VI.E	x																	
Mttj	646-8	VI.E			x															
Mḥw	619-22	VI.E	x																	
ššsš.t	617-9	VI.E	x																	
Wr-nw	519	VI.M-VI.L	x																	
Rmnj	---	VI.M-VI.L	x																	

[1] Ziegler, *Louvre*, 96-103.

[2] Stevenson Smith, HESPOK, Plate 34c, in the upper register the person is not carrying anything and this contradicts the remarks in ibidem page 151 were the men are called offering bearers, for this reasons these persons are interpreted as attendants.

[3] Fischer, Metropolitan Museum Journal, 10 (1975), Figures 12 and 13.

[4] Mariette, *Mastaba*, 175 mentions the offering bearers and not the butchers. PM, III/2, 486 mentions the butchers and not the offering bearers.

[5] On this entrance thickness cattle is walking in the direction of the chapel without visible guidance. Realizing that they are in fact guided by persons that are not depicted, this theme is interpreted as "offering bringers".

Name	PM	Date	E1	E2	E3	E4	E5	E6	E7	E8	E9	E10	E11	E12	E13	E14	E15	E16	E17	E18
Ḫwj	519	VI.M-VI.L	x						x											
Nb-kꜣw-ḥr	627-9	VI.L													x					
ꜣẖtj-ḥtp	633-4	VI.L									x									
ꜣẖtj-ḥtp	634-7	VI.L	x		x				x		x	x	x		x	x				
total	**44**		**23**	**2**	**12**				**4**	**3**	**14**	**6**	**5**	**3**	**6**	**2**	**2**			
		%	**52**	**5**	**27**				**9**	**7**	**32**	**14**	**11**	**7**	**14**	**5**	**5**			

Table III. Portico decoration

				Person signalling									Purpose signalling											
	Name	PM	Date	1	2	3	10	12	15	16	18	%	4	5	6	7	8	9	11	14	17	13	%	chapel
1	*R*ʿ*-wr*	265	V.E-V.M					x				100											0	x
2	*Nn-sḏr-k*ꜣ*.j*	72	V.M	x								50	x										50	x
3	*Nj-*ʿ*nḫ-ẖnmw*	641-4	V.M-V.L	x				x		x	x	50	x						x	x		x	50	x
4	*K*ꜣ*.j-m-ṯnnt*	489	V.L	x	x			x				100											0	x
5	*ṯjj*	468-78	V.L	x		x		x		x		67					x				x		33	x
6	*R*ʿ*-špss*	496	V.L							x	x	100									x		0	x
7	*ḥsj*	---	V.L				x	x		x	x	57						x			x	x	43	x
8	*šnḏm-jb Mḥj*	87-8	V.L			x	x	x		x		67						x			x		33	x
9	*šnḏm-jb Jntj*	85	V.L	x			x	x		x	x	83									x	x	17	x
10	*Nfr-mḏr-ẖwfw-*	---	V.L	x								100											0	x
11	*ššm-nfr [IV]*	223-4	V.L-VI.E	x			x	x		x	x	83						x					17	x
12	*Nḫbw* [1]	89-90	VI.E	x			x	x		x		80										x	20	x
13	*ꜣḫt-mḥw* [2]	87	VI.M-VI.L		x	x				x	x	50	x					x	x	x			50	---
14	*Mrw-k*ꜣ	118	VI					x				100											0	x
15	*Ṯtw*	66-7	VI	x				x				29	x			x		x	x	x			71	---
				9	2	3	5	11	---	9	6		4	---	---	1	1	5	3	3	5	4		
	%			60	13	20	33	73	---	60	40		27	---	---	7	7	33	20	20	33	27		

1 Whether the boat scene belongs to no. 15 or no. 13 cannot be determined.

2 Giza Archives, Photo AAW1539.

Table IV. Giza. Themes on the entrance door jambs

Name	PM	date	D1	D2	D3	D4	D5	D6	D7	D8	D9	D10	D18
Ḥm-jwnw	122-3	IV.E	x										
K3.j-wꜥ b[1]	187-8	IV.E	x										
Ḫwfw-ḫꜥ.f [I]	188-90	IV.E		x	x				x		x	x	x
3ḫtj-http	200-1	IV.E	x										
ḏ w3-n-Ḥr	200	IV.L		x									
Nb.j-m-3htj	229	IV.L		x									
W3š-ptḥ	273	IV.L-V.E			x								
Mr-jb.j	71-2	IV.L-V.E			x								
K3.j-nfr	77-8	V.E		x	x				x		x		
šḫm-k3-Rꜥ	233-4	V.E	x										
K3-pw-nswt :Kꜥj	135	V.E/M		x									
Nfr-b3w-ptḥ	169-70	V.M/L	x	x									
Rdj	---	V.M/L	x		x								
Wp-m-nfrt	281-2	V-M/L		x	x								
K3.j-m-nfrt [2]	263-4	V-M/L	x										
Nfr [3]	258-9	V-M/L		x	x								
Jj-nfrt	298-9	V.L[4]	x						x				
Ỉnpw-http	106-7	V.L		x							x		x
Ḫww-wr [5]	254-5	V.L		x									
Nj-m3ꜥt-Rꜥ	282-4	V.L	x										
Jjḏf3	61	V.L/ VI.E			x								
Nfr-ḥtp	286 - 7	V	x										
Total	**22**		**10**	**10**	**9**	**---**	**---**	**---**	**3**	**---**	**3**	**---**	**1**
		%	**45**	**45**	**41**				**14**		**14**		**5**

[1] In Simpson, *Gmast 3*, Figure 4, the passage from vestibule C to room B is considered to be the entrance of the chapel.

[2] For the decoration the entrance of the "south tomb" (PM, III/1, plan XXXIV, no. 2ab) has been taken.

[3] In plan PM, III/1, XXXIV the rooms II and III are considered as "corridor", the room with wall 5 in it is known as the "sloping passage" (Hassan, *Giza III*, Figure 167). Only room I is considered to be a chapel.

[4] This date is based on the surface of the tomb of 230m^2 (Schürmann, *Ii-nefret*, 7; Roeten, *Economic decline*, Figure 107.

[5] The false door consists of a niche (PM, III/1, plan XXXV, 10abc) that itself can be considered to be a chapel.

Table V. Giza. Themes on the entrance thicknesses

	Name	date	PM	E 1	E 2	E 3	E 4	E 5	E 6	E 7	E 8	E 9	E 10	E 11	E 12	E 13	E 14	E 15	E 16	E 17	E 18
IV	*Ḥm-jwnw*	IV.E	122-3				x										x				
	Ḫwfw-ḫꜥ.f [I]	IV.E	188-90			x				x											
	Ḫntj-kꜣ.j	IV.E	74-5	x																	
	ꜣḫtj-ḥtp	IV.E	200-1				x														
	G 7750	IV.E-IV.L	203	x	x																
	Mn-ḏd.f	IV.L	203-4		x																
	D wꜣ-n-Rꜥ	IV.L	148	x									x	x							
	D wꜣ-n-Ḥr	IV.L	200		x	x															
	Mrs-ꜥnḫ [III]	IV.L	197-9	x								x	x								
	Dbḥnj	IV.L	235-6			x				x		x									
	Nj-wsr-Rꜥ	IV.L	234			x															
	Kꜣ.j-m-sḫm [1]	IV.L	201-2					x													
	Nfr	IV.L	72-4	x			x			x		x									
	Jꜥn	IV.L	65		x	x															
	Snfrw- ḫꜣ.f	IV.L-V.E	183-4			x															
	Wꜣš-ptḥ	IV.L-V.E	273		x	x															
	Jttj [2]	IV.L-V.E	193	x	x					x											
	Mr-jb.j	IV.L-V.E	71-2			x							x								
	Kꜣw-nswt [3]	IV.L-V.E	274			x															
19	%			32	32	47	16	5	---	21	---	16	16	5	---	---	5	---	---	---	---
V.E	*Sšꜣt-ḥtp*	V.E	149-50		x	x				x											
	Sḫm-kꜣ-Rꜥ [4]	V.E	233-4		x					x		x									
	Kꜣ.j-nfr	V.E	77-8	x			x			x		x									
	G 4411	V.E	127			x				x			x								
	Wḥm-kꜣ.j	V.E	114-5		x																
	Kꜣ.j-nj-nswt [I]	V.E	78-9				x			x											
	Sṯw	V.E	135-6				x			x		x									
	Kꜣ-pw-nswt :Kꜣj	V.E/M	135	x		x															
	T ntj	V.E/M	141-2	x																	
9	%			33	33	33	33	---	---	67	---	33	11	---	---	---	---	---	---	---	---
V.M	*Rꜥ- ḫꜥ.f-ꜥnḫ*	V.M	207-8			x															
	Kꜣ.j-nj-nswt [II]	V.M	79-80	x						x		x									
	Jtj	V.M	174-5		x																
	Ḫwfw-ḫꜥ.f [II)	V.M	190-1		x																
	Rꜥ-wr [I]	V.M	158	x								x									
	Nfr-bꜣw-ptḥ	V.M/L	169-70		x	x						x									
	Sḫm-kꜣ.j	V.M/L	127			x				x			x								
	Rdj [5]	V.M/L	---	x		x															
	Tomb H	V-M/L	257			x				x		x	x	x							
	Jtj-sn	V.M/L	252-3		x	x															
	Kꜣ.j-m-nfrt	V.M/L	263-5			x						x									
	Nj-(mꜣꜥ)t-Rꜥ	V.M/L	241-2			x															
12	%			25	25	58	---	---	---	25	---	42	17	8	---	---	---	---	---	---	---
V.L	*Kꜣ.j-dwꜣ*	V.L	244-5		x	x															
	Sꜣ-jb	V.L	70	x																	

	Name	date	PM	E 1	E 2	E 3	E 4	E 5	E 6	E 7	E 8	E 9	E 10	E 11	E 12	E 13	E 14	E 15	E 16	E 17	E 18
	Tntj [I] [6]	V.L	---	x																	
	ʿnḫ-m-ʿ-Rʿ	V.L	206	x						x		x									
	Nfr-msḏr-ḫwfw	V.L	---			x															
	Sšm-nfr	V.L	249			x															
	Nḫt-kꜣ.j	V.L	240		x																
	Snḏm-jb: Jntj	V.L	85-7			x															
	Ḫww-wr	V.L	254-5	x																	
	Nfr	V.L	258-9	x																	
	Ḥmt-rʿ	V.L	243-4									x				x					
	Nfr-ḥtp	V.L	286-7	x	x																
	Nj-mꜣʿt-Rʿ	V.L	282-4		x	x						x									
	Nfr.s-rs	V.L	284	x																	
	Mr-sw-ʿnḫ	V.L	269-70	x																	
	Dwꜣ-Rʿ	V.L	287-8	x																	
	G 2087 (Gmast 6)	V.L	---	x								x									
	Kꜣ.j-m-ʿnḫ	V.L	131-3	x																	
	Nfr [I] [7]	V.L-VI.E	137-8	x						x		x	x								
	Kꜣ.j-mnj	V.L-VI.E	260			x						x									
	ʿnḫ-m-sꜣ.f	V.L-VI.E	246			x															
	Ḫwj-n-ptḥ	V.L-VI.E	237		x																
	ꜣḫtj-mrw-nswt	V.L-VI.E	80-1		x																
	ʿnḫ-ḥꜣ.f	V.L-VI.E	60	x																	
	Jrj-n-Rʿ	V.L-VI.E	144-5	x																	
	Jrrw	V.L-VI.E	280		x							x									
	Sšm-nfr [IV]	V.L-VI.E	223-6			x															
	Nfr-ḥr-nj-ptḥ	V.L-VI.E	63-4			x															
	Ḥmw	V.L-VI.E	245		x	x					x										
29	%			48	28	34	---	---	---	7	3	24	3	---	---	3	---	---	---	---	---
VI	*Snḏm-jb: Mḥj*	VI.E	87-9			x															
	Jdw	VI.E	185-6	x		x															
	Nfr-Jdw [I]	VI.E	165	x																	
	Mr-ʿnḫ.f	VI.E	278-9		x	x															
	Sḫm-ʿnḫ-ptḥ	VI.E	272		x																
	Ḥtp-nj-ptḥ	VI.E	94-5	x																	
	Jꜣsn	VI.E	82		x																
	ꜣbdw [8]	VI.E	51	x																	
	Mrjj-Rʿ-nfr : Qꜣr	VI.E/M	184-5	x																	
	Kꜣ-ḥj.f	VI.M	76		x																
	Ṯtw : Kꜣ.j-nswt	VI.L	66-7	x																	
	Mn-ḫbw	VI	168	x						x		x									
	Nj-ʿnḫ- Hnmw	VI	247-8			x															
	Hnmw-ḥtp [II]	VI	105		x					x											
	S-nfr	VI	108		x																
	Inpw-ḥtp	VI	106-7		x							x									x
	Nswt-wsrt [9]	VI	272		x																
	Smꜣ-ʿnḫ	VI	251			x															
	Sšm-nfr	VI	250	x						x		x									
	Hnmw-ḥtp	VI	164-5		x																

	Name	date	PM	E 1	E 2	E 3	E 4	E 5	E 6	E 7	E 8	E 9	E 10	E 11	E 12	E 13	E 14	E 15	E 16	E 17	E 18
	Qd-ns [II]	VI	152	x		x															
21	%			43	43	29	---	---	---	14	---	14	---	---	---	---	---	---	---	---	5
	Total 90			**35**	**30**	**36**	**6**	**1**	---	**18**	**1**	**7**	**2**	---	**1**	**1**	---	---	---	---	**1**
			%	**39**	**33**	**40**	**7**	**1**	---	**20**	**1**	**8**	**2**	---	**1**	**1**	---	---	---	---	**1**

[1] In Reisner, *Giza I*, 318(16) it is stated that the "door-jamb" (= entrance thickness) decoration is nearly obliterated; yet he puts there only being two persons forward as a certainty.

[2] In the available literature the date of this tomb is controversial; some scholars place it in the later part of the 5th dynasty, others in the transition from the 4th to the 5th dynasty.

[3] The tomb owner is depicted walking *into* the chapel (Hassan, *Giza II*, Figure 88 (page 84), Plate XXIV(2)). A possible explanation is that the depiction is placed on the entrance thickness of the main entrance from a pillared hall in front of the east façade of the rock cut tomb into the chapel.

[4] The chronological place of this monument is disputable but decided as early in V.E according to Baud, *Famille royale*, 575.

[5] The tombs of *Rdj*, *Nfr-msḏr-ḫwfw* and *S3-jb* are described in Roth, *Gmast 6*.

[6] Kormysheva, *Lepsius tombs*, Figure 7.

[7] If the date of IV.2 (contemporary Khufu (IV.2)) as proposed by Cherpion, *Mastabas*, 233 is accepted, the chronological development of theme C becomes much more logical. However, preliminary studies based on other criteria corroborate a V.L – VI.E date.

[8] The date of this tomb is based on the 6th dynasty date given in PM, III/1, 51; Harpur, *DETOK*, 265; Kanawati, *Administration*, combined with the V.6-V.8 date in Roth, *Gmast 6*, 103.

[9] The tomb owner walks *into* the chapel (Hassan, *Giza II*, Plate IX).

Table VIa. The width of the entrance of chapels others than corridor chapels (m).

	Name	PM, III/1	Dating	Width entrance
IV	G 7130 + 7140	188	IV.E	0.75
	Ḫntj-k3 (G 2130)	74-5	IV.E	0.83
	K3.j-nfr (G 1203)	57	IV.E	0.70
	G 7110 + 7120	187	IV.E	0.94
	G 4160	124-5	IV.E	0.72
	G 4260	125	IV.E	0.73
	Ḫwfw-nḫt (G 1205)	57	IV.E	0.56
	Ḥm-Jwnw (G 4000)	122 – 3	IV.E	0.81
	Nfr	58	IV.E	0.47
	Wp-m-nfrt (G 1201)	57	IV.E	0.80
	Jnj	61	IV.E	0.52
	K3.j-m-ˁḥ (G 1223)	59	IV.E	0.81
	ˁnḫ-ḥ3.f (G 7510)	196	IV.E	0.95
	3htj-ḥtp (G 7650)	200-1	IV.E/M	0.63
	Nfr-m3ˁt (G 7060)	183	IV.E/M	0.95
	Mn-ḫˁ.f	195	IV.E/M	0.94
	G 7330 + 7340	192	IV.M/L	0.76
	Nfr (G 1207)	58	IV.M/L	0.61
	G 4350	126	IV.M/L	0.81
	G 2135	75	IV.M/L	0.84
	G 4660	135	IV.M/L	0.62
	Nfrt-k3.w (G 7050)	182-3	IV.M/L	0.82
	Nfr (G 2110)	72-4	IV.L	0.75
	Dw3-n-Ḥr (G 7550)	200	IV.L	0.63
	Mr-ḥtp.f	127	IV.L/V.E	0.70
V.E	S*š3t-ḥtp*	149-50	V.E	0.72
	K3.j-nfr	77-8	V.E	0.65
	S*šm-nfr* [I]	142-3	V.E	0.82
	K3.j-nj-nswt [I]	78-9	V.E	0.63
	Špss-k3.f-ˁnḫ	175	V.E/M	0,72
	Jj-mrjj	170-4	V.E/M	0.85
V.M	*Jtj*	174	V.M	0.72
	Nfrj	50-1	V.M/L	0.51
	Nfr-b3w-Ptḥ	169-70	V.M/L	1.00
	*Nj-ḥtp-*Hnmw	50	V.M/L	0.70
V.L	S*šm-nfr* [III]	153-4	V.L	0.96
	S*ṯw* (G 4710)	135-6	V.L	0.69
	Nḫt-s3-rˁ (Abusir, XII)	---	V.L	0.79
	Nbtj-m-nfr.s (Abusir XII)	---	V.L	0.60
	Ꞽnpw-ḥtp (Abusir XXIII)	---	V.L	0.54
	Nfr-jḥjj	---	V.L	0.61
	Nfr [I]	137-8	V.L/VI.E	0.75
	Hs*j*	---	V.L/VI.E	0.61
	Jdw	185-6	VI.E	0.60
VI	*3nḫ-tj.fj*	275	VI	0.55
	3bdw	51	VI	0.61

	Name	PM, III/1	Dating	Width entrance
	Mjnww	140	VI	0.77
	ꜣḫtj-ḥtp	49	VI	0.61
	H*nmw*	121	VI	0.56
	Wrj	121	VI	0.58
Total 50	**Mean = 0.72m**			**35.80**

Table VIb. The width of entrances of corridor chapels (m)

	Name	PM, III/1	Dating	Width entrance
	Nfr [I]	137 - 8	V.L – VI.E	0.73
	Jrrw	280	V.L – VI.E	0.86
	K*ꜣ.j-m-ʿnḫ*	191 - 2	V.L – VI.E	0.46
	Mrw-kꜣ.j	118 - 9	VI	0.66
	W*rj*	121	VI	0.44
	J*dw*	185 - 8	VI.M/L	0.60
	anx-tj.fj	275	VI	0.51
	Mjnww	140	VI	0.78
	Nj-ʿnḫ-H*nmw*	247 - 8	VI	0.57
	H*nmw*	121	VI	0.56
Total 10	**Mean 0.62m**			**6.17**

Table VII. Chronological development themes entrance thicknesses and western wall (Giza)

				ww		Ent. thickness			Ent. thickness		
	Theme[1]			1	3	A	B	C	D	E	F
	name	date	PM								
IV	*Ḥm-jwnw* [2]	IV.E	122-3						▲		
	Ḫwfw-ḫꜥ.f [I]	IV.E	188-90		■		▲				
	Ḫntj-k3.j	IV.E	74-5						▲[3]		
	3ḫtj-ḥtp	IV.E	200-1				○				
	G 7750	IV.E-IV.L	203				○				
	ꜥnḫ-ḫ3.f	IV.L	196						▲		
	Mn-ḏd.f	IV.L	203-4				▲				
	D w3-n-Rꜥ	IV.L	148					▲			
	Mrs-ꜥnḫ [III]	IV.L	197-9		■			○			
	Dbḥnj	IV.L	235-6					○			
	Nj-wsr-Rꜥ	IV.L	234				○				
	Nfr	IV.L	72-4					○			▲
	Jꜥn	IV.L	65				▲				
	Snfrw- ḫ3.f	IV.L-V.E	183-4				○				
	W3š-ptḥ	IV.L-V.E	273				○	▲			
	Jttj [4]	IV.L-V.E	193		■		▲				
	Mr-jb.j	IV.L-V.E	71-2				○	○			
	K3w-nswt [5]	IV.L-V.E	274					○			
V.E	*Sš3t-ḥtp*	V.E	149-50		■		▲				▲
	Sḫm-k3-Rꜥ [6]	V.E	233-4					▲			
	K3.j-nfr	V.E	77-8		■			▲			▲
	Wḫm-k3.j	V.E	114-5		■		○				
	K3.j-nj-nswt [I]	V.E	78-9		■						▲
	Sṯw	V.E	135-6	○							▲
	K3-pw-nswt :K3j	V.E/M	135		■		▲				
	K3j	V.E/M	277				○				
	Ṯ ntj	V.E/M	141-2	○	■				▲		
V.M	*Rꜥ- ḫꜥ.f-ꜥnḫ*	V.M	207-8		■		○[7]				
	K3.j-nj-nswt [II]	V.M	79-80		□		▲	▲			
	Jtj	V.M	174-5				○				
	Ḫwfw-ḫꜥ.f [II)	V.M	190-1				○				
	Rꜥ-wr [I]	V.M	158					○			
	Nfr-b3w-ptḥ	V.M/L	169-70		□			▲			
	Sḫm-k3.j	V.M/L	127					○			
	Rdj [8]	V.M/L	---	○			○				
	Tomb H	V-M/L	257					▲			
	Jtj-sn	V.M/L	252-3				○				
	K3.j-m-nfrt	V.M/L	263-5				○	○			
	Nj-(m3ꜥ)t-Rꜥ	V.M/L	241-2				○				
V.L	*K3.j-dw3*	V.L	244-5	○	□			○			
	S3-jb	V.L	70		□	○					
	Ṯntj [I] [9]	V.L	---			▲					
	ꜥnḫ-m-ꜥ-Rꜥ	V.L	206		□			▲			
	Nfr-msḏr-ḫwfw	V.L	---		□		○				
	Sšm-nfr	V.L	249				○				

				ww		Ent. thickness			Ent. thickness		
	Theme[1]			1	3	A	B	C	D	E	F
	name	date	PM								
	Nḫt-kꜣ.j	V.L	240		□		○				
	Snḏm-jb (Jntj)	V.L	85-7				○				
	Nfr	V.L	258-9				○				
	Nfr-ḥtp	V.L	286-7			○					
	Nj-mꜣꜥt-Rꜥ	V.L	282-4		□		○				
	Nfr.s-rs	V.L	282-4					○			
	Mr-sw-ꜥnḫ	V.L	269-70			○					
	Dwꜣ-Rꜥ	V.L	287-8				○				
	G 2087	V.L	---			○					
	Kꜣ.j-m-ꜥnḫ	V.L	131-3			○					
	Hnmw-ḥtp [II]	V.L	105				○				
	Nfr [I][10]	V.L-VI.E	137-8		□			▲[11]			
	Kꜣ.j-mnj	V.L-VI.E	260					○			
	ꜥnḫ-m-sꜣ.f	V.L-VI.E	246				○				
	Ḫwj-n-ptḥ	V.L-VI.E	237				○				
	Šfwj	V.L-VI.E	106			○					
	ꜣḫtj-mrw-nswt	V.L-VI.E	80-1				○				
	ꜥnḫ-ḥꜣ.f	V.L-VI.E	60			○					
	Jrj-n-Rꜥ	V.L-VI.E	144-5			○					
	Jrrw	V.L-VI.E	280		□		○				
	Htj	V.L-VI.E	163-4		□		○				
	Sšm-nfr [IV]	V.L-VI.E	223-6				○				
	Nfr-ḥr-nj-ptḥ	V.L-VI.E	63-4				○				
	Ḫmw	V.L-VI.E	245				○				
VI	*Snḏm-jb: Mḥj*	VI.E	87-9				○				
	Jdw	VI.E	185-6		□	○	○				
	Kꜣ-ḫr-ptḥ	VI.E	166-7			○					
	Nfr-Jdw [I]	VI.E	165			○					
	Mr-ꜥnḫ.f	VI.E	278-9				○				
	Sḫm-ꜥnḫ-ptḥ	VI.E	272				○				
	Ḥtp-nj-ptḥ	VI.E	94-5			○					
	Jꜣsn	VI.E	82		□		○				
	ꜣbdw	VI.E	51			○					
	Mrjj-Rꜥ-nfr : Qꜣr	VI.E/M	184-5			○					
	Kꜣ-ḥj.f	VI.M	76		□		○				
	Snfrw-ḥtp	VI.L	96			○					
	Ṯtw : Kꜣ.j-nswt	VI.L	66-7			○					
	Mn-ḥbw	VI	168			○					
	Nj-ꜥnḫ- Hnmw	VI	247-8		□		○				
	Hnmw-ḥtp [II]	VI	105		□		○				
	S-nfr	VI	108				○				
	Inpw-ḥtp	VI	106-7				○				
	Nswt-wsrt [12]	VI	272				○				
	Smꜣ-ꜥnḫ	VI	251		□		○				
	Ḫwfw-snb [II]	VI	153				○				
	Sšm-nfr	VI	250				○				

				ww			Ent. thickness				Ent. thickness		
	Theme[1]			1	3		A	B	C		D	E	F
	name	date	PM										
	Hnmw-ḥtp	VI	164-5					○					
	Qd-ns [II]	VI	152					○					
				1	3		A	B	C		D	E	F

▲ = the tomb owner sitting　□ = theme 3 on the western wall
○ = the tomb owner standing　■ = theme 3 on the southern wall

[1] In some tombs it is evident that decoration is present on the entrance thicknesses, but this is either unfinished or too damaged to be of use in this table (e.g. *Nswt-nfr*, PM III/1, 143-4).

[2] The decoration of the northern entrance thickness of the chapel of the tomb of *Ḥm-jwnw* (PM, III/1, 122-3) and the dimensions of the exterior wall of the chapel as they are visible in the photo made during the excavation (Junker, *Giza I*, Plate XVb) show that there is room enough to place the tomb owner before the offering table. Also see: Der Manuelian, *Hemiunu.*

[3] The state of preservation of the decoration on the entrance thicknesses (Der Manuelian, *Gmast 8*, 253) makes it impossible to determine whether other persons were present, although there Figures 8.41 and 8.42 show that enough space is available to place persons and/or an offering table in front of the sitting tomb owner. The presence of the goose as part of the ideographic offering list makes the presence of an offering table probable.

[4] In the available literature the date of this tomb is controversial; some scholars place this tomb in the later part of the 5th dynasty, others in the transition from the 4th to the 5th dynasty.

[5] The tomb owner is depicted walking *into* the chapel (Hassan, *Giza II*, Figure 88 (page 84), Plate XXIV(2)). A possible explanation is that the depiction is placed on the entrance thickness of the main entrance from a pillared hall in front of the east façade of the rock cut tomb into the chapel.

[6] The chronological place of this monument is disputable, but here is placed early in V.E according to Baud, *Famille royale,* 575.

[7] On both entrance thicknesses the tomb owner has been depicted, but on one of them as a young man and on the other as an elderly man (LD, *II*, 8ab).

[8] The tombs of *Rdj*, *Nfr-msḏr-ḫwfw*and *S3-jb*are described in Roth, *Gmast 6*.

[9] Kormysheva, *Lepsius tombs*, Figure 7.

[10] If the date of IV.2 (contemporary Khufu (IV.2)) as proposed by Cherpion, *Mastabas*, 233 is accepted, the chronological development of theme C becomes much more logical. However, preliminary studies based on other criteria corroborate a V.L – VI.E date.

[11] The mastaba of *Sḫm-ˁnḫ-ptḥ* (PM, III/1, 191) which has two statues of the sitting tomb owner flanking the entrance (Der Manuelian, *Giza archives*, photo B6177_NS) should be placed in this period.

[12] The tomb owner walks *into* the chapel (Hassan, *Giza II*, Plate IX).

Table VIII-1. Northern and southern entrance thicknesses (theme numbers according to Figure 11.9)

period	name	PM III/1	Standing (theme 1)		Sitting (theme 2)		Table scene (theme 3)	
			north	south	north	south	north	south
IV	*Dwꜣ-n-Rꜥ*	148	-	-	x	x	-	-
	Mrs-ꜥnḫ [III]	197-9	x	x	-	-	-	-
	Dbḥnj	235-6	x	x	-	-	-	-
	Kꜣ.j-m-sḫm	201-2	-	-	-	-	x	x
	Nfr	72-4	x	-	-	-	-	x
	Wꜣš-ptḥ	273	-	x	x	-	-	-
	Mr-jb.j	71-2	x	x	-	-	-	-
	Kꜣw-nswt	274	x	x	-	-	-	-
	Ḥm.t-Rꜥ	243 - 4	-	-	-	-	-	-
	CG 1538-9	309	-	-	-	-	-	-
V.E	*Sšt-htp*	149-50	-	-	-	x	x	-
	Sšm-nfr [I]	142 - 3	-	-	-	-	-	-
	Sḫm-kꜣ-Rꜥ [1]	233-4	-	o	x	x	-	o
	Kꜣ.j-nfr	77-8	-	-	-	x	x	-
	Kꜣ.j-nj-nswt [I]	78-9	-	-	-	-	x	x
	Stw	135-6	-	-	-	-	x	x
V.M	*Kꜣ.j-nj-nswt* [II]	79-80	-	-	x	x	-	-
	Rꜥ-wr [I]	158	x	x	-	-	-	-
	Nfr-bꜣw-ptḥ	169-70	-	-	x	x	-	-
	Sḫm-kꜣ.j	127	x	x	-	-	-	-
	Tomb H	257	-	-	x	x	-	-
	Kꜣ.j-m-nfrt	263-5	x	x	-	-	-	-
	Sšm-nfr [II]	146 - 8	-	-	-	-	-	-
V.L	*Kꜣ.j-dwꜣ* [2]	244-5	x	x	o	o	o	o
	ꜥnḫ-m-ꜥ-Rꜥ	206	-	-	x	x	-	-
	Nj-mꜣꜥt-Rꜥ	282-4	x	x	-	-	-	-
	Dwꜣ-Rꜥ	287-8	o	x	-	-	-	-
	Nfr [I]	137-8	-	-	x	x	-	-
	Kꜣ.j-mnj	260	x	x	-	-	-	-
	Jrrw [3]	280	x	x	-	-	-	-
	Ḥmw	245	x	x	-	-	-	-
VI	*Mn-ḥbw* [4]	168	x	x	-	-	-	-
	Jj-nfrt	298 - 9	x	x	-	-	-	-
	Nj-ꜥnḫ-Hnmw	247-8	x	x	-	-	-	-
	Jnpw-ḥtp	106-7	x	x	-	-	-	-
	ꜥnḫ-wḏꜣ	167	-	-	-	-	-	-
	Sšm-nfr	250	x	x	-	-	-	-
	placements		18	19	9	9	5	4
FO			50	53	25	25	14	11

x = present on the complete or incomplete entrance thicknesses
– = not present on the complete entrance thicknesses
o = not present on the incomplete entrance thicknesses

[1] The state of conservation of the decoration of the entrance thicknesses is such that it cannot be determined whether on the southern entrance thickness the tomb owner is standing or sitting. Taking into account the overall symmetry of these two postures, it is likely that the tomb owner is depicted in a sitting position.

[2] Based on a diachronically growing symmetry, it is probable that the tomb owner was depicted in a standing posture.

[3] The presence of the standing tomb owner on the southern entrance thickness is an assumption that is based on the prevailing symmetry of this type of depictions on the entrance thicknesses.

[4] The offering bearers pose a problem here, because Junker, *Giza VIII*, 159 – 65 does not mention any decoration on the entrance thicknesses; LD, *Erg.*, 24 shows a standing tomb owner with a register of five figures underneath of which four are clearly designated as *ḥm-kꜣ* although all of them carry items that are typically those of offerings bearers. PM, III/1, 168 only mentions offering bearers.

Table VIII-2. Northern and southern entrance thicknesses (theme numbers according to Figure 11.9)

period	name	PM III/1	Offering bearers (theme 4)		Priests (theme 5)		Scribes (theme 6)		Butchery Scene (theme 7)	
			north	south	north	south	north	south	north	south
IV	*ḏwꜣ-n-Rꜥ*	148	x	x	o	o	x	o	x	o
	Mrs-ꜥnḫ [III]	197-9	x	x	-	-	-	x	-	-
	ḏbḥnj	235-6	x	x	-	-	-	-	-	-
	Kꜣ.j-m-sḫm	201-2	o	o	o	o	o	o	o	o
	Nfr	72-4	-	-	-	x	x	-	-	-
	Wꜣš-ptḥ	273	x	x	o	o	o	o	o	o
	Mr-jb.j	71-2	x	-	-	-	x	-	-	-
	Kꜣw-nswt	274	o	x	o	o	o	o	o	o
	Ḥm.t-Rꜥ	243 - 4	x	x	-	-	-	-	-	-
	ŚG 1538-9	309	x	x	-	-	-	-	-	-
V.E	*ššt-ḥtp*	149	-	-	x	-	-	-	-	-
	ššm-nfr [I]	142 - 3	x	o	-	-	-	-	x	o
	šḫm-kꜣ-Rꜥ	233-4	x	x	o	x	o	o	-	-
	Kꜣ.j-nfr	77-8	-	x	x	-	-	x	-	-
	Kꜣ.j-nj-nswt	78-9	-	x	x	x	-	-	-	-
	šṯw	135-6	-	-	x	-	-	-	-	-
V.M	*Kꜣ.j-nj-nswt [*	79-80	-	-	x	x	-	-	-	-
	Rꜥ-wr [I]	158	x	x	o	o	o	o	-	-
	Nfr-bꜣw-ptḥ	169-70	-	x	-	x	-	-	-	-
	šḫm-kꜣ.j	127	-	o	x	o	x	o	-	-
	ṯqmb ḥ	257	o	x	x	o	x	o	o	x
	Kꜣ.j-m-nfrt	263-5	o	o	x	o	o	o	-	-
	ššm-nfr [II]	146 - 8	x	x	o	o	-	-	-	-
V.L	*Kꜣ.j-dwꜣ*	244-5	o	o	o	o	o	o	-	-
	ꜣnḫ-m-ꜥ-Rꜥ	206	-	x	-	-	-	-	-	-
	Nj-mꜣꜥt-Rꜥ	282-4	x	x	-	-	-	-	-	-
	ḏwꜣ-Rꜥ	287-8	o	o	o	o	o	o	o	o
	Nfr [I]	137-8	-	x	-	-	x	-	-	-
	Kꜣ.j-mnj	260	x	-	-	-	-	-	o	-
	Jrrw	280	x	x	-	-	-	-	-	-
	Ḥmw	245	x	x	-	-	-	-	-	-
VI	*Mn-ḥbw*	168	x	x	-	-	-	-	-	-
	Jj-nfrt	298 - 9	x	x	-	-	-	-	-	-
	Nj-ꜥnḫ-ḫnmw	247-8	-	-	-	-	-	-	-	-
	Jnpw-ḥtp	106-7	x	x	-	-	-	-	-	-
	ꜥnḫ-wḏꜣ	167	x	o	-	-	-	-	-	-
	ššm-nfr	250	x	x	-	-	-	-	-	-
	plꜥšements		20	23	8	5	6	2	2	1
FO			65	77	29	19	21	8	6	3

Table IX. Northern chapel wall, presence tomb owner

			theme	1	2	3
	name	**PM**	**date**			
IV	*Ḫwfw-ḫꜥ.f* [I]	188-90	IV.E	-	○	-
	ꜣḫtj-ḥtp	200-1	IV.E	○	-	-
	Nb-m-ꜣḫt	230-3	IV.E	-	○	-
	Abu Rawash F48 [1]	---	IV.E	-	○	-
	Kꜣ.j-m-sḫm	201-2	IV.L	-	-	-
	Ḏbḥnj	235-6	IV.L	○	-	-
	ḏꜣtj	204-5	IV.L/V.E	-	●	-
	Mr-jb.j	71-2	IV.L/V.E	●	-	-
	Jttji	193	IV.L/V.E	-	-	●
V.E	*Sšꜣt-ḥtp*	149-50	V.E	-	●	-
	Kꜣ.j-m-nfr	77-8	V.E	-	○	-
	Wḥm-kꜣ.j	114-5	V.E	-	○	-
	Sšm-nfr [I]	142-3	V.E	-	○	-
	Kꜣ.j-nj-nswt [I]	78-9	V.E	-	○	-
	Nswt-nfr	143-4	V.E	-	●	-
	Kꜣ-pw-nswt	135	V.E/M			
	Ṯntj	141-2	V.E/M	-	-	●
V.M	*Rꜥ-ḫꜥ.f-ꜥnḫ*	207-8	V.M	○	-	?
	Kꜣ.j-swḏꜣ	159	V.M	●	-	-
	Nfr-bꜣ.w-ptḥ	169	V.M	○	-	-
	Jj-mrjj	170-4	V-M/L	-	-	-
	Jtj-sn	252-3	V-M/L	-	-	●
	Kꜣpj	69-70	V.M/L	○	-	-
	Rdj	---	V.M/L	-	○	-
	Sšm-nfr [II]	146	V-M/L	-	-	-
V.L	*Kꜣ.j-dwꜣ*	244-5	V.L	-	-	-
	Ṯntj [I]	---	V.L	-	○	-
	Sšm-nfr	249	V.L	-	-	-
	Nḫt-kꜣ.j	240	V.L	-	-	-
	Sšm-nfr [III]	153-4	V.L	-	-	-
	Nfr-ḥwj	---	V.L	-	-	-
	Nj-mꜣꜥt-Rꜥ	282-4	V.L	-	-	-
	Nj-mꜣꜥt-Rꜥ	70	V.L	-	-	-
	ꜣnḫ-m-ꜥ-Rꜥ	206	V.L	-	○	-
	Ḫww-wr	254-5	V.L	●	-	-
	Kꜣ.j-m-ꜥnḫ	131-3	V.L	-	-	-
	Ns-m-nꜣw	209	V.L/VI.E	-	○	-
	Htj	163-4	V.L/VI.E	○	-	-
	Sḫm-kꜣ.j	221-2	V.L/VI.E	-	●	-
VI	*Htp-nj-Ptḥ*	94-5	VI.E	-	-	●
	Jꜣsn	82	VI.E	○	-	-
	Kꜣ-ḥj.f	76	VI.M	-	○	-

○ = tomb owner standing
● = tomb owner sitting

[1] Gourdon, *Djedefra*, Plate 2.

Bibliography, Abbreviations and Technical Terms

Abdou, *Nebkauhor* A. M. Abdou Mohamed, *The tomb of Akhethotep Hemi re-used by Nebkauhor-Idu* (Doct. Thesis Prague University, 2011).

Abu-Bakr, *Giza* A-M. Abu-Bakr, *Excavations at Giza, 1949-1950* (Cairo, 1953).

Adams, *Djet* B. Adams, 'Possible *s3*-signs from the Tomb of Djet (Uadji), JEA, 80(1994), 183 - 7.

Adams, *Protodynastic* B. Adams and K. M. Ciałowicz, *Protodynastic Egypt* (Princes Risborough, 1997).

Adams, *Mummies* B. Adams, *Egyptian Mummies* (Princes Risborough, 1998).

Adams, *Shunet el-Zebib* M. D. Adams and D. O'Conner, 'The Shunet el-Zebib at Abydos: Architectural conservation at one of Egypt's oldest preserved royal monuments' in S. H. D'Auria (ed.), *Offerings to the Discerning Eye. An Egyptological Medley in Honor of Jack A. Josephson* (Leiden, Boston, 2010), 1 - 8.

Aeragram Newsletter of the Ancient Egypt Research Associates (Cambridge, MA).

ÄF Ägyptologische Forschungen, Glückstadt, Hamburg, New York.

AJA American Journal of Archaeology, Norwood.

Andelković, *Political organization* B. Andelković, 'Political Organization of Egypt in the Predynastic Period', in E. Teeter (ed.), *Before the Pyramids. The origins of Egyptian Civilization* (Chicago, 2011), 25 - 32.

Aldred, *Egyptian art* C. Aldred, *Egyptian art in the Days oft he Pharaohs 3100 - 320 BC* (London, 1966).

Alexanian, *Chasechemui* N. Alexanian, „Die Reliefdekoration des Chasechemui", in N. Grimal (ed.), *Les critères de datation stylistiques à l'Ancien Empire* (Le Caire, 1997), 1 - 30.

Alexanian, *Netjeraperef* N. Alexanian, *Dahschur II, Das Grab des Prinzen Netjer-aperef. Die Mastaba II/1 in Dahschur* (Mainz, 1999).

Alexanian, *Tomb and social status* N. Alexanian, „Tomb and social status. The textual evidence" in M. Bárta (ed.), *The Old Kingdom Art and Archaeology. Proceedings of the conference held in Prague, May 31 - June 4, 2004* (Prague, 2006), 1 - 8.

Alliot, *Isi* M. Alliot, *Rapport sur les fouilles de Tell Edfou (1933)* (Le Caire, 1935).

Alliot, *Divinisé* M. Alliot, „Un nouvel example de vizir divinisé dans l'Égypte ancienne", BIFAO, 37(1937), 93 - 160.

Altenmüller, *Geburtsschrein* H. Altenmüller, „Geburtsschrein und Geburtshaus", in P. Der Manuelian (ed.), *Studies in Honor of William Kelly Simpson*, Vol. I (Boston, 1996), 27 - 37.

Altenmüller, *Mehu* H. Altenmüller, *Die Wanddarstellungen im Grab des Mehu in Saqqara* (Mainz, 1998).

Andreu, *Akhethetep* G. Andreu - Lanoë, „Le dépot de tables d'offrandes et de bassins devant le mastaba d'Akhethetep", in C. Ziegler (ed.), *Fouilles du Louvre à Saqqara, Volume I. Le Mastaba d'Akhethetep* (Louvain, Paris, 2007), 176 - 92.

AoF Altorientalische Forschungen, Berlin.

Arnold, *Pyramidentempel* D. Arnold, "Ritual und Pyramidentemple", MDAIK, 33(1977), 1 - 15.

Arnold, *Building* D. Arnold, *Building in Egypt. Pharaonic stone maconry* (Oxford, 1991).

ASAE Annales du service des antiquités de l'Egypte, Le Caire.

Assmann, *Tod, jenseits* J. Assmann, *Tod und Jenseits im alten Ägypten* (München, 2001).

Association The tendency of themes to be placed together on the same wall, or wall section, or on the false door or a part of it.

Badawy, *Stèle funéraire* A. Badawy, „La stèle funéraire sous l'Ancien Empire: son origine et son fonctionnement", ASAE, 48(1948), 213 - 43.

Balík, *Ptahshepses* M. Balík, B. Vachala, "The scientific restitution of Ptahshepses' mastaba at Abusir - an ideal reconstitution", in M. Barta and J. Krejči (eds), *Abusir and Saqqara in the year 2000* (Prague, 2000), 317 - 30.

Bárta, *Serdab* M. Bárta, "Serdab and Statue Placement in the Private Tombs down to the Fourth Dynasty", MDAIK, 54 (1998), 65-75.

Bárta, *Abusir V* M. Bárta, *Abusir V. The Cemeteries of Abusir South I. The cemeteries at Abusir South I* (Prague, 2001).

Bárta, *Hetepi* M. Bárta and B. Vachala, "The tomb of Hetepi at Abu Sir South", EA, 19 (2001), 33-5.

Bárta, *Funerary rites* M. Bárta, "Funerary rites and cults at Abusir South", BSAK, 9(2003), 17 - 30.

Bárta, *Afterlife* M. Bárta, "A new gateway to the afterlife", in K. Daoud, S. Bedier and S. Abd el-Fatah (eds), *Studies in Honor of Ali Radwan* (Cairo, 2005), 1 - 9.

Bárta, *Inty* M. Bárta, "The Sixth Dynasty tombs in Abusir. Tomb complex of the vizier Qar and his family", in M. Bárta (ed.), *The Old Kingdom Art and Archaeology. Proceedings of the Conference held in Prague, May 31 - June 4, 2004* (Prague, 2006), 45 - 62.

Bárta, *Abusir XIII* M. Bárta *et al.*, *Tomb Complex of the Vizier Qar, his sons Qar junior and Senedjemib, and Ikai* (Prague, 2009).

Bárta, *Abusir XIX* M. Bárta *et al.*, *Abusir XIX, Tomb of Hetepi (AS 20), Tombs AS 33 - 35, and AS 50–53* (Prague, 2010).

Bárta, *Rock-cut tomb* M. Bárta, "A new Old Kingdom rock-cut tomb from Abusir and its Abusir-Saqqara context", in N. Strudwick and H. Strudwick (eds), *Old Kingdom, New Perspectives. Egytian Art and Archaeology 2750 - 2150 BC* (Oxford, 2011), 9 - 21.

Bárta, *Journey* M. Bárta, *Journey to the West. The world of the Old Kingdom tombs in Ancient Egypt* (Prague, 2011).

Bárta, *Abusir XXIII* M. Bárta *et al.*, *Abusir XXIII. The Tomb of the Sun Priest Neferinpu (AS 37)* (Prague, 2014).

Bárta, *Punctuated equilibrium* M. Bárta, "Ancient Egyptian History as an Example of Punctuated Equilibrium: An Outline", in P. Der Manuelian and T. Schneider (eds), *Towards a New History for the Egyptian Old Kingdom* (Leiden, Boston, 2015), 1 - 17.

Bárta, *Afterlife existence* M. Bárta, "The Afterlife Existence Captured in Stone", in P. Jánosi and H. Vymazalová (eds), *The Art of Describing. The World of Tomb Decoration as Visual Culture of the Old Kingdom* (Prague, 2018), 53 - 84.

Bárta, *Opferliste* W. Bárta, *Die altägyptische Opferliste von der Frühzeit bis zur griechisch-römische Epoche* (Berlin, 1963).

Bárta, *Opferformel* W. Bárta, *Aufbau und Bedeutung der altägyptische Opferformel* (Glückstadt, 1968).

Baud, *F 19* M. Baud, "Le cimetière F d'Abou Rawach, nécropole royale de Rêdjedef (IVe dynastie) », BIFAO, 103 (2003), 17-71.

Baud, *F 48* M. Baud, *La nécropole royale d'Abou Rawach* (publication www.egypt.edu).

Baumgartel, *Prehistoric Egypt* E. J. Baumagartel, *The Cultures of Prehistoric Egypt, Volume II* (Westport (Conn.), 1960).

BD Book of the Dead.

Beaux, *Portico* N. Beaux, « The decoration in the portico of Ti's mastaba at Saqqara. An innovative introduction to the tomb » in M. Barta, F. Coppens and J. Krejči (eds), *Abusir and Saqqara in the year 2010* (Prague, 2011), 223-32.

Berger, *Culte de reines* C. Berger - el-Naggar, "Cultes des Reines et cultes privés dans le cimetière de la famille royale de Pépy Ier", in *Des Néferkarê aux Montouhotep. Travaux archéologiques en cours sur la fin de la Vie dynastie et la Prmière Période Intermédiaire. Actes de colloque CNRS - Université Lumière Lyon 2, tenu le 5 - 7 juillet 2001*, TMOM, 40(2005), 15 - 29.

BIFAO Bulletin de l'Institut Français d'Archéologie Orientale, Le Caire.

BMFA Bulletin of the Museum of Fine Arts, Boston.

BMSAES British Museum Studies in Ancient Egypt and Sudan, London.

Bolshakov, *Tomb cult* A. O. Bolshakov, "The Moment of the Establishment of the Tomb-cult in Ancient Egypt", AoF, 18(1991), 204 - 18.

Bolshakov, *Ankh-haf* A. O. Bolshakov, "What Did the Bust of Ankh-haf Originally Look Like?", Journal of the Museum of Fine Arts, Boston, 3(1991), 4 - 14.

Bolshakov, *Man and double* A. O. Bolshakov, *Man and his Double in Egyptian Ideology of the Old Kingdom* (Wiesbaden, 1997).

Borchardt, *Denkmäler I* L. Borchardt, *Catalogue Général des Antiquités Egyptiennes de Musée du Caire. Denkmäler des Alten Reiches,* Teil I (Berlin, 1937).

Borchardt, *Denkmäler II* L. Borchardt, *Catalogue Général des Antiquités Egyptiennes de Musée du Caire. Denkmäler des Alten Reiches,* Teil II (Berlin, 1964).

Breasted, *Ancient records* J. H. Breasted, *Ancient Records of Egypt,* Volume I (Chicago, 1906).

Brovarski, *Doors of heaven* E. Brovarski, "The Doors of Heaven", Orientalia, 46(1977), 107 -15.

Brovarski, *South Saqqara* E. Brovarski, *The Late Old Kingdom at South Saqqara,* in *Des Néferkarê aux Montouhotep. Travaux archéologiques en cours sur la fin de la VIe dynastie et la Première Période Intermédiaire. Actes du colloque CNRS - université Lumière Lyon 2, tenu le 5-7juillet 2001* (Lyon : Maison de l'Orient et de la Méditerranée, 40), 31 -71. http://www.persee.fr/doc/mom_1955-4982_2005_act_40_1_2393.

Bruyère, *Sennedjem* B. Bruyère, *La Tombe N° 1 de Sennedjem à Deir el Medineh* (Le Caire, 1959).

Brunton, *Badarian* G. Brunton, G. Caton - Thompson, *The Badarian Civilisation and Predynastic remains near Badari* (London, 1928).

BSAK Beihefte Studien zur Altägyptischen Kultur, Hamburg.

Bussmann, *Door bolt sealing* R. Bussmann, "Locking and Control: A Door Bolt Sealing from Hieraconpolis", JARCE, 50(2014), 95 - 101.

CAA Corpus Antiquitatum Aegyptiacarum, Pelizaeus-Museum, Hildesheim, Mainz.

Callender, *Queen Tatjet* V. G. Callender, "Queen Tatjet: an exercise in chronology"" in H. Vymazalová, M. Bárta (eds), *Chronology and Archaeology in Ancient Egypt (The third Millennium B.C)* (Prague, 2008), 107 - 9.

Capart, *Primitive art* J. Capart, *Primitive Art in Egypt* (London, 1905).

Capart, *Rue des tombeaux II* J. Capart, *Une Rue de Tombeaux à Saqqarah,* Vol. II (Bruxelles, 1907).

Chauvet, *Tomb environment* V. Chauvet, "Decoration and Architecture: the definition of private tomb environment", in S. H. D'Auria (ed.), *Servant of Mut. Studies in Honor of Richard A. Fazzini* (Leiden, Boston, 2008), 44 - 52.

Chauvet, *Portico-chapels* V. Chauvet, « Entrance-porticoes and Portico-chapels : The creation of an Outside Ritual Stage in Private Tombs of the Old Kingdom », in M. Barta, F. Coppens and J. Krejči (eds), *Abusir and Saqqara in the year 2010* (Prague, 2011), 261 - 311.

Cherpion, *Mastabas* N. Cherpion, *Mastabas et hypogées d'Ancien Empire* (Bruxelles, 1989).

Clark, *Tomb security* R. Clark, *Tomb security in Ancient Egypt from the Predynastic to the Pyramid age* (Oxford, 2016).

Clarke, *Construction* S. Clarke, R. Engelbach, *Egyptian Construction and Architecture* (New York, original edition 1930, 2nd edition 1990).

Coffin A long narrow box, not made of stone, in which a dead body is buried or cremated (Oxford dictionaries).

(compound) *serekh* false door A *serekh* false door flanked at both sides by a group of three plain compound niches.

CP Abbreviation for "Co-occurrence Percentage", the number of co-occurrences between two (sub) themes expressed as a percentage of the maximum number of co-occurrences possible between the two of them.

CPSD "Co-occurrence percentage surrounds discrepancy", a calculated value giving the quantified difference between a CP value and the CP values surrounding it in a table of CP values.

CRIPEL Cahier de recherches de l'Institut de papyrologie et égyptologie de Lille, Lille.

Davies, *Amarna II* N. de G. Davies, *The Rock Cut Tombs of El Amarna. Part II. The tombs of Panehesy and Meryra II* (London, 1905).

Davies, *Townhouse* N. de G. Davies, "The Townhouse in Ancient Egypt", Metropolitan Museum Studies, Vol. I, 2(1929), 223 – 55.

Davies, *Rekh-mi-Re'* N. de G. Davies, *Paintings from the tomb of Rekh-mi-Re'* (New York, 1935).

Dawood, *Burial chamber decoration* K. Dawood Khaled, "Animate Decoration and Burial Chambers of Private Tombs during the Old Kingdom. New Evidence from the Tomb of Kairer at Saqqara", in *Des Néferkarê aux Montouhotep. Travaux archéologiques en cours sur la fin de la VIe dynastie et la Première Période Intermédiaire. Actes du colloque CNRS – université Lumière Lyon 2, tenu le 5-7juillet 2001* (Lyon : Maison de l'Orient et de la Méditerranée Jean Pouilloux, 2005), 107-127. http://www.persee.fr/doc/mom_1955-4982_2005_act_40_1_2395.

Deglin, *Wood* F. Deglin, *Wood exploitation in ancient Egypt: where, who and how?* In H. Abd el-Gawad, *et al.* (eds), "Current Research in Egyptology 2011. Proceedings of the Twelfth Symposium Durham University 2011 (Oxford, 2012), 85 – 96.

Der Manualian, *Redi-nes* P. Der Mauelian, "The Giza Mastaba Niche and full frontal view figure of Redi-nes in the Museum of Fine Arts, Boston", in D. P. Silverman (ed.), *For his Ka. Essays offered in memory of Klaus Baer* (Chicago, 1994), 55 – 78.

Der Manuelian, *Presenting scroll* P. Der Manuelian, "Presenting the Scroll: Papyrus Documents in Tomb Scenes of the Old Kingdom" in P. Der Manuelian (ed.), *Studies in Honor of William Kelly Simpson* (Boston, 1996), 563-88.

Der Manuelian, *Giza slab stelae* P. Der Manuelian, "The Problem of the Giza Slab Stelae", in H. Gunksh and D. Polz (eds), *Stationen, Beiträge zur Kulturgeschichte Ägyptens. Rainer Stadelmann gewidmet* (Mainz, 1998), 115-34.

Der Manuelian, *Hemiunu* P. Der Manuelian, "Hemiunu, Pehenptah, and German/American Collaboration at the Giza Necropolis (Giza Archives Gleanings: II)", in A. Spiekermann (ed.), *"Zur Zierde gereicht...." Festschrift Bettina Schmitz zum Geburtstag am 24. Juli 2008"* (Hildesheim, 2008), 29 – 57.

Der Manuelian, *Gmast 8* P. Der Manuelian, *Mastabas of Nucleus Cemetery G 2100. Part I: Major mastabas G 2100 – G 2200* in W. K. Simpson and P. Der Manuelian (eds), Giza Mastabas, Vol. 8 (Boston, 2009).

Der Manuelian, *Wadi cemetery* P. Der Manuelian, «On the early history of Giza: The « lost » Wadi Cemetery (Giza Archive gleanings, III), JEA, 95(2009), 105 – 40.

Davies, *Akhet-hotep I* N. de Garis Davies, *The Mastaba of Ptahhetep and Akhethetep* (London, 1900).

Davies, *Amarna II* N. de Garis Davies, *The rock tombs of El Amarna. Part II. The tombs of Panehesy and Meryra II.* (London, 1905).

Dissociation The tendency of themes not to be placed together on the same wall, or wall section, or on the false door or a part of it.

Dobrev, *Tables d'offerandes* V. Dobrev and J. Leclant, "Les tables d'offerandes de particuliers découvertes aux complexes funéraires des reines près de la pyramide de Pépi Ier", in N. Grimal (ed.), *Les critères de datation stylistique à l'Ancien Empire* (Le Caire, 1997), 143-7.

Dodson, *Tomb* A. Dodson, S. Ikram, *The Tomb in Ancient Egypt* (London, 2008).

Donadoni, *Sarcofagi* A. M. Donadoni Roveri, *I Sarcofagi Egizi dalle origini alla fine dell'Antico Regno* (Roma, 1969).

Drenkhahn, *Handwerker* R. Drenkhahn, *Die Handwerker und ihre Tätigkeiten im Alten Ägypten* (Wiesbaden, 1976).

Dreyer, *Abydos, Den* G. Dreyer, "Umm el-Qaab. Nachuntersuchungen im frühzeitlichen Königsfriedhof. 3./4. Vorbericht", MDAIK, 46(1990), 53 – 89.

Dreyer, *U-j* G. Dreyer, "Umm el-Qaab. Nachuntersuchungen im frühzeitlichen Königsfriedhof. 5./6. Vorbericht", MDAIK, 49 (1993), 23 - 62.

Dreyer, *Messergriffe* G. Dreyer, "Motive und Datierung der dekorierten prädynastischen Messergriffe", in C. Ziegler (ed.), *L'art de l'Ancien Empire égyptien* (Paris, 1999), 195 – 226.

Dreyer, *Royal burial* G. Dreyer, « Tomb U-j : A royal burial of dynasty 0 at Abydos », in E. Teeter (ed.), *Before the Pyramids. The origins of Egyptian Civilization* (Chicago, 2011), 127 – 36.

Dreyer, *Dewen* G. Dreyer, "Eine Statue des Konigs Dewen aus Abydos ? », in S. d'Auria (ed.), *Offerings to the Discerning Eye. An Egyptological medley in Honor of Jack A. Josephson* (Leiden, 2010), 73 – 8.

Drioton, *Ishethi* E. Driotin and J. – Ph. Lauer, "Un groupe de tombes à Saqqara", ASAE, 55(1958), 207 – 51.

Duell, *Mereruka I* P. Duell, *Mereruka, part I, Chambers A 1-10, plates 1-103* (Chicago, 1938).

Duell, *Mereruka II* P. Duell, *Mereruka, part II, Chambers A 11-13, plates 104-219* (Chicago, 1938).

Dunham, *Prince Ankh-haf* D. Dunham, "The Portrait Bust of Prince Ankh-haf", BMFA, 37 (1939), 41 – 6.

Dunham, *Gmast 1* D. Dunham, W. K. Simpson, *The mastaba of Queen Meresankh III, Giza Mastaba, Vol. 1* (Boston, 1974).

EA Egyptian Archaeology, The Bulletin of the Egypt Exploration Society, London.

El- Fikey, *Re'-wer* S. A. El – Fikey, *The tomb of the Vizier Re'-wer at Saqqara* (Warminster, 1980).

El- Tayeb, *Rashepses* H. El- Tabey, "Some Rare Scenes in the Tomb of Rashepses at Saqqara", in P. Jánosi and H. Vymazalová (eds), *The Art of Describing. The World of Tomb Decoration as Visual Culture of the Old Kingdom* (Prague, 2018), 289 – 307.

Emery, *Hor-Aha* W. B. Emery, *Excavations at Saqqara, 1937 - 1938. HOR-AḤA* (Cairo, 1939).

Emery, *Archaic Egypt* W. B. Emery, *Archaic Egypt* (London, reprint 1991).

Emic The point of view when a system is studied employing criteria being inherent to the system itself.

Endesfelder, *Entstehung staates* E. Endesfelder, *Beobachtungen zur Entstehung des altägyptischen Staates,* IBAES, XIV(2011).

Etic The point of view when a system is studied employing criteria being inherent to a system other than the system under study.

Fischer, *Varia nova* H. G. Fischer, *Varia Nova. Egyptian Studies III* (New York, 1996), 91 – 102.

Fisher, *Minor cemetery* C. S. Fisher, *The Minor Cemetery at Giza* (Philadelphia, 1924).

Flentye, *Ankh-haf* L. Flentye, "The Mastabas of Ankh-haf (G 7510) and Akhethetep and Meretites (G 7650) in the Eastern Cemetery at Giza: A Reassesment" in Z. Hawass and J. Richards (eds), *The Archaeology and Arts of Ancient Egypt. Essays in Honor of David B. O'Connor* (Cairo, 2007), 291 – 308.

Flentye, *Statuary* L. Flentye, "Royal and non-royal statuary of the Fourth Dynasty from the Giza Necropolis" in M. Bárta, F. Coppens and J. Krejčí (eds), *Abusir and Saqqara in the year 2015* (Prague, 2017), 123 – 44.

Forschler, *Wood preference* Tae-Young Lee and B. T. Forschler, « Ranking Wood Preference of subterranean termite *Reticulitermes virginicus* (Banks) tsing Two-, Four-, and No-Choice Experimental Designs", in B. T. Forschler (ed.), *Proceedings of the 10th Pacific-Termite Research Group Conference*

FO Abbreviation for "Frequency of Occurrence", the frequency with which a subject under study occurs in a population, expressed as a percentage of a defined number of attributes, the character of which is determined by the subject under study.

Forshaw, *Lector* R. Forshaw, *The role of the Lector in Ancient Egyptian Society* (Oxford, 2014).

Friedman, *Djoser* F. D. Friedman, "The Underground Relief Panels of King Djoser at the Step Pyramid Complex", JARCE, 32(1995), 1 – 42.

Friedman, *Cosmos* F. D. Friedman, "Notions of Cosmos in the Step Pyramid Complex", in P. Der Manuelian (ed.), *Studies in Honor of William Kelly Simpson,* Vol. I (Boston, 1996), 337 – 51.

Friedman, *Hierakonpolis* R. Friedman, "Hierakonpolis", in E. Teeter (ed.), *Before the Pyramids. The origins of Egyptian Civilization* (Chicago, 2011), 33 – 44.

Funerary container A long narrow box intended to contain the mortal remains of the deceased

Funerary All architectural expressions and cultic activities which are connected with the burial of the tomb owner (for the definition of cult see Verma, *Cultural expression,* 269).

Funerary offerings The grave goods that are brought to the tomb on the day of the burial, and that were intended to stay with the tomb owner in his house for eternity.

Garstang, *Bêt Khallâf* J. Garstang, *Mâhasna and Bêt Khallâf* (London, 1903).

GM Göttinger Miszellen, Beiträge zur ägyptologischen Diskussion, Göttingen.

Gourdon, *Djedefra* Y. Gourdon, "The Royal Necropolis of Dejedefra at Abu Rawsh (seasons 2001 – 2005)", in M. Bárta, F. Coppens, J. Krejčí (eds), *Abusir and Saqqara in the year 2005* (Prague, 2006), 247 – 56.

Grajetzki, *Tarkhan* W. Grajetzki, "The architecture and the signification of the Tarkhan mastabas", Archéo-Nil, 18(2008), 103 – 12.

Great door niche (= *serekh* type false door) A unit of three plain compound niches, of which the niche in the middle has been elongated.

Gunn, *Inscriptions* B. Gunn, "Inscriptions from the Step Pyramid site", ASAE, 26(1926), 177 – 96.

Handoussa, *Abu Bakr cemetery* T. Handoussa, E. Brovarski, "New research in the Abu Bakr cemetery at Giza", EA, 27(2005), 34 – 6.

Hannig, *Handwörterbuch* R. Hannig, *Grosses Handwörterbuch Ägyptisch - Deutsch* (Mainz, 2001).

Harpur, *DETOK* Y. Harpur, *Decoration in Egyptian Tombs of the Old Kingdom* (London, New York, 1987).

Harpur, *Maidum* Y. Harpur, *The Tombs of Nefermaat and Rahotep at Maidum* (Oxford, 2001).

Harvey, *Wooden statues* J. Harvey, *Wooden Statues of the Old Kingdom. A typological Study* (Leiden, Boston, Köln, 2001).

Hassan, *Giza* S. Hassan, *Excavations at Giza,* 10 Vols (Oxford, Cairo, 1932-1960).

Hawass, *Dwarf statue* Z. Hawass, "The Statue of the Dwarf *Pr-n(j)-ʿnḫ(w)* Recently Discovered at Giza", MDAIK, 47(1991), 157 -62.

Hawass, *Khafre* Z. Hawass, "Discoveries in Front of Khafre's Lower temple: The *jbw* and *R-š*" in V. Verschoor, A. J. Stuart and C. Demarée (eds), *Imaging and Imagining The Memphite Necropolis. Liber Amicorum René van Walsem* (Leiden, 2017), 9 - 29.

Hays, *Funerary rituals* H. M. Hays, « Funerary Rituals (Pharaonic Period), , in J. Dieleman, W. Wendrich (eds),*UCLA, Encyclopedia of Egyptology , Los Angeles* (UEE, 2010).

Hayes, *Scepter I* W. C. Hayes, *The Scepter of Egypt,* Volume I (New York, 1978).

Hendrickx, *Decorated pottery* S. Hendrickx, « Checklist of predynastic « Decorated » pottery with human figures », Cahiers Caribéens d'Egyptologie, 3-4(2002), 29 - 50.

Hendrickx, *Royal scene* S. Hendrickx *et al.*, "A lost Late Predynastic-Early Dynastic royal scene from Gharb Aswan", Archéo-Nil, 19(2009), 169 - 78.

Hoffmann, *Amratian house* M. A. Hoffmann, "A rectangular Amratian house from Hierakonpolis and its significance for predynastic research", JNES, 39(2) (1980), 119 - 37.

Hölscher, *Chephren* U. Hölscher, *Das Grabdenkmal des Königs Chephren* (Leipzig, 1912).

Hornung, *Book of the dead* E. Hornung, *Die Unterwelts-Bücher der Ägypter* (Düsseldorf, 2002).

IBAES Internet-Beiträge zur Ägyptologie und Sududanarchäologie, Berlin, London.

ICMOAPS Institut des Cultures Méditerranéennes et Orientales de l'Académie Polonaise des Sciences, Warszawa.

Ikram, *Food* S. Ikram, "Food and Funerals sustaining the dead for eternity", PAM, 20 (Research 2008), 361 - 71.

JAEA The Journal of Ancient Egyptian Architecture.

Jánosi, *Giza* P. Jánosi, *Giza in der 4. Dynastie. Die Baugeschichte und Belegung einer Nekropole des Alten Reiches. Band I : Die Mastabas des Kernfriedhöfe und die Felsgräber* (Wien, 2005).

Jánosi, *Burial chamber* P. Jánosi, H. Vymazalová, "The Decorated Burial Chamber of *Ppy-ʿnḫ S̱tw* at South Saqqara", in P. Jánosi and H. Vymazalová (eds), *The Art of Describing. The World of Tomb Decoration as Visual Culture of the Old Kingdom* (Prague, 2018), 215 - 34.

JARCE Journal of the American Research Center in Egypt, Boston.

JEA Journal of Egyptian Archaeology, London.

Jéquier, *Pyramides reines* G. Jéquier, *Fouilles à Saqqara. Les Pyramides des Reines Neit et Apouit* (Le Caire, 1933).

JNES Journal of Near Eastern Studies, Chicago.

Jones, *Index I* D. Jones, *An Index of Ancient Egyptian Titles, Epithets and Phrases of the Old Kingdom,* Vol. I (Oxford, 2000).

Junker, *Vorbericht 1914* H. Junker, *Vorläufiger Bericht über die Grabung bei den Pyramiden von Gizeh von 3. Januar bis 23. April 1914* (Wien, 1914).

Junker, *Giza* H. Junker, *Giza, Grabungen auf dem Friedhof des Alten Reiches,*12 Vols (Wien, Leipzig, 1922-1955).

Kaiser, *Königsfriedhof* W. Kaiser, G. Dreyer, „Umm el-Qaab. Nachuntersuchungen in frühzeitlichen Königsfriedhof. 2. Vorbericht", 38(1982), 211 - 69.

Kanawati, *Teti cemetery V* N. Kanawati and M. Abder - Raziq, *The Teti cemetery at Saqqara, Volume V, The Tomb of Hesi* (Warminster, 1999).

Kanawati, *The tomb* N. Kanawati, *The tomb and Beyond. Burial Customs of Egyptian Officials* (Warminster, 2001).

Kanawati, *Giza I* N. Kanawati, *Tombs at Giza, Volume I, Kaiemankh (G 4561) and Seshemnefer I (G 4940)* (Warminster, 2001).

Kanawati, *Giza II* N. Kanawati, *Tombs at Giza, Volume II, Seshathetep/Heti (G 5150), Nesutnefer (G 4970) and Seshemnefer II (G 5080)* (Warminster, 2002).

Kanawati, *Conspiracies* N. Kanawati, *Conspiracies in the Egyptian Palace. Unis to Pepy I* (London, 2005).

Kanawati, *Teti cemetery VIII* N. Kanawati, *The Teti Cemetery at Saqqara, Volume VIII. The Tomb of Inumin* (Oxford, 2006).

Kaplony, *Methethi* P. Kaplony, *Studien zum Grab des Methethi* (Bern, 1976).

Kayser, *Mastaba* H. Kayser, *Die Mastaba des Uhemka* (Hannover, 1964).

Kemp, *Ancient Egypt* B. J. Kemp, *Ancient Egypt. Anatomy of a Civilization* (London, 1989).

Kloth, *Biographische Inschriften* N. Kloth, *Die (auto) biografische Inschriften des ägyptischen Alten Reiches: Untersuchungen zu Phraseologie und Entwicklung* (Hamburg, 2002).

KMKG Koninklijke Museum voor Kunst en Geschiedenis (Royal Museum for Art and History), Brussels.

Koeningsberger, *Tür* O. Koeningsberger, *Die Konstruktion der ägyptische Tür,* ÄF 2, (Glückstadt, 1936).

Kormysheva, *Lepsius* E. Kormysheva and S. Malykh, "Lepsius Tombs in the Giza necropolis rediscovered: Preliminary report on the Russian Archaeological Mission at Giza Excavations 2006 - 2008", JEA, 96(2010), 49 - 70.

Krejči, *Abusir XI* J. Krejči, *The Architecture of the Mastaba of Ptahshepses* (Prague, 2009).

Krejči, *Abusir XII* J. Krejči, *et al., Minor Tombs in the Royal Necropolis. The Mastabas of Nebtyemneferes and Nakhtsare, Pyramid Complex Lepsius no. 24 and Tomb Complex Lepsius no. 25* (Prague, 2008).

Krejči, *Abusir XVIII* J. Krejči, *Abusir XVIII. The Royal necropolis on Abusir* (Prague, 2010).

Krejči, *AC 31* J. Krejči, "Archaeological excavations of tomb AC 31 in Abusir Centre. A preliminary report", PES, 17(2016), 12 - 23.

Kuentz, *Bassins* C. Kuentz, "Bassins et tables d'offrandes", BIFAO, 81.1(1981), 243 - 82.

Kuraszkiewicz, *Practical, ritual* K. O. Kuraszkiewicz, "The practical behind the ritual. Observations on the Sixth Dynasty funerary architecture", in M. Barta, F. Coppens and J. Krejči (eds), *Abusir and Saqqara in the year 2010* (Prague, 2011), 530 - 6.

Kuraszkiewicz, *Ikhti* K. O. Kuraszkiewicz, "The Tomb of Ikhi/Mery in Saqqara and Royal Expeditions During the Sixth Dynasty, ICMOAPS, XXVII(2014), 202 - 16.

LÄ W. Helck and E. Otto, *Lexikon der Ägyptologie,* 7 Vols. (Wiesbaden, 1975-1986).

La Loggia, *Engineering* A. S. La Loggia, *Engineering and Construction in Egypt's Early Dynastic Period. A review of Mortuary Structures. Vol. I* (Sydney, 2012).

Lauer, *Saqqara* J.- Ph. Lauer, *Saqqara. The Royal cemetery of Memphis. Excavations and discoveries since 1850* (London, 1976).

Lauer, *Imhotep* J.- Ph. Lauer, „Remarques concernant l'inscription d'Imhotep gravée sur le socle de statue de l'Horus Neteri-khet (roi Djoser)", in P. Der Manuelian (ed.), *Studies in Honor of William Kelly Simpson*, Vol. II (Boston, 1996), 493 - 8.

LD K.R. Lepsius, *Denkmäler aus Aegypten und Aethiopien*, (plates), 6 Vols (Berlin, 1849-1859).

LD, *Erg.* K.R. Lepsius, *Denkmäler aus Aegypten und Aethiopien*, Ergänzungsband (Leipzig, 1913).

Legros, *Cultes privés* R. Legros, „La disparition d'une élite? Les cultes privés de la nécropole de Pépy Ier à Saqqara", CRIPEL, 28(2009 - 2010), 1 - 21.

Lehmann, *Serdab III* K. Lehmann, *Der Serdab in den Privatgräbern des Alten Reiches*, Doctoral Thesis, University of Heidelberg (Heidelberg, 2000).

Lehner, *Hetep-heres* M. Lehner, *The Pyramid Tomb of Hetep-heres and the Satellite Pyramid of Khufu* (Mainz, 1985).

Lehner, *Khentkaues* M. Lehner, *et al.*, "Re-examining the Khentkaues Town" in N. Strudwick and H. Strudwick (eds), *Old Kingdom, New Perspectives. Egytian Art and Archaeology 2750 - 2150 BC* (Oxford, 2011), 143 - 91.

Lehner, *Shareholders* M. Lehner, "Shareholders: The Menkaure Valley Temple Occupation in Context", in P. Der Manuelian, T. Schneider (eds), *Towards a New History for the Egyptian Old Kingdom* (Leiden, Boston, 2015), 227 - 314.

Lehner, *Giza* M. Lehner, Z. Hawass, *Giza and the Pyramids* (London, 2017).

Lichtheim, *Literature I* M. Lichtheim, *Ancient Egyptian Literature, Vol. I: The Old and Middle Kingdom* (Berkeley, Los Angeles, London, 1975).

Lieven, *Deified humans* A. von Lieven, "Deified Humans" , in J. Dieleman, W. Wendrich (eds),*UCLA, Encyclopedia of Egyptology , Los Angeles* (UEE, 2010).

Lutz, *Offering stones* H. F. Lutz, *Egyptian tomb and offering stones of the Museum of Anthropology and Ethnology of the University of California* (Leipzig, 1927).

Mawdsley, *Tarkhan* L. Mawdsley, "Rediscovering Tarkhan", WAMCEAS, 9(2012), 23 - 32.

Marée, *Edfu* M. Marée, « Edfu under the Twelfth to Seventeenth Dynasties : The monuments in the National Museum of Warsaw », BMSAES, 12(2009), 31 - 92.

Mariette, *Mastaba* A. Mariette, *Les Mastaba de l'ancien Empire* (Paris, 1885).

Marochetti, *Coffin Gebelein* E. F. Marochetti *et al.*, ""Le Paquet" : Sépulture anonyme de la IVe dynastie provenant de Gébélein", BIFAO, 103(2003), 235 - 56.

Marochetti, *Gebelein* E. F. Marochetti, « Gebelein », in J. Dieleman, W. Wendrich (eds),*UCLA, Encyclopedia of Egyptology , Los Angeles* (UEE, 2013).

Martin, *CAA 3* K. Martin, *CAA, Pelizaeus-Museum Hildesheim, Lieferung 3* (Mainz, 1978).

Martin, *CAA 8* K. Martin, CAA, *Pelizaeus-Museum Hildesheim, Lieferung 8* (Mainz, 1980).

McFarlane, *Kaiemheset* A. McFarlane, *Mastabas at Saqqara. Kaiemheset, Kaipunesut, Kaiemsenu, Sehetepu and Others* (Oxford, 2003).

MDAIK Mitteilungen des Deutschen Archäeologischen Instituts, Abteilung Kairo, Kairo.

MET or MMA Metropolitan Museum of Art, New York.

Mohr, *Hetep-her-akhty* H. T. Mohr, *The Mastaba of Hetep-her-akhty. Studies on an Egyptian Tomb Chapel in the Museum of Antiquities, Leiden* (Leiden, 1943).

Monnet Saleh, *Tomb 100* J. Monnet Saleh, « Remarques sur les Représentations de la peinture d'Hierakonpolis (Tombe No 100), JEA, 73(1987), 51 - 8.

Montet, *Vie privée* P. Montet, *Les scenes de la vie privée dans les tombeaux égyptiens de l'Ancien Empire* (Paris, 1925).

Morales, *Veneration* A. Morales, "Traces of official and popular veneration to Nyuserra Iny at Abusir. Late Fifth Dynasty to the Middle Kingdom", in M. Bárta, F. Coppens, J. Krejčí (eds), *Abusir and Saqqara in the year 2005* (Prague, 2006), 311 - 41.

Morgan, *Ptah-chepsés* J. de Morgan, "Découverte du mastaba de Ptah-chepsés dans la nécropole d'Abou-Sir", Revue Archéologique, 24(1894), 18 - 33.

Morris, *Saqqara mastabas* E. F. Morris, "On the Ownership of the Saqqara Mastabas and the Allotment of Political and Ideological Power at the Dawn of the State", in Z. A. Hawass and J. Richards (eds), *The Archaeology and Art of Ancient Egypt. Essays in Honor of David B. O'Connor*, 2 Vols. (Le Caire, 2007), 171 - 90.

Morris, *Sacrifice* E. F. Morris, "Sacrifice for the State: First Dynasty Royal Funerals and the Rites at Macramallah's Rectangle", in *Performing Death. Social analyses of Funerary Traditions in the Ancient Near East and Mediterranean* (Chicago, 2007), 15 - 37.

Mortuary All architectural expressions and cultic activities which are connected with the regular offerings made to the tomb owner for the sustenance of the *k3*.

Mortuary offerings The regular offerings as described in the term "Mortuary" (Ritual Opfer).

Mourad, *Ptahhotep I* A.-L. Mourad, *The tomb of Ptahhotep I* (Oxford, 2015).

Moussa, *Craftsmen* A. M. Moussa, F. Junge, *Two Tombs of Craftsmen. Old Kingdom Tombs at the Causeway of King Unas at Saqqara* (Mainz, 1975).

Moussa, *Nianchchnum* A. M. Moussa, H. Altenmüller, *Das Grab des Nianchchnum und Chnumhotep* (Mainz, 1977).

Munro, *Unas-Friedhof* P. Munro, *Der Unas-Friedhof Nord-West I* (Mayence, 1993).

Naville, *Deir el Bahari II* E. Naville, *The Temple of Deir el Bahari, Part II* (London, 1897).

Nour, *Cheops boats* M. Z. Nour, *et al.*, *The Cheops Boats, Part I* (Cairo, 1960).

Nováková, *Sarcophagi* V. Nováková, "Old Kingdom sarcophagi – The Abusir corpus", in I. Incordino *et al.*, *Currrent Reasearch in Egyptology 2017. Proceedings of the Eighteenth Annual Symposium. University of Naples, "L'Orientale" 3 – 6 May 2017* (Oxford, 2018), 139 – 60.

O'Brian, *Serekh* A. O'Brian, *The Serekh as an Aspect of the Iconography of Early Kingship*, JARC, 33(1996), 123 – 38.

O'Connor, *Abydos* D. O'Connor, *Abydos. Egypt's First Pharaohs and the Cult of Osiris* (London, 2011).

Odler, *Tomb Abusir* M. Odler *et al.*, "New Egyptian tomb type found at Abusir South? Report on the excavations of mud brick complex AS 103", PES, XXI(2018), 73 – 93.

OEE Oxford Expedition to Egypt: Scene-details Database (Linacre College, Oxford (2006) Oxford Expedition to Egypt: Scene-details Database [data-set]. York: Archaeology Data Service [distributor] (https://doi.org/10.5284/1000009).

OIM Oriental Institute Museum, Chicago.

O'Neill, *Setting the scene* B. O'Neill, *Setting the Scene: The deceased and regenerative cult within offering table imagery of the Egyptian Old to Middle Kingdom* (Oxford, 2015).

PAM Polish Archaeology in the Mediterranean, Warsaw.

Papazian, *Eight dynasty* H. Papazian, "The State of Egypt in the Eight Dynasty", in P. Der Manuelian and T. Schneider (eds), *Towards a New History for the Egyptian Old Kingdom* (Leiden, Boston, 2015), 393 – 428.

Payne, *Tomb 100* J. Crowfoot Payne, "Tomb 100: The decorated tomb at Hierokonpolis confirmed", JEA, 59 (1973), 31-43.

Perrot, *Histoire*, G. Perrot, C. Chipiez, *Histoire de l'Art dans l'antiquité, Tome I, L'Egypte* (Paris, 1882).

PES Prague Egyptological Studies, Prague.

Petrie, *Kahun* W. M. Flinders Petrie, *Kahun, Gurob, and Hawara* (London, 1890).

Petrie, *Medum* W. M. Flinders Petrie, *Medum* (London, 1892).

Petrie, *Naqada, Ballas* W. M. Flinders Petrie and J. E. Quibell, *Naqada and Ballas* (London, 1896).

Petrie, *Deshasheh* W. M. Flinders Petrie, *Deshasheh* (London, 1898).

Petrie, *Royal tombs I* W. M. Flinders Petrie, *The Royal Tombs of the First Dynasties*, Vol. I (London, 1900).

Petrie, *Royal tombs II* W. M. Flinders Petrie, *The Royal Tombs of the earliest Dynasties*, Vol. II (London, 1901).

Petrie, *Sinai* W. M. Flinders Petrie, *Researches in Sinai* (New York, 1906).

Petrie, *Gizeh and Rifeh* W. M. Flinders Petrie, *Gizeh and Rifeh* (London, 1907).

Petrie, *Arts & crafts* W. M. Flinders Petrie, *The Arts and Crafts of Ancient Egypt* (Edinburh and London, 1909).

Petrie, *Meydum and Memphis* W. M. Flinders Petrie, *Meydum and Memphis (III)* (London, 1910).

Petrie, *Labyrinth* W. M. Flinders Petrie, *The Labyrinth, Gerzeh and Mazhuneh* (London, 1912).

Petrie, *Tarkhan I* W. M. Flinders Petrie, *Tarkhan I and Memphis V* (London, 1913).

Petrie, *Tarkhan II* W. M. Flinders Petrie and G. A. Wainwright, *Tarkhan II* (London, 1913).

Petrie, *Courtiers* W. M. Flinders Petrie *et al.*, *Tombs of the Courtiers and Oxyrhynhos* (London, 1925).

Petrie, *Memphite chapels* H. Flinders Petrie and M. A. Murray, *Seven Memphite tomb chapels* (London, 1952).

PM, I B. Porter and R. L. B. Moss, *Topographical Bibliography of Ancient Egyptian Hieroglyphic Texts, Reliefs and Paintings*, Vol. I, part I, The Theban Necropolis, Part 1. Private Tombs (2nd ed., revised and augmented, Oxford, 1970).

PM, I/2 B. Porter and R. L. B. Moss, *Topographical Bibliography of Ancient Egyptian Hieroglyphic Texts, Reliefs and Paintings*, Vol. I, part II, The Theban Necropolis, Part 2. Royal Tombs and smaller cemeteries (2nd ed., revised and augmented, Oxford, 1964).

PM, III/1 B. Porter and R. L. B. Moss, *Topographical Bibliography of Ancient Egyptian Hieroglyphic Texts, Reliefs and Paintings*, Vol. III, part 1, Memphis, Abû Rawâsh to Abûsir, (2nd ed., revised and expanded by J. Málek, Oxford, 1994).

PM, III/2 B. Porter and R. L. B. Moss, *Topographical Bibliography of Ancient Egyptian Hieroglyphic Texts, Reliefs and Paintings*, Vol. III, part 2, Memphis, Saqqâra to Dahshûr, (2nd ed., revised and expanded by J. Málek (Oxford, 1981).

PM, IV B. Porter and R. L. B. Moss, *Topographical Bibliography of Ancient Egyptian Hieroglyphic Texts, Reliefs and Paintings*, Vol. IV, Lower and Middle Egypt (Oxford, 1968).

PM, V B. Porter and R. L. B. Moss, *Topographical Bibliography of Ancient Egyptian Hieroglyphic Texts, Reliefs and Paintings*, Vol. V, Upper Egypt: Sites (Oxford, 1962).

PT R. O. Faulkner, *The Ancient Egyptian Pyramid Texts* (Warminster, 1969).

Ptahshepses, *Preliminary report Preliminary Report on Czechoslovak Excavations in the Mastaba of Ptahshepses at Abusir* (Prague, 1976).

Quibell, *El Kab* J. E. Quibell, *El Kab* (London, 1898).

Quibell, *Hierakonpolis I* J. E. Quibell, *Hierakonpolis*, Part I (London, 1900).

Quibell, *Hierakonpolis II* J. E. Quibell and F. W. Green, *Hierakonpolis*, Part II (London, 1902).

Quibell, *Hesy* J. E. Quibell, *Excavations at Saqqara (1911-12). The Tomb of Hesy* (Le Caire, 1913).

Quirke, *Religion* S. Quirke, *Ancient Egyptian Religion* (London, 1992).

Radwan, *Abusir* A. Radwan, "Ein Treppengrab der 1. Dynastie aus Abusir", MDAIK, 47(1991), 305 – 8.

Radwan, *Mastaba XVII* A. Radwan, "Mastaba XVII at Abusir (First Dynasty) preliminary results and general remarks", in M. Barta and J. Krejči (eds), *Abusir and Saqqara in the year 2000* (Prague, 2000), 509 – 14.

Randell, *El Amrah* D. Randell – Maciver, *El Amrah and Abydos* (London, 1902).

Reisner, *Preliminary report* G. A. Reisner, C. S. Fisher, "Preliminary report on the work of the Harvard - Boston Expedition in 1911 - 1913", ASAE, 13(1913), 227 - 52.

Reisner, *Meresankh* G. A. Reisner, "The Tomb of Meresankh, a Great-Granddaughter of Queen Hetep-Heres I and Sneferuw", BMFA, 25(1927), 64 - 79.

Reisner, *Mycerinus* G. A. Reisner, *Mycerinus. The temples of the third pyramid at Giza* (Cambridge (Mass.), 1931).

Reisner, *Estate stewards* G. A. Reisner, "A Family of Royal Estate Stewards of Dynasty V", BMFA, XXXVII (1932), 29-35.

Reisner, *Grave stelae* G. A. Reisner, "The position of the Grave stelae", in S. R. K. Glanville, N. Macdonald Griffith (eds), *Studies presented to F. Ll. Griffith* (London, 1932), 324 - 331.

Reisner, *History mastaba* G. A. Reisner, "The history of the Egyptian mastaba" in *Mélanges Maspero,* Vol. I, (Cairo, 1934), 579-84.

Reisner, *Tomb development* G. A. Reisner, *The Development of the Egyptian Tomb down to the Accession of Cheops* (Cambridge (Mass.), 1936).

Reisner, *Giza I* G. A. Reisner, *A History of the Giza Necropolis,* Vol. I (Oxford, London, 1942).

Roeten, *Functions* L. H. Roeten, "Special functions of the decoration of Old Kingdom mastabas", GM, 228 (2011), 65 - 75.

Roeten, *Decoration* L. H. Roeten, *The Decoration of the Cult Chapel Walls of the Old Kingdom Tombs at Giza. A New Approach to their Interaction* (Leiden, Boston, 2014).

Roeten, *Economic decline* L. H. Roeten, *Chronological development in the Old Kingdom tombs in the necropoleis of Giza, Saqqara and Abusir* (Oxford, 2016).

Roeten, *Osiris* L. H. Roeten, *Loaves, beds, plants and Osiris. Considerations about the emergence of the Cult of Osiris* (Oxford, 2018).

Romano, *Royal sculpture* F. F. Romano, « Sixth dynasty royal sculpture », N. Grimal (ed.), *Les critères de datation stylistiques à l'Ancien Empire* (Le Caire, 1997), 235 - 303.

Rosso, *Vipère sans tête* B. Rosso, "La vipère à cornes sans tête. Étude paléographique et considerations historiques", BIFAO, 110(2010), 251 - 74.

Roth, *Opening of the mouth* A. M. Roth, "The *pšs-kf* and the 'opening of the mouth' ceremony", JEA, 78(1992), 113 - 47.

Roth, *Social change* A. M. Roth, "Social change in the fourth Dynasty", JARCE, 30(1993), 33 - 41.

Roth, *Gmast 6* A. M. Roth, *Cemetery of Palace Attendants. Including G 2084-2099, G 2230 + 2231 and G 2240* in W. K. Simpson and P. Der Manuelian (eds), Giza Mastabas, Vol. 6 (Boston, 1995).

Rusch, *Grabsteinformen* A. Rusch, "Die Entwicklung der Grabsteinformen im Alten Reich", ZÄS, 58(1923), 101 -24.

Rzeuska, *Funerary customs* T. Rzeuska, "Funerary customs and rites on the Old Kigdom necropolis in West Saqqara" in M. Bárta, F. Coppens, J. Krejčí (eds), *Abusir and Saqqara in the year 2005* (Prague, 2006), 353 - 84..

Sarcophagus A stone box, meant to hold a body, with or without decoration or inscription.

SBAW Sitzungsberichte der Bayerischen Akademie der Wissenschaften, Phil.-hist. Kl., Berlin.

Scharff, *Wohnhaus* A. Scharff, *Das Grab als Wohnhaus in der ägyptischen Frühzeit,* SBAW, Jahrgang 1944/46, Heft 6 (München, 1947).

Signalling role The function of some themes to signal the ownership of the tomb by means of depiction and text.

Simpson, *Gmast 2* W.K. Simpson, *The Mastabas of Qar and Idu. G 7101 and 7102,* Giza Mastabas, Vol. 2 (Boston, 1976).

Simpson, *Gmast 3* W.K. Simpson, *The Mastabas of Kawab, Khafkhufu I and II,* Giza Mastabas, Vol. 3 (Boston, 1978).

Simpson, *Gmast 4* W. K. Simpson, *Mastabas of the Western Cemetery: Part I,* Vol. 4 (Boston, 1980).

Snape, *Egyptian tombs* S. Snape, *Ancient Egyptian Tombs. The Culture of Life and Death* (Chichester, 2011).

Soleiman, *Ptahshepses* S. Soleiman, « The Inscribed Lintel of Ptahshepses at Saqqara », JEA, 103/1(2017), 103 - 16.

Sourouzian, *L'iconographie* H. Sourouzian, "L'iconographie du roi dans la statuaire des trois premières dynasties », in *Kunst des Alten Reiches* (Mainz, 1995), 50 -6.

Spencer, *Naos Nekhthorheb* N. Spencer, "A Naos of Nekhthorheb from Bubastis. Religious Iconography and Temple Building in the 30th Dynasty » (London, 2006).

Stadelmann, *Pyramiden* R. Stadelmann, *Die ägyptischen Pyramiden. Vom Ziegelbau zum Weltwunder* (Mainz, 1991).

Stadelmann, *Strenge Stil* R. Stadelmann, „Der Strenge Stil der frühen Vierten Dynastie" in *Kunst des Alten Reiches* (Sonderschrift 28, Mainz, 1995), 155 - 66.

Stadelmann, *Famille royale* R. Stadelmann, „Représentations de la famille royale dans l'Ancien Empire", in C. Ziegler (ed.), *L'art del'Ancien Empire égyptien* (Paris, 1999), 169 - 92.

Staring, *Personal choice* N. Staring, „Fixed rules or personal choice? On the composition and arrangement of daily life scenes in Old Kingdom elite tombs", in N. Strudwick and H. Strudwick (eds), *Old Kingdom, New Perspectives. Egytian Art and Archaeology 2750 - 2150 BC* (Oxford, 2011), 256 - 69.

Steindorff, *Ti II* G. Steindorff, *Das Grab des Ti. Zweiter Band* (Leipzig, 1913).

Stevenson Smith, *HESPOK* W. Stevenson Smith, *A History of Egyptian Sculpture and Painting in the Old Kingdom* (London, 1946).

Stevenson Smith, *Archaic sculptures* W. Stevenson Smith, "Two Archaic Egyptian Sculptures", BMFA, 65(1967), 70 - 84.

Stevenson Smith, *Art and architecture* W. Stevenson Smith, *The Art and Architecture of Ancient Egypt* (revised edition with additions by W.K. Simpson) (New Haven, London, 1981).

(Sub)theme One of the (basic) items of the decoration of the architectural elements and the parts of the false door. With other (sub)themes it can form a group or scene and it consists of attributes.

Tavares, *House* A. Tavares and L. Yeomans, "A House Through Time: Building, Abandonment, and Intermingling", Aeragram, 10.2(2009), 10 -3.

Taylor, *Coffins* J. H. Taylor, *Egyptian Coffins* (Princes Risborough, 1989).

Taylor, *Papyrus Panebmontu* J. H. Taylor, « The Amduat Papyrus of Panebmontu », BMSAES, 23(2016), 135 – 51.

Teeter, *Origins* "Catalog of Objects", in E. Teeter (ed.), *Before the Pyramids. The origins of Egyptian Civilization* (Chicago, 2011), 162 – 3.

Theme A theme is the basic item of decoration; together with other themes it can from a group (a scene) and itself consist of attributes. An example is the theme of the standing tomb owner with family, the attributes are family, staff, scepter, name, title(s); the scene consists of the family group, offering bearers, dog, monkey.

Troche, *Letters to the dead* J. Troche, "Letters to the Dead", in J. Dieleman, W. Wendrich (eds),*UCLA, Encyclopedia of Egyptology , Los Angeles* (UEE, 2018).

TT Theban Tomb.

Verner, *Abusir I* M. Verner, *Abusir I. The Mastaba of Ptahshepses, Reliefs I/1* (Prague, 1977).

Verner, *Abusir III* M. Verner, *Abusir III. The pyramid complex of Khentkaus* (Prague, 2001).

Verner, *Abusir VI* M. Verner, V. G. Callender, *Djedkare's Family Cemetery* (Prague, 2002).

Verner, *Pyramids* M. Verner, *The Pyramids. Their Archaeology and History* (Prague, 1997, English edition, London, 2003).

Verner, *Abusir IX* M. Verner, *The Pyramid Complex of Raneferef. The Archaeology* (Prague, 2006).

Verner, *Chronology* M. Verner, "The system of dating in the Old Kingdom" in H. Vymazalová and M. Bárta (eds), *Chronology and Archaeology in Ancient Egypt (The third millennium B.C.)* (Prague, 2008), 23 - 43.

Vlćková, *Abusir south* P. Vlćková, "Abusir South and the End of the Old Kingdom", in K. Piqette and S. Love (eds), *Current Research in Egyptology 2003* (Oxford, 2005), 163 – 78.

Walsem, van, *Iconography* R. van Walsem, *Iconography of Old Kingdom Elite Tombs. Analysis & Interpretation, Theoretical and Methodological Aspects* (Leyden, Louvain, 2005).

Walsem, van, *Mastabase* R. van Walsem, Mastabase or The Leiden Mastaba Project (Leuven, Leiden, 2008).

WAMCAES Western Australian Museum Centre for Ancient Egyptian Studies, Welshpool (Australia).

Warden, *Serdab* L. A. Warden, "Serdab, cult and "home": Domestic life and relationships in Old Kingdom mastabas" in M. Bárta, F. Coppens and J. Krejčí (eds), *Abusir and Saqqara in the year 2015* (Prague, 2017), 467 – 88.

Weeks, *Gmast 5* K. R. Weeks, *Mastabas of Cemetery G 6000. Including G 6010 (Neferbauptah); G 6020 (Iymery); G 6030 (Ity); G 6040 (Shepseskafankh)* in W. K. Simpson and P. Der Manuelian (eds), Giza Mastabas, Vol. 5 (Boston, 1994).

Wiebach, *Scheintür* S. Wiebach, *Die Ägyptische Scheintür. Morphologischen Studien zur Entwicklung und Bedeutung der Hauptkultstelle in den Privat-Gräbern des Alten Reiches.* Dissertation Universität Hamburg (Hamburg, 1981).

Wilkinson, *Early dynastic* T. A. H. Wilkinson, *Early Dynastic Egypt* (London, New York, 1999).

Williams, *A-group* B. B. Williams, *The A-Group royal cemetery at Qustul: Cemetery L* (Chicago, 1986).

Willems, *Djehutinakht* H. Willems, Deir el-Barsha: the tomb of Djehutinakht (III?)", EA, 44(2014), 36 – 8.

Winlock, *Models* H. E. Winlock, *Models of Daily Life; from the tomb of Meket-Re at Thebes, Metropolitan Museum of Art, Egyptian Expedition* (Cambridge (Mass.), 1955).

Wood, *Archaic tombs Helwan* W. Wood, "The archaic stone tombs at Helwan", JEA, 73(1987), 59 – 70.

Woods, *Rattling papyrus* A. Woods, *sšš w3ḏ scenes of the Old Kingdom revisited,* in N. Strudwick and H. Strudwick (eds), *Old Kingdom, New Perspectives. Egytian Art and Archaeology 2750 - 2150 BC* (Oxford, 2011), 314 – 9.

Žabkar, *Ba concept* L. V. Žabkar, *A study of the Ba concept in Ancient Egyptian Texts,* Studies in Ancient Oriental Civilizations, no. 34 (Chicago, 1968).

ZÄS Zeitschrift für Ägyptische Sprache und Altertumskunde, Leipzig, Berlin.

Zelenkova, *Stiftungsinschriften* L. Zelenkova, *Die privaten Stiftungsinschriften des funerären Bereichs des Alten Reiches und der 1. Zwischenzeit,* Doctoral Thesis (Wien, 2008).

Ziegler, *Saqqara* C. Ziegler, *et al.* "La mission archéologique du Musée du Louvre à Saqqara. Résultats de quatre campagnes de fouilles de 1993 à 1996, BIFAO, 97(1997), 269 – 92.

Ziegler, *Saqqara, Louvre* C. Ziegler, "Recherches sur Saqqara au musée du Louvre: bilan et perspectives", in M. Barta and J. Krejči (eds), *Abusir and Saqqara in the year 2000* (Prague, 2000), 43 – 54.

Ziegler, *Akhethetep* C. Ziegler, « The architectural complex of Ahkhethetep at Saqqara: the last discoveries » in M. Bárta (ed.), *The Old Kingdom Art and Archaeology. Proceedings of the Conference held in Prague, May 31 - June 4, 2004* (Prague, 2006), 375 – 81.

General Index

General items

Gods, Goddesses

Kings

Non-royal persons

Tombs